EMPATHY

EMPATHY

A History

SUSAN LANZONI

Yale
UNIVERSITY PRESS

New Haven and London

Published with assistance from the Mary Cady Tew Memorial Fund.

Yale University Press books may be purchased in quantity for educational, business, or promotional use. For information, please e-mail sales.press@yale.edu (U.S. office) or sales@yaleup.co.uk (U.K. office).

Set in Janson type by Integrated Publishing Solutions, Grand Rapids, Michigan.
Printed in the United States of America.

Library of Congress Control Number: 2018934079
ISBN 978-0-300-22268-5 (hardcover : alk. paper)

A catalogue record for this book is available from the British Library.

This paper meets the requirements of ANSI/NISO Z39.48-1992 (Permanence of Paper).

10 9 8 7 6 5 4 3 2 1

For Bruce, Natalia, Conrad

Men can do nothing without the make-believe of a beginning. Even Science, the strict measurer, is obliged to start with a make-believe unit, and must fix on a point in the stars' unceasing journey when his sidereal clock shall pretend that time is at Nought. His less accurate grandmother Poetry has always been understood to start in the middle; but on reflection it appears that her proceeding is not very different from his; since Science, too, reckons backwards as well as forwards, divides his unit into billions, and with his clock-finger at Nought really sets off in medias res.

—GEORGE ELIOT, *Daniel Deronda*

The failure of earlier psychologists and philosophers to make empathy the prime philosophical project of modernity opened the door to its becoming exactly that.

—MARK JARZOMBEK, *Psychologizing Modernity*

Contents

Preface   ix
Acknowledgments   xi

INTRODUCTION   I

PART I EMPATHY AS THE ART OF MOVEMENT

1. The Roots of Einfühlung or Empathy in the Arts   21
2. From Einfühlung to Empathy   46
3. Empathy in Art and Modern Dance   68

PART II MAKING EMPATHY SCIENTIFIC

4. The Limits of Empathy in Schizophrenia   101
5. Empathy in Social Work and Psychotherapy   126
6. Measuring Empathy   158

PART III EMPATHY IN CULTURE AND POLITICS

7. Popular Empathy   193
8. Empathy, Race, and Politics   216
9. Empathic Brains   251

CONCLUSION   277

Notes   281
Index   381

Preface

IT WAS NOVEMBER 2004, and I was rushing through the New Haven station to board an evening train, returning home to my young children in Boston from my visiting teaching post. I paused at a newsstand to pick up *O* magazine and discovered an interview with recently elected United States Senator Barack Obama. He worried about America's "empathy deficit," he told Oprah, more than the trade or budget deficit. He had always urged his students to try and look out through another's eyes, declaring, "We have to build a society on the belief that you are more like me than different from me."

This call for empathy caught my eye, as I already knew from my dissertation research that the English word—empathy—first appeared only in the early years of the twentieth century as a translation of the German *Einfühlung*. Einfühlung, or "in-feeling," was a central concept in German aesthetics and captured a viewer's projection of feeling and movement into paintings, objects of art, and nature.

As I hurried through that train station, I pondered the path from Einfühlung, with its surprising aesthetic meaning, to its early English translation, and then to its use in contemporary American culture. My research subsequently revealed that psychologists disagreed as to how to translate the German term, and "empathy" emerged as one among a number of alternatives. Empathy, as well as its precursor, Einfühlung, possessed multiple meanings. I followed the threads of empathy's varied definitions, conceptualizations, and practices through the fields of art, psychology, social science, psychiatry, and psychotherapy, ending up in the neuroscience of today.

As I complete this book, the empathy deficit seems larger than many of us had imagined even a decade ago. Obama counseled then that in matters of empathy "images, actions and stories always speak the loudest." In tracking and telling the many stories of empathy over the past century, I have discovered that empathy has been a tool, a technique, a practice, and an aspiration. It has enlisted the body and feeling as well as thought and the imagination. Empathy has sometimes relied on self-expression, and at other times on self-restraint. Although its dimensions are still vigorously debated, empathy links us to other beings and to things, and it is as vital today as it was a century ago.

Acknowledgments

THIS BOOK TOOK SHAPE over a number of years. In it I have drawn together ideas and inspiration sparked by many scholars and mentors during my doctoral studies in the history of science, psychology, and neuroscience. I am greatly indebted to my history of science mentors: Peter Galison, who taught me to interweave history with philosophy; Anne Harrington, who inspired me to study the history of psychiatry and neuroscience; and Robert Brain, whose investigations of aesthetics and science were formative. Other professors who taught me the tools of the historical trade include Robert Martenson, Paula Findlen, Alfred Tauber, and Allan Brandt. I would also like to extend my gratitude to my professors at the Harvard Divinity School: Francis Fiorenza, Margaret Miles, Larry Sullivan, and Richard Niebuhr, who nurtured my interest in world religions, hermeneutics, and philosophical pragmatism.

This history could not have been written without the crucial assistance of the following archivists and librarians, who were extremely generous with their time and attention: Pat Burdick, Miller Library, Colby College, Waterville, Maine; Adam C. Green and Sandy Paul, Trinity College Library, University of Cambridge, Cambridge, England; Eleanor Brown, Division of Rare and Manuscript Collections, Carl A. Kroch Library, Cornell University, Ithaca, New York; Pauline Adams, Somerville College, Oxford University, Oxford, England; Lizette Royer Barton, Center for the History of Psychology, University of Akron, Akron, Ohio; Dr. Christopher Hilton, Wellcome Library, Welcome Trust, London, England; Jack Ekert,

Center for the History of Medicine, Francis A. Countway Library of Medicine, Boston, Massachusetts; Stephen Horrocks, Karnes Archives and Special Collections, Purdue University, West Lafayette, Indiana; Rebecca Y. Martin, Monroe C. Gutman Library, Harvard Graduate School of Education, Cambridge, Massachusetts; Sarah Hartwell, Rauner Special Collections, Dartmouth University, Hanover, New Hampshire; Arlene Shaner, Historical Collections, New York Academy of Medicine Library, New York, New York; Sara Keckeisen, Kansas Historical Society, Topeka, Kansas; Rachael Dreyer, American Heritage Center, University of Wyoming, Laramie, Wyoming; Tom McCutchon, Columbia University Rare Book and Manuscript Library, New York, New York; Lewis Wyman, Manuscript Division, Library of Congress, Washington, D.C. Thanks also go to Rosalind Dymond Cartwright for interviews and comments on drafts, and to Michael G. Allport, Robert G. Hoskins and Roger Taft for permission to cite material from the unpublished writings of Gordon Allport, Roy Hoskins, and Jessie Taft.

The research for this book was funded by a National Science Foundation Scholar's Grant awarded to me for "The Emergence of Empathy," Award No. SES-0750603. This grant provided support to conduct research and to visit historical archives. As I pursued various threads in empathy's history I greatly benefited from the skills of three efficient and engaging research assistants—Steven Randy Anderson, Daniel Dempski, and J. Juniper Friedman—who collected and reviewed material for this project while they were students at the Harvard Extension School. Thanks also go to the Newhouse Center for the Humanities at Wellesley College for providing a yearlong research and writing fellowship, and for the good company and inspiration of humanities scholars there, among whom Rebecca Bedell, Ling Hon Lam, Eva Hoffman, and Carol Dougherty were particularly helpful.

This book drew insights from the vibrant exchange of ideas that took place at the workshop "Varieties of Empathy in History, Science and Culture" that I initiated and planned with the integral assistance of Robert Brain and Allan Young. This interdisciplinary workshop, held in October 2008 with funding from the Peter Wall Institute at the University of British Columbia and from the Canadian Social Science Research Council, welcomed scholars from history, philosophy, neuroscience, anthropology, architecture, and visual studies, among other fields. A great many perspectives on empathy were presented in those few days, and I would like to thank each participant for sharing his or her ideas: Robert Brain, Robin Curtis, Carolyn Dean, Jean Decety, Adam Frank, Shaun Gallagher, Laurence Kirmayer, Ruth Leys, Elizabeth Lunbeck, Steven Meyer, Harry Mallgrave, Gordon McOuat, Amir Raz, Kim Schonert-Reichl, Frank Stahnisch, Karsten Stueber, Evan Thompson, Stephen Turner, Marga Vicedo, Allan Young, and Daniel Zahavi.

I was happy to participate in a 2012 conference on empathy sponsored by the Zentrum für Literatur- und Kulturforschung Berlin, organized by Sigrid Weigel and Vanessa Lux. I greatly benefited from the presentations and exchanges with the following participants: Thomas Fuchs, Marianne Leuzinger-Bohleber, Mark Solms, David Freedberg, Vittorio Gallese, Helmut J. Schnieder, Christian Allesch, Andrea Pinotti, and Patrizia Manganaro. The volume *Empathy: Epistemic Problems and Cultural-Historical Perspectives of a Cross-Disciplinary Concept*, ed. Vanessa Lux and Sigrid Weigel (London: Palgrave Macmillan, 2017), stands as a valuable record of this intellectual exchange.

I have presented numerous portions of this book to a variety of audiences, which have offered insightful comments and questions, including: the History of Science Society; the Society for Science, Literature, and the Arts; the American Historical Association; the American Association for the History of Medicine; the Society for U.S. Intellectual History; and the New York Metro American Studies Association. I also presented material from this book at specialized conferences, among which were "The Stimulated Body and the Arts," Durham, U.K.; "The Transmission of Emotion in the Nineteenth Century," Queen Mary University of London; the Twenty-Fourth International Congress of History of Science, Technology, and Medicine, Manchester, England; the Newhouse Center for the Humanities at Wellesley College, Wellesley, Massachusetts; and the Cornell Council of the Arts Biennial, Ithaca, New York.

The following presses generously gave permission to include in this book revised material from my previously published articles: Palgrave Macmillan for "Empathy's Translations: Three Paths from *Einfühlung* into Anglo-American Psychology," in *Empathy: Epistemic*

Problems and Cultural-Historical Perspectives of a Cross-Disciplinary Concept, ed. Vannessa Lux and Sigrid Weigel; University of Toronto Press for excerpts from "Imagining and Imaging the Social Brain: The Case of Mirror Neurons," *Canadian Bulletin of Medical History* 33, no. 2 (September 2016): 447–464; Cambridge University Press for permission to reprint revised excerpts from "Empathy in Translation: Movement and Image in the Psychological Laboratory," *Science in Context* 25, no. 3 (2012): 301–327; and John Wiley and Sons for permission to include revised portions of my article "Practicing Psychology in the Art Gallery: Vernon Lee's Aesthetics of Empathy," *Journal of History of the Behavioral Sciences* 45, no. 4 (2009): 330–354. This material has been updated and composed anew for this book.

At Yale University Press, Jennifer Banks provided unflagging support in addition to astute and gentle critiques of my manuscript; Heather Gold gracefully assisted with the nuts and bolts of the publication process; and Eliza Childs was extremely patient and careful with my many last-minute copy edits. Anonymous reviewers provided helpful commentary and feedback along the way. I greatly appreciate the critique and commentary of early chapter drafts suggested by members in a coterie of independent scholars (IWSS), namely, Joy Harvey, Debbie Weinstein, Debra Levine, Rachael Rosner, Martha Gardner, Conevery Bolton Valencius, Kara Swanson, and Nadine Weidman. Thanks also go to Bruce Fischl and Marga Vicedo for reading and responding to book outlines and portions of the manuscript, and to Nina Gerassi-Navarro for innumerable walks and talks about book writing and publishing. A special shout-out to Sean Marrett for his many-year empathy "news-clipping service." I would like to thank Tracy Behar, who walked me through the ins and outs of book contracts, and Nadine Weidman, for reviewing many final chapter drafts.

I am immensely indebted to my family as well as countless friends and neighbors who have heard me talk about empathy for a very long time! This book fulfills a promise I made many years ago. I offer my infinite gratitude to Bruce, Natalia, and Conrad, who taught me the most about every important thing, including empathy.

EMPATHY

Introduction

"WHERE DOES THE MIND stop and the rest of the world begin?" asked the philosophers Andy Clark and David Chalmers in 1998, considering the case of Otto, a patient suffering from Alzheimer's disease. Otto always carried with him a simple spiral notebook as a memory aid, in which he recorded his thoughts and experiences. To retrieve his memories, he paged through his notes. Clark and Chalmers describe the notebook as an extension of Otto's self—it serves as a storehouse of memories just as the mind and brain do for an unimpaired person. The philosophers then ventured the surprising suggestion that our minds normally function as this kind of "extended system."[1] This idea is at once ordinary but also quite radical: How can our minds, usually identified with the workings of our individual brains and enclosed within the skull, exist in some fashion beyond these bounds?

Today, we might readily grasp the notion of an "extended mind" given our increasing reliance on and fascination with our various devices, smart phones, and computers that function as our "memories" and our mental aids. But if our minds can extend into old-fashioned spiral notebooks as well as flashy electronic devices, might this call into question a narrow, contained notion of selfhood? What if we imagine ourselves according to a network model of "distributed human being" along these lines? What would it mean to see ourselves as intimately enmeshed in the world and with others?

Even absent these new technologies, it is possible to imagine one's distributed, expansive nature. Once your child enters your life, isn't your selfhood immediately and irrevocably distributed? How is it that feeling your child's pain can sometimes be more agonizing than feeling your own? How is it that we sometimes move in synchrony with a dancer on the stage or an athlete running down a field? Do we at times lean to one side in an effort to alter the course of the bowling ball spinning down the lane? Do we feel the heaviness when observing a painted or digital image of someone lifting a weighty object? How is it that we experience a mountain as if rising or a path as if stretching out before us? And why do we find ourselves in the stories we read, the films we watch, the dramas we view?

Over the past century, a host of social scientists, psychologists, medical practitioners, and art theorists have explored these extensions of the self—imagined, projected, or extended—into others and the world. These connections, bound by feeling, and often incorporating knowing and bodily awareness, have linked us to others as well as to natural and artistic objects. This connection or extension has most often been called "empathy," even though the word first appeared only in 1908 as a translation of the German art historical term *Einfühlung*, or literally, "in-feeling." Einfühlung captured the aesthetic activity of transferring one's own feeling into the forms and shapes of objects. This was empathy's earliest meaning, one that has been covered over and for the most part forgotten.

From the time of the coining of "empathy," empathic practices have coursed through a stunning number of fields from aesthetic psychology to social work and psychotherapy, to politics, advertising, and the media. These practices, diverse as they are, make clear that extending the mind and feeling, as well as the self and bodily movements to others and objects, has been imagined to be possible for a long time. The history of empathy shows us that in scientific, therapeutic, political, and everyday settings, empathy has been credited with the power to shift the shape of the self so as to enter into alien forms, to transform into art objects, to inhabit other realities, and to take on the experiences of other persons. To look back at empathy in all its varieties is to witness, directly and obliquely, the diffusion of the self across its feeling connections.

Empathy Today

As many understand it today, empathy is our capacity to grasp and understand the mental and emotional lives of others. It is variably deemed a trained skill, a talent, or an inborn ability and accorded a psychological and moral nature. Among its many definitions are: emotional resonance or contagion, motor mimicry, a complex cognitive and imaginative capacity, perspective taking, kinesthetic modeling, a firing of mirror neurons, concern for others, and sometimes, although rarely, aesthetic self-projection, its earliest meaning. But even this list does not exhaust its possible definitions!

This abundance of meanings does not hamper the fact that we readily call upon empathy in everyday exchanges. It figures in political discourse, in anti-bullying curricula in schools, in psychotherapy, in business, and in personal relationships. Declarations have been made that we live in the age of empathy, or in an empathic civilization, as book titles attest.[2] Cultural critic Jeremy Rifkin professed in 2009 that empathy is a social value that will remake our businesses, our neighborhoods, even our biosphere. Drawing on Daniel Goleman's work on emotional intelligence, Rifkin tells us that an "empathic sensibility lies at the heart of the new management style." It is more important to have a caring boss and emotionally satisfying office exchanges than material gain.[3] Rifkin claimed that this "new empathic spirit" is evidenced by required community service for high school students, efforts to expose children to people of diverse backgrounds, and a new theatrical sense of the self, evident in social media.[4] Goleman has long argued that a capacity for empathy is key to successful leadership, and in a 2017 Harvard Business Review publication he once again highlights the importance of empathy.[5]

Other cultural critics are less sanguine that we are entering a new era of global empathy. A study of American college students from 1979 to 2010 documented a sharp drop-off in self-reported empathy scores on measures of empathic concern and perspective taking.[6] Some attribute this decline to the fact that Americans spend more time alone, that they read fiction less often, and that neoliberal capitalism has significantly eroded our natural tendencies toward empathy.[7] "Where is the empathy?" Nicholas Kristof asked in a *New York Times* op-ed piece, describing the tendency to blame rather than understand those who fall on hard times, telling the story of his friend who lost his job, went on disability, and died poor at the age of fifty-four.[8]

Empathy continues to be a popular topic, from psychology to education, from literature to philosophy, from business to product design.[9] Literary scholars have declared that the act of reading complex literary fiction can increase one's empathy by encouraging "readers to make inferences about characters and be sensitive to emotional nuance and complexity."[10] Researchers postulate that this exercise might lead to better real-life empathy and to understanding the beliefs and intentions of others. David Kelley, founder of the Stanford University d.school (Design School) and his brother Tom describe empathizing as an essential design practice. They offer "empathy maps" as a brainstorming tool: one records what consumers say and do on Post-its and then one infers what these users think and feel. These insights of empathy are jotted down on still another set of Post-its that are displayed in order to trigger design inspirations.[11] The MIT agelab developed empathy age suits (Age Gain Now Empathy System, or AGNES), complete with a heavy helmet, cloudy goggles, compression knee bands, and uneven plastic shoes. While wearing the age suit, one actually feels the physical trials of a seventy-four year old, an aid to brainstorming innovative products. And fathers-to-be and others can purchase the "empathy belly" to "try on" the experience of pregnancy by donning the enlarged plastic belly.[12]

If debates continue as to whether our society has grown more empathic or not, empathy is still regularly promoted as a critically important capacity. In fact, calls for empathy have become more urgent in our current political climate with its steep rise in hate crimes, intolerant speech, and overt racism. Some argue that empathy offers a way to understand one's political opponents; others contend that if citizens imagine each child as one's own, gun violence can be reduced; and still others claim that empathy can foster a connectedness that can ameliorate climate change.[13] The cognitive psychologist J. D. Trout integrates insights from social policy, economics, and neuroscience to point to the presence of an "empathy gap," or an inability to use emotional understanding to grasp others' lives that are culturally or temporally distant from us. This gap results in acute failures of effective social policy.[14] He claims that one can predict congressmen's voting records on women's issues on the basis of whether or not they have daughters. The cognitive neuroscientist Emile Bruneau and collaborators at MIT report on a neurological empathy gap for those inhabiting cultural groups different from one's own, especially those in conflict groups.[15] Others have linked income inequality, steadily growing in the past few decades, and other forms of social inequality to a failure of empathy. Studies have demonstrated that the more powerful often feel less empathy for those lacking power.[16]

In 2009, empathy became a decisive political player during the confirmation debates of Supreme Court nominee Sonia Sotomayor.[17] President Barack Obama praised empathy as a way to appreciate and understand the lives of those marginalized from social and political power.[18] Senator Orrin Hatch countered: "What does that mean? Usually that's a code word for an activist judge."[19] Conservative critics saw an empathy standard as a dangerous substitution of emotion for rational judgment. During her confirmation hearings, Sotomayer downplayed the role of emotion, seeming to recognize that a wholehearted embrace of empathy might jeopardize her appointment to the court. The columnist William Safire weighed in that spring to clear up the distinction between "empathy" and "sympathy" in his *New York Times* column "On Language." He explained that sympathy was aligned with pity, but empathy, which he put in scare quotes, comprised a stronger emotional identification.[20]

Empathy and sympathy are still confused, although back in the eighteenth century "sympathy" was the moral and aesthetic concept debated by the philosophers David Hume, Adam Smith, and Edmund Burke. Nineteenth-century psychologists spoke of "sympathy" as an interpersonal value in evolutionary and physiological frameworks.[21] By the early twentieth century "empathy" first appeared and connoted an aesthetic experience. Just a few decades later, however, empathy was introduced to the broader American public as a more powerful capacity than sympathy. Rather than feeling bad for someone else's misery, empathy enabled a comprehensive grasp of another's experience. "Empathy" soon took over the meanings of "sympathy" even as it extended beyond them. Today sympathy is usually defined as a distanced feeling of pity for another, whereas empathy is a deeper-going ability to engage with a variety of feelings and to inhabit, sometimes even bodily, the other's perspective. Empathy carries with it a spatial dimension—the ability to dwell in another's place and to see from this vantage point. Social psychologist Lauren Wispé explains that empathy entails "perspective-taking," or "role-taking," and is the more empirical concept.[22]

One of the biggest recent boosts to the study of empathy has come from scientific quarters—primatology, the medical humanities, and the growing field of social neuroscience. The primatologist Frans de Waal has argued that apes, elephants, dolphins, and whales possess empathy, findings that have been taken up in popular accounts.[23] He recorded numerous incidents of animals helping and providing consolation to each other, behavior informed by intensities of feeling nearly impossible to duplicate in a laboratory.[24] For de Waal, empathy is a complex, layered capacity that comprises basic emotional contagion, efforts of consolation, concern or targeted helping behaviors, as well as advanced cognitive models where one takes on another's perspective. He counters the common perception that humans harbor a competitive, callous, "inner ape," pointing out that we have overlooked our ancient heritage of empathy and social connectedness, rooted deep in our evolutionary past, and localized to the prefrontal cortex as well as to the evolutionarily older parts of the brain.[25] Remarkably, empathy makes it difficult to maintain a clear distinction between altruism and selfishness: "Empathy hooks us into the other's situation. Yes, we derive pleasure from helping others, but since this pleasure reaches us via the other, and only via the other, it is genuinely other-oriented."[26]

If de Waal offers us a view from primatology, physicians have looked to empathy as a vital factor in a caring and productive doctor-patient relationship. Rita Charon and colleagues in the medical humanities have championed empathy as central to understanding the stories of illness that patients tell.[27] Empathy emerges through attentiveness: doctors put themselves at the disposal of another and give up on their own egos in order to become receptive to the meanings relayed by the patient.[28] Bioethicist Jodi Halpern has examined the physician's complicated role of employing empathy to gain information about the patient's condition, which not only improves diagnostic ability but also promotes therapeutic dialogue.

She rejects the position of detached concern, elaborated in the 1960s as the best strategy for doctors positioning themselves vis-à-vis patients. Neither detachment nor simple emotional resonance is helpful, she argues. Rather, physicians should imaginatively engage with the patient's story, using sophisticated emotional reasoning to gain insight into the patient's situation.[29] To train empathy in medical contexts in one study, actors assisted radiologists to speak to parents about difficult diagnoses.[30]

Over the past two decades, neuroscientists have sparked keen interest in empathy by charting putative empathy circuits in the brain. In 1992, Giacomo Rizzolatti and collaborators at the University of Parma in Italy identified a type of neuron in the prefrontal cortex of the macaque monkey that fired not only when the monkey performed an action but also when the monkey *observed* a person or another monkey performing that action. Dubbing these "mirror neurons," these researchers, among many others, have launched an impressive number of studies on mirror neurons and the human mirror neuron system.[31] Some neuroscientists postulate that such systems may form a neural substrate for the human behaviors of imitation, social learning, and empathy. Other neuronal models of empathy, linked to the perception of pain in others, have also been hypothesized.[32] In the interdisciplinary new field of social neuroscience, cognitive, social, and developmental psychologists, as well as philosophers, have joined spirited debates on the best ways to characterize empathy and to chart its neural underpinnings.

Empathy has been so championed that it now has its own set of detractors. Psychologist Paul Bloom warns that feeling empathy for an individual—the young girl who fell down a well, for instance—can cause one to lose sight of a rational approach to effective political and moral intervention on a broad scale.[33] Empathy may be a poor guide to moral action. New studies have questioned whether reading literary fiction indeed makes us more empathic and if empathy can be put to work as an effective political tool.[34]

In the social, psychological, and neurological sciences, the meanings and scope of empathy are vigorously debated. Disagreements about the importance and effectiveness of empathy often reflect very different understandings of the capacity. The social psychologist C. Daniel Batson enumerates at least eight different phenomena, all of which have been labeled empathy.[35] Some scholars devise their own variants: Jodi Halpern rejects the Oxford English Dictionary meaning of empathy as the projection of one's personality into another, redefining it as "an essentially experiential understanding of another person that involves an active, yet not necessarily voluntary, creation of an *interpretative* context."[36] The appearance of a number of interdisciplinary volumes on empathy over the past ten years reflects the growing interest in the topic as well as empathy's proliferating meanings.[37]

We have a lot riding on empathy today, even if we don't fully understand its mechanisms or its scope. "Empathy" is part of our everyday language and our exchanges with others, and captures something vital, even protean, that speaks to the relationships between people and, historically, the relationship between people and objects. It is used, adopted, challenged, redefined, and enrolled for one purpose or another but nonetheless remains difficult to pin down. Given this ambiguity in the understanding of empathy today, it is essential to ask: How did we get here? And can history shed light on what empathy means today?

A History of Empathy

The history of empathy reveals right away that today's multiplicity of meanings is itself not new. In 1936, the psychoanalyst Theodor Reik wrote, "The conception of empathy has become so rich in meanings that it is beginning to mean nothing at all."[38] One social psychologist looked at the history of empathy only to conclude that empathy has "generally suffered from the lack of a clear, compelling, organizational framework.[39] Another bemoaned the fact that a "generally accepted definition of empathy would be hard to find."[40] One historian of the emotions calls empathy an emotion "found" or "invented" in the eighteenth century, which became a resource for civil society, although the term was not even in use back then.[41] A look into empathy's history shows us that empathy was never one simple thing, and its meanings have been molded and reshaped by generations of researchers for particular projects and aims. In fact, the meanings of empathy shifted so radically that its original meaning transformed into its opposite!

"Empathy" is a relatively new English word. Anglo-American psychologists coined "empathy" as the best translation of the German *Einfühlung* (in-feeling) only in 1908. In the late nineteenth century, psychologists began to examine aesthetic response as a bodily engagement with form, which engaged a spectator's muscles, breath, and posture. Einfühlung was defined by Theodor Lipps, one of its main theorists, as the projection of inner feelings of striving and movement into objects, key to all forms of aesthetic experience. The amateur psychologist, novelist, and travel writer Vernon Lee wrote extensively on aesthetic empathy for English-speaking audiences. By the dawn of the twentieth century, psychologists probed the nature of Einfühlung: Was it an actual bodily imitation or an imagined mimicry? Did it take place in the mind or the muscles? How did one project feelings and movements into objects of contemplation? German phenomenologists, philosophers, and sociologists considered the viability of empathy as a means for knowing others and as an interpretative method for the social sciences, but discussion on these topics was more limited in Anglo-American circles.[42]

Scientific advances in German psychology greatly influenced American psychology, as most late nineteenth-century American psychologists trained in German laboratories. German émigrés soon came to teach at North American universities.[43] English translations were therefore needed for many German psychological terms, among them Einfühlung. At first, psychologists suggested a number of competing translations including "aesthetic sympathy," "play," "semblance," and "animation." In 1908, the Cornell psychologist Edward B. Titchener offered "empathy" as a translation, although it was first misspelled as "enpathy" in a philosophical journal and overlooked. That same year, the psychologist James Ward at the University of Cambridge in England also suggested "empathy" to his colleagues. In 1909 the term appeared in psychological textbooks, and by 1913 it became the generally accepted translation.[44]

Early empathy signified animation or personification and was often linked to the panpsychic view that mind suffused matter. Empathy opened up the interior of objects by allowing for the possibility that mind existed within matter—either projected or there to be grasped. At Titchener's Cornell laboratory, empathy was defined through the lens of sensory psychology as a mental image of bodily movement, what he called the kinesthetic image. Observers assiduously examined the contents of their own minds with the new method of systematic introspection and added the mental image of bodily movement to the more commonly known visual, auditory, and olfactory images.

In the early twentieth century, empathy was closely tied to the aesthetic meanings of Einfühlung and its capacity for "feeling-into" various forms and shapes in art and nature. Psychologists of art explained that one could feel empathy by projecting one's feeling of moving upward into the "rising" mountains or by transferring one's own, often unconscious, undulating movements into the "waviness" of lines. The University of Wyoming psychologist June Downey recorded the experiences of her experimental subjects who "felt themselves into" poetic fragments, and Herbert Langfeld taught Harvard undergraduates to appreciate Renaissance and medieval art by empathically projecting feelings of weight, force, and activity into the depicted figures. This aesthetic experience created the object in the image of the subject, blurring the lines between the self and perceived form. Empathy thus formed a kinesthetic, imaginative entry to painting, poetry, sculpture, and modern dance.

As American psychologists moved away from documenting the inner workings of the mind in favor of behaviorist descriptions, however, empathy came to narrowly signify only an observable bodily imitation. In one 1939 psychology textbook, for instance, empathy was illustrated with a photograph of a coach raising his own leg while watching an athlete launch himself over a high jump bar.[45]

Even as empathy's aesthetic meaning was in the forefront in these early decades, some medical practitioners explored empathy's interpersonal aspects. The Boston neuropathologist E. Ernest Southard, an avid student of social and pragmatic philosophy, developed an "empathic index" in 1918 as a guideline for psychiatric diagnosis. According to Southard, if a psychiatrist could imagine behaving as the patient did, the patient scored high on the empathic index. But if the patient's behavior was so outlandish that the psychiatrist could not imagine acting in a similar way, the patient was deemed to be beyond empathy. These patients, Southard concluded, were likely to be suffering from schizophrenia. Over the next decades, psychiatrists classed the schizophrenic as the quintessential "other," who stood beyond the reach of understanding and likewise suffered from an inability to empathize with others. The neuroendocrinologist Roy Hoskins directed a twenty-year-long, multidisciplinary research program on schizophrenia only to conclude in 1946 that the defining symptom of schizophrenia was a lack of empathy—the biosocial ability to connect with others of one's own species.

One might think psychoanalytic theory would be a central locus for the development of empathy concepts, but emotional connection was marginalized in orthodox Freudian psychoanalysis. When the analysts Sandor Ferenczi and Otto Rank underscored the importance of the emotional bond rather than the patient's insight into his or her condition, they were soon ousted by psychoanalytic orthodoxy. These analytic notions were instead welcomed by social workers, nearly all of them women. Jessie Taft, director of the University of Pennsylvania School of Social Work, melded her doctoral training in social philosophy with these psychoanalytic ideas to pioneer a form of therapy centered on emotional connection. Her innovative "relationship therapy," devised with her colleagues, is rarely discussed today, but it was a major contribution to the empathic psychotherapy techniques developed by clinical psychologist Carl Rogers. For Rogers, empathic practice resisted labeling, judging, or even diagnosing clients' maladies in favor of more deeply engaging with clients' experiences. Rogers's approach had great influence on an array of counselors after World War II, and by the end of the 1950s, empathy had become a staple of much psychotherapy.[46]

Along a parallel historical trajectory, in the late 1920s, Chicago sociologists Ernest Burgess and Leonard Cottrell, students of the social psychologist George Herbert Mead, struggled to operationalize empathy. They aimed to more reliably access the life histories of their subjects in social science interviews. It was only in 1948, however, that psychologist Rosalind Dymond Cartwright, a student of Cottrell's, developed the first experimental tests of empathy. She explicitly rejected empathy's aesthetic meaning to measure "empathy" as one student's ability to predict another's response to a personality assessment. The following decade saw a flurry of studies in which psychologists separated out measures of self-projection from what they called "true empathy." Empathy was now operationally defined as the *accurate* prediction of another's opinion or preference.

Empathy's flights of imagination into forms of art were traded in for empathy's ability to deliver a realistic appraisal of another person. Empathy and projection were now opposed.

Along with this important shift from the projection of the self into objects to a realistic immersion in another's experience, empathy was introduced to popular readers just after World War II. In 1940, a philosopher of science had complained that the concept "has gone begging for recognition" and devised an empathy equation to remedy this neglect: "I = ec." Insight (I) could be produced by empathy (e), or putting "putting ourselves inside" of things, combined with contemplation (c).[47] His equation never became popular, of course, but it was only a decade later that the term "empathy" began to appear in advice columns, advertising campaigns, and in the new media world of television. Because it was so new, however, "empathy" was nearly always accompanied by a definition, spelled in different ways, and often asterisked and explained in a footnote to puzzled readers.

The increased public presence of the concept of empathy resulted from the postwar popularization of psychology and the explosive growth of a culture of psychological experts.[48] Empathy had cachet after the turbulent war years: not only did it reflect psychological expertise, but it offered new possibilities for connection, identification, and understanding that might improve social relations of all kinds. *Reader's Digest* defined "empathy" in 1955 as the "ability to appreciate the other person's feelings without yourself becoming so emotionally involved that your judgment is affected."[49] Empathy could enhance employer-employee relations, forge connections between consumers and advertisers, sell products, and model harmonious family bonds. It was hyped as an advertising technique that enabled women to imagine themselves in Revlon face cream ads, and that presented African American models to engage the African American consumer. Seen as more specialized and scientific than sympathy, empathy soon became the dominant and galvanizing concept. "Empathy" became so prominent at this time that the English term was translated back into the German as "Empathie" to replace the now-outdated Einfühlung.[50]

Empathy became an aspirational value, and was expected to do political work. For social scientists committed to community improvement, fostering empathy in intercultural educational projects could help eradicate prejudice and increase tolerance. The social psychologist Gordon Allport, well versed in the German literature on Einfühlung, connected the study of aesthetics, form, and personality to an ability to show tolerance toward other ethnic and racial groups. By the mid-1960s, Kenneth B. Clark, the African American psychologist and civil rights activist, ardently championed empathy as a form of social sensitivity sorely lacking in his white liberal colleagues and more broadly in the competitive nature of American educational institutions. Exercising empathy could minimize the impact of one's privileged racial identity, expert knowledge, and social power to entertain the possibility of feeling similar to a person of color living at the margins of society.

In the postwar years, psychologists developed various scales and measures of empathy and charted bodily and physiological markers of the ability. It was not until the early 1990s, however, that the work of neuroscientists in Parma, Italy, provided what some deemed to be the decisive neuroscientific evidence for empathy. Mirror neurons, observed to fire when a macaque monkey performed an action *and* when he watched another act, were purported to be the neurobiological underpinning not only of action imitation but also of empathy. Today there is an immense and growing literature on the neural correlates of empathy, and the popular press has enthusiastically reported on these studies. Recently, however, critiques have emerged of some of the broad claims made for mirror neurons.[51] Researchers are still debating how to operationalize empathy for scientific study and where exactly empathy is localized in the brain.

This hundred-year history uncovers a general narrative arc: empathy was first understood as the extension of the self, or a projection of one's own implicit movements into forms, lines, and shapes, but by mid-century, empathy lost its projective meaning and its intimate connection to the arts. By the postwar period, influenced by a therapeutic and scientific ethos, empathy captured a way to understand another more objectively on his or her own terms. No longer concerned with things, empathy became almost exclusively about other people. This is not to say that empathy was not taken up in literary studies, theater, and the arts after World War II, for it most assuredly was.[52] But since that time empathy was no longer predominantly an expressive projection of the self into things, nature, or objects. Rather than an expansion of the self into a form or shape, empathy came to mean the very opposite: the reining in of the self's expressiveness to grasp another's emotion in service to a therapeutic goal or moral imperative.[53]

Empathy's postwar meaning as the restraining of the self to privilege the understanding of another lent itself to associations with women as mothers and teachers, but more significantly to the disenfranchised of all kinds. Empathy became a watchword for those with little power, from patients desiring to be heard in a medical or therapeutic dyad, to religious minorities, to African Americans abiding in a racist society. Empathy became allied to the social virtues of egalitarianism, tied to the recognition of the inherent rights of others. The recent turn to neurological models of empathy demonstrates another iteration of the changing psychological landscape. It is now commonplace to translate the social phenomenon of empathy into descriptions of the firings of neurons and the lighting up of specific brain areas.[54]

Staging the Forgotten Scenes of Empathy

In the history of the sciences, empathic relation, with its close connection to feeling and emotion, has been overlooked. Empathy has been difficult to measure and to systematize, and it has been associated with subjectivity more frequently than objectivity. Because it entails the emotional, kinesthetic, or embodied underside of rational decision making, it was for many years a marginalized topic of study for scientists and psychologists.[55] More recently, however, there has been an upsurge of interest in emotion and its contribution to rational thought among social neuroscientists. In addition, there has been growing recognition across the academy of the importance of emotional understanding for many kinds of social, economic, and political endeavors.[56] Some recent literature on affect has emphasized its automatic nature, although other theorists view emotions as closely linked to cognitive appraisal. Philosopher Martha Nussbaum contends that emotions are, in fact, "upheavals of thought."[57] Empathy stands at the intersection of these competing theories—it sometimes has been deemed a narrow emotional response but just as often has been accorded cognitive elements.

If contemporary theorists are now giving emotion new intellectual weight, over the past century a small set of art theorists, social scientists, and psychologists consistently touted the importance of empathy as a feeling connection that could also transmit knowledge. Their forays into the scope and practices of empathy have been both rudimentary and sophisticated and comprise an important legacy that warrants a closer look. Tracking the history of empathy means unearthing forgotten episodes, sometimes examining figures marginal to the history of the sciences, sometimes looking at fault lines between disciplines and sometimes venturing into popular realms. And, of course, this history could never comprise an exhaustive treatment of such ideas, practices, and venues—similar practices, under slightly different names, were also taking place in alternate contexts across this century.

The best way to understand empathy's historical complexity is not to unearth a set of definitions set out in dusty psychological tomes but to paint the vivid scenes and settings in which empathy was taken up and engaged. It is appropriate to think of empathy with theatrical tropes, given that taking on the role of the other is one of its many definitions. Empathy has been a central theme in drama theory, notably in German playwright Bertolt Brecht's 1930s campaign against empathy as a viewer's mindless absorption in a theatrical performance. He deemed an unconscious empathic identification with actors on the stage politically dangerous, and instead cultivated alienation and critical response in the audience.[58]

Psychologists have nonetheless implicitly and explicitly relied on theatrical models and metaphors to describe the workings of empathy. In this book I describe nine historical stagings of different empathic practices over the past century. I begin each chapter with a set design comprising an image, scene, dialogue, or literary excerpt that crystallizes the way empathy was understood and carried out by social scientists and psychologists at that time. As we move through the chapters, we thus transition from the art gallery, where spectators empathically contemplated objects and paintings, to the psychological laboratory, where trained introspectors looked into their own minds to detect fleeting images of movement, understood to be the basis for empathy. We visit the theater where the abstract movements of modern dancers elicited imitative empathic movements of entranced viewers. We sit in on interviews between social worker and client and listen to psychotherapy protocols that trained therapists in empathic listening. We travel to Harlem where scenes of struggle were strategically disclosed in order to evoke white empathy, and to schools where intercultural education groups invented forums and festivals to foster empathy during World War II. We encounter a variety of public voices defining empathy for the first time in advice columns in newspapers and magazines, on TV, and in advertising after the war. And, of course, we visit the contemporary neuroscientific laboratory where empathy is imaged under controlled conditions with brain scans.

Understanding empathy in the sites in which it is elaborated, or put into practice is key to discerning a concept's meanings, as the philosopher Ian Hacking reminds us.[59] The psychologist Lauren Wispé also advises that empathy and sympathy be understood according to "the systems of thought in which they were embedded and the times in which they flourished."[60] By encountering empathic investigations in different scenes over the past century we experience a richness and complexity impossible to convey with a short definition or through a schematic history of ideas.[61]

Delving into the specific contexts in which empathy was enacted allows us to go deep into particular historical moments—and then to draw back and see how varied forms of empathy are linked by an overall historical shift from empathy with objects to people, from art to the social sciences, from the academy to public discourse, from a mode of often unconscious self-projection to a controlled effort to occupy the other's position. My approach is akin to historian David Armitage's method of serial contextualism: a way of delving into significant historical moments with detail yet still holding to an expansive view.[62] But even as I adhere to this general narrative, the links between individual settings are loose, demonstrating that tracking a concept over time often describes not a smooth evolution, as Michel Foucault reminds us, but a jagged and discontinuous path. We examine the "singularity of events," as he puts it, "not in order to trace the gradual curve of their evolution but to isolate the different scenes where they engaged in different roles."[63] This history is thus better captured by a model of family resemblances or a complex genealogy.

Because this history illuminates empathy's profusion of meanings, it does not seek to secure one definitive conception of empathy for all time. Recognizing with other historians of the emotions that even presumed universal human capacities have a history, I unearth the conditions in which empathy was deployed as a means of knowledge gathering, a way of appreciating art, a predictive capacity, a psychotherapeutic attitude, an innate human capacity, and a political stance. Empathy has been frequently wedded to the body—as an imagined movement or kinesthetic response—but at other times has been a way of grasping an abstract idea. Some psychologists deem empathy to be inherently therapeutic, for others it is an epistemological venture, and for yet others, a political and aspirational value. It is sometimes seen as an automatic and unconscious response, other times deliberate and controlled. One theorist declares that empathy signifies a "constellation of phenomena."[64] Empathy, as revealed in this book, holds together an array of ideas and practices to form a textured weave rather than a uniform fabric.

Studying empathy raises a host of questions: What is at stake in identifying sameness and difference across an empathic divide? How close are we to our empathic objects or other persons? Does empathy mean a merging with another, or a necessary delineation of the self and the other? What role does the body and its organic and physiological responses play in what has been deemed a meeting of minds? And a critical epistemological question lurks: Can an activity originally based in self-projection yield reliable information about another?

Despite shifts in empathy's definition and its complex genealogy, repeated themes emerge over the course of a century of writing, theorizing, and evoking empathy. Empathy depends on movement between the poles of similarity and difference, of distance and closeness, of immersion and alienation. Empathy marks a relation between the self and other that draws a border but also builds a bridge. In its many varieties, empathy continues to present us with an intriguing paradox: we project ourselves to be something other than ourselves. If at first we might see empathy as a sharing of sim-

ilarities, empathy also hinges on difference. To see another accurately means to recognize that I am not you. The empathic aesthetic
appreciation of a landscape, Gothic column, or weaving tendril, for
instance, reveals that empathy can take place between two very different beings. The philosopher Ted Cohen points out that empathic
connection is not about making equivalences. Rather, it works like a
metaphor, where "metaphorical identity is not symmetrical."[65]

Practices of empathy are best understood as modifications of
the self-in-relation, often requiring a shift or change in the self.[66]
Psychologists of art debated how deeply one could participate in
paintings and poetry, and counselors and social workers fashioned
the self into an empathic therapeutic agent. The very ways in which
empathy was construed helped to make possible empathy's enactment. And of course empathy has been closely entwined with questions of power and morality.

It is illuminating to rethink empathy as the stuff of art and imagination, as it was first envisioned over a hundred years ago. Within
the aura of this early aesthetic meaning, empathy challenges us to
stretch the limits of the self, but more audaciously, the understanding of our human-ness. Can we envision radical and new forms of
connection with objects and the world around us? If contemporary
philosophers have urged us to think of the mind as extended, aesthetic empathy asks us to relax the familiar borders of the self to
embrace objects, nature, even perhaps to reimagine the nature of
matter, as did some of its early proponents.

Today the language of neuroscience has been privileged as a way
to understand empathy, but this history encourages us to see empathy's many facets through a diverse set of approaches and disciplines. What remains the case is that we are still grappling with what
empathy is and what it means to us. Today, as was true in the past,
we can benefit from the rich languages of history, social psychology,
philosophy, and the arts to take hold of empathy's full potential and
dimensions. A number of dedicated historical actors have provided
us with vivid insights into empathy's many meanings; it would be
foolish to move forward without also looking back. This book in-
vites us to embrace many empathies.

PART I

Empathy as the Art of Movement

CHAPTER ONE

The Roots of Einfühlung or Empathy in the Arts

Empathy [tr. G. *Einfühlung* (see EINFÜHLUNG) (T. Lipps *Leitfaden d. Psychol.* (1903) 187), ad. Gr.] "The power of projecting one's personality into (and so fully comprehending) the object of contemplation."

—*Oxford English Dictionary*

SOMETIME IN 1895 OR 1896, the Victorian novelist and art historian Violet Paget positioned her artist friend and lover Clementina Anstruther-Thomson, or Kit, in front of a sturdy mahogany chair with "curved arms, rather a high square seat and a square panel on the back. The two top corners reach some inches higher than the panel and are terminated by carved foliated clumps" (figure 1).[1] While taking in the form of the chair, Kit made careful note of her bodily reactions. As she followed the horizontal lines of the chair seat, she felt her eyes move apart, her chest expand, and her breathing deepen. And when she traced the rising back of the chair, she felt as if she were growing taller.

Violet and Kit were conducting a psychological experiment on the bodily effects of aesthetic perception, joining scholars and psy-

Figure 1. Print of a chair, used by Vernon Lee and Kit Anstruther-Thomson in aesthetic experimentation around 1897. Photographic print accompanying unpublished papers on Beauty and Ugliness. Vernon Lee Archive, Colby College Special Collections, Miller Library, Waterville, Maine.

chologists of the period who sought empirical data for the understanding of aesthetics. Aesthetics had been historically defined as the domain of sensory or perceptual experience in contrast to that of conceptual thought or reason, but by the mid-eighteenth century, the term became associated with art and the beautiful.[2] A century later, scientists delved into empirical investigations to pinpoint physiological and psychological responses to works of art.[3]

The German psychophysicist Gustav Fechner insisted in the 1870s that aesthetics had to be conducted "from below," meaning from the results of psychophysical experiments rather than from the speculations of philosophers sitting in armchairs. He tested subjects' perception of the golden section, thought from the time of antiquity to be the most pleasing ratio for a rectangular shape. His observers found rectangles with a ratio of 1 to 1.168 most agreeable.[4] Across the Channel, Victorian psychologists evaluated aesthetic appreciation through evolutionary schemas and by aligning beauty along the bodily axis of pleasure and pain. They employed new brass instruments in psychophysiology laboratories to chart and time their subjects' bodily movements, respiration, circulation, and attention as they perceived art objects.[5] Psychologists had also, at this time, pioneered the new mental technique of systematic introspection to provide reliable reports of the images, feelings, and sensations passing through the mind. Scholars took to diaries to document their own aesthetic reactions and distributed questionnaires to art connoisseurs.[6]

This burgeoning science of aesthetics centered on the spectator's response to the work of art rather than on the work itself.[7] One theorist pointed out that "the beautiful is not a thing, it is an act."[8] By the 1890s, the Einfühlung response, or the ability to feel-into objects, came to dominate aesthetic discourse in Germany, and it soon spread to international circles.[9] Einfühlung described how the spectator "felt-into" or extended the self into the swirling lines of a design, into a mountain rising upward toward the skies, or into the curving line of an archway.[10] One of the central architects of the theory, Theodor Lipps, described Einfühlung as the projection of one's own unconscious feelings and inner imagined movements into the art object, which were then experienced within the object itself. He believed that this impulse of self-transfer was sui generis and key to aesthetic experience. Other scholars asserted that the response resulted from the mind's tendency to associate ideas.[11] Questions swirled as to whether the body actually moved in response to art objects, leading to vigorous debates in academic circles. Although Violet and Kit stood outside the academy, they were deeply cognizant of these debates and soon carried out their own aesthetic experiments.

Violet Paget/Vernon Lee

Violet Paget was a brilliant young writer, who in 1880, at the tender age of twenty-four, published her exposition of eighteenth-century music and drama under the male pseudonym "Vernon Lee" (figure 2). Born to English parents, Violet and her family enjoyed

Figure 2. John Singer Sargent, portrait of Vernon Lee, 1881.
Wikipedia Commons.

a peripatetic existence, settling for extended periods in Nice, Bologna, Padua, and Rome. As a child, she visited the art museums of Florence and greater Europe, often accompanied by her friend, the painter John Singer Sargent and his family. In 1873, the family settled near Florence, and a decade later moved nearby to "Casa Paget," where Violet would live for the rest of her life.[12]

Violet welcomed writers, artists, and scholars to her home, soon a cosmopolitan intellectual salon. She became a prolific writer, moving fluidly between the genres of art history, aesthetic theory, novels, short stories, and travelogues. The novelist Henry James was so impressed with her intelligence that he confided to his psychologist brother William, "She is as dangerous and uncanny as she is intelligent, which is saying a great deal. Her vigour and sweep of intellect are most rare and her talk superior altogether. . . . She is far-away the most able mind in Florence."[13]

Known to the intellectual world by her pseudonym Vernon Lee, she had by 1887 turned from her early forays into art history to the study of the psychological underpinnings of the beautiful. She was fascinated by the growing field of psychology, absorbing reports of psychophysical experiments carried out in German laboratories as well as of cures achieved through suggestion and hypnotism in French and Viennese clinics. She found the psychological principle of the association of ideas both dangerous and delightful: "Association, I have said, makes art, makes our capacity of enjoying it; nay makes our minds."[14] She immersed herself in the works of the new physiological psychologists William James and Giuseppi Sergi and traveled to London to attend the 1892 International Congress of Experimental Psychology. Neurology and psychophysics formed one main section of the Congress, and hypnotism took up another.[15] The famed physicist Hermann Helmholtz and psychologists James Sully, Alexander Bain, and Francis Galton were all in attendance. Lee found intriguing the experiments on suggestion and hypnotism for the treatment of nervous disorders, excitedly relaying to her mother that there might be hope for her half-brother who suffered from an untreatable paralysis and neurasthenia.[16]

Lee devoured new scientific works detailing physiological and bodily effects on mental function, informing her mother that she was developing a facility for mental science.[17] She plunged into the first volume of William James's massive *Principles of Psychology* in the winter months of 1893 and was soon reading James's shorter work on psychology. Lee accepted James's influential view that emotion was at its core a physiological response, whether it accelerated heartbeats, quickened respiration, or inspired bodily movement. Emotion was in essence a bodily reaction: without fear's racing pulse, it would not be fear; without the sobs, grief would not be grief. As James famously explained in 1884, "We feel sorry because we cry, angry because we strike, afraid because we tremble, not that we cry, strike, or tremble, because we are sorry, angry, or fearful, as the case may be."[18] Years later, Lee confessed to James how significant his work was to her own thinking (even if she strongly disliked his later, pragmatic philosophy). "Has not your *Psychology* read, re-read till it is almost falling to pieces, made an epoch in whatever philosophical thought I am capable of?"[19] By the summer of 1895,

Lee wrote to her friend Kit Anstruther-Thomson, "I am working with delight at psychology."[20]

Lee became convinced that bodily movement was instrumental not only to emotion but also to aesthetic experience. She credited the French psychologist Alfred Fouillée for highlighting "the importance of the motor element in intellectual processes."[21] In her commonplace books, she reflected: "Many people, I am sure, could like myself, distinguish a faint muscular consciousness whenever they reason." This faint "muscular consciousness" was evident, she outlined, when "we speak of the *positions* for argument, the *grip* of a thinker."[22]

Early in the nineteenth century, the anatomist and artist Charles Bell had added the muscle sense to the common five senses. This sixth sense, as it was called, judged weight, resistance, and the awareness of the body's movement. By 1880, it was labeled "kinaesthesis" by the pathological anatomist H. Charlton Bastian.[23] The kinesthetic sense had become so important in psychology by this date that it comprised one of the five subsections of the 1889 First International Congress of Physiological Psychology held in Paris, where members offered toasts on the platform of the newly constructed Eiffel Tower.[24] (The other subsections were heredity, hypnotism, hallucinations, and abnormal association of sensations.)

Psychologists debated how the kinesthetic sense was experienced and how it related to brain function.[25] Psychologists Alexander Bain and Wilhelm Wundt connected the kinesthetic sense to the will, localized centrally in the brain, from which the impulse to move originated. But William James and his colleague Hugo Münsterberg pinpointed myriad sensations from the eyes and from moving limbs as sources for the feeling of effort or the kinesthetic sense that only secondarily registered in the brain. They did acknowledge, however, that thought in an "ideal" form could spur movement.[26]

Psychologists were not alone in championing the kinesthetic sense. Artists saw the viewer's eye movements as critical to the perception of form as well as the third dimension in painting and relief sculptures. The German sculptor Adolph von Hildebrand, who worked in a studio near Florence and was acquainted with Lee, declared that pictorial arrangements directly stimulated the spectator's movements, sensations, and breathing.[27] Lee borrowed Hildebrand's description of Titian's *Sacred and Profane Love* in her writing to stress the ways the painting carried its viewer into the scene by creating a sense of the third dimension.[28] The art connoisseur Bernard Berenson, adviser to Isabella Stewart Gardner, famously wrote that a painter must give "tactile values to retinal impressions," which meant that to successfully see a painting was to also feel it in one's muscles.[29] When a painting activated the viewer's tactile imagination, it not only produced a more vivid sense of the painting but also heightened the viewer's vitality. Lee and Anstruther-Thomson visited galleries in Florence accompanied by Berenson, and all agreed that art could stimulate a vitalizing power in a viewer without producing the exhaustion of actual movement.

Lee linked perception to the muscular sense, explaining in her notes, "We see with the eye but realise movement only through the muscles."[30] When one felt the body "shrinking at the narrative of an operation," one might experience imitative movements, what Lee called a "sympathetic realization."[31] These everyday imitative responses, she believed, were heightened and integrated in aesthetic experience. By spring 1895, Lee and Anstruther-Thomson began experimenting in art galleries to document the bodily effects of art.[32] They explored the spectator's physiological reactions while perceiving a nude model and antique sculptures.[33] In these experiments, Anstruther-Thomson took on the difficult role of the introspective observer. As their investigations grew more ambitious, she painstakingly reported her sensations while perceiving Doric columns, Gothic arches, Renaissance paintings, a chair, a jar, even a blank wall.

Neither Kit nor Violet had undertaken academic instruction in psychology, but Anstruther-Thomson's training as a visual artist enabled her to attend to her subtle bodily responses while she perceived forms and shapes. Using the introspective method, she assiduously isolated, slowed down, repeated, and compared her individual perceptions. Lee later clarified that their scientific endeavors necessitated a "long course of special training [that] had magnified not only her [Kit's] powers of self-observation, but also most probably the normally minute, nay, so to speak, microscopic and imperceptible bodily sensations accompanying the action of eye and attention in the realisation of visible form."[34]

Lee herself had trouble implementing the method, reporting that she did not often feel sensations while viewing a painting. As a friend remembered, the "robustness of Kit's appreciation of art was what first set Vernon Lee on the track of realizing art's psychological (and physiological) significance."[35] Lee, however, did experience bodily reactions when scanning architecture or hearing music, and she divulged, "It was largely the habit of recognizing bodily sensations in myself while hearing and particularly recollecting music that had prepared me to welcome Miss A. T.'s discoveries."[36]

In one experiment, Anstruther-Thomson meticulously described her perception of a chair, while reporting at the same time her eye movements, breathing patterns, feelings of pressure, tension, and balance. As her eye followed the lines of the chair, her eyes and chest felt as if they were pulling apart. Her feet automatically pressed hard against the ground, as if she was imitating the front legs of the chair, and she felt her balance shift. As she scanned the height of the chair, she experienced an accompanying upward stretch of her body, suddenly checked by the sight of the leaf ornaments on the top of the chair's corners.[37] The researchers concluded that breathing and balance were key to the perception of form. Aesthetic pleasure was produced through cerebral activity as well as from organic activity of the viscera, especially of the heart and lungs.[38] Furthermore, when Kit's bodily sensations harmonized and were in equilibrium she found the form agreeable.[39] She did not experience triangular shapes as congenial but discovered a rounded jar to be highly pleasing—an object that became the focus of another experiment (figure 3).

While perceiving the jar, Anstruther-Thomson reported: "The curve outwards of the jar's two sides is simultaneously followed by an *inspiration* as the eyes move up to the jar's widest point. Then *expiration* begins, and the lungs seem slowly to collapse as the curve inward is followed by the eyes, till, the narrow part of the neck being reached, the ocular following of the widened out top provokes a short inspiration."[40] Her body and breathing synchronized with her scan of the jar: the "lift up" of the jar accompanied the "lift up" of the body; a "downward pressure on the head" mimicked the "downward pressure of the widened rim on the jar's top."[41] The integrated organic movements of breath, eyes, and body comprised her sense of the jar as a harmonious and pleasing shape. The investigators

Figure 3. Print of a vase, used by Vernon Lee and Kit Anstruther-Thomson
in aesthetic experimentation around 1897. Photographic print accompanying
unpublished papers on Beauty and Ugliness. Vernon Lee Archive, Colby College
Special Collections, Miller Library, Waterville, Maine.

concluded that forms that served the health of the bodily organism
were aesthetically preferred, a fact that explained the ubiquity of the
rounded jar in antiquity and in modern peasant ware.

Lee mused on their findings in her commonplace book in January 1897: "Do we perceive form through cardiac-respiratory movements, or do cardiac-respiratory movements result from the action of whatever perceives form?"[42] By November, when she and
Anstruther-Thomson published their experimental results in the
popular periodical *The Contemporary Review*, they resolved that
bodily adjustments were not merely a *reaction* to the form of the
object but rather *constituted* the perception of form. The striking
coordination between Kit's own bodily responses and the shape of the
object revealed that bodily reaction was part and parcel of aesthetic
pleasure. "These adjustments of breathing and balance are the actual physical mechanism for the perception of Form, the sense of

relation having for its counterpart a sense of bodily tension."[43] To perceive form thus required a breathing, feeling body. Even more striking, bodily experience transmuted into objective form: "the objective terms, *height, breadth, depth*," along with "the more complex terms *round, square, symmetrical, unsymmetrical*" referred to subjective states that in turn could be analyzed "into more or less distinct knowledge of various and variously localised bodily movements."[44]

Objective perception was thus shot through with subjective feeling and physiological reaction; likewise form, shape, and color had direct bodily effects. One might "inhale color," which stimulated the eye, the nostrils, and the throat and made things warmer and easier to see.[45] A landscape adorned with bright squares of color caused a disturbance in respiration, closely linking the eye and the breath. The experience of being inside a large church created a synchrony of self and object to the point of a confusion of boundaries: "The total effect is that of feeling the *church as a larger circumference of ourselves,* and this is the specific sensation of architecture considered as spatial enclosure."[46] To move while perceiving a form altered one's aesthetic response: "When we adjust our muscles in imitation of the tenseness or slackness of the statue's attitude, the statue immediately becomes a reality to us."[47] Art could also induce the viewer to move: when Lee viewed Gothic arches, lintels, and columns she felt inclined to shift her posture to find a new bodily equilibrium, which in turn produced mental lucidity. Viewing art, she concluded, could "improve our consciousness of existence by literally forcing us to more harmonious movements."[48]

Einfühlung Theory in German Aesthetics

Lee and Anstruther-Thomson did not directly invoke Einfühlung theory in their 1897 experiments, but their findings captured the attention of the Munich psychologist and philosopher Theodor Lipps. Lipps was a major proponent of aesthetic Einfühlung and one of the most influential psychologists of his day. He forged his theory of Einfühlung in the 1890s through a study of 175 optical illusions. To feel into the form meant that one animated the illusion by unconsciously projecting movement into the lines.[49] So, for instance, subjects saw the lines of the Müller-Lyer illusion *as if* they

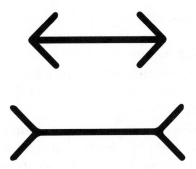

Figure 4. Müller-Lyer illusion, composed of two horizontal lines of the same length with arrows at the ends pointing in different directions, producing the illusion that one line is longer than the other. Brentano Stimuli, Wikimedia Commons.

were in movement: the lines either seemed to stretch toward the ends of the figure or to move inward toward the middle, depending on the direction of the arrows (figure 4). This dynamic perception, of which one was generally unaware, Lipps claimed, accounted for the illusion that the lines were of different lengths even as they were identical.[50]

Lipps soon extended the perceiver's capacity to animate optical illusions to the perception of all lines. Lines were seen to contain mechanical forces that contracted and compressed, expanded and extended. So, for instance, when viewing a Doric column one un-consciously perceived the forces gather together in its circumfer-ence and rise upward. This movement, however, was actually one's *own* inner activity, along with feelings of vigor, strength, or constric-tion, transferred into the object. "I feel myself, generally speaking, in a movement that is perceptively striving after completion. This fact we name *Einfühlung*. In this constitutes at the same time the aesthetic insight of what is optically perceived."[51] Aesthetic pleasure was in fact our own enjoyment, projected into the object.

Lipps fashioned and refashioned his theory of Einfühlung over the course of many years, but one central and unchanging feature was the idea that the way one apprehended objects imparted mean-ing to those objects.[52] Put another way, seeing was based not only on the nature of objects themselves but crucially also on the *act* of perception, or "what they 'signify' for us from some point of view."[53] Lipps's empirically rooted, descriptive psychology spurred later developments in phenomenological philosophy and influenced Sigmund Freud's conception of the unconscious. Freud's notion of transference as the projection of one's feelings onto others shares intriguing links with Lipps's conception of Einfühlung as a projective, illusory perception.[54]

Even as Lipps wrote extensively on Einfühlung, the concept predated him. Its origins go back to the Romantic philosophers Arthur Schopenhauer and Johann Herder. In the 1870s, the philosopher Friedrich Theodor Vischer and his son, Robert, brought Einfühlung into wide-ranging discussion in aesthetics.[55] Vischer was inspired by Karl Scherner's *The Life of the Dream*, which Freud consulted a couple decades later. Scherner explained that a dream objectified the body in a spatial form: for instance, a house might symbolize one's body. Vischer extended this capacity beyond the dream to a natural human capacity to feel our way into objects. If we projected ourselves into a large form we felt expansive; alternatively, feeling into a broken object evoked feelings of oppression. To encounter an object was to "mediate its size with my own, stretch and expand, bend and confine myself to it."[56] With Einfühlung, Vischer explained, one "traces the object from the inside (the object's center) to the outside (the object's form)."[57]

Aesthetic viewing stimulated the muscles and nerves of the eye into congenial movements, producing pleasurable sensations. These bodily sensations in turn evoked various levels of feeling, which were then projected into, and experienced within, the object itself. Vischer described the common phenomenon of confusing our own feelings with that of nature and things. We feel the warmth of light on our skin and speak of warm shades of color, thus mixing together "our own stimulation with the thing that produces the stimulus: light and color in themselves appear to be angry, to jubilate, to mourn, and so on."[58] He elaborated a complex hierarchy of sensations and feelings to capture these nuances, Einfühlung being only one of them.

If Vischer charted eye movements, and Lee and Anstruther-Thomson documented the importance of breath and movement in aesthetic perception, Lipps anchored Einfühlung in the mind and not in bodily reactions.[59] Lipps reviewed Lee's and Anstruther-Thomson's experiments in 1900 only to decry what he called the "cult" of bodily sensations and the fact that the body had become a mania in psychology.[60] To Lipps, Einfühlung was not a matter of activating muscular sensations or stimulating actual movements but rather the projection of the self's inner sense of activity into the perceived object. The viewer did not actually move but rather experienced a mental awareness of striving or effort within the object of contemplation. At the highest level of Einfühlung, the spectator merged with the object. Lipps described a spectator watching an acrobat on a tight-wire: "I am, according to my direct (unmediated) awareness in him; I am there high up. I am transported there. Not next to the acrobat, but exactly within him, where he is. This is thus the full meaning of '*Einfühlung.*'"[61] One's actual, practical self remained in one's seat, but one's "ideal" or contemplative self was transported into the ac-robat. This fusion of self and object comprised the apogee of aes-thetic Einfühlung for Lipps.

Other psychologists defined Einfühlung as this kind of fusion: Mary Whiton Calkins, founder of the first psychological laboratory at Wellesley College surveyed schoolchildren and college students who reported their peak aesthetic experience as an "almost indescribable merging of self and thing, of ego and alter, of subject and object."[62] But if Einfühlung meant one was wholly absorbed in the object and had forgotten the body, how did Lee and Anstruther-Thomson ex-plain the many bodily accompaniments to aesthetic viewing that they had so assiduously recorded? It would take Lee another decade of research to figure this out.

The Question of Imitation

After receiving Lipps's blistering critique, Lee began to wonder whether bodily movements felt during aesthetic viewing were, in fact, universal. Anstruther-Thomson's responses may have simply been idiosyncratic. Psychologists had discovered in reaction time experiments that individuals could be cued by different sensory channels—auditory, visual, and motor—and had different response tendencies.[63] Lee was familiar with the so-called motor type demon-strated in patients with amnesia who could not access visual and auditory memories but still possessed memories for movement.[64] If

Kit was a motor type, then her experience might not generalize to other aesthetic spectators.

To address these concerns, Lee and Anstruther-Thomson circulated a questionnaire at the Fourth International Congress of Psychology in Paris that asked respondents to assess whether they experienced eye movements or inner muscular adjustments while feeling aesthetic pleasure or displeasure.[65] They collected only a few completed questionnaires, however, which Lee attributed to a lack of interest in aesthetics, the questionnaire's technical language, and its presumption of the existence of a motor type.[66] Lee then solicited responses from acquaintances with an appreciation for art and received forty-eight written responses over the next few years.[67] Almost half of her respondents reported that they were aware of bodily sensations when they saw perceived lines as moving during an aesthetic experience.[68]

One of Lee's respondents was Karl Groos, a professor of philosophy at the University of Giessen who had written extensively on aesthetics. Groos judged aesthetic enjoyment as a form of play that traded in imitation and illusion, a view that drew directly from Friedrich Schiller's influential eighteenth-century theory.[69] Both children and animals engaged in play behavior, a biologically rooted activity he deemed necessary to prepare the organism for later developmental tasks. The impulse to imitate, according to Groos, was not always expressed in actual movements but could take place as an inner (or mental) imitation or simulation.[70] He deemed inner imitation akin to Einfühlung but preferred to use the term *Miterleben*, meaning "feeling or experiencing with."

Groos completed Lee's questionnaire by reporting movements of his eyes, neck, and face and breathing sensations during aesthetic experiences.[71] But he cautioned Lee that her survey might be unreliable. Respondents had to pay attention to their aesthetic responses even as the experience usually required a self-forgetting. He pointed to the further danger in asking respondents explicitly to focus their attention on movement, which might lead them to enact movements that ordinarily would not have taken place.[72] Groos then suggested to Lee that because she possessed an exceptional aesthetic receptivity she should chart her own aesthetic responses. She could then determine if her responses aligned with those of Anstruther-Thomson.[73]

It may have been Groos's advice that prompted Lee to begin composing her own "Gallery Diaries" in 1901, which she penned for the next three years. At this time, Kit was suffering from mental and physical exhaustion and declined to participate further in aesthetic experiments. She thought that her ailments may have been triggered by their intensive investigations. Even more troubling, Kit's and Violet's intimate bond was unraveling. After a number of separations, the two permanently parted in 1904.[74]

Lee now took on the role of psychological observer while frequenting the museums of Rome and Florence. She jotted down her moods, the tunes that coursed through her head, her level of attentiveness, thought-associations, and motor reactions while she scanned a variety of antique sculptures. She was convinced that this method of introspection allowed her to attend to her own responses without unduly interrupting the perceptive process. On this matter she cited psychologist E. B. Titchener, the foremost authority on introspective technique, who claimed that he could make mental notes while reading without losing the thread of the discussion. Lee found that her own internal spectator did not interfere with her aesthetic responses but rather heightened them.[75]

In March 1902, Lee visited the Uffizi Gallery in Florence and contemplated the painting of Saint Sebastian by the High Renaissance painter Il Sodoma (Giovanni Antonio Bazzi) (figure 5). She addressed what she called the "Question of Inner Mimicry" by evaluating whether she experienced a bodily imitation: "The arrow through the throat of Sodoma's Sebastian ought to give me a slight sense of discomfort in my throat. The fact that it doesn't points to something else diverting my attention. What is that something? When I say to myself, 'The arrow cut into the flesh, crashed through the bone, and cut through the arteries,' I feel a vague sickness." When she verbally described the arrow's trajectory, Lee amplified her own sickly feeling. But she found that the angel hovering about Saint Sebastian's head mitigated these feelings: "When I cover the angel the arrow business becomes more painful; that cheerful, busy, very alive angel sets up, I think, a feeling which destroys the arrow feeling." In addition to analyzing the bodily effects of the painting's compositional elements, Lee attended to her shifting attention, mood, even the inner beat of a tune hammering in her head. She

Figure 5. Il Sodoma, Saint Sebastian, *1525. Wikimedia Commons.*

discovered that all these mental goings-on tempered her experience. "Coming upstairs and after, I had a certain Neapolitan popular song in my head. It fitted on to the beating of my heart. As long as those palpitations went on, and that song, I couldn't see the Saint Sebastian properly."[76]

Lee soon enlisted the aid of an assistant, Irene Cooper Willis to corroborate her findings. Willis described how she was "dispatched, almost under subpoena, on my afternoons out, to the galleries in Florence to record my impressions before a Botticelli or a Simone Martini." Willis knew that Lee was testing out Groos's theories of inner mimicry, which was that "complete aesthetic enjoyment of a work of art produces bodily accompaniments and mimetic processes in the observer." Willis later declared in a biographical essay that she was happy that "'remarkable specimens of modern art' had not then asserted themselves or the inner mimicry evoked might have been painful. Even Botticelli used to give me the stitch."[77]

Experiments on Einfühlung

As Lee embarked upon her own aesthetic introspections, she began reading Lipps's monumental *The Aesthetics of Space*, as she explained, "to clear up my ideas about the *theory* of *Einfühlung*."[78] Lee described Einfühlung as "*sympathy, with-feeling—(einfühlen,* 'feeling into,' the Germans happily put it)," which comprised the phenomenon "when our feelings enter, and are absorbed into, the form we perceive; so that (very much as in the case of sympathy with human vicissitudes) we participate in the supposed life of the form while in reality lending *our* life to it."[79] She agreed with Lipps that Einfühlung entailed the attribution of the self's energies and activities to objects. Lee dated the phenomenon back to the early German Romantics and discerned its effects in the visual arts as well as in poetry.[80]

Lipps and Lee may have met in Rome at the Fifth International Congress of Psychology in 1905. Lipps delivered the opening address, and explained that Einfühlung was not only the animation or projection of activity into objects but also a way to understand the emotions of others.[81] Already in 1903 Lipps had extended the purview of Einfühlung beyond aesthetics to encompass four different varieties: he identified a general Einfühlung for common objects, one for nature, another for moods, and a fourth for the perception of other people's expressions, offering a path to understand their emotions.[82] The scope and meanings of Einfühlung were expanding rapidly in the German-speaking world. At the 1910 Fourth Congress for Experimental Psychology in Innsbruck, the phenomenologist Moritz Geiger warned that if researchers did not spell out what they meant by Einfühlung, it was not at all clear what they were talking about![83] In subsequent years, German philosophers Edith Stein, Edmund Husserl, Max Scheler, and Martin Buber proposed sophisticated formulations and critiques of Einfühlung.[84] Soon thereafter, European psychiatrists drew on the theory to understand their patients, and sociologists counted Einfühlung as among the methods of interpretation and understanding (*Verstehen*) for the social sciences.[85]

At the 1905 congress, however, Lee centered her remarks on aesthetic Einfühlung.[86] She was introduced as Miss Paget in a session on introspective psychology, and she told her audience that she had conducted twenty years of aesthetic psychological research. She urged the congress to establish a section wholly dedicated to artistic phenomena. She advised that it was better to analyze the effects of particular works of art—the ceiling of the Sistine Chapel, Wagner's Trilogy, even the circles and triangles described in Lipps's *Aesthetics of Space*—than to hold forth on art in a general way. She duly credited Lipps for creating a new science of beauty based on Einfühlung but pointed out that a work of art did not always elevate or purify the spectator. Sometimes it tired, bored, or even degraded the viewer. The spectator was nonetheless an active participant in a work of art, standing at only one remove from the artist who had created it for the first time.

Again and again, Lee brought attention to a spectator's actual encounter with a specific work of art, undertaken in a certain mood and tenor of mind. Lipps had maintained that during heightened moments of aesthetic contemplation one was fully absorbed in the object and oblivious to bodily sensations. This transcendent experience put aesthetics beyond the practical realities that Lee highlighted. She acidly countered Lipps's claim: "I fear that this notion of being so *Versunken* [immersed] in contemplation of columns merely shows how little even great aestheticians have observed their normal degree of aesthetic attention."[87] Lee insisted that even while she was lost in aesthetic contemplation she could still feel the tightness in her boot![88] If aesthetic experience included moments when the self dissolved into the object, Lee found that she could not easily forget the body nor mental distractions such as tunes running through her head while in an aesthetic reverie.

If Lee had doubts as to the extent to which Einfühlung could take place without bodily accompaniments, others put the question to experiment. Already in 1903, Oswald Külpe, the head of the psychological laboratory in Würzburg, had tested whether Lipps's Einfühlung could be demonstrated with three aesthetically sophisticated observers. Subjects viewed twenty-eight slides, each for three seconds, of Doric, Corinthian, and Ionic columns; temples from Corinth; the Parthenon; and altar reliefs of Zeus and Athena.[89] The reports of their aesthetic responses revealed no spontaneous responses of Einfühlung, even when Külpe pointedly asked his subjects if they perceived the columns to rise—one of Lipps's favorite examples.[90] Three years later at the Fourth Congress for Experimental Psychology in Innsbruck, Külpe held forth on various methods for the experimental study of aesthetics.[91] Lipps, sitting in the audience, protested that the method of presenting images for very short durations simply did not allow the process of Einfühlung to unfold.[92]

Although Külpe had not found direct evidence for Einfühlung, his subjects did report imitative bodily movements and organic sensations when viewing a human posture. All three observers in his 1903 experiment described these imitations to total nineteen instances over eighty-four trials, or 22 percent. These responses emerged when subjects viewed human forms or when an unusual or lively position was displayed. Another experiment conducted in Zurich found that eight subjects relied on bodily and organic sensations to select the rectangles, triangles, and straight or zigzag lines that they found pleasing.[93] One subject scanned a triangle and sensed that it might collapse at the same time she felt her chest constrict; other subjects felt they were able to breathe more freely in the presence of certain shapes. These findings supported Groos's inner imitation theory—that feelings in the body were part and parcel of aesthetic experience.

Lipps's Einfühlung was also put to the test by the British psychologist Charles Valentine. He asked eighty subjects to compare an individual square (A) to another placed underneath a stack of blocks (B) (figure 6). Sixty percent of his subjects viewed the square topped by a stack of blocks (B) as taller than one without the blocks, although the squares were the same size. The results could be explained by the subjects' perception that square (B) raised itself up vigorously against the weight of the stack of blocks, thus confirming the phenomenon of Einfühlung.[94] According to Einfühlung theory, these subjects viewed the vertical lines of square (B) as taller than they were wide. This assumption, however, was not confirmed in a further test, undermining Einfühlung as the explanation for the illusion. Valentine admitted, however, that, "Lipps's theory of the illusion seems incapable of direct disproof by means of experiment."[95]

Einfühlung was also popularly invoked in these years to explain "one of the burning controversies of aesthetics"—or why curved lines were seen to be pleasing.[96] The eye was thought to follow curves

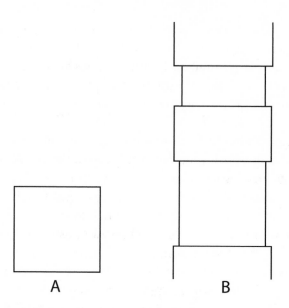

A   B

*Figure 6. Image of single box and stacked boxes used in 1913 experiments
to test for Einfühlung in the viewer. C. W. Valentine,* An Introduction
to the Experimental Psychology of Beauty
(London: T. C. and E. C. Jack, 1913), 50.

with its own smooth movements, producing a calming physiological response attributed to and felt within the curves themselves. But in 1902 George Stratton demonstrated to the surprise of many psychologists that eye movements bear "but a crude resemblance" to the curved figures. Stratton's photographic recordings of the eye showed jerky movements and a course "wild and broken" when tracking curves. The sense that the eye moved smoothly was a "most striking introspective illusion."[97]

But even this finding did not lead to an outright rejection of Einfühlung. Stratton concluded that rather than stemming from eye movements, Einfühlung was a more generalized, "faint bodily reaction" that "helps us realize and appropriate the imagined movement in the object, so that it thereby becomes, in some literal sense, flesh of our flesh."[98] To support this claim, Stratton cited Lee's and Anstruther-Thomson's experiments. He attributed the preference for the curved line to "movements of the attention and imagination, and with the activity of comprehension and sympathy."[99] The graceful curve continued to suggest life and movement not by mirroring eye movements but by evoking "organic vasomotor or muscular response."[100]

In 1904, the head of the Harvard psychological laboratory, Hugo Münsterberg, explained how aesthetic Einfühlung was tied to motor response. When a spectator followed the shape of a line, aesthetic responses did not occur if motor impulses were inhibited, or if practical movements resulted such as grasping a door handle or stepping onto the sidewalk.[101] But if antagonistic muscles were stimulated, and if the subject projected muscular tensions and contractions into the line or object, this produced aesthetic Einfühlung. In this case, muscular responses became qualities of the lines themselves through aesthetic transference: "The energies which we feel in the lines are external projections of our own energies."[102] Münsterberg elaborated, "We ourselves are contracting our muscles, but we feel as if the lines were pulling and piercing, bending and lifting, pressing down and pushing up."[103] In a similar vein, psychologists of the period often referred to perceived "*forces* in the picture or the line" as the spectator's "forces of attention."[104]

Münsterberg's student Ethel Puffer also subscribed to the existence of Einfühlung. Puffer had traveled to Berlin to study psychology in 1895, but as a woman she had to obtain special permission to attend lectures.[105] She began work in Münsterberg's home laboratory in Freiburg and returned to Harvard with him to write her dissertation on symmetry and beauty. In her 1906 book, *The Psychology of Beauty*, Puffer asked, "How do we think of a tall pine-tree?" She answered, "By sweeping our eyes up and down its length, and out to the ends of its branches."[106] While viewing a work we carry out motor suggestions, and when this system of energies balance, aesthetic repose is produced.[107] Symmetrical forms roused a harmonic response as they reflected the energy of the human bilateral organism.[108]

Puffer called Einfühlung "expression theory" or "sympathetic reproduction" and saw it as a fundamental, though limited, aesthetic response.[109] To feel the energy of the line meant that a certain mood and moral quality was conveyed, but this did not always transmit the form's meaning.[110] The sweep of a curving line might convey strength or energy, but one gleaned a very different meaning if the curve delimited the arc of a drapery rather than the line of an infant's limb.[111]

Puffer wrote on Einfühlung theory into the 1910s, but her academic career was abruptly cut short when the offer of an academic post at Barnard College was rescinded due to her engagement to be married. She later outlined the dilemma of the professional woman in a popular magazine as the "persistent vicious alternative, marriage *or* career—full personal life *versus* the way of achievement."[112] In 1913, she reviewed the aesthetic literature on Einfühlung. which she called "a field already pretty well exploited."[113] She reported that there was little doubt that Einfühlung existed, but its mechanism of action was still opaque: "Not *that* we sympathetically reproduce ('Miterleben'), or 'feel ourselves into' a form ('Einfühlen'), but *how* we do so, is the question."[114]

If psychologists attested to the existence of Einfühlung, so too did art historians and artists. The Munich architect and Jugendstil designer August Endell studied with Lipps and created border designs that evoked a feeling-into-forms, resonant with Einfühlung (figure 7).[115] Wilhelm Worringer's influential 1908 dissertation on abstraction and empathy argued that Lipps's Einfühlung exemplified a style of art that generated an identification with organic, representational figures, in contrast to the geometric style that reflected an urge to abstraction.[116] Wassily Kandinsky and his Blue Rider collective in Munich promoted ideas that resonated with the literature on Einfühlung, and the expressionist painter Hans Hofmann invoked empathy as key to aesthetics even after he relocated to New York from Munich in 1932.[117] By 1914, Einfühlung theory had so permeated aesthetics that one Oxford philosopher declared that it "in various forms may be said to be the most commonly accepted of our time."[118] The popularity of the Einfühlung tradition extended well into the 1930s; in his 1933 overview of psychological aesthetics, the Earl of Listowel devoted the longest section to Einfühlung.[119]

In 1912, Vernon Lee gathered and amended her aesthetic essays in a new compilation, *Beauty and Ugliness*. These updated findings were informed by her continuing experiments, by her contact with Groos, and by her visit to Külpe's laboratory in Bonn.[120] By this time, Lee resolved that there were two types of empathy (she had adopted the English translation from psychologist Edward Titchener).

FORMENSCHÖNHEIT UND DEKORATIVE KUNST

A. ENDELL

Figure 7. Decorative motif designed by August Endell, inspired by Theodor Lipps's writings on Einfühlung. August Endell, "Formenschönheit und Dekora-tive Kunst," in Dekorative Kunst: Illustrierte Zeitschrift für Angewandte Kunst, *vol. 1 (Munich: H. Bruckmann, 1898), 76.*

One was formal and abstract, the other gestural and representational. The first—formal-dynamic empathy—was aligned to Lipps's theory, whereby one projected enlivening feelings into the lines of a statue, column, or painting. The second—imitative or gestural empathy—relied on the body's organic and kinesthetic sensations and accorded well with her own experiments, those she conducted with Anstruther-Thomson, and Groos's approach. Lee argued that the two forms of Einfühlung could work separately or in tandem. If formal-dynamic Einfühlung comprised the more elevated aesthetic engagement, Lee never rejected the notion that the body played a role in aesthetics, if not always in immediate experience, then in memories of movement.

Her book garnered a mixed response. The *New York Times* described it as "simply a 'terrible' book" with "long, involved sentences, long scientific terms, queerly inverted thoughts, French words, and Latin and German." As Europe lurched toward war, one reviewer couldn't fathom why any American art student would care for the "frightful labors of Prof. Külpe." Even if the title was deceptively simple, it asked too much of the general public.[121] Puffer more positively branded Lee's book "The Adventures of a Mind with the *Einfühlung*-Theory."[122] Despite its pastiche-like quality,

Puffer called it a "treasure-house of material" that provided bold "suggestions for new departures."[123]

Einfühlung had unquestionably made its mark on Lee's writings. In these years, Lee continued to write her signature travel essays, tracking her peregrinations across Europe, expounding on its natural beauties, architectural wonders, and artistic splendors.[124] She celebrated the motorcar in one essay as giving "the rapture of mere swift movement" and the "sense of triumph over steepness."[125] But moving so quickly, she reflected, did not allow for a deeper-going bodily connection with the landscape, one very like Einfühlung: "In motoring things remain ocular, mere visions, unaccompanied by the sympathizing measuring of our muscles and will."[126]

In 1913, Lee published *The Beautiful,* an accessible, popular book on aesthetics. In it, she waxed eloquent on aesthetic empathy. Empathy explained how it is that we see shapes, "at some definite angle to our own axis and to the ground on which we stand."[127] Lee described the aesthete as a traveler who moved actively through the worlds of sense, sound, touch, and vision, moving her head and body and adjusting her focus like an opera glass. Unlike the scientist who scanned the landscape to seek evidence of its volcanic history, or the engineer who scrutinized the terrain to fix the placement of irrigation equipment, the aesthetic traveler had no instrumental aims and was unattached to particular ends. The aesthete simply attuned herself to the beauties of the landscape, "satisfied with the wonderfully harmonized scheme of light and colour, the pattern (more and more detailed, more and more co-ordinated with every additional exploring glance) of keenly thrusting, delicately yielding lines, meeting as purposefully as if they had all been alive and executing some great, intricate dance."[128] The lines and patterns of the landscape came to life and moved in an erotic dance of light, form, and color.

Lee told her readers that the "best example [of empathy] was when I said that opposite to the man there was a distant mountain *rising* against the sky."[129] The rising is actually the man's own rising, the lifting of his eyes, neck, and head to see the mountain. A spectator usually did not recognize these origins in him or herself and translated them into objective terms, thus merging "the *activities* of the perceiving subject with the qualities of the perceived object."[130] The movement of rising gathered together associated thoughts and emotions of rising, imbued by past experience as well as with expectations of the future. Each empathic act was therefore a mini-drama complete with its own history and anticipated future.

Lee declared that we simply could not see the world without reference to our bodily positioning, linked to our memories and expectations embedded in movements like rising. She drew on empathy when she described "a skyline '*dropping down merely to rush up again in rapid concave curves*'; to which I might have added that there was also a plain which *extended*, a valley which *wound along*, paths which *climbed* and roads which *followed* the *undulations* of the land."[131] She italicized the verbs to reveal the crystallization of empathic movement within language itself.

It would not be an exaggeration to say that for Lee Einfühlung formed a psychological and aesthetic groundwork that bodied forth in language, modes of expression, and in everyday life. It constituted a good portion of our consciousness and was critical to both logical thought and the power of poetry. Empathy palpably demonstrated how inner experience shaped outer perception. It had so permeated our thinking, Lee surmised, that it had not yet been given its due. "Indeed if Empathy is so recent a discovery, this may be due to its being part and parcel of our thinking; so that we are surprised to learn its existence as Molière's good man was to hear that he talked prose."[132]

CHAPTER TWO

From Einfühlung to Empathy

IN A DARK ROOM at the psychology laboratory at Cornell University in May 1919 the observer H faced a blank wall and closed his eyes. Helen Sullivan, the experimenter, sat near a window where a streak of light illuminated the notepad on which she recorded responses. After saying, "ready," she instructed the observer to feel "yourself making a hundred yard leap on a pair of skis." H imagined he took off in the leap, but then felt as if someone else hurtled through the air on skis. Because H had never leaped on skis before, he imagined someone else carrying out the jump. To the Cornell researchers, this ability to imagine another person executing an unfamiliar movement signified "empathy."[1]

This was only one of many such experiments in mental imagery and empathy carried out at the Cornell laboratory in the first decades of the twentieth century. The British-born Edward Titchener, director of the laboratory, had helped to fashion a new scientific psychology that aimed to uncover the building blocks of thinking with the method of systematic introspection. With this technique, trained observers in the laboratory painstakingly reported on the visual, auditory, olfactory, and kinesthetic images passing through their minds. Titchener concluded that kinesthetic images—those of bodily movement—were at the root of empathic response.

Most psychologists of this era had trained at cutting-edge German laboratories, and as the new field of experimental psychology grew, it became increasingly important to formulate terminology for programs at Anglophone universities. In 1908, Titchener suggested the new English translation "empathy" for Einfühlung, and early the next year he explained his translation in a series of public lectures. Although psychologists and historians have attributed the translation solely to Titchener, he was not the only one to suggest empathy or other translations at this time.[2]

"Aesthetic sympathy" appeared in 1901 as the first translation of Einfühlung in the *Dictionary of Philosophy and Psychology*. Psychologist James Mark Baldwin compiled this dictionary with help from his colleagues in order to establish a standardized nomenclature for the new science. But Baldwin found the term "semblance" more apt because it captured the idea of aesthetics as a form of play, key to his developmental psychology. And, at Trinity College at the University of Cambridge, psychologist James Ward also proposed the term "empathy" in 1908. He deemed empathy a mythic impulse that personified and animated objects, which still persisted in modern-day thinking and philosophy.[3] These early meanings of empathy reflect its rich history, largely forgotten today.

James Mark Baldwin and Semblance

One of the first attempts to find an English translation for Einfühlung was ventured by the American psychologist James Mark Baldwin, who took up the enormous task of standardizing psychological nomenclature at the dawn of the twentieth century. Between 1901 and 1905, he enlisted the expertise and collaboration of over sixty colleagues in the overlapping fields of psychology and philosophy to compile the *Dictionary of Philosophy and Psychology*, later called "Baldwin's Dictionary."

Baldwin was a developmental (then called "genetic") psychologist who completed his undergraduate degree at Princeton and studied experimental psychology with Wilhelm Wundt in Leipzig. He returned to Princeton to earn his doctorate, founded the *Psychological Review* with James McKeen Cattell in 1894, and set up a psychological laboratory at the University of Toronto in 1889. He studied the development of his own child's capacity for imitation and sympathy with others, and he linked individual development with that of the human species, or phylogeny.[4] His evolutionary theory, called the "Baldwin effect," argued that adaptations made by an individual could produce further variations that were selected for as instincts and then passed on through natural selection.[5] By 1903, Baldwin was teaching psychology and philosophy at Johns Hopkins University.

Baldwin was convinced that the confusion in the new science of mind was due to the "lack of well-defined terms." Older nineteenth-century expressions, such as "soul, reason, cause, creation, vital force," evoked metaphysical notions and were thus problematic for the new psychology.[6] Baldwin considered various strategies to develop a new psychological language from William James's attempt to retool familiar terms, to the logician Charles Peirce's creation of "a clear and consistent terminology for the mental and moral sciences as had been done for mathematics and symbolic logic."[7] Baldwin opted for a middle ground between the creation of neologisms and the adaptation of the older terminology to the new discipline.

In his *Dictionary*, Baldwin listed the English equivalents and translations for French, German, and Italian psychological terms. On the matter of a translation for "Einfühlung," however, there was little agreement. Baldwin reported in 1906 that "the committee of the *Dict. of Philos.* failed to find any available term for *Einfühlung*," and therefore the loose translation, "aesthetic sympathy" was adopted.[8] The *Dictionary* showcased psychologists' agreement on a translation by posting their initials at the end of an entry. The initials WMU and EBT followed the entry "aesthetic sympathy," indicating assent from Wilbur M. Urban, Baldwin's former student, a philosopher at Ursinus College, and E. B. Titchener at Cornell. But the entry also mentioned another translation: "animation," which some saw as a more accurate rendering of *Beseelung*, Lipps's synonym for Einfühlung. To add to the mix, the German psychologist Karl Groos penned an addendum to the entry, protesting that Lipps's Einfühlung did not specify the locale of feeling, which could be either in oneself or in the object.[9] Far from authoritatively pinning down the meaning of Einfühlung, then, the entry echoes with the contentious voices of psychologists, disagreeing not only on the translation but on the meaning of the German term as well.

Once the *Dictionary* was completed, Baldwin moved to another consuming project: his dense, four-volume work on genetic (or developmental) logic, entitled *Thoughts and Things*. He published the first volume in 1906 and completed the series in 1915 with *The Genetic Theory of Reality*.[10] Throughout these volumes, Baldwin emphasized the importance of Einfühlung, defining it as a play sensibility and repeatedly offering his preferred translation of "semblance." Child's play was "sembling," or creating a make-believe situation set against the backdrop of the real world. Baldwin described the play object as an "experimental object" that existed in the real world but at the same time could be imaginatively controlled by the child. He explained: "Broadly understood, the process of 'sembling' consists in the reading into the object of a sort of psychic life of its own, in such a way that the movement, act, or character by which it is interpreted is thought of as springing from its own inner life."[11] The child intertwined his imagination with objects in the actual world, animating playthings as living animals or persons. "There is a certain feeling-into the given object (*Einfühlung*), now made semblant, of the subject's own personal feeling: an attribution to it of the inner movement which its construction requires."[12] The play or semblant object thus possessed a real and an imaginary status at the same time.[13] Baldwin's ideas were closely allied to Karl Groos's writings on play, inner imitation, and illusion in animals and children, which Baldwin and his wife translated and introduced to an English speaking audience.[14]

Baldwin continued to speak of Einfühlung as semblance, even suggesting it as a good translation in 1906.[15] He noted in his *Dictionary*: "The committee of the Dict. of Philos. failed to find any available term for *Einfühlung*, and the rendering here made has since then occurred to me."[16] And back in 1902, his definition of "semblant," not surprisingly, was synonymous with that of aesthetic sympathy: "the indulgence in the temporary acceptance of a mental construction as real, with the knowledge, at the same time, that it is not. This is characteristic of much play and art enjoyment; one feature of which is that it throws the observer into a voluntary treatment of an artificial situation as real. Cf. Sympathy (aesthetic)."[17]

If semblance was central to child's play, it was also key to art and aesthetics. According to Baldwin's developmental schema, the play sensibility first appeared in the child's prelogical modes of thinking, and after the logical phase of development, it reemerged in the highest or hyperlogical stage. Art, just as play, operated in the field of the "as if actual," meaning that it was suggestive of reality but not actual reality. Art marked out a real situation and transformed it at the same time. "The aesthetic interest presumes a modicum of suggested actuality, existence, reality, truth."[18] By this measure, the photograph was not art because it did not depart from actual reality. At the other pole, Baldwin explained, the abstractions of the "mere ink-spot or the mere noisy crash—loses interest, whether in play or in art." Both extremes lacked the quality of semblance.[19]

Baldwin's use of the term "semblance" for Einfühlung, however, did not catch on. His student Wilbur Urban saw semblance as only "one stage of the total process" and not broad enough to cover what he saw as the more expansive scope of Einfühlung.[20] It was also the case that many American psychologists were moving away from Baldwin's dense philosophical treatment and into more experimental, applied realms. But likely the most compelling reason Baldwin's suggestions were not taken up was that scandal engulfed him in June 1908: he was caught visiting an African American brothel and was arrested.[21] In the ensuing days, he abruptly resigned his professorship at Johns Hopkins and fled to Paris. His direct influence on American psychology declined, although his developmental schema was of considerable interest to psychologists Jean Piaget and Lev Vygotsky.[22]

Living in Paris, Baldwin still kept tabs on new psychological terminology, reporting in 1911, "Both Titchener and James Ward have suggested 'empathy' as English translation of *Einfühlung*."[23] The term "empathy" had already appeared in October 1908, in the Philosophical Periodicals section of the British journal *Mind*, likely written by either Ward or Titchener, both contributing editors.[24] Titchener was the American editorial representative and Ward was on the journal's advisory committee. Titchener had penned these periodical sections in 1894, although it is not clear if he was still doing so in 1908.[25] That same month—October 1908—James Ward was credited for suggesting "empathy" for Einfühlung in an experiment on color perception printed in the *British Journal of Psychology*, which he edited.[26] And in November of that year, the term appeared in the *Philosophical Review*, a Cornell publication.[27] "Empathy" was printed as the correction to a footnote in the journal's July issue, which had read: "Professor E. B. Titchener has suggested the introduction of the term 'enpathy' as an equivalent for *Einfühlung*."[28]

Sometime in 1908, then, both Ward and Titchener suggested "empathy" as a translation; it is unclear if they discussed it or if they independently turned to the Greek *empatheia* for inspiration.[29] But even as Baldwin acknowledged in 1911 that both psychologists had suggested "empathy," he resisted using the new term. He pointed to the "great confusion" on Einfühlung in the German literature and advised that a proper English equivalent be found only when consensus was reached on its meaning. In a final bid for his own "semblance," Baldwin suggested that "empathy" was "the best term for the strictly aesthetic movement," whereas it would be better for a "more general word such as 'semblance' being used for the entire group of analogous imaginative processes."[30] In the minds of most psychologists, then, "empathy" still signified an aesthetic phenomenon.

Baldwin continued to invoke semblance as key to his developmental schema, and to the aesthetic sensibility—the highest, most integrated stage of development. Aesthetic feeling, he explained in the final volume of his series, should at last be elevated to "its true dignity as an organ of the apprehension of reality."[31] Aesthetic semblance bridged mind and matter, affect and cognition, truth and value. It linked the self with objects in the world: with semblance/empathy, "the object is not merely presented to me for my observation or criticism; but in it I find the inner world mirrored; in it I feel my own cognitive and active powers establishing themselves."[32] We imaginatively took hold of the world through semblance and through the process could also connect with others. As Baldwin put it, "in this world, presently semblantly to my gaze, I find realized my community with other selves.[33]

James Ward and Personification

If "semblance" was Baldwin's preferred translation of Einfühlung, the British psychologist James Ward suggested "empathy" in 1908.

Ward was one of the first psychologists in England to embrace physiological principles, although he had initially trained in theology. After preaching for only one year, he abandoned his post as a Congregational minister and turned to psychology.[34] He studied the moral sciences at Trinity College at the University of Cambridge and conducted experimental studies on crawfish in Michael Foster's physiological laboratory.[35] Foster promoted a monism that highlighted the continuities between the protoplasm of unicellular organisms and the bodies of more complex animals; over the course of evolution protoplasmic movement was thought to transform into the rhythmic beating of the heart in higher organisms.[36] This argument for evolutionary continuity would soon become a central plank in Ward's psychology.

Ward began lecturing in psychology in 1878. In 1886 he wrote a highly influential account of the new psychology that appeared in the ninth edition of the *Encyclopedia Britannica*, in which he critiqued the regnant discourse on sensationism and associationism, central to British philosophy and psychology of mind. He instead elaborated on a psychology of experience based on the idea that the mind did not merely passively receive stimuli but actively responded to the world. In an attempt to put psychology on an empirical foundation, Ward requested funds from the university for a psychophysical apparatus and set up a small space for a laboratory in 1891, which in 1893 moved to the physiology department. A fully appointed Cambridge laboratory, however, was not constructed until 1912, after a petition launched by Ward and psychologist Charles S. Myers in 1908 and funded by a significant contribution from Myers's family.[37]

A number of Ward's collaborators and students in the laboratory attributed the new translation of "empathy" to him. Edward Bullough's experiments on aesthetics found that subjects described colored lights as possessing a particular temperament or character, which he called "empathy" responses on Ward's suggestion. In early 1909, Myers credited Ward with proposing the term "empathy" in his textbook on experimental psychology, writing, "Professor James Ward suggests to me this convenient translation of the German *Einfühlung*." Myers defined empathy as a process of "living into" the object, in which "the subject feels in himself the suggestions of strain, movement or rest in the object, and makes them part of himself."[38] And Charles Valentine, a student of Ward's, conducted experiments on Lipps's aesthetic Einfühlung at the Cambridge laboratory and called the capacity to read activity into vertical lines "empathy as Dr. Ward translates it."[39]

Ward developed a descriptive psychology of consciousness and experience, as he put it, "to ascertain, describe, and analyze the invariable factors of psychical life."[40] His view of evolutionary continuity linked the world of matter with that of the mind. Just as protoplasm grew into differentiated tissue, Ward speculated, so too did the infant experience the world as a unified continuum, which over the course of development differentiated into specialized functions. One could therefore never return to one's childhood's experience of the world, as this would mean returning to a confused and indistinct set of perceptions. Mental development altered consciousness as an integrated whole, a view taken up by Ward's student Frederic Bartlett, who developed an influential theory of memory. Bartlett held that memories were not pocketed in some corner of the mind but were continually assimilated into one's experience over time; it was a "constantly changing active-memory system as opposed to a 'store-house' of past experiences."[41]

In 1897 Ward became a professor of mental philosophy and logic at Trinity College and twice gave the prestigious Gifford Lectures. Linking matter with mind, Ward argued that nature's laws were very like psychological habits: "All nature is regarded as plastic and evolving like mind: its routine and uniformity being explained on the analogy of habit and heredity in the individual, and of custom and tradition in society."[42] If others thought this was merely a mistaken attribution or projection of the mind's properties to matter, Ward disagreed. It was indeed true that humans imputed human concepts to nature: "We attribute to extended things a unity which we know only as the unity of an 'enduring' subject; we attribute to changes among these extended things what we know only when we act and suffer ourselves."[43] But Ward took this tendency as evidence of the fact that matter demonstrated mind-like qualities, a view called "panpsychism."

Panpsychism was advocated by a number of psychologists and philosophers in these years, among them C. S. Peirce, Josiah Royce, and William James.[44] Ward cited with approbation Peirce's declaration that "matter is effete mind, inveterate habits becoming physical laws." He also agreed with Royce's notion that "evolution would be a vast series of processes suggesting to us various degrees and types of conscious process."[45] Ward admitted that this philosophical view was not scientific, and yet there was nothing in science that could reject out of hand this "panpsychic view." A significant support for panpsychism, as Ward saw it, lay in the continuity of evolutionary processes. Because no sharp lines could be drawn between animals of a lower and higher order, it was also improbable that a stark distinction existed between matter and mind. If the theory of evolution was first thought to be a leveling down of the human to his animal origins, Ward pointed out that it might be better understood as a leveling up. "At first it appeared as if man were only to be linked with the ape, now it would seem that the atom, if a reality at all, may be linked with man."[46]

Ward adopted Leibniz's view that the smallest units of reality, or monads, possessed psychical properties and individual peculiarities. He didn't specify the nature of these monads, only cautioned that one should not dismiss the theory out of hand on the basis that chairs or stones were not alive.[47] If matter was indeed undifferentiated mind, it was likely that inanimate objects possessed psychic qualities, even if in a still inexplicable fashion.[48] As Ward put it, "All things were animated albeit in divers degrees."[49]

Ward's conception of animation was closely linked to his understanding of empathy, which he described in a 1915 letter to his close friend, the anthropologist James Frazer. Ward wrote that he had purposed to translate what German psychologists nowadays call Einfühlung as "empathy." Instead of typing "empathy," however, he typed "sympathy" and then directly over the letters *sy* he printed the letter *e* as a correction (figure 8). Ward's letters of a few years earlier were handwritten, suggesting either that an assistant typed the letter and was unfamiliar with the new word, or that Ward himself was not used to the new contraption and simply made a mistake by typing the more common "sympathy." He corrected the error by writing a large *e* and also bolding the faint *n* in the word "Einfühlung." The error at once reveals the close connection between the new term and "sympathy," as well as the deliberate attempt to coin the new translation "empathy."[50]

Aд.М. b.37 331

```
                    6 Selwyn Gardens,
                       Cambridge.

                               19.xi.15.

My dear Frazer,

    Perhaps one of the most telling facts in favour of
your interpretation of personification is what German
psychologists nowadays call Einfühlung - a term I have
purposed to translate by empathy.  It is evidence of the
original impulse having 'survived'.  I will try and explain
when we next meet.

                            D
```

Figure 8. Facsimile of letter written by James Ward and sent to James Frazer,
November 19, 1915. Trinity College Archive, the Master and Fellows of
Trinity College Cambridge.

Ward and Frazer knew each other as undergraduates, when Ward suggested that Frazer explore anthropology by reading Edward B. Tylor's book *Primitive Culture*. Frazer spoke of "my friend, James Ward (with whom I have walked and talked on all subjects in earth and heaven on an average once a week for many years)."[51] Their friendship was sustained through their long mutual connection with Trinity College as well as their participation in an informal Cambridge anthropological circle.[52] They swapped ideas with Henry Jackson, philosopher of ancient Greek; the classicist W. H. D. Rouse; and Robertson Smith, the biblical scholar and anthropologist.[53] Jackson found Ward's psychological writings of use to him when he lectured on Aristotle's *De Anima*—on the souls of living things, including animals and plants.[54]

Beginning in 1890, Frazer published his multivolume *The Golden Bough: A Study in Comparative Religion*, a world-renowned work that went through many editions. Frazer discovered the impulse to personification in many May Day festivals manifest in diverse cultures from Bavaria and Alsace to Transylvania and Bengal: "The names May, Father May, May Lady, Queen of the May, by which the anthropomorphic spirit of vegetation is often denoted, show that the idea of the spirit of vegetation is blent with a personification of the season at which his powers are most strikingly manifested."[55]

Ward linked empathy to this kind of anthropomorphic person-ification in his letter, but in his other writings he did not restrict the impulse to the primitive or mythic mind, nor even to a religious sensibility. Ward likely explained in one of his weekly walks with Frazer that the impulse to personification understood as Einfühlung or empathy was unmistakable in modern philosophical discourse. As he elaborated in an introductory text on philosophy: "We seem justified then, in maintaining the presence of anthropomorphism or 'poetical metaphysics' not only in the speculation of primitive man but even in those of philosophers down to our own time."[56] Empa-thy captured a habit of thinking or tendency toward anthropomor-phic projection that persisted in everyday experience as well as in contemporary philosophy. Ward reinforced this notion in his letter to Frazer, declaring that empathy in its current form was proof of this "original impulse having 'survived.'"[57]

Ward's understanding of empathy has been for the most part forgotten. But some contemporary thinkers have found value once again in this anthropomorphic impulse. Philosophers have launched technical arguments refuting a strict dualism of mind and matter, and others have ventured that embracing panpsychism might lead to a new ecological sensibility. As one theorist contends, to personify the natural world is to communicate with it, providing an avenue for an encounter with nature rather than a way to gather knowledge.[58] This impulse, which Ward declared to have survived in 1915, may be still with us.

E. B. Titchener and the Kinesthetic Image

If Ward viewed empathic personification as reflective of the larger philosophical truth that mind and matter were not all that different, and Baldwin saw semblance/empathy as essential to aesthetic expe-rience, the psychologist E. B. Titchener catalogued "empathy" ac-cording to its mental constituents. He argued that the basic building blocks of thought could be uncovered through systematic introspec-tion carried out by trained psychologists in the laboratory. Titchener was born in England, studied the classics at Oxford, and then com-pleted his graduate degree in physiological psychology with Wil-helm Wundt in Leipzig. Beginning in 1892, Titchener established a vibrant experimental psychological training program at Cornell, and he headed the laboratory until his death in 1927.[59] Titchener's laboratory protocols became standard practice for generations of experimental psychologists, and his findings were published in the *American Journal of Psychology*.[60] Introspective methods dominated American academic psychology up until World War I, when psychologists turned away from the inner workings of the mind to study observable behavior and applied psychology.

Back in 1902, Titchener had appended his initials to the translation of Einfühlung as "aesthetic sympathy" in Baldwin's *Dictionary*. Six years later, however, he decided that the German term deserved a new translation. He had dedicated 1908 to the study of the imagination at Cornell, complaining to a colleague that there existed "as yet no psychology of the imagination."[61] The imagination played a central role in Titchener's understanding of Einfühlung, a view also put forth by his mentor Wundt in his extensive volumes on language, myth, and art that comprised his everyday psychology (*Völkerpsychologie*). Wundt's 1908 volume on art, for instance, explored how the mythic projection of subjective feelings into objects was intensified in aesthetic perception.[62]

By 1908, Titchener had already translated a number of classic German psychological texts for the training of American students of psychology. He declared that German psychophysical terms were best translated into English by way of their Latin-Greek origins, in order to mirror the languages of physics and chemistry. Titchener reasoned that new translations of this kind would provide prestige to the new scientific psychology.[63] So when Titchener suggested a new translation of Einfühlung, he turned to the Greek *empatheia* with its meaning of strong "pathos" or "feeling" to derive the English "empathy."

Titchener publicly introduced his translation in a series of lectures he gave at the University of Illinois at Urbana in March 1909. These lectures comprised a fierce argument against his psychological competitors at the Würzburg laboratory, headed by Oswald Külpe, the psychologist who had conducted experiments on aesthetic Einfühlung just a few years earlier. The debate revolved around whether it was possible to think without relying on mental images. Psychologists at Würzburg believed it was indeed possible, arguing that abstract forms of thought such as surprise, expectation, familiarity, even Einfühlung could not be reduced to more elementary sensations or images.[64]

Titchener, however, judged it impossible. He held that all thought processes were rooted in the basic building blocks of images, feelings, and sensations. The Würzburg psychologists had simply carried out faulty introspections, Titchener alleged, and had specifically overlooked kinesthetic and bodily images in the thinking process. These kinesthetic images, it turned out, were key not only to Titchener's polemic against his psychologist rivals but also to his conception of empathy. Titchener may well have adopted the term "kinaesthetic image" from Lipps as a way to capture the ways perception and the feeling of movement were intertwined in Einfühlung.[65]

Kinesthetics, or the awareness of bodily movement, was first identified in the early nineteenth century, and it was often referred to as the sixth sense. By the end of the century, psychologists avidly took up its study. The psychologist John B. Watson, soon to become a well-known behaviorist, experimented on mice in 1906 to see if they could reach the end of a maze, modeled after the seventeenth-century Hampton Court hedge maze, using only their kinesthetic sense. Watson blinded the mice, knocked out the pads in their feet, destroyed tympanic membranes in their ears, and punctured their olfactory bulbs. An editorialist in the *New York Times* decried his method as torture not sufficiently warranted by the scientific results. Watson nonetheless reported that the desensitized mice managed to orient through the maze, affirming the existence of the kinesthetic sense.[66] In 1907, Titchener began to test observers in a kinesthetics room in his laboratory. Observers sat in a Mach rotation apparatus—a chair mounted in rectangular frame that could be pivoted on a vertical axis—and reported on their feelings of bodily movement.[67]

To his audience in Urbana, Titchener emphasized the ubiquity of mental images by proclaiming that his own mind was a "fairly complete picture gallery,—not of finished paintings, but of impressionist notes."[68] He told his audience that he could not read or write a paragraph without hearing imagined musical accompaniment—usually the sound of the woodwind, as he was keen on the oboe.[69]

When he tried to understand complex psychological theories, he explained, he imagined a visual image of a dull red pattern with angles rather than curves. This visual image helped him to evaluate the integrity of an argument by seeing either "neatness or confusion where the moving lines come together."[70]

Images comprised the necessary psychological vehicles for thinking. Titchener declared that to think "horse" was to imagine the shape of "a double curve and a rampant posture with a touch of mane about it." Cow was "a longish rectangle with a certain facial expression, a sort of exaggerated pout."[71] Even "meaning" had a visual equivalent—"the blue-grey top of a kind of scoop, which has a bit of yellow above it . . . and which is just digging into a dark mass of what appears to be plastic material."[72] Titchener attributed this image to his classical training in which he had to ferret out Greek and Latin meanings of words. One of his graduate students visualized "meaning" as the unfurling of a white scroll, and another saw "meaning" as a horizontal line with two short verticals at each end.[73]

But if visual images like these were commonly experienced, kinesthetic images were far more difficult to identify. Titchener declared that this was precisely the error of the Würzburg school. Just as a trained introspectionist knew the difference between seeing a red square and imagining a red square, Titchener argued that a psychological expert should be able to distinguish between feeling a movement or a sensation and having an image of that movement.[74] An image was, indeed, less distinct than a sensation; it was "relatively pale, faded, washed out, misty; and its intensity and duration are markedly less" than the sensation.[75] If sensations rooted one to the actual perception of one's surroundings, an image was a mental picture that carried ideas and concepts. Images were key to memory and imagination, and they enabled travel to the past or into the future; they went beyond sensation and characterized the more advanced mind.[76]

Titchener then enticed his audience to imagine kinesthetic images in the form of mental nods and frowns. A kinesthetic image of a nod, he claimed, was limited to specific muscles, but the sensations felt in an actual nod of the head engaged many more muscles than were necessary.[77] Kinesthetic images also grounded abstract concepts such as doubt, hesitation, and belief.[78] Titchener offered the example of the concept "stately," which called up in his mind the image of a heroine—a tall figure with a hand holding up a steely gray skirt.[79] This mental image was not only visualized but felt, as he imagined the gesture and physical posture of the heroine. Titchener explained: "Not only do I see gravity and modesty and pride and courtesy and stateliness, but I feel or act them in the mind's muscles. This is, I suppose, a simple case of empathy, if we may coin that term as a rendering of *Einfühlung*."[80] His metaphor of the "mind's muscles" aptly conveyed the idea that imagined movement comprised the core of empathy. Empathy joined the optical with the kinesthetic, so that in the mind's eye, stateliness was linked to felt bodily movement.

Empathy could also extend from an image to holistic "attitudinal feels," or organic and whole body responses to experimental materials and everyday situations.[81] Titchener explained that his movements and kinesthetic representations were quite different when he sat down at his desk to write a letter than to compose a lecture. Even the word "but" was connected to a mental image, which Titchener described as comprising an attitude of suspension or the feeling of being stuck between two opposing movements. This inner feeling or attitude of suspended movement Titchener called "motor empathy."[82]

At the end of his lectures, Titchener polled his audience to find that one-third of the attendees possessed kinesthetic ideation and could form a mental image of a movement.[83] His host, Stephen Colvin, confessed later that year that although he had previously believed it possible to think without images, he came to believe in "those kinaesthetic experiences (whether central or peripheral in their origin) which we employ at times in our thinking and which constitute the mind-stuff of certain of our ideational processes."[84] Some psychologists reported mental images of coldness, which included the cool spray of the surf and the cold shock of a shower bath. Images of heat for one psychologist included the "hot and stuffy interior of another bathing-house" and warm water touching his feet in a bay.[85]

Karl Dallenbach, a curious undergraduate at the University of Illinois, "attended every one of [Titchener's] lectures and was entranced by them."[86] Two years later, he arrived at Cornell with a fellowship in hand to begin his doctoral studies. One of Dallenbach's first tasks was to explore the attribute of "clearness" in attention, as outlined by Titchener in his 1910 *Lectures on the Elementary Process of Feeling and Attention*. Dallenbach soon recognized, however, that Titchener's term "clearness" erroneously imputed a cognitive element to attention. When Dallenbach asked Titchener why he chose the term, Titchener replied that he made the decision based on empathy, or the kinesthetic feeling he had for the words: "the word 'clearness' was round and forward-flowing, whereas 'vividness' was angular and prickly."[87] Titchener agreed with Dallenbach that "vividness" was in fact better suited to describe the mental process of attention, and they changed the term.[88]

When Dallenbach met with Titchener to discuss his dissertation, Titchener became enthralled by his offhand mention that he played chess blindfolded. The dissertation was quickly forgotten and the meeting was "chiefly devoted that evening to blindfold chess."[89] Titchener urged his student to systematically examine his mental processes while playing the game. Dallenbach was able to identify a large number of kinesthetic images while playing, which "consist in the projection upon the board of 'lines of force,' peculiar to the game, and weave themselves over the board like a 'cat's-cradle.'"[90] During one game, Dallenbach noticed that his opponent had twice overlooked the opportunity to take a pawn with his bishop. Once he became aware of this missed move, Dallenbach felt "strain sensations or images (I know not which) in the shoulders, that carried this meaning. In character they were like those in wrestling; it was as if I wanted to interpose my body along the diagonal between the bishop and the pawn."[91] Dallenbach converted a sedentary game into a mental wrestling match by imagining that he occupied lines of force in the midst of the board. He felt kinesthetic empathy with the chess pieces, as if they possessed their own motive power, and he went as far as to say that "the meaning of 'chessness' was carried by the kinaesthesis."[92]

If the Cornell researchers were convinced that kinesthetic images underlay abstract thought, psychologists at Würzburg were not persuaded. But at the crux of the debate on the possibility of thinking without images stood the question of whether kinesthetic and organic imagery existed, as the psychologist June Downey remarked.[93] And, of course, kinesthetic imagery was key to empathy.

By the fall of 1909, Titchener published his Urbana lectures as the *Experimental Psychology of the Thought-Processes*, enshrining his translation and definition of empathy in print. A year later, reports documenting the existence of kinesthetic imagery and empathy began to pour out of the Cornell laboratory.

Beginning in 1910, psychologists and students at Cornell, all highly trained in the method of systematic introspection, documented empathic kinesthetic images.[94] In these experiments, introspectors, called "observers," sat in laboratory spaces and dark rooms, fixated lights, watched shadowy shapes appear from projected lantern slides, and focused their attention while prompted verbally or visually with a stimulus word or image. Respiration was often measured with a kymograph, and reactions were timed with a chronometer. Observers meticulously reported the stream of thoughts, feelings, and sensations going through their minds, responses inscribed by experimenters in the room.

Observers were categorized as verbal, auditory, visual, or kinesthetic types and were identified in published papers by name and position. Observers ranged from established psychology professors, to newly minted PhDs serving as assistants in the laboratory, to graduate students working toward their doctorates, including a significant number of women. In the 1890s, a handful of universities had opened their doors to women for graduate study. The discipline of psychology soon became a popular new scientific field, boasting more doctorates by 1897 than any science other than chemistry.[95]

Systematic introspection required observers to describe the perceived colors, shapes, and tones of the stimulus object and not the object itself.[96] For instance, an observer would report on the perceived color and shape of a red apple—the stimulus object—while never mentioning the apple itself. This meticulous description of the contents of consciousness was the ambit of the new scientific psychology, which, Titchener explained, was not to be confused with already existing philosophical or logical approaches to the mind.[97] Scientific psychology was new precisely because it described the elements of consciousness "not as they mean but as they are."[98]

Empathic kinesthetic images were sometimes attributed directly to the stimuli, sometimes identified with the introspector's own bodily images, and sometimes experienced as a startling sense of a bodily fusion or confusion between self and stimuli. In a 1910 study of belief, the graduate student Alma De Vries reported an empathic kinesthetic response: a "visual image of a trick elephant dancing. Felt big and clumsy myself, as if I were the elephant."[99] De Vries was a frequent participant in imagery studies at the Cornell lab, and she was credited with the capacity to respond with visual, tactual, and verbal images, as well as with kinesthetic and organic sensations.[100] Another observer, an instructor in psychology, listened to a phrase about drinking alcohol and reported empathic kinesthetic images: "There was a very vague, kinaesthetic and motor attitude, representing a woman of the total-abstainer kind, with disgust for drunkard, turning away her face and head and wrinkling her forehead: these things seemed to occur in my own case (feeling of disgust, tendency to turn head and wrinkle forehead)."[101]

The 1910 experiments conducted by Titchener's student Cheves Perky on the relation of imagination, perception, and memory also elicited empathic responses. Observers in these experiments, both trained and naive, described shapes they thought they imagined but which had actually been presented to them as stimuli. Subjects described the faint yellow shape of a banana projected from the lantern slide as imaginary, and they declared that the trickle of a stream of water continued even after it had stopped.[102] Perky concluded that the imagination called up powerful, stable, even photographic images, accompanied by imagined bodily participation and feelings of strangeness or surprise. Participation could extend to a merging with the object, signaling empathy: "The object spreads all over me and I over it; it is not referred to me but I belong to it."[103] One experimental subject was told to imagine a bunch of grapes and reported "a cool, juicy feeling all over"; when she imagined a fish, she described a "slippery feeling in my throat, coolness in my eyes."[104] Perky contrasted these invented mental images with those from memory, which were unstable, laden with personal meanings, and often accompanied by actual bodily movement. Perky's findings made their way into Titchener's 1915 textbook on psychology, in which he distinguished memory and imagination in good part by the presence of empathy. "Memory was characterized by the feeling of familiarity and by imitative kinaesthesis; imagination by the feeling of strangeness and by empathy."[105]

Figure 9. Stimuli for 1917 experiments on kinesthetic empathy and shape perception conducted by Anna Rogers at the Cornell Psychology Laboratory. Anna Rogers, "An Analytic Study of Visual Perceptions," American Journal of Psychology *28, no. 4 (1917): 551.*

A few years later, the graduate assistant Anna Sophie Rogers demonstrated that with an empathic kinesthetic sense one could ascertain the meaning of shapes. Observers viewed inkblots, hieroglyphs, and shapes with representational elements and then introspected their visual, kinesthetic, and auditory images (figure 9).[106] Observer Helen Clarke reported that while perceiving the shapes, "I felt myself (general empathic kinaesthesis) standing erect and rigid, and then the meaning 'grass' came."[107] Rogers classed empathic kinesthetic responses of this type as interpretative perceptions, which meant the observer tried to read meaning into the figures. In Titchener's psychology, meaning was most often carried by a kinesthetic response, a bodily attitude, or a sensation.[108] Rogers published her results in Titchener's flagship journal in 1917, a use of inkblots in psychology that predated the publication of Swiss psychiatrist Hermann Rorschach's more famous ones by four years. In a striking parallel, Rorschach also invoked kinesthetic empathy to explain why some subjects perceived movement in the inkblots.[109]

In another Cornell study, observers looking at squares responded with empathic kinesthetic responses. One observer reported that the squares possessed "stability" or "compactness" directly related to the sensations and imagined feelings he experienced in his chest and throat. Another felt that the lack of balance in an oblong shape was mirrored and even determined by images and sensations of pressure felt in the chest.[110] Other empathic responses included feelings of imbalance or solidity felt in the shapes themselves rather than as the observer's own feeling.[111] When students at Cornell were asked to picture the passing of time, they reported wheels, a stream, a crawling snake, a zigzag, climbing a hill, hurtling through space, and a moving line. More than half reported moving images, and researchers concluded that it was empathy that enabled these observers to experience time as "traversed space."[112] In another study, an assistant in the laboratory reported "rather vague empathic feelings which had something sharp about them" that helped him pair nonsense words and figures.[113]

As frequent as these kinesthetic images were in laboratory reports, they were nonetheless difficult to pin down. Sometimes they were experienced in the mind of the observer, sometimes within the object, and sometimes in a merging of the two. Alice Sullivan's doctoral work of 1921 tried to sort out these differences.[114] She instructed observers to *feel* rather than to think in order to prompt kinesthetic imagery. "Feel: yourself running downstairs; Feel: an acrobat walking a tight rope; Feel: Laocoön struggling in the coils of the serpent; Feel: yourself stooping to pick up a pencil."[115] She then classed kinesthetic images according to whether they referred to oneself (resident) or to something or someone else (projected).

Sullivan concluded that empathy was best characterized by a *projected kinesthesis*—a feeling one projected onto another. To empathize meant to imagine another performing an action, or to imagine how it might feel to move in the way an object might move. If the action was unusual, and one the observer had never performed, an observer typically projected it into someone else. When asked to feel a farmerette (a Canadian term for a young woman working on a farm) pitching hay, for instance, one observer responded: "The kinaesthetic image belongs to the farmerette, it is a kind of empathy."[116] And when another observer was asked to imagine Tantalus of Greek myth bending down to drink from the pool in which he was standing while the water incessantly ebbed away, he reported: "The imagery was in me and then in Tantalus, but somehow it was transferred from the right side of my neck to the left side of Tantalus, who was out in front and facing me. It seems as if the kinaesthesis is lifted bodily out of me and put into someone else."[117]

To empathize was therefore to project kinesthetic images into others rather than feeling them for oneself. The mental images of one's own actions were fleeting and passive, whereas empathy took focus and mental work. Sullivan concluded that empathy required "an attitude which is active, exploratory, detached, scrutinising."[118] One was more prone to adopt empathy's exploratory attitude when encountering the unknown. Titchener explained to beginning psychology students that with empathy, we could enter into an unfamiliar situation in order to understand it better. He suggested we might "*become* the explorer; we feel for ourselves the gloom, the silence, the humidity, the oppression, the sense of lurking danger; everything is strange, but it is to us that the strange experience has come."[119]

Herein lay the difference between empathy and sympathy. Titchener explained: "This tendency to feel oneself *into* a situation is called **empathy**,—on the analogy of sympathy, which is feeling *together with* another."[120] Sympathy meant to identify *with* another, often a familiar, interpersonal experience, whereas empathy meant to enter *into* a situation, often one that was unfamiliar or alien. Titchener called empathy our "natural tendency to feel ourselves, often bodily, into what we perceive or imagine." It was a capacity that extended to objects as well. He described it as "humanizing objects, of reading or feeling ourselves into them."[121] He instructed his students to examine their own empathic experiences while reading, while contemplating art or architecture, in the theater, even while daydreaming. "We are told of a shocking accident, and we gasp and shrink and feel nauseated as we imagine it; we are told of some new and delightful fruit, and our mouth waters as if we were about to taste it."[122]

Titchener acknowledged that he often resorted to figurative language to capture empathic response, but that nonetheless, "in broad outline and on the average, we may hope that it is true to the psychological facts."[123] If empathy eluded precise scientific definition, it still had the power to transform the mute presence of an object with feeling, life, and movement. One projected the mind's image into the object. "Take the empathic tendency: what lover of books has not shifted the place of certain volumes on a shelf, because he could not bear to put good and bad, sound and trivial, side by side,—as if the *books* would feel the incongruity?"[124]

Titchener's readers were quick to adopt the kinesthetic image as the root of empathic response. Vernon Lee found that the kinesthetic image made possible a formal-dynamic empathy with abstract line and shape in distinction to representational empathy for the human form.[125] A speaker at the International Congress of Psychology in 1929 declared that the kinesthetic image allowed an actor to employ empathy to simulate emotions rather than to rely on sensations that produced the actor's actual emotions.[126]

By 1913, most psychologists had adopted "empathy" as the accepted translation of Einfühlung. That year, Vernon Lee showcased the concept in her popular book, *The Beautiful*. But the new term, "empathy," had its critics. James and Alix Strachey, translators of Freud's writings, called it a "vile word."[127] The British journal *Notes and Queries* listed it as a new word in 1926 yet could not locate it in any dictionaries. The authors found its definition confusing and not in line with the meaning of the original Greek. They explained that the new word meant that one felt an awkwardness while watching someone with an awkward gait, which one then projected into that person.[128] The term was simply an "unfortunate attempt to force a meaning on the English word, which is not expressed by the Greek."[129] Another scholar called empathy "a doubtful Graecism," and yet another wanted to substitute the term "ecpathy" for empathy, to clearly denote the aesthetic appraisal of action. Art theorist Ernest Mundt dubbed it an "artificial word."[130]

And yet "empathy" stuck, carrying with it the intertwined ideas of semblance, projection, and aesthetic perception. In these early years, empathy offered the possibility of imagining or projecting oneself into unfamiliar situations, and into objects or shapes quite unlike the human. Early empathy emerged from the mind's ability to form kinesthetic images. For some psychologists, empathy possessed the power to animate and to personify objects, and it could even bridge mind and matter. The concept was still closely tied to its roots in aesthetic Einfühlung, however, and for the next two decades in American psychology, this projection model of empathy would continue to be alive and well.[131]

CHAPTER THREE

Empathy in Art and
Modern Dance

Oh, it is joy to say

To the clod of earth, "Thou art I:"

And to mirror myself in each tree.

—JUNE DOWNEY, "Monism," 1904

WHEN THE WRITER REBECCA West strolled down the Odéon to the Boulevard Saint-Germain in Paris, her "eye lit on a dove that was bridging the tall houses by its flight." She "felt that interior agreement with its grace, that delighted participation in its experience, which is only possible when one is in a state of pleasure."[1] West called the feeling of being in flight with the dove "empathy" even as she acknowledged that the word was "absent from most dictionaries." She borrowed the term from Vernon Lee, the travel writer, novelist, and aesthetician. West defended her use of the term against her critics, explaining that "empathy" was simply a convenient rendering of the familiar feeling of "entering into the experience of objects outside ourselves." If "empathy" was a term unknown to the general public in 1928, it had already captured the imagination of writers, art psychologists, and dance critics as a way to blend the self and object through aesthetic experience.

Psychology was still only a subdiscipline in most university philosophy departments in the early twentieth century, but it had been rapidly gathering adherents and growing laboratories. Psychologists continued to broaden their academic inquiries, moving the profession toward applied projects in industry, intelligence, and advertising, as well as in art education and appreciation. Building on the nineteenth-century tradition of psychological aesthetics, psychologists analyzed mental and physiological responses to art and tested creativity, literary ability, and the workings of empathy in the laboratory. The psychologization of art was fast becoming a dominant twentieth-century trend.[2]

Experimental subjects experienced empathy by projecting inner images of movement laden with emotion into visual art, literature, and poetry. Empathy was described more often in these years with the lines of paintings or the shape of an object than with persons. Kinesthetic empathy captured the audience's ability to feel into and grasp the new abstract forms of modern dance.[3] Empathy also informed the study of personality: according to analyst Carl Jung, the penchant for empathy made one an extrovert, and psychologists found empathy to be a holistic, aesthetic approach to understanding personality. Empathy theorists of this period were kinesthetic modernists who stressed experiential values in the encounter with form, line and verse. The aesthetic spectator was moved by empathy, as we will see, in ways literal and metaphoric.[4]

Empathic Projection in Poetry

The Wyoming psychologist and poet June Downey declared that the puzzles of aesthetic creation and appreciation "might be solved in the laboratory." Even better, such a science would not "unweave the rainbow."[5] Over the course of three decades, Downey sought empirical evidence for empathic engagement in poetry, and aimed as well to help the writer unlock creative capacities.[6] She came to see the importance of mental imagery through her training in introspective methods at the University of Chicago and during a summer

session spent at the Cornell laboratory.[7] Downey established and
chaired the Department of Psychology and Philosophy at the University of Wyoming, the only woman to head such a department in
the country. She did not marry or have children, devoting her time
to teaching, research, and creative pursuits, as was required of successful women psychologists of the period. She was unflatteringly
memorialized at her death at fifty-seven as a "frail little woman"
with "almost paralyzing physical difficulties" but with a remarkable
ability to labor for hours in a "dingy attic workroom."[8]

Downey was fascinated by mental imagery, which formed a central theme of her scientific investigations, played a key role in her
own poetry, and accounted for her love of modern Imagist poets.
Downey found the Imagists' use of images to be crisp, clear, and in-
ventive, and she fashioned her own poems in this style.[9] She was cap-
tivated by synesthesia and wrote an intensive case study of a college
student who experienced tastes as colored images.[10] Downey called
those who were adept at creating visual images the "eye-minded"
sensory type, whose thoughts, she explained, "resemble flickering
movies."[11]

In 1919, Downey created the Individual Will-Temperament
Test, one of the first psychological tests to measure temperament
in an era when testing of all kinds had become psychology's central
mission. A decade earlier, Henry H. Goddard adapted the French
Binet-Simon intelligence tests for use with feeble-minded children,
tests that were soon tailored for children in public schools, for immigrant adults, and for screening soldiers during World War I.[12]
Downey's test correlated handwriting to personality by measuring
the speed, flexibility, impulsion, and detail of writing movements.
She tested more than two hundred subjects, including thirty patients
at the Boston Psychopathic Hospital, although she based her final
norms on college subjects.[13] She was well aware that graphology had
a dubious scientific reputation, and she leveled critiques against the
bolder claims made for the science, correcting the popular notion
that a back-slant to one's writing signaled a chilly personality. She
contended that it was a more reliable indicator of being left-handed
as a child or of having a dominant left eye.[14]

Downey nonetheless identified four different temperaments
with her writing test: the mobile, rapid-fire person; the accurate,

deliberate type; a complex, mixed type; and a phlegmatic or slow type. These motor types revealed one's personality as well as one's aesthetic propensities. The slower, deliberate types tended to engage in greater visualization, contemplation, and aesthetic enjoyment. When movement was slowed or inhibited, inner imagery was heightened. She explained: "In aesthetic enjoyment, with a failure in practical attitude and its motor sequences, visual images develop to the verge of hallucinatory vividness."[15] Downey found this true for herself; when she was fatigued and not inclined to move, she experienced all kinds of visualizations, some even infiltrating her dreams.

Downey determined that visual images were critical to aesthetic experience, but so too were images of movement, or kinesthetic images. Downey agreed with Titchener that kinesthetic images made empathic engagement possible, what she called "psychic participation" in the aesthetic object. Such participation might involve imitating the movements of a statue or feeling subtle organic and bodily feelings while perceiving the lines of a building. These inner movements could induce an intricate array of emotions, moods, and perceptual complexes.[16] "It is not merely that we grow breathless with the runner on canvas as we do when watching him upon the field; not only that we writhe with Laocoön, or sink into a contemplative mood with Michelangelo's 'Thinker,' but every arch of stone, every cedar box, every curving vase induces subtle personal reactions." When we see a ruined form, we feel it bodily: "We pause at sight of the broken column. Our sense of its meaning is realization of the arrested eye, the checked breath." Empathic feeling meant that we felt pressure when viewing weighty forms: "The slender pillar topped with heavy cornice overweighs us; we too yield under a too heavy burden."[17] Downey conveyed the range of empathic feeling in this literary style, but she also employed technical psychological terms to explain that "optical-kinaesthetic imagery in which the movement or mood-complex humanizes the object is empathic."[18]

To pin down the features of empathic response, Downey assessed a dozen subjects on their sensory and mental imagery while they read more than four hundred lines of poetry by Keats, Schiller, Poe, Swinburne, and Blake. Subjects reported auditory images while reading Poe, but they felt more bodily and cutaneous images while reading Keats. Downey explained that bodily imagery accounted for the common depiction of Keats's poetry as "statuesque."[19] She then asked subjects if they felt any bodily movements or shifts in posture when they read the depiction of Saturn in Keats's unfinished poem *Hyperion*:[20]

> Upon the sodden ground
> His old right hand lay nerveless, listless, dead,
> Unsceptred; and his realmless eyes were closed;
> While his bowed head seem'd list'ning to the Earth,
> His ancient mother, for some comfort yet.

Subject D reported that she had a "perfectly clear-cut visual image of the old man in the posture described" and described her empathic response: "Tactual and kinaesthetic feeling of the sodden ground. Feeling of weight and relaxation in right hand. Kinaesthetic feeling of bowed head and of closed eyes."[21] Subject M described how she "put self into the old man and [had a] slight tendency to get outside and see old man." And Subject J reported, "As Observer I am northeast of visualized self and of old man. Visual self about one hundred feet off, looking at old man who is twenty feet farther off. No imitation of old man's posture."[22]

Some subjects saw or felt themselves in the scene, while others felt as if they themselves were the old man. To empathize meant that one went beyond seeing oneself in the scene to feeling *bodily* present. It was, according to Downey, a "'feeling-in,' in which motor and emotional attitudes, however originating, are projected outside of the self."[23] In another experiment Downey gave her subjects a short excerpt from Edgar Allan Poe's poem "For Annie" to read:

> And I rest so composedly
> Now, in my bed
> That any beholder
> Might fancy me dead.

While reading these lines, subjects reported visual images of a man in bed and the reader lying in bed or standing near it. Some readers reported the feeling that they were lying on the bed with another person looking at him or her. When the reader described a *felt-sense* of occupying the bed or another position in the scene empathy occurred.[24]

Downey chose one highly empathic subject (M) to read lines from Percy Shelley's *Prometheus Unbound:*

Wheeled clouds, which as they roll
Over the grass, and flowers, and waves, wake sounds,
Sweet as a singing rain of silver dew.

The subject's introspective response was: "Movement in chest; spreading forward of hands in space. Feet not on ground. Become the cloud; feel of the cloud. The cloud, if conscious, would feel thus."[25] When the subject then read a description of a rainstorm, he reported: "I go out and am there. Kinaesthetic consciousness. Dripping; I become the little drops; small and ethereal."[26] Subject M epitomized empathic engagement by bodily feeling himself into the scene. Downey explicated: "He identified himself in kinaesthetic terms, with waving flowers, palpitating trees, flying insects and the like." As one of the more successful experiencers of empathy, this subject was versed in the German aesthetic theory. It was typical in these early years of psychology to test well-trained subjects because they were deemed the most incisive observers of the contents of their own minds. In another report, this subject revealingly uttered "'*Einfühlung.*' I become blue and turn to silver."[27]

Downey's observers not only imagined feeling with other persons but also felt subsumed in clouds, trees, and in abstract shapes. This phenomenon entailed "an actual fusion of the self-kinaesthetic content with visual content not-the-self."[28] Fusion comprised the highest level of empathic engagement, accomplished when the subject's feeling was transmuted into the object. Just as sweetness was seen as a property of sugar, or the color yellow as inherent to the petals of a sunflower, emotional and sensory qualities were experienced as integral to the objects themselves. Even "delicate personal emotions" could be felt as actual features of the object.[29] One psychologist explained empathic self-object fusion as the melding of visual images with kinesthetic and organic experiences to produce a kind of synesthesia.[30]

Subjects could also empathically feel into words. Downey instructed nine subjects to become absorbed in the words "twilight, halcyon, drowsy, nightingale, and mystic," and then to offer their reactions, images, attitudes, completions, or associations.[31] One response to "twilight" was: "Gleaming color. Sparkly lights from house. Feeling of sleepiness. Word looks half asleep. Blinky." To "thunder" a subject responded: "Voice deepens in speaking it. Smell of rain. Incipient auditory image. Word looks heavy and dark."[32] When subjects projected their own feelings into the words, it was as if the words themselves resonated with these qualities.

The idea that one's own emotions could be experienced within objects was central to Theodor Lipps's empathic aesthetics, and in these years the phenomenon was subject to testing and analysis by psychologists. The scholar of Italian, Edward Bullough taught the first course on aesthetics at the University of Cambridge and also carried out studies on color perception at the Cambridge laboratory. He presented his subjects with colored plates lighted through incandescent gas burners and with patches of reflected light on colored wallpapers and on colored silk. Introspecting subjects responded to colors in one of four ways. Those who offered "objective" perceptions attended to the saturation or brightness of the color, and subjects who gave "associative" responses likened the color to natural objects like the sun, sky, garden, as well as to lamps, railway signals, and, in two unique cases, crackers and skating. Other subjects observed the color's warmth, coolness, or restfulness, which were dubbed "physiological" responses. In the final group, the colors themselves were seen to be "insipid, stubborn, treacherous, energetic, jovial," which Bullough identified as empathic "character" or "temperament" responses.[33] Subjects saw the color red as intrinsically affectionate: it will "come out to you with openness and frankness." Blues were "more reserved, distant." Yellow was lightness of heart, but also fidgety, "almost impossible to take it seriously."[34]

Bullough classed these responses along a spectrum of what he called psychical distance. Subjects who gave "objective" responses stood at the greatest distance to the color, whereas those with "character" or empathic responses were the closest.[35] Even if the apparent heaviness of a color was due to the color's luminosity, it was empathy that caused subjects to see a golden yellow color as light in weight and a rich blue color as heavy.[36] Empathy took place through the fusion of physiological and optical elements so that "the individual projects himself into the object and rediscovers himself in it."[37] Bullough found empathic responses to be least frequent, but he deemed them the most sophisticated. Downey drew on Bullough's research in combination with her own findings to conclude that with empathy "we pass from detached intellectual evaluation of content, through emotional realization, into aesthetic objectivity."[38] Empathy humanized the object and at the same time objectified the self.[39]

Empathy into Form

Just as Downey saw kinesthetic imagery as central to empathy, the Harvard psychologist Herbert Langfeld rooted empathy in "the motor theory of mind, namely that to every stimulus which the organism receives from without, it makes a definite response."[40] For Langfeld and other functional psychologists, thinking was intimately tied to action. Drawing from studies of children and "primitives," Langfeld argued that attention developed adaptively from eye movements, and word meanings evolved from action descriptions. Functionalists took inspiration from John Dewey's conception that the entire reflex arc was involved at all stages of thought, rather than only a sensory or motor component.[41] Consciousness thus encompassed both incoming sensations and outgoing motor movements, even if motor responses were too weak to create actual movements.[42]

In 1920, Langfeld published *The Aesthetic Attitude* and gave pride of place to aesthetic empathy. He amassed material from his undergraduate lectures, pitched it to a general audience, and included seventy high-quality prints, an unusual presentation for the time.[43] Langfeld had trained in psychology at the University of Berlin under Carl Stumpf, a pioneer of early Gestalt psychology.[44] Langfeld first traveled to Berlin as a young naval attaché based at the American Embassy, and after his psychological training, arrived at Harvard

University in 1909 to teach and to begin a research fellowship. In 1924, he became head of the Princeton psychology laboratory and went on to coauthor a series of introductory textbooks in psychology and to edit the *Psychological Review*. In 1930 he became president of the APA.[45] One of his students described him as a Germanic type, who sported a goatee and lived on an extensive estate outside the university.[46]

The central insight of his 1920 book was that aesthetics comprised a relation or an attitude toward an object. Humans were always interacting with their environment in either a practical or aesthetic manner. One overcame obstacles in the practical attitude, but in the aesthetic attitude one harmoniously engaged with the world. If one encountered a classical statue with its hand extended in a practical attitude, for example, one would feel an impulse to return the handshake. But if one were feeling aesthetically inclined, one would instead mimic the pose. To reach out and still a moving branch entailed a practical reaction, but to sway along with the moving branches of a tree was aesthetic. Simply put, moving *toward* a form was practical, *with* or *in* the form was aesthetic.[47]

If aesthetics was a matter of one's stance, the intrinsic nature of the object receded in importance. It followed for Langfeld that an aesthetic attitude could "be assumed toward any object from fountain pens to Paradise Lost."[48] Every kind of spectator, then, whether it be "the rich and the poor, the prude and the libertine," could relate aesthetically to all kinds of objects including, "jazz or symphony, melodrama or classic tragedy, folk song, or polyphonic prose."[49] And further, empathy was essential to the aesthetic attitude. To empathize was to feel into the dynamic forces present in a panorama of lines and shapes, not merely to identify with a human figure. While watching a drama, the spectator should relate to *every* character, so that "one is swayed back and forth by the conflicting forces. One is successively hero, villain, and clown." Langfeld advised that one should feel into the work with an active passivity, as if one were "rowing downstream with the current and following its windings."[50]

Empathic response while viewing art could best be understood as embodied perceptions of force, movement, and weight. Langfeld demonstrated this phenomenon with examples of Renaissance paintings in his 1920 book. As one gazed at the image of the body of Jesus in the *Pietà* of Perugino (figure 10) and in *The Entombment* by Raphael (figure 11), empathy enabled one to feel marked differences in the weight of Jesus's body. In the Perugino, Jesus's body hovers above Mary's lap and the viewer feels a sense of lightness. Saint John the Evangelist, who supports his head, shows no signs of exertion or strain. This empathic perception was similar to watching as a talented ballet dancer "move[s] in the air with the lightness of a leaf blown by the wind."[51] Raphael's painting, in contrast, depicts so much strain and muscular exertion that the viewer empathizes violent force and with it, emotional vehemence.

Empathy as this kind of bodily projection into form soon was codified in psychology textbooks. In a 1933 textbook on general psychology, Langfeld and his colleagues depicted empathy with a schematic illustration and called it the "tendency of the observer to project himself" into objects and bodies. In this diagram, the figure on the left with its narrow base topped by a wide rectangle looks as if it was "carrying an insufferable burden" because, as Langfeld explicated, "we tend to think of *ourselves* as carrying such a burden, after the manner of Atlas" (figure 12).[52] The paired figure on the right was perceived to be "preposterous" because the strength of the column was too great for the weight of the thin capital (or block) on top. A well-proportioned, aesthetically pleasing form required that "the relations between a task and a muscular adjustment is one which the observer himself could handle."[53]

A few years later, Langfeld coauthored another psychology textbook in which empathy was depicted with a photograph of an athlete clearing a pole while his trainer raised his own leg in the background. The image was simply captioned "Empathy" (figure 13). Empathy was invoked to explain why an enthusiastic spectator at a football game pushed on his neighbor while watching his team at the one-yard line, and why viewers would sway back and forth while watching a climber scale a pole.[54]

The psychologist Kate Gordon developed a "brief and simple means of illustrating the experience" of empathic projection in 1934 by showing subjects a series of eight photographs of a Mexican figu-

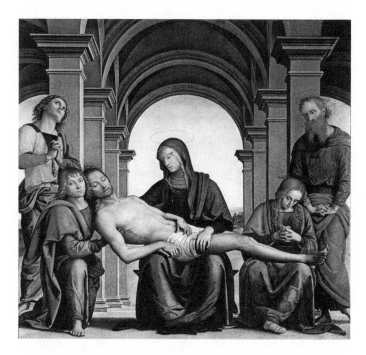

Figure 10. Pietro Perugino, Pietà. *Image printed in Herbert Langfeld's 1920* The Aesthetic Attitude *to demonstrate viewer empathy with the perceived weight of the figure of Jesus. Wikimedia Commons.*

rine raising one arm, four of which were mirror images of the others (figure 14). She asked her subjects, "Is it the right arm or the left arm which the statue is lifting in the air?"[55] Subjects felt themselves gesturing, making slight movements, or feeling their muscles twitching as they tried to answer the question. As Gordon explained, empathy was the projection of the viewers' own subtle movements into the statues or the tendency "to throw ourselves into attitudes or gestures which in a sense imitate or reproduce the object."[56]

Empathy had become a motor imitation. The Harvard personality psychologist Gordon Allport collected photographs in his personal file marked "Muscle tension/Empathy Pictures" presumably for use in psychology textbooks. One image depicted a baby about to topple over, and another, from a 1939 *Life* magazine, showed a weightlifter watched by an onlooker. The onlooker, even while sit-

Figure 11. Raphael, The Entombment. *Image printed in Herbert Langfeld's
1920* The Aesthetic Attitude *to demonstrate viewer empathy with the perceived weight of the figure of Jesus. From Julia Cartwright,* The Early Work
of Raphael *(London: Seeley, 1895), Internet Archive Book Images, Wikimedia
Commons.*

ting down, mimics the lifter with his legs spread out and his mouth
wide open. Given his own postdoctoral training in Germany, Allport was well aware that imitative motor empathy was a behaviorist simplification of Einfühlung's original meaning. He later elaborated: "*Empathy* arrived in a portmanteau packed in Munich"
embedded in a complex social philosophy, but "*motor mimicry* was
all we wanted."[57]

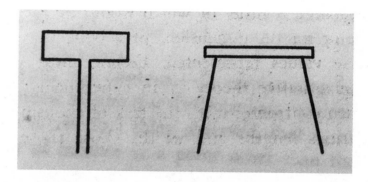

Figure 12. Image printed in 1933 psychology textbook to illustrate empathy as a feeling of weight and balance experienced within the geometric forms. Gardner Murphy, General Psychology *(New York: Harpers and Brothers, 1933), 238.*

FIG. 24. EMPATHY.

Figure 13. Photograph, showing a trainer extending his own leg while watching an athlete leap over a bar, used to depict "empathy." Edwin G. Boring, Herbert S. Langfeld, and Harry Porter Weld, Introduction to Psychology *(New York: John Wiley and Sons, 1939), 274.*

Figure 14. A series of Mexican figurines with arms raised used as stimuli to evoke empathic movements in subjects. Kate Gordon, "A Device for Demonstrating Empathy," Journal of Experimental Psychology *17, no. 6 (1934): 893.*

Empathy in Modern Dance

Although motor mimicry was a narrow interpretation of empathy, this meaning was nowhere more vivid than in modern dance. John Martin, one of the major dance critics of the period, drew on the empathy literature to uncover links between a spectator's felt inner movements and the performances taking place on the stage. He was hired by the *New York Times* to be its first dance critic in 1927, a year when the major New York City daily newspapers hired dance critics for the first time.[58] Martin had studied violin and Stanislavsky's acting methods, directed experimental theater, and tirelessly advocated for the artistry of modern dance.

In the early years of the twentieth century modern dance carved out a new niche between Isadora Duncan's romantic dance, with its emphasis on emotion and expressiveness, and the classical dance, or ballet, that had for years encompassed a standard vocabulary of movement. By 1928, modern dance had come into its own: Martha

Graham formed her own school and company in New York City; Doris Humphrey established a company with Charles Weidman; and Tamiris (Helen Becker) created a concert group.[59] These new companies, along with a growing focus on group dance, more intricate choreography, and the self-conscious adoption of forms that would appeal to modern life, ushered in a surge of popularity in the modern dance in the late 1920s.

Modern dance was not about ornamentation, story, or even musical accompaniment. Martin explained that it "abstracts its material to the most pungent essences and presents it sparsely and directly," to become, as he put it, "the art of movement."[60] He called modern dance, the "absolute dance," a term derived from German expressionist sources and used by Martha Graham to signify that dance was independent of other forms of art.[61] Graham urged that her dances not be interpreted with conceptual or narrative content, but with attention to the significance of the movement itself.[62]

John Martin pitched modern dance as a quintessentially American art form in his newspaper columns, books, and speaking engagements. He recognized that modern dance required new and demanding forms of aesthetic reception on the part of the spectator, and he took pains to win over skeptical audiences. He called the years after World War I the "Power Age," stirred by a new vitalism, in which dance drew on mechanistic models of efficiency and physical training regimens.[63] Martin advised the student dancer to develop an exquisite and powerful set of physical movements not simply by imitating the teacher, but by innovating.[64] The "impulses to move for one's own pleasure," as Martin put it, accounted for the explosion of interest in folk dance, in the ragtime of the dance hall, as well as in professional performance.

Martin gave a series of lectures at the New School for Social Research, published in 1933 as *The Modern Dance*. He outlined four discoveries of the new art form: the centrality of movement; the importance of "metakinesis," or the direct transmittal of emotion to the viewer's own body through movement and gesture; dynamism, or the constant activity of the dance; and the abolishment of traditional forms. Martin drew on prominent empathy theorists—Theodor Lipps, Karl Groos, and Vernon Lee—to account for the ways emotion and meaning were conveyed to the spectator through "inner mimicry" and "sympathetic muscular memory."[65] Inner mimicry was the "faculty for transferring to our own consciousness those motor experiences which an inanimate object before us would undergo if it were capable of undergoing conscious experiences."[66] A viewer might elongate the body when looking at a tall building, or broaden him- or herself before a low structure. The appreciation of architecture and the judgment of proportion were accomplished through the body: "The building becomes for a moment a kind of replica of ourselves and we feel any undue strains as if they were in our own bodies."[67]

Martin's language of empathic dynamism described inert objects like rocks as *lying* on the ground or *standing*, as if they were animate forms. Paraphrasing Vernon Lee, Martin explained, "Hills roll and mountains rise, though they are perfectly stationary; the rolling and the rising are activities in us when we look at them. The wind howls and whistles shriek, because those are what we would call our actions if we were producing similar sounds."[68] Objects implied actions, or at least subtle movements: "standing or lying or sitting or spreading or rising or waving or flowing—or something of the sort."[69] While describing a spiral staircase, for instance, it was typical to make small circles with one's hands in the air to enact the structure. Movement was the most elementary physical experience and dance distilled this dynamism into art.[70] One philosopher of the period explained that "dancing is the most direct elaboration of empathy (those movements by which we seek to become one with the object we contemplate)."[71]

Martin educated his audience to be empathic viewers and not idle spectators.[72] Viewers should go to modern dance performances to feel movement. He penned guidelines entitled "Layman's Guide: How to Look at Dancing" and "How Not to Look at Dancing," instructing his audience that movements of the dance should echo in the muscles of the viewer. The viewer had to "feel through" the dance with a sensitive body and fill in the space and complete the form.[73] To watch Martha Graham dance, as Martin wrote, one could "not sit limp and inactive" but had to follow along. The dance will "frighten away somnolescence." Graham's moods and movements were "concentrated to the highest degree. She gives less and less of the full dimensions of her meanings; she indicates, she suggests, she leads you on with her."[74]

Watching dance enticed the viewer into an inner imitation of the movement. Martin explained that "through kinaesthesis, any bodily movement arouses a sympathetic reaction in the mind of a spectator."[75] Kinesthetic sympathy or empathy activated movement-sense receptors in the spectator, prompting emotional associations leading to a grasp of the underlying intention of the movement. Martin declared: "We shall cease to be mere spectators and become participants in the movement that is presented to us, and though to all outward appearances we shall be sitting quietly in our chairs, we shall nevertheless be dancing synthetically with all our musculature."[76] It was a mistake, however, to focus on one's own muscle movements while attending to the dance. To do so was to lose the sense of the overall performance. This aesthetic error, against which Langfeld and Lipps had also warned, resulted in an incomplete empathic entry into the art form. As Langfeld explained, "in aesthetic contemplation such experiences are not felt as sensations within the body" but experienced within the object itself.[77] To deliberately attend to one's own kinesthetic sensations could shatter empathy.

Martin assured his audience, however, that with practice and perseverance, one could feel one's own movement while at the same time attending to the dance. In doing so, the viewer occupied the object; in Martin's words, "We look out from it, in a sense, instead of looking merely at it."[78] Educating the viewer to fine-tune his or her own motoric engagement enhanced individual aesthetic response while simultaneously securing the modern dance as an art form in its own right. Bodily empathy was key to the aesthetic respectability of modern dance, as Martin saw it, because a nonexperiential view of dance did injury to the work. Martin's account of kinesthetic empathy has recently received new scrutiny by dance theorists, who see striking consonances between his approach and current neuroscientific accounts of movement and empathy.[79]

Empathy into Line

Viewers empathized not only with forms, objects, and dancers on the stage but also with lines—both abstract and representational. Langfeld explained that while following the lines in a painting, a spectator could powerfully engage bodily feelings. He explained that while viewing a painting of the Dream of Saint Ursula, a spectator's gaze was diverted by the bend of the saint's elbow and the corner of the bedstead, evoking a contemplative feeling. At the Harvard laboratory, the postdoctoral researcher Helge Lundholm discovered that subjects attributed affective qualities to abstract lines.[80] Lundholm was born in Sweden, went to Paris to paint, and then earned a degree in the history of art before he turned to the study of psychology.[81] In one experiment he instructed eight subjects to draw lines that exemplified the emotions of melancholy, quiet, lazy, merry, agitating, furious, dead, weak, gentle, hard, serious, and powerful. He asked subjects to draw "pure" or abstract lines that did not symbolize or represent part of an object. Subjects drew lines with short waves or angles to convey the emotions "merry, furious or hard," and sketched long wavy lines to depict laziness or melancholy.[82] Lundholm found that the direction of the lines also carried meaning: "upwards expresses strength, energy, force, ambition, uplifting feelings, etc., direction downwards, weakness, lack of energy, relaxation, depression, etc."[83] Lundholm surmised that the shape of the line coordinated with the actual movements made when expressing the corresponding emotion.

Columbia psychologists A. T. Poffenberger and B. E. Barrows further examined this "feeling-tone of lines" by asking five hundred subjects to connect a series of lines with various emotions (figure 15).[84] They wanted to know how lines produced affective responses "to a work of art, a piece of architecture, or an advertisement." The most significant factor turned out to be the lines' directionality. Slow, descending curves were designated "sad," "weak" or "lazy," and slow, horizontal curves were "quiet" and "gentle." Rapid or medium rising angled lines were classed as "agitating," "furious," and "powerful."[85] Subjects also described the lines using expressions such as "down in the dumps," "sharp tongue," or "up in the air."[86] Poffenberger called these descriptions "immediate or fundamental": curves intrinsically gave off a warmth or glow, and sharp angles directly conveyed roughness or conflict. One did not first see a shape and then subsequently associate an emotion to it, but the emotion was already present in the perception of the line. Because these perceptions simply "could not be further analyzed," the authors suggested that these responses were instinctual.[87] This view

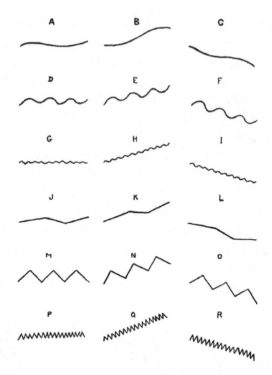

Figure 15. Lines presented as stimuli to subjects who described the lines as expressing emotions. A. T. Poffenberger and B. E. Barrows, "The Feeling Value of Lines," Journal of Applied Psychology 8 *(1924): 192.*

was in accord with Theodor Lipps's claim that empathy was sui generis, or directly intuited in shapes and lines, and not reducible to associations between ideas. Poffenberger's study has resurfaced in a contemporary book on aesthetics as evidence of the ways we "grasp the embodied meaning of a visual scene without the use of propositions of language."[88]

Lundholm's lines were adopted in another study that asked children to describe how "you would feel if you felt the way the line feels."[89] The researchers found that young children had a pronounced ability to empathically feel into the lines, but older children "felt themselves less and less into their surroundings."[90] Empathy was considered to be a regressive capacity, which was circumscribed to aesthetic experience by the time one reached adulthood. This view was not uncommon at the time; psychological projection or animation was frequently attributed to the less "advanced" mind of the child or primitive and viewed as only residually present in the adult.

Empathy and the Extrovert

Aesthetic empathy occurred when subjects became absorbed in the object, and psychologists began to wonder whether some personality types were more prone to empathize than others. Bullough had already identified different perceptual types in his experiments on color, but did these tendencies map onto broader personality differences? It lay to Carl Jung, acolyte of Freud and founder of analytic psychology, to draw on empathy for the creation of one of the most influential personality typologies of the century, that of the introvert and extrovert.

Jung first developed his personality typology by contrasting the pathologies of hysteria and schizophrenia. He explained in a 1913 lecture to the Psychoanalytic Society that the hysteric's abundance of feeling starkly differed from the apathy of the schizophrenic patient. This difference went beyond an emotional variance to signify a difference in the direction of the libido, a sexual and spiritual energy. Hysterics directed their energy outward, toward the world, whereas schizophrenics turned it inward, toward the self. Jung labeled these directed energies "extroversion" and "introversion," judging them to be "simple psychic mechanisms" that could also characterize the "normal human type." Only at extremes did these directed energies signal pathology. The extrovert, although well-adjusted, could transform into the hysteric, "caught up in objects, wholly losing himself in their toils" and possessing an "exaggerated rapport with members of his circle." The introvert tended toward paranoia or schizophrenia and acted "as though the object possessed a superior power over him against which he has to defend himself."[91]

Jung formulated this typology from his patients' pathology, but he also drew directly from the young art historian Wilhelm Worringer's extremely popular 1908 dissertation on art history.[92] Worringer's dissertation, published as *Abstraction and Empathy: A Contribution to a Psychology of Style*, outlined Lipps's theory of empathy but then offered a counterpoint—abstraction. Worringer asserted that Einfühlung was not the universal aesthetic principle that Lipps had affirmed but rather was circumscribed to the Graeco-Roman and Western style of representational art. With empathy, one projected one's own "organically beautiful vitality" into representational forms. Einfühlung was a harmonious aesthetic enjoyment experienced "in a sensuous object diverse from myself" but was only operative in this naturalistic artistic style.[93]

Worringer insisted that Lipps had overlooked empathy's opposing impulse—that of abstraction. Abstraction was the deliberate refusal of a harmonious projection into forms inspired by "an immense spiritual dread of space," or a "great inner unrest inspired in man by the phenomena of the outside world."[94] Rather than leading one to extend oneself into forms in the world, the urge to abstraction produced a withdrawal from a chaotic and unsettling world. This chaos prompted the creation of repose and order in a new crystalline, geometric style, which was typical of the Byzantine mosaic or the Egyptian pyramid. If Worringer deemed empathy the predominant impulse in Western representational art, abstraction was prevalent in Eastern and primitive art.

Worringer described empathy and abstraction as differing psychological orientations that produced contrasting artistic styles. He was inspired by art historian Alois Riegl who argued that the will to create was a central principle in the making of art, with technique, raw material, and purpose all playing subsidiary roles.[95] Worringer mapped the historical progression of art styles onto a developmental psychological template. The ancient, abstract, ornamental style progressed into the medieval Gothic style, which Worringer called an intermediary, pubertal stage. At this pivotal stage, the Gothic style embodied the transitional point from the early will for abstraction to the later urge for empathy. The Gothic cathedral, Worringer explained, was structured according to abstract laws, which "have become living, i.e. they have acquired expression. Man has transferred his capacity for empathy onto mechanical values."[96] Worringer argued that the abstract Gothic pointed arch had become empathizable.

At this historical juncture, the viewer could first empathically feel into the abstract form. It was not until the next phase, however —the naturalistic style of the Renaissance complete with representational figures—that empathy fully flowered. In Worringer's historical schema, empathy and representational art arose from abstraction. Worringer added one caveat to this stark historical opposition between empathy and abstraction—but only in a footnote. Even if the creative urge for abstraction produced geometric forms, a perceiver might in fact feel empathy with crystalline forms, for instance, the abstract shape of a pyramid.[97] But once a spectator felt empathy for a geometric form, it no longer held the same abstract value for that spectator.

Worringer's exposition of the primitive, geometric style supported modernist theories of abstraction, and his analysis of the two dimensions of the creative will provided Jung with a psychological groundwork for personality. Jung simply mapped Worringer's concepts of empathy and abstraction onto the traits of extroversion and introversion. The extrovert "gives his whole interest to the outer world, to the object, and attributes an extraordinary importance and value to it."[98] In distinction, the "inner easiness" and "spiritual dread of space" constituted the "primary tendency towards introversion." The introvert found the universe disquieting, withdrew libido from the object, and exalted "the intellect to offset the devaluation of external reality."[99] Jung found additional evidence for the link between introversion and artistic abstraction in the similarities between drawings made by schizophrenics and by "primitive humanity." The withdrawn, asocial schizophrenic patient—at empathy's opposite pole—had become a dominant type in psychiatry.

Jung expanded his theory of psychological types in his 1921 book of that name, translated into English two years later.[100] He explained that one either battled the world with abstraction or harmoniously accepted it with empathy. Abstraction emphasized the power of the object, whereas empathy put power in the subject. With empathy "some essential psychic content is projected into the object, so that the object is assimilated to the subject . . . so that he feels himself, as it were, in the object."[101] Jung soon complicated this picture, however, arguing that the two opposing psychological impulses were both powered by the deeper desire for self-alienation. One could escape the self through empathy by transforming into the object, or one could lose the self in a created abstraction.[102] Jung explained that to project into the object, one had to first empty or rob the object of its own spontaneity; likewise the forbidding animating world of the primitive was already an unconscious projection.

Despite these complications, Jung continued to chart introversion and extroversion as general-attitude types.[103] The introvert was taciturn, impenetrable, and shy, and the extrovert was sociable and open, on good terms with the world. These types were independent of class, gender, and other social determinants, and Jung speculated that they might be biological. The British art critic Herbert Read, editor of Jung's works and a friend to Worringer, explained in his popular books on art and psychology that we empathize with objects; we "feel into their shape, conform to it, and react to its limits, its mass, its rhythmic convolution; and so we invent the word *empathy*."[104] The empathic impulse, he declared, was common to the personality type who read him or herself into the world.[105]

Personality as Art

If empathy characterized the extroverted personality type, it also served as a method for aesthetically grasping the "undivided" whole or "form-quality" of another's personality, according to the psychologist Gordon Allport.[106] Allport was a student of Langfeld's at Harvard and completed a lengthy dissertation in 1922 on the experimental study of the personality.[107] He employed Jung's association tests to measure extroversion and introversion, characterizing subjects' responses as objective or egocentric. Egocentric responses could be empathic when, as Allport explained, the "imagery of self participat[ed] in the situation called up by stimulus word."[108] If this tendency became extreme and exhibited marked self-interest, it became a pathological complex. In another test that required the skills of empathy and imagery, Allport timed his subjects' ability to make associations while they read passages of shipwreck from *David Copperfield* and of despairing love from Dostoyevsky's *The Gambler*.[109]

After completing his dissertation, Allport traveled to Berlin to undertake postdoctoral studies and the study of the person.[110] He adopted Lipps's conception of Einfühlung as a route to aesthetic pleasure as well as a way to understand others through the "unconscious imitation of gesture, gait, and manner of speech."[111] To report that a "Gothic spire *soars* heavenward" or that a "waterfall *leaps*" or a "storm cloud *weighs heavily*" was to project one's own kinesthetic experience onto the object. This kind of kinesthetic understanding also extended to other people. Allport melded the aesthetic tradition of empathy with his psychology of personality, writing, "It has often been said by the advocates of empathy that the understanding of a personality is like the understanding of a work of art."[112]

Allport appreciated June Downey's experimental studies of aesthetic empathy and praised the "psychoesthetic panorama" of her 1929 *The Creative Imagination*, a compilation of many of her earlier papers. In a review of her book, Allport remarked that "with a work of such horizon and such understanding available there should be less complaint from artists concerning the sterility and 'impudence' of the psychological method."[113] Allport and Downey began a correspondence and shared their intent to find holistic methods for the study of personality. Downey was discouraged by "the narrowness and dogmatism of so many American psychologists" and complained to Allport that students were "actually writing their doctors' dissertations by formula."[114] She suggested a collaboration in early 1931, asking Allport, "I wonder what you would think of an endeavor to approach the study of the Undivided Personality—to use your striking expression—by way of Graphology?"[115]

Allport and Downey, along with the British psychologist Philip Vernon, temporarily based at the Harvard Psychological Clinic, soon began a collaboration on handwriting and personality. Downey analyzed the script of twenty-three Yale freshmen for clues to their personalities. She performed better than the professional graphologist they had hired. Allport found the results to be a "slight, but unmistakable success," although they were not statistically impressive.[116] Vernon argued that they were on the right track but needed to further refine their analytic methods. At the bottom of a typewritten letter to Downey, he enthusiastically scribbled, "Your 'visual image' of subject No. 9 describes him exactly."[117]

The next year, Downey delivered a paper on the handwriting of introverts and extroverts at the Third International Congress of Eugenics in New York.[118] She tentatively correlated extroversion and introversion with body types and speculated that temperament, as intelligence, had a "native endowment" that might be correlated to racial and ethnic groups, despite the vicissitudes of temperament, age, sex, fatigue-level, and other factors. She ventured that questions such as "Is the Irishman really a bit more belligerent than the Englishman?" or "Is the negro fundamentally excitable, impulsive, uncontrolled?" might be answered in the future.[119] Downey did not continue this line of research, however, as just a few months after the congress, she died suddenly of stomach cancer.[120]

If Downey saw a path from a holistic study of the individual personality to a biological typology of ethnic and racial groups, Allport moved decidedly in the opposite direction. He was more interested in individual portraits than in group assessment. With his collaborator Vernon, Allport conducted an extensive study of the expressive movements of twenty-five male undergraduates: walking, strolling, arranging cubes, tapping, compressing a stylus, drawing, and estimating sizes. The researchers compiled a large set of group statistics, and at the end of their 1933 book appended four intensive case studies. The case studies revealed that each individual exhibited what they called a "psychomotor congruence," or a movement style that infused the person's handwriting, drawing, postures, and gestures.[121] This individual movement style reflected the personality as a whole. Allport was convinced that one could understand the individual personality not by listing traits but by grasping the *"relation* of these features to one another and their inter-consistency."[122] He came to see the case study as the "most complete and most synthetic of all methods for the study of personality" and bemoaned the fact that it was not widely accepted in psychology.[123]

Allport was so taken by the case study method that he designed an undergraduate course at Harvard centered on one lengthy self-study, "The Locomotive God." This narrative depicted the author's agoraphobia and told the story of his early life and possible causes of the disorder. Allport contended that reading this one narrative allowed his students to discern the psychological principles of conditioning, the laws of learning as well as Freudian theories. But even more important, his students gained a holistic sense of the author's personality. A good judge of personality, Allport explained, needed experience, intelligence, and insight, but the most gifted judges were also aesthetically inclined. Aesthetic perception allowed one to grasp the "intrinsic harmony of any object," a method that relied on empathy.[124] By the time of World War II, as we will see, Allport's vision of empathy as a means to access a unique personality became a central trait of the tolerant, nonprejudiced person.

The Waning of Empathy Aesthetics

The dominance of empathy theories in the psychology of art had already begun to ebb by the war's start. In 1941, a résumé of major experiments in design reported that empathy research had come to a halt in England, overtaken by the new trends toward formalism and a statistical approach.[125] Museum curators were advised that empathy was a "now outmoded aesthetic" even if many had been schooled in the empathy tradition.[126] One philosopher critiqued empathy theory as engaging only a "thin aesthetic man" who entered into forms, leaving behind the everyday self with its practical interests. This image of empathy harked back to Lipps's notion of the ideal self that empathically entered into the object, leaving the real self behind.[127] The German-born Ernest Mundt, director of the California School of Fine Arts, was well acquainted with empathy theory but found it more "mystical" than conceptual. Another critic agreed, calling it a mystic union.[128] One art educator found American formulations of European empathy theory lacking in philosophical sophistication. Other critiques undercut empathy's originality: it was merely a modern version of the eighteenth-century sublime or the expansiveness of the soul.[129]

In art criticism, abstract formalism trumped the focus on the subject's encounter with art, evidenced in the postwar popularity of abstract expressionism. The influential critic Clement Greenberg defined modern painting in pictorial, flat, and purely optical terms, shunning the sculptural and tactile, as well as kinesthetic appreciation and empathic response.[130] The trend was to bracket the subject's response to art and to focus instead on the object. One German theorist saw Lipps's empathy theory as too psychological, opting instead for a view "which insures to the object an existence of independent worth."[131]

Empathy was nonetheless still relevant to art appreciation and art education, but often without explicit reference to the older theories. Art educators invoked empathy as a method of training students by cultivating one-ness with the object of attention, developing warmth and enthusiasm, and as "a force for projecting one's consciousness into others."[132] Art historian Mark Jarzombek points out that "art pedagogy was one of the principal carriers of the empathy message" in its celebration of authentic seeing.[133] One educator saw empathy as the counterpart of a science education, a "sympathetic identification, in imagination, with the unique qualities of the form, by which the content is intuited."[134] Empathy could help educate an artist's grasp of form, which in turn could enrich one's understanding of other people in everyday life. One literary critic found empathy useful for understanding motor and kinesthetic imagery in the poetry of Keats and Shelley, citing in 1946 the same excerpts from Keats's poem *Hyperion* that June Downey had studied thirty years earlier.[135]

Gestalt psychologists were perhaps closest to empathy theorists in their exploration of the perception of form, but they too began to depart from empathy's projection model. At a symposium on art in 1939, the émigré Gestalt psychologist Kurt Koffka argued that the perceiver did not have to project structure and feeling into the art object as it inhered in the object itself.[136] Empathy could not be "entirely subjective," as the self existed as only one feature "in a dynamic field."[137] Art psychologist Rudolf Arnheim contended that the movements, tensions, and forces perceived within forms emerged from inherent structural patterns and were not projected there by a subjective eye.[138] The gesture of moving one's hand in a parabola, for instance, possessed the inherent dynamic forces of compromise or yielding that produced the perception of "gentleness" in the viewer. Structural similarities linked the actual forces of yielding in the movement with the retinal image in the eye of the perceiver, as well as with the mental images in the perceiver's mind.[139]

Arnheim credited Lipps's projective empathy theory with anticipating his view of structural similarity, or isomorphism, and advocated for a kind of empathy without projection. He found inanimate objects to be naturally expressive: "A flame, a tumbling leaf, the wailing of a siren, a Louis XV chair, the cracks in a wall, the warmth of a glazed teapot, a hedgehog's thorny back, the colors of a sunset, a flowing fountain, lightning and thunder, the jerky movements of a bent piece of wire—they all convey expression through the various senses."[140] Another Gestalt psychologist identified movement-like qualities as inherent in music. Subjects directly perceived music to "rise, fall, ascend, mount, leap, bound, spring, shoot, tower, soar, drop, sink, slide, swoop, tumble, shift, swerve, tremble, quiver, flutter, pulsate, *etc.*"[141] These physical movements appeared in a variety of sensory modalities: "A swift, uneven, agitated, upward movement, increasing rapidly in intensity, may run through visual sensation, auditory sensation, and bodily sensation, giving to all three a similar form."[142]

Empathy theorists were not always consistent—sometimes they embraced a projective model and other times they regarded objects themselves as naturally expressive. These differences emerged from the angle from which they described empathy—whether from the position of subject or object. The philosopher John Dewey found both these positions wanting, however. To understand abstract lines as expressive meant that one perceived the meanings of the lines already as "constituent parts" of familiar objects.[143] He explained: "Lines express the ways in which things act upon one another and upon us; the ways in which when objects act together, they reinforce and interfere. For *this* reason, lines are wavering, upright, oblique, crooked, majestic . . . they are earthbound and aspiring; intimate and coldly aloof; enticing and repellent."[144]

Dewey welcomed Vernon Lee's emphasis on physiological engagement with form and shape, but he rejected her claim that such activity was projected into the object. He highlighted her subjectivist leaning by italicizing her own words: "The dramas enacted by lines and curves and angles, take place not in the marble or pigment embodying the contemplated shapes, but *solely in ourselves.*"[145] Dewey concluded that localizing aesthetic experience in either the subject or the object spoiled the experience and delivered only a partial account. Self and world were inextricably intermeshed: "The world we have experienced becomes an integral part of the self that acts and is acted upon in further experience."[146]

Some Gestaltists judged empathic viewing to be an uneducated perception. Wolfgang Köhler pointed out that when one described events as "sudden or smooth, jerky or continuous," it was indeed true that "from a descriptive point of view they are therefore no less objectively localized, are no less aspects of events themselves." But if this seemed to validate empathy theory, Köhler quickly rejected what he labeled a naive, realist view. A primitive might perceive a cloud as menacing, but a modern had enough scientific knowledge to perceive it in terms of measured distances and the velocities of physics.[147] Empathy was therefore a primitive, mistaken anthropomorphism that the scientist and the modern should properly leave behind.

In 1946, Langfeld rallied to the defense of empathy one last time, arguing that the theory had been radically misunderstood.[148] If empathy was a projection of the spectator's movements into the object, the shape of the object mattered as well. "Clues from the physical object arouse movement, either overt or covert, and that these movements are projected into the object in the sense that they form the basis for the characteristics of movement and force which are perceived in the phenomenal object."[149] The key to empathy was not projection, he insisted, but movement. To see circles, rooms, or colors empathically was to perceive "rotating circles, abrupt corners, expanding colors, rippling tones, heavy books and confining rooms."[150] Langfeld's position was close to Arnheim's depiction of the artist's way of seeing objects as "vehicles of behavior, embodied initiatives" exhibiting a "dynamic nature."[151]

But if Langfeld hoped that the dynamism central to empathy might be salvaged, by the postwar years, empathy had traded in this emphasis on movement and activity to become almost exclusively the coin of interpersonal understanding. Empathy, Langfeld complained, had been distorted into a pale synonym of sympathy. He blamed this shift on the term's increasing popularity in these years: "As usually happens when a technical word is widely and popularly used, it is sometimes misused or at least the concept for which it stands is misunderstood."[152]

Empathy was still discussed in aesthetics, but now it entailed a spectator's grasp of the underlying intention of the *artist*, no longer an immersion in the dynamic qualities of line or shape. Empathy joined viewer and artist, and the work dissolved between them. In 1947, the philosopher Geddes MacGregor contested the idea that one could empathize with objects: "One cannot live in the Nelson column [in Trafalgar Square], although one might possibly be said to live in the mind of the artist who designed it."[153] A few decades later, an art theorist found it necessary to remind his audience that Langfeld's empathy with form and line was quite different from the common notion of a viewer's empathy with the artist.[154]

If the aesthetic definition of "empathy" was still listed as primary in the 1943 *Dictionary of World Literature*, a caveat quickly followed: "In our own day, empathy is a term of expanding implications." The author of the entry elaborated: "One of the strongest empathic experiences of my life occurred in hearing a radio description of a Japanese smashing a prisoner's foot with the butt of his rifle."[155] In a world riven by war, empathy was no longer confined to the realm of artifice and the imagination but became bound to real circumstances and to actual conflict.

PART II

Making Empathy Scientific

CHAPTER FOUR

The Limits of Empathy in Schizophrenia

WHEN CLARA GOLDBERG WAS admitted to the Boston Psychopathic Hospital in 1918, she had not eaten for several days. She said she was a "bad girl" and "a flirt" and wore a "silly expression." Her head was inclined forward and saliva ran from her mouth. "Now and then her hands and arms would shake violently. Her pupils were dilated. For the rest, the physical examination was not remarkable."[1] Clara had first come to the outpatient clinic three years earlier and had been diagnosed as psychoneurotic. She then found work in a biscuit factory, but her employers soon found her "impossible." She began to say peculiar things: "I have burned my sister inside of me." The staff of the hospital could not agree as to whether she was still psychoneurotic or now suffered from schizophrenia.

Precisely to help diagnose puzzling cases of this sort, the director of the hospital, Elmer Ernest Southard, designed what he called an empathic index. The index guided the psychiatrist through a series of questions, such as: "How far can you read or feel yourself into the patient?" "Can you see the 'ither' as you see 'yersel' i.e. can you see yourself acting under some circumstances precisely as he is acting?" "Can you put yourself in his place?"[2] Southard was invoking Robert Burns's poem "To a Louse," which pictured a self-satisfied lady sitting in a church pew, blissfully unaware of the louse crawling on her bonnet as the wandering eyes of others watched the insect with amusement.[3] In his poem Burns urged the reader to dispel haughty airs, and "to see ourseles as ithers see us!" But Southard turned this dictum around and asked the psychiatrist to imagine that he was the patient. If a psychiatrist found the patient "peculiar, eccentric, exceptional or difficult" and could not imagine behaving as the patient did, this empathic index indicated that the patient was likely to be suffering from schizophrenia.[4]

Southard, along with most early twentieth-century psychiatrists, categorized schizophrenic thinking as bizarre: a "primitive," childlike mentality that stood beyond the realm of everyday understanding. These patients failed at making social connections. The analyst Carl Jung deemed these patients extreme introverts in his personality typology. The neuroendocrinologist Roy Hoskins, the director of a wide-ranging interdisciplinary research program on schizophrenia at Worcester State Hospital, arrived at a similar conclusion in 1945. After decades of intensive research, researchers at the hospital had "tried as yet in vain to solve" the puzzling disorder of schizophrenia. The essence of the disorder, Hoskins concluded, lay in the patient's astonishing lack of the psychobiological capacity for empathy.[5]

E. E. Southard and "Psycho-Sociology"

Southard developed his index in the final months of the Great War, when new psychiatric classification schemes were in the making, psychiatric social work was getting its start, and psychiatrists began to apply their expertise to social problems. Psychiatrists had shifted their attention from a narrow nineteenth-century focus on the asylum to mental hygiene, a new science of intervention, prevention, and treatment of mental disorders. As the ambit of psychiatry widened, those with socially maladaptive behaviors were now cast together in a new diagnostic category of "psychopathy." This term was coined by the Swiss psychiatrist Adolf Meyer for those manifesting social maladjustments, constitutional or personality disorders, delinquency, vagrancy, prostitution, alcoholism, or general waywardness.[6] It was pinned on those without severe mental illness but who nevertheless stood at the margins of proper social behavior.

In 1912, the Boston Psychopathic Hospital opened its doors on Fenwood Road and Vila Street in Boston with a mission to conduct research and to serve as a clearinghouse for examining and diagnosing patients for further treatment.[7] Southard oversaw the hospital and, as chief neuropathologist, dissected and photographed over five hundred brains in search of anatomical evidence for mental disease. He wrote books on shell shock, neurosyphilis, and social work, and he developed his own psychiatric classification system that was implemented at the hospital.[8] As an undergraduate at Harvard, Southard had pursued philosophy under the tutelage of William James and Josiah Royce, and during a long walk with James from McLean Hospital in Belmont back to Cambridge in 1896, he had made up his mind to study abnormal psychology.[9]

Southard's friend, the physician Richard Cabot, described him as "just like a boy, round red cheeks, and always making jokes and the most tremendous mind you ever saw."[10] But his ebullient temperament was marred by low-grade headaches, "with much restlessness and a flight of ideas," and sometimes near-convulsive attacks.[11] Despite, or perhaps due to his mental agility and agitation, Southard wrote prolifically on logic, philosophy, pragmatism, and social psychology. He composed experimental poetry and hobnobbed with the modernist artists Marcel Duchamp and Francis Picabia.[12] He gave a 1917 lecture at the exhibition of the Society of Independent Artists in New York and teasingly asked, "Are cubists insane?"[13]

For thirteen years Southard faithfully attended Josiah Royce's Logic Seminary, a gathering of scholars who met monthly at the Harvard Club for dinner and group discussion.[14] Cabot remarked that the strength of the group was the "transference of concepts" from one field to another, and topics stretched from "mechanical and electrical theories/Structure versus function, vitalism, speculative psychology, statistics, the mathematics of order, to say nothing of epidemiology, ontology, cosmology, sociology."[15] The Yale brain surgeon Harvey Cushing "always came home simply exhausted" after a meeting. He reflected, "I enjoyed it all greatly, but it was a club in which I was wholly outclassed, and I wasn't even always a good listener."[16]

At one meeting, Southard presented diagrams of a patient's delusions to show how mental disorders fundamentally shifted a patient's relation to the world around him. He wholeheartedly ascribed to Royce's conviction that an awareness of others formed a constituting aspect of one's own consciousness.[17] In another study, Southard catalogued a delusional patient's use of the active or passive voice, finding that grammatical elements disclosed underlying psychological inclinations.[18] Southard paid close attention to the social dimensions of psychiatry, intending to develop what he called a "true social psychology" or "psycho-sociology."[19]

In 1918, he elaborated on the uses of an empathic index for diagnosis in the *Journal of Abnormal Psychology*. Empathy, he explained, was a manner of "read[ing] or feel[ing] ourselves into" objects or others, drawing on Titchener's use of the term. Southard cited the importance of kinesthetic images in empathy discovered by the Cornell experimenters, arguing that these images made it possible to "realize ourselves in other persons, races, or even animals or inanimate objects."[20]

A few years earlier, Southard had identified his own kinesthetic images through introspections he conducted with the aid of the hospital psychologist Robert Yerkes, who had adapted the Binet intelligence tests for psychopathic patients and developed his own mental scales for adolescents and adults.[21] Southard donned a blindfold and played chess while relaying the images and feelings passing through his mind.[22] He was no stranger to the game: as an intercollegiate chess champion he had won every game he played over a period of four years.[23] When Southard examined his sense of doubt about a chess move, he discovered "a slight feeling of tension with possibly the vaguest schematic visual image of two dog's ears pricked up."[24] When he imagined a knight hovering over a square, he reported: "I seem to both feel something, curiously enough, in right upper arm muscles (a feeling most nearly resembling a pressure skin sensation plus something else) combined with a visual image of a moved dark long object, on arm presumably, running from right to left toward the Knight in question."[25] Southard found that these imaginary kinesthetic images did not mirror the activation of actual muscles, but instead they reflected movements on the board; as he put it, they were "rather referred by preference to some external surface."[26]

Southard's discovery of his own kinesthetic images led him to affirm Lipps's empathy for the perception of visual illusions and Vernon Lee's empathic art theories. But Southard believed that the significance of empathy stretched beyond aesthetics to spin "a web of relation with all sorts of philosophical concepts."[27] Empathy was implicated in animism, Leibniz's monads, doctrines of magic, nature worship, fetishism, solipsism, pantheism, and anthropomorphism. It was also similar, Southard thought, to Freudian narcissism —the reading of oneself into objects and others. Empathy, Southard concluded, was a profoundly important concept: "It is not too much to say that ideas of this sort stick very deeply into life, and that the whole front that we present in our practical human interests (such as that time-honored question of egoism and altruism) depends upon what stand we take on this matter of reading oneself into another object."[28]

Empathy was distinct from sympathy. Sympathy was the ability to feel *with* another, often to feel bad *for* another, and Southard saw it as "often chargeable with being a bit superior to the person sympathized with."[29] Empathy was more challenging. It required "a translation *into*" another, a task Southard deemed "more intellectual than emotional."[30] One might sympathize with the Belgians for the atrocities that took place during the recent German incursion, he explained, but empathy required the conscious effort of imagination, which was much more difficult to accomplish. With respect to fathoming wartime cruelties, he noted, "We have not memories enough for that level of imagination." Empathy's intellectual and imaginative components were so essential to Southard that empathy might even require putting emotion aside in order to "stop at a coldly rational view of its object."[31]

Southard intended to make empathy useful for psychiatric diagnosis. Beyond the tests to identify the spirochete that caused syphilis, or those to measure feeblemindedness and intelligence, psychiatric diagnosis was a difficult task. Because psychiatric diagnostics lacked clear biological markers, the social dimensions of diagnosis took on inordinate significance. Accurate diagnosis relied to a great extent on clinical acumen and insight. And if clinical judgment was dependent on social perception, Southard thought these perceptions should be spelled out. "What we do here practically, ought to be studied theoretically."[32]

How did empathy operate, then, in the diagnostic encounter? The clinician projected himself into the patient to see if the patient's utterances and behavior made sense, as something the clinician himself might do. To empathize meant that the clinician was to "homologize himself with this man, animate him, as it were, with his own type of soul."[33] It was not a matter of grasping the logic of the patient's state of mind but an attempt to see similarities, if they existed, between the patient and the clinician. In stark distinction to our contemporary understanding of empathy, Southard conceived it as a *narcissistic* notion of realizing *oneself* in objects or in another.

If the clinician successfully projected himself into the patient, he could see himself acting as the patient did. The patient then earned a high score on the empathic index. Patients who scored low on the index, however, displayed inscrutable ideas and strange behaviors. Nineteen-year-old Dora Hadley was a prostitute and lost numerous jobs, but she was deemed intelligent. She was one of one hundred patients assessed in Southard's book, *The Kingdom of Evils*, coauthored with Mary Jarrett, director of social services at the hospital, and published after Southard's death.[34] Dora scored high on the empathic index because she voluntarily put herself in an institution, discontinued prostitution, and became a nurse in training. "The story would not be properly told if Dora's beauty of physique and vivacity of behavior should not figure therein. Everybody's empathic index (as someone has called it) for Dora was high—one somehow liked to see oneself in such a guise."[35] The alcoholic John Sullivan who suffered from hallucinations also scored high on the empathic index. He was an amiable man who was in hospital care for five weeks and demonstrated insight into his condition. He improved, and received counseling in a Men's Club after his release.[36] Another patient, addicted to alcohol and morphine and repeatedly hospitalized was also judged to have a high empathic index rating, linked to her overall attractiveness.[37]

As a measure of successful projection, Southard's empathic index in these cases served as a crude likeability or attractiveness scale. It drew uncritically from common social, gendered, and ethnic biases. The index thus ensconced social norms for psychiatric classification in a deliberate fashion. If historians of psychiatry have unmasked the intertwining of medical authority and normative understandings as an insidious and often unacknowledged feature of medical practice, Southard thought that the two were necessarily and unproblematically enmeshed.[38] The "general impression" made by the patient, commonly invoked in medical practice, was, according to Southard, "nothing but a phrase for the basis of the empathic test."[39] Because a psychiatrist's determination of the patient's general impression was to a significant degree dependent on social expectations, Southard intended to make these norms explicit. He was neither surprised nor critical of the fact that the psychiatrist, almost always white and male, exercised both medical and social authority in delimiting the acceptable bounds of normality.

To some of Southard's contemporaries, however, empathic projection was inadequate to produce verifiable knowledge. This was not because the psychiatrist's social insights might be biased or prejudical, but rather because social judgments simply did not rise to the level of science. Southard's colleague, the philosopher Clarence I. Lewis, catalogued empathy as just another version of art critic John Ruskin's pathetic fallacy of projecting the self into forms of nature: "I seek to interpret other minds by empathy or einfühlung [sic], and inference from behavior. That such sympathetic comprehension is not pathetic fallacy, there is—so far as I can see—no theoretical assurance. It transcends the possibility of verifiable knowledge."[40] William James, too, warned his colleagues about the psychological fallacy, or the belief that one's own psychological responses were identical to those of the subject being investigated.[41] And the nineteenth-century discovery that astronomers measured the passage of stars in slightly different ways had to be taken into account as the individual's "personal equation."[42]

Southard nevertheless construed patient diagnosis as deeply indebted to tacit social understanding and clinical experience. It was indisputable that an experienced practitioner or expert relied on hunches or tips that were grounded in accumulated experience.[43] Even if one could not fully spell out all the moves in diagnosis, as in chess, one acquired skill through intensive practice. Empathic projection was thus "neither naiveté nor analysis," as Southard put it, but "a synthetic general result of a reaction made upon the analytic data."[44]

The psychiatrist William A. White, superintendent of St. Elizabeth's Hospital in Washington, D.C., saw value in Southard's empathic index but urged caution in using it. It was "to be thought through before it can be improved upon."[45] White was an eclectic psychoanalyst who edited the wide-ranging journal *Psychoanalytic Review* and wrote *Principles of Mental Hygiene* in 1917. He believed that improvement in social conditions would help reduce neuroses, and he opposed popular eugenicist measures.[46] He called empathy "a process of introjection, since it brought the object into an intimate relation with the subject." Empathy drew on natural, emotional impulses, but it also had an intellectual component that helped one grasp the total situation. It stood a step above the common sympathy, which for White was only "sentimentalism plus ignorance" and a watchword of the anti-vivisectionists who opposed animal experimentation.[47] One of White's analysands, a free speech lawyer, elaborated on empathy in psychoanalysis as a way of finding an "accurate memory duplication of, or emotional identity with something in the psychological experience of another."[48]

But if some psychiatrists thought empathy could be corralled for diagnosis, most psychoanalysts relegated empathy to a primitive form of identification. Two years after Southard published his index, the orthodox Freudian psychoanalyst Abraham A. Brill described his own empathic index in the *Medical Record*.[49] Brill was one of the first psychoanalysts to practice in the United States, translated Freud's works for the American public, and founded the New York Psychoanalytic Society. To compose his index, he asked his male patients "what personage from history or legend do you admire most, or whom would you consider your ideal?" Brill found that 90 percent of his patients identified with men of action—Napoléon, Lincoln, Caesar, Washington, or Frederick the Great. Napoléon was the most popular figure and represented the "very acme of primitivity." These famous figures had enacted impulses that the patient dared not or could not carry out himself.[50] Brill found this kind of primitive empathic identification common to his patients, children, and the lower classes.

Brill credited empathy for instigating the popular craze for questionnaires and quizzes in the 1920s. He was cited in a *New York Times* article as the psychiatric expert who explained that empathy, more than sympathy, was feeling for a thing to such an extent that one became part of it oneself. "Empathy," the article explained, was one of the "newest pet words of the psychologists."[51] Brill clarified that people took quizzes to measure themselves against others. After receiving a good score one "feels for the time being that he, too, is one of the best minds, a great thinker. That's empathy."[52] Empathy made it possible for a crowd watching a prizefight "to feel itself one with the men in the ring," the next best thing to actually fighting. Brill declared, "Tell me your empathic index, and I will tell you who you are."[53]

One of White's students, psychoanalyst Harry Stack Sullivan, also promoted empathy as a primitive form of emotional connection. Sullivan developed an interpersonal approach to psychiatry while working with schizophrenic patients, and he founded and co-edited the interdisciplinary social science and medical journal *Psychiatry*, first published in 1938.[54] For Sullivan, empathy was "emotional contagion or communion" that passed from the mother to the infant.[55] A nonverbal, emotional link, it "vitally changed" the infant, sometimes by heightening muscle tone through the communication of "worry, fear, anxiety, happiness, security from mother to infant."[56]

The notion that empathy was unique to the mother-infant bond, however, was limited to psychoanalysts. One reviewer pointed out in 1940 that Sullivan's definition was not the "classic" one, which was "the thinking or feeling oneself into some situation that provokes strong feelings."[57] Sullivan continued to tout empathy as an important emotional vector from the mother to infant but admitted that he could not specify the mechanism by which this transfer occurred. He told an audience in 1946 that even if "empathy may sound mysterious, remember that there is much that sounds mysterious in the universe, only you have got used to it, and perhaps you will get used to empathy."[58]

Empathy's Limits: Classifying "Queer" Patients

If Southard's empathic index helped guide the diagnosis of psychopathic patients, he deemed it best suited to help make the difficult differential diagnosis between manic depression and dementia praecox (or schizophrenia). Dementia praecox and manic depression were the two pillars of psychiatric disease consolidated in a series of psychiatric textbooks beginning in 1896 by the German psychiatrist

Emil Kraepelin. The Swiss psychiatrist Eugen Bleuler introduced the term "schizophrenia" for dementia praecox in 1911, reflecting the fact that the disease did not always entail an inevitable downward spiral into dementia. Bleuler painted a psychological picture of the disorder that included bizarre trains of thought, flat affect, delusions, and autistic tendencies. Psychiatrists used the two terms interchangeably well into the 1930s, although Southard preferred the term "schizophrenia."[59]

Psychiatrists and general practitioners found manic depression and schizophrenia, the "sister" groups of mental disease, difficult to differentiate.[60] At the psychopathic hospital, these cases were confused 15 to 20 percent of the time. One physician might be "found triumphantly proclaiming dementia praecox on the basis of schizophrenic symptoms, whereas his colleague with equal triumph claims manic-depressive psychosis on the basis of cyclothymic symptoms."[61] Southard's neuropathological studies showed nearly 86 percent more brain lesions and convolutional abnormalities in dementia praecox than in manic depression, but these findings did not provide diagnostic certainty, and more important, they could not assist in diagnosing living patients.[62]

Further, psychiatric diseases boasted few if any indicator or pathognomonic symptoms, as a pock did for the disease of smallpox or a tubercule bacillus did for tuberculosis. More than one mental disease presented with symptoms of mania, depression, persecutory ideas, grandiosity, and hallucinations. Remarkably, nearly a quarter of the patients diagnosed at Boston Psychopathic Hospital received a different diagnosis upon admittance to the state hospital.[63] There was thus a pressing need for "accurate observation and intelligent interpretation" as well for a unification of diagnostic standards.[64] This was particularly urgent at the psychopathic hospital because under the temporary care law, a diagnosis had to be given in seven to ten days.[65] Classification was also required for patient aftercare, needed by two-thirds of patients and arranged by social workers.[66]

Southard had found impractical the classification of mental disease devised by the American Medico-Psychological Association, taught in medical schools and adopted in many hospitals.[67] Twenty-two disease categories were simply too many for the practitioner to assimilate (twenty-one for mental diseases and one for "not insane"). Southard constructed his own system of psychiatric classification with only ten disease categories or "orders" and an eleventh, residual category labeled psychopathy.[68] His diagnostic "key" logically and pragmatically guided diagnosis by a process of orderly exclusion. The key began with the most determinative diagnosis and ended with the least. The psychiatrist thus moved systematically down the list, excluding one diagnosis after another until he or she discovered the best fit for the patient's symptoms. Southard continued to tackle the puzzle of disease classification throughout his life, calling it more of an art than a science. He later embarked on a classification scheme based on the effects of disease rather than on its causes, but the project was cut short by Southard's untimely death.[69]

Using Southard's key, the clinician first ruled out neurosyphilis by administering the Wasserman test to identify the spirochete that caused the disease. If this test was negative, feeblemindedness would next be excluded with results from the Binet-Simon intelligence test.[70] When the practitioner came to the eighth category of mental disease, or schizophrenia, it was to be rejected before the ninth, manic depression, because symptoms of schizophrenia were "more 'pathognomonic' than cyclothymic symptoms."[71] At this stage, Southard's empathic index came into play. Southard described group 8, or schizophrenia, as exhibiting "dissociation of personality," "queer," and "empathy low." He explained that the "examiner can almost never put himself in patient's place" (figure 16).[72] Case records of dementia praecox patients were littered with these kinds of evaluations: patients "talked incoherently" or "talked strangely," one was "always peculiar," another was "queer after 34 years of age." Many patients uttered incomprehensible ideas: "head and brain sawdust" or "Oh! Yes slumosee," when asked if she slept well. This patient reported that she was a "piano which played without hands."[73]

If the schizophrenic's behavior was "queer and not easily understood," the manic depressive, as Southard explained, "can be readily understood by the layman."[74] Southard informed third-year medical students that the manic depressive exhibited exaggerations of normal feelings, but the dementia praecox patient "seems queer." He explained, "Dementia praecox is different, he is not more or less."[75] The patient's reactions were radically unlike those "which a

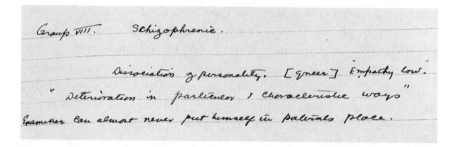

Figure 16. Notes written by neuropathologist E. E. Southard around 1918 describing the patient with schizophrenia. E. E. Southard, "Key for History Reading," E. E. Southard Papers, GA 81, box 2, Center for the History of Medicine, Francis A. Countway Library of Medicine, Boston.

reasonably normal fellow finds himself to possess," and it was these "peculiarities in the patients that lead to a lack of 'empathy.'"[76]

One New York psychoanalyst made use of Southard's empathic index to describe how her schizophrenic patient's "opaque surface" made him so inaccessible that she was thoroughly exhausted in attempting to read herself into his thoughts. She became "almost incapacitated for work on other patients."[77] She imputed to the patient an inability to "experience a plastic interchange between the self and another person."[78] The failure of empathy, as she described it, occurred on the part of the clinician as well as on that of the patient. One contemporary psychologist has described the clinician's feeling of disconnection with a schizophrenic patient as a *"shared alienation,"* meaning that the clinician feels the alienation that the patient is feeling him or herself.[79]

Although Southard did not speculate on the schizophrenic's own feelings of disconnection, he noted that the usefulness of the empathic index lay in the hands of the diagnostician. If a patient stood outside the empathic range of one psychiatrist but not another, it pointed to a deficit in the observer. The exploration of a psychiatrist's capacity for empathy would then, "in a peculiarly intimate way," as he clarified, "allow psychiatry to begin where it always should, namely, at home."[80] Southard knew that his empathic index was an "all too rough statement," but it was to remain rudimentary. Just two years after he introduced his index, while on a visit to

New York City he became seriously ill with septicemia, a blood infection. He died in his hotel room at the age of forty-three.[81]

Southard was not alone in finding the schizophrenic mentality beyond the reach of projective empathy. In 1913, the German psychiatrist Karl Jaspers at Heidelberg published his lengthy textbook on psychopathology, claiming that clinicians simply could not empathize with the schizophrenic's mental processes. Just as an average person could distinguish the genuinely crazy (*verrückt*) from those with less severe disturbances, the psychiatrist drew on tacit social norms to place the schizophrenic patient outside the bounds of understanding.[82] The Munich psychiatrist Emil Kraepelin described feeling an abyss in the presence of a dementia praecox patient, as if no one were there, and the Swiss psychiatrist Ludwig Binswanger, who pioneered an existential approach to psychiatry, felt thrown back into himself while trying to communicate with a patient with schizophrenia. European psychiatrists even named their bizarre sense of disconnection while sitting with a schizophrenic patient the "praecox feeling."[83] In these years, the terms "bizarre" and "queer" functioned as technical psychiatric terms identifying those whose mental processes were utterly unlike what they considered rational, common sense, adult ways of thinking.[84]

If the schizophrenic mentality exemplified the radically "other," it was often grouped together with the child's animistic thinking and the "primitive" belief in occult forces and a diffused sense of self. Nineteenth-century psychiatrists had hammered home the links between mental illness and primitivism in their tracts on degeneration in their account of mental illness as a regression to earlier evolutionary forms. Psychiatrists warned that mild mental deficiency in one generation could increase in severity in subsequent generations, culminating in idiocy and sterility. Freud questioned degenerationist models, but he too assessed schizophrenia as a regression to an earlier infantile state. He explained in *Totem and Taboo* how difficult it was to empathize with primitive modes of thinking.[85] Child psychologists also connected mental pathology, the child's immature mind, and the racially primitive.[86]

According to this formulation, the civilized, rational, European adult was unable to empathically grasp these radically "other" ways of seeing the world. William White declared, "We cannot hope to understand the child, the savage, or the psychotic by a process of projecting, so to speak our own methods of thinking upon him and then trying to understand him in terms of ourselves."[87] One of White's dementia praecox patients believed that his body parts corresponded to different sections of the universe, making him the creator of all races and elements, a view White found similar to that of a "savage tribal king" who was the source of vital energy for the entire tribe.[88] His patient experienced "voices in the walls or in the trees" and lived in a "misty haze of indistinctness."[89] Animistic thinking was believed to be common to both the schizophrenic and the child. The failures of empathic projection revealed to White that the child was *not* a little adult; the savage did not have the same potentialities as the civilized, and the psychotic was not just crazy or vicious.[90]

If psychiatrists found schizophrenic thinking bizarre, they also saw it as a potent source of fascination. The German psychiatrist and art historian Hans Prinzhorn collected and analyzed more than 4,500 paintings and drawings created by 435 patients living in German and Swiss asylums, three-quarters of whom were suffering from schizophrenia or related disorders. In his immensely popular 1922 book, *Artistry of the Mentally Ill*, Prinzhorn provided a glimpse into a mentality strikingly unlike the normal. The paintings exhibited the themes of play, ornamental elaboration, patterned order, obsessive copying, and an adherence to symbolic systems (figure 17).[91] Psychiatrists interpreted these paintings as embodying an emotional renunciation of the outside world and a turn inward toward the self. This turn inward epitomized Carl Jung's introverted psychological type in contrast to the extroverted, empathic type. As Jung observed, introversion at its pathological extreme manifested as schizophrenia. Modern artists and the general public found the paintings compelling; the painter Paul Klee described the paintings as a "sublime art" that illuminated a "direct spiritual vision."[92]

But if the fascination with these paintings marked an interest in expanding the scope of a narrow human rationality, it also reinforced the pathological nature of these creations.[93] Prinzhorn's collection contributed to the development of the nascent Art Brut movement later known as "outsider art," which garnered interest in great part due to the diagnostic labels of the artists themselves. The trope that "schizophrenic thinking resembled the pre-logical thinking of

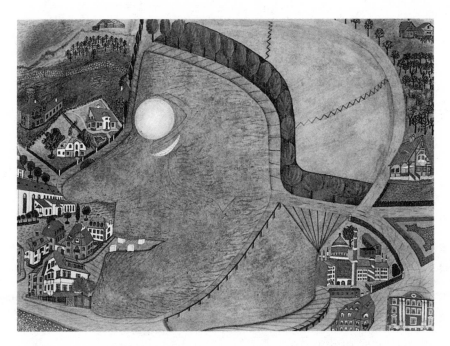

Figure 17. Painting composed by patient with schizophrenia, collected by psychiatrist and art historian Hans Prinzhorn in 1920s Germany. August Natterer, Witch's Head, c. 1915, Prinzhorn Collection, Wikimedia Commons.

children and primitive people" remained popular for decades, aired as late as 1939 at a meeting of the American Psychiatric Association.[94]

Southard's empathic index, in concert with the pronouncements of many psychiatrists, enshrined the schizophrenic as the ultimate outsider. Schizophrenic thinking and behavior simply thwarted comprehension. Over the next decades, psychiatrists and mental health professionals continued to view the disorder through the lens of an impossible empathy—on the part of both the clinician and the patient.

Researching Schizophrenia at Worcester State Hospital

Southard's empathic index pinpointed the clinician's failure of empathy, but already in 1911 Bleuler had identified the patient's emotional withdrawal from others, or "autism," as a key symptom of the disease.[95] In 1945, the neuroendocrinologist Roy G. Hoskins broadcast to his listeners at the New York Academy of Medicine: "Perhaps as fundamentally characteristic as anything about the psychosis is the failure of the subject either to achieve or to retain an adequate breadth and depth of empathy. Whatever else he may be, the schizophrenic is an egregious egoist."[96]

Hoskins ventured this assessment after overseeing a twenty-year research program that produced hundreds of physiological, social, biological, endocrine, and experiential studies of 175 schizophrenic patients at the Worcester State Hospital in Massachusetts.[97] Hoskins was perfectly frank when responding to plans for his 1945 lectures with the organizers: "No large, single group of schizophrenic patients elsewhere has ever been so thoroughly studied as those who have gone through our Service, but we have experienced the same frustrations as has everyone else in the field. We do not know in any adequate fashion either the etiology or the rational therapy of the disorder."[98] Despite intensive research, the project had failed to find either cause or cure.

Hoskins had trained at Harvard with the pioneering physiologist Walter Cannon, who explained that it was Hoskins's interest in the endocrine system that prompted him to begin work on the "ductless" glands. Together they conducted experiments on cats, finding that secretions from the adrenal medulla produced emotional excitement, leading to Cannon's important discovery of the fight-or-flight response.[99] Hoskins went on to obtain his medical degree at Johns Hopkins and chaired the physiology department at Ohio State University for seven years. Hoskins's first wife died of a narcotics overdose, and just a few years later, his second wife passed away from a blood clotting disease.[100] Despite personal tragedy, in 1927 Hoskins signed on as research director of the Memorial Foundation for Neuroendocrine Research to study schizophrenia. The foundation was established by Katherine Dexter McCormick, the first woman to graduate from MIT with a biology degree.

Katherine had married Stanley McCormick, heir to his father's Harvester Reaper fortune, but soon after their marriage, Stanley began to show signs of schizophrenia. He was hospitalized at McLean Hospital in Belmont, Massachusetts, and then transferred to Riven Rock, the family estate in California.[101] Stanley was examined by many psychiatric luminaries of the day: Adolf Meyer, August Hoch, Smith Ely Jelliffe, and Emil Kraepelin, the latter of whom traveled from Munich in 1908 and again in 1925 to pronounce upon his case.[102] The consensus was that Stanley suffered from schizophrenia of the catatonic type, which Kraepelin distinguished from manic depression by "the loss of contact between the patient's acts and the situation."[103] Stanley also underwent psychoanalysis with William White and his colleague Edward Kempf.

Katherine was convinced that her husband's illness stemmed from adrenal problems on the opinion of endocrinologist Allan Rowe and given her own training in biology. When the psychoanalysts treating Stanley refused to give him hormone therapy, Katherine sued. She won the right to end the medical contract, and soon thereafter Katherine established the Memorial Foundation. The foundation funded biological and physiological research into schizophrenia and stridently rejected a psychoanalytic, or even a psychological, approach to treatment.[104] Katherine's philanthropic leanings later turned to women, and she donated two million dollars for the development of a contraceptive pill.[105]

As research director of the Memorial Foundation at Worcester State Hospital, Hoskins carried out a great many neuroendocrine studies in search of a causal relationship between hormonal action and schizophrenia.[106] He studied the thyroid, pituitary, adrenal, and pancreatic hormones at the Harvard laboratory, and he applied these findings to experimental treatment regimens for Worcester patients. In 1931, he reported that 171 schizophrenic patients at the hospital had undergone extensive metabolic testing, and 62 percent (107) had shown some endocrine deficiency. Of these, 54 had shown improvement with a variety of endocrine gland derivatives.[107] He posited that the cause of the disorder was likely a toxic handicap of an organic or endocrine nature.[108] He reassured Katherine McCormick at a foundation meeting that he too did not believe in a psychological cause: "Schizophrenia is due, almost certainly, to organic anomalies and the solution of the problem will come from the organic side."[109]

At first, researchers found that treating patients with thyroid hormones improved their psychotic symptoms. But the effects faded quickly, and the patients who had left the hospital were forced to return.[110] Hoskins gave 39 patients manganese chloride in another trial, but it failed to alleviate psychotic symptoms.[111] At the 1932 annual meeting of the foundation, Hoskins reported that he "felt no great confidence in the endocrine approach, and turning to Mrs. McCormick at the meeting, he said that if she were only interested in a possible endocrine etiological factor in dementia praecox, he guessed she had her answer already."[112] McCormick expressed dismay that she had been funding three psychiatrists, as she was intensely skeptical of a mental approach to the disease. Hoskins explained that one psychiatrist documented personality changes in patients, and the other two corroborated the findings. The discussion grew acrimonious as Hoskins defended the use of psychological tests to increase diagnostic accuracy, and Dr. Rowe, a proponent of hormonal causes of the disease, questioned their importance.[113] Hoskins later expanded on the importance of psychological measures: "The patients come to the hospital because of abnormalities at the psychologic level, are kept in the hospital because of vagaries in personality manifestations, and are sent home—if they be so fortunate—because of changes of the same order. The 'end-points' therefore even in physiologic investigations have to be found in psychologic changes."[114] The contentious meeting ended near one in the morning, with one member running to catch a train "without any solution of the difficulties" and "without having been formally adjourned."[115]

Hoskins continued to emphasize the importance of a psychological understanding of schizophrenia. He calculated that there were at least 140,000 schizophrenic cases in American hospitals, each one of which represented "a wrecked life and a grave social maladjustment."[116] He described schizophrenia as a persistent dream state, in which patients suffered from a loss of self-respect and reacted to others in futile attempts at self-protection. A 1933 poll of his research team on putative causes of the disease ranged from adrenal deficits and deficient oxygenation of brain cells, to inadequate training in childhood, undischarged affects, and failures of adaptation.[117] This assortment of causes reflected the interdisciplinary team of biologists, physiologists, psychiatrists, psychologists, and even theologians at Worcester. The neuroendocrine foundation funded only about a third of the research at the hospital, with additional funds for research coming from the state of Massachusetts and a grant from the Rockefeller Foundation.[118]

The senior psychologist on staff, David Shakow, called the research program at Worcester a "little graduate school," complete with journal clubs, departmental and cross-departmental seminars, and luncheon meetings. During its peak years of research from 1935 to 1940, the program boasted seventy staff members.[119] Courses were given on psychopathology, the history of psychopathology, psychoanalytic therapy, and mental adjustment, taught by the chief of the psychology laboratory at Boston Psychopathic Hospital.[120] At Worcester, the first sound-recorded psychotherapies were developed along with the first studies of the new insulin treatment for schizophrenia.[121]

In this multidisciplinary setting, Hoskins reflected on his "unique privilege as a physiologist to have observed from a favorable vantage point many cases of the disorder and the efforts of a group of workers from several disciplines to elucidate the problems presented."[122] Many of the patients at Worcester arrived by way of Boston Psychopathic Hospital. The difficulties Southard had described a decade earlier in diagnosing schizophrenia continued to loom large. Shakow called it "our most fundamental problem."[123] The hospital did not implement Southard's empathic index, but Hoskins was aware of Southard's attempt to provide guidelines to clinicians for diagnosis. Worcester researchers developed a five-point rating system to strengthen diagnostic regimens and drew from in-depth psychiatric interviews, ward observations, patients' social history, and a large battery of psychological tests to assist diagnosis.[124]

Psychological and biological approaches to schizophrenia had been intertwined at the hospital ever since 1896, when the Swiss émigré Adolf Meyer served as head psychiatrist. Meyer restructured the primarily custodial institution into a teaching hospital dedicated to research and close observation of patients and stressed the psychobiological approach.[125] In 1933, Shakow argued for the "virtue of embracing studies at both the psychological and physiological levels" and posited that schizophrenia was "due to a differential rate and method of adjustment to environmental changes from the normal."[126] Shakow began working at Worcester as a graduate student, mentored by Gordon Allport at Harvard and the psychologist Frederic Wells at Boston Psychopathic.[127] He published his long-delayed dissertation on deterioration in schizophrenia in 1946, which demonstrated that schizophrenics did not show adaptation in learning studies, nor did they habituate to physical pain—their heart rates did not diminish to successive stimulation as did controls.[128] This "adaptive difficulty," Shakow postulated, was likely triggered by some kind of "an innate liability factor."[129] He suggested that the disorder could best be understood at the integrated level of the organism or person. While at Worcester, Shakow trained a hundred clinical psychologists and in 1947 drafted his famous "Shakow" report, which became the official American Psychological Association (APA) training manual for clinical psychologists.[130]

Worcester hospital was also the first in the country to hire a chaplain. Anton Boisen arrived in 1924 after training at Union Theological Seminary and at the Boston Psychopathic Hospital. At Worcester, he recorded the intense feelings of isolation and alienation relayed to him by schizophrenic patients. He himself had endured psychotic episodes, describing "three weeks of violent delirium," when "I myself was more important than I had ever dreamed of being; I was also a zero quantity."[131] Boisen was institutionalized at a psychopathic hospital and emerged "much as one awakens out of a bad dream." The experience of psychosis, he explained, was to "have been forced off the beaten path of common sense and have traveled through the little-known wilderness of the inner life."[132]

Boisen listened intently to his patients as "living human documents" and developed a protocol and a standardized form to record patients' moods, behavior, and utterances that was adopted for research purposes across the hospital. Patients described their overwhelming feelings of isolation, which Boisen believed to be socially rooted. As he explained, patients "are isolated from their fellow through a social judgment which either consciously or subconsciously they accept and pronounce upon themselves."[133] Boisen was soon training theological students at the hospital, and not long afterward he and Richard Cabot set up the Council for the Clinical Training of Theological Students, the seed of the new profession of clinical pastoral education.[134]

The Laws of Empathy

The consensus at Worcester was that schizophrenic patients suffered from feelings of isolation, a biological and psychological inability to adapt, and from an "inadequate manipulation of environmental situations."[135] Because these patients demonstrated wide physiological variability at different times on measurements of blood sugar, blood pressure, and arterial and venous oxygen, it was difficult to identify one pathognomic symptom for the disease.[136] This variability signified the schizophrenic's overall "physiological clumsiness" and intolerance to stress.[137]

Hoskins saw this variability as a sign of an abnormal homeostatic index. The idea of a regulated homeostatic index had emerged from Walter Cannon's work on the adrenal medulla, the gland that secretes individual steroids, in addition to biochemist Hans Selye's "general adaptation reaction," which identified the adrenal cortex as responsive to stressful situations. The schizophrenic patient's adrenal glands were simply ill-equipped to respond to the body's changing needs given the strains of daily life. Hoskins explained that it was like driving through traffic with only one setting for the throttle, unable to adjust the speed to changing traffic patterns.[138] Because schizophrenic patients used up their energy to achieve an "organic adaptation," there was little if any remaining for "successful adaptation in the social field."[139] Hoskins concluded that schizophrenia was quintessentially a biological failure to adapt to the environment, which in turn produced social withdrawal and feelings of isolation.

In 1945, Hoskins proclaimed that "the primary defect in schizophrenia—a defect from which the remainder of the symptomatology stems—is inadequate empathy."[140] Schizophrenic patients had a history of being aloof and odd, and they had displayed tantrums and emotional instability as children.[141] This oddness developed into manneristic behavior, emotional dulling, and withdrawal. Echoing Southard two decades earlier, Hoskins wrote that the schizophrenic patient presented "a picture of inexplicable queerness. It is at this stage that a failure of empathy becomes unmistakably and bafflingly evident."[142] Augmenting the patient's lack of empathy were the additional symptoms of general immaturity, autistic escape mechanisms, concrete thinking, and inadequate reality testing.

Hoskins explained that empathy was a social capacity rooted in biology: a "consciousness of co-identification in a social group of two or more members."[143] If the impulse seemed at odds with an organism's evolutionary impulse to survive and reproduce, it nonetheless could explain the strange behavior of the pronghorn antelope standing as a sentinel on "a sandhill top," a sight familiar to Hoskins growing up on a farm on the Kansas prairie. The fact that "this hungry animal sacrificed his immediate welfare to that of the herd feeding safely below presents a biological problem of major significance."[144] This puzzling behavior could be attributed to empathy, or the biologically based "consciousness of *belongingness*."

But how did Hoskins connect empathy to the consciousness of belonging? It is likely that one of his Worcester colleagues, the Viennese-born psychiatrist Andras Angyal, was the source of inspiration. Angyal left Vienna to join the culture and personality research group at Yale University before coming to Worcester. He wrote of "empathy" in his 1941 *Foundations for a Science of Personality*, putting the English term in quotes to signal its unfamiliar status. Angyal described empathy as a projection into persons and things in accord with its early aesthetic meaning. It was evident in the way a child "imitates and places himself in the role, not only of human personages but also of a horse or a locomotive." The underlying motive of this impulse was "to feel oneself as one with something outside of the narrower self: to be oneself and at the same time to be somebody or something else, too."[145] Empathy was akin to what Angyal called the "homonomous impulse," which was "a tendency to submerge, participate, and share in those larger units and to conform to them," embodying "the basic human need for 'belonging.'"[146]

In choosing the word "empathy" to characterize this vital impulse of belonging, Hoskins acknowledged that he had bypassed its primary, aesthetic meaning. "Perhaps the best available term—though used in one of its secondary meanings—is the word *empathy*, signifying literally, 'feeling into' the meaning connoted in Southard's term, the 'empathic index.'"[147] He cited this second meaning as "a mental state in which one identifies or feels himself in the same state of mind as another person or a group."[148]

Hoskins placed empathy at the crux of psychology and evolutionary biology, as well as of sociology and ethics. Empathy made social bonding possible—from love and friendship to patriotism, group morale, and mutual helpfulness. It explained the cocktail hour, the religious revival, patriotism, and military morale, which Hoskins allowed was "driving thousands of soldiers to their death."[149] By mobilizing individual feelings in the service of larger goals, the evolutionary impulse of empathy "drain[ed] off individual egoistic emotions" and enlarged the "I" through a championing of the "we."[150] But empathy could also render people liable to suggestion, and demogogues could manipulate it for nefarious ends. Just as the term "consciousness" expressed the bare minimum of intra-individual awareness, so too did "empathy" indicate only a basic awareness of another. Hoskins warned that it could evolve into either love or hate.

As empathy was pinpointed as the key deficit in schizophrenia, efforts were made to nurture the capacity at Worcester State Hospital. Psychiatrists placed patients into groups or grades, like elementary schoolchildren, in an attempt to foster a "sense of group consciousness" and emulation within the group.[151] The groups were arranged according to assessments of a patient's personal hygiene, compliancy, and flexibility. Patients in Grade A demonstrated the most independence and those in the Grade E, the least. A patient that was placed in Grade C, for instance, was "on parole" but "working and playing well. Getting new ideas and interests. Making the best of everything. Cooperating well and obeying rules." Those in Grade B or above were allowed to go home. Patients in Grade A got along with family, were able to work, and could "act like normal people." Membership in these grades was designed to promote a "we mentality" or empathy.[152]

Hoskins charged the psychotherapist with the development of the laws of empathy and with skill in utilizing them, as they were "the chief, if not sole, stock in trade of the psychotherapist in his dealings with the schizophrenic patient."[153] He was dubious about the effectiveness of shock therapies for schizophrenic patients and called lobotomy a partial decerebration, the experimental procedure carried out on dogs in Cannon's laboratory many years earlier. The *New York Times* review of Hoskins's book reinforced the importance of fostering empathy as one of the few avenues for hope in the treatment of the "vexing problem of schizophrenia."[154] Hoskins suggested a "systematic study of techniques for the promotion of empathy rather than continuation of the haphazard exploitation of this factor."[155]

Psychiatrist Nathan Blackman at the Worcester Hospital strengthened patient connections with some of the first trials of group therapy, and he supported an improvised literary group organized by schizophrenic patients in 1940.[156] He believed that group therapy mitigated schizophrenic patients' exaggerated, introspective thinking and found patients more readily accepted the advice of other patients than that of the psychiatrist.[157] In 1954, Blackman drafted a paper on empathy with schizophrenics, which he shared with Hoskins, suggesting that therapists abandon the search for "psychodynamic leads" when treating patients and instead invest their own feelings in the relationship.[158] It was only when "therapists left 'technique' behind and became more sensitive toward patients' feelings that progress was noted." The onus was on the therapist to cultivate empathy as patients had difficulty doing so; a patient usually relied on "projections of his own feeling and experiences rather than of concern and understanding of somebody else's feelings."[159]

Just a year after Hoskins published his lectures on the biology of schizophrenia, Stanley McCormick died and Katherine closed the doors of the foundation. Hoskins suffered from a small coronary event. He had already begun to delve into the growing field of psychosomatic medicine, and his research interests had turned to gerontology.[160] He confessed to a friend, "I am fed up with research on psychosis."[161]

But by this time, psychotherapists and psychiatrists had already begun to call upon empathy more frequently. Its meanings were still unclear, however, and in 1958 Blackman felt compelled to clarify in print that empathy was not a matter of projection, identification, nor of sympathy. To project meant to escape from one's own situation; to identify was to take the other's place but to improperly remain there; and to sympathize was to observe from a distance and simply agree with the other's sentiments. Empathy was instead the "ability to step into another person's shoes and to step back just as easily into one's own shoes again" and, in so doing, to "feel along with, to understand, and to insinuate one's self into the feelings of another person."[162] Empathy required flexibility, and no longer signaled the transfer of one's own feelings and movements into another or an object. As we will see, the psychotherapeutic rendering of empathy traded self-projection for its opposite: one now had to bracket the self's feelings and judgments in order to more fully occupy the position of another.

CHAPTER FIVE

Empathy in Social Work and Psychotherapy

WHILE UNDERGOING PSYCHOTHERAPY IN 1954, Mrs. Oak wondered why it was that parents so often told their children to stop crying. She herself began to cry and described the root of her problem: "It's just being *terribly hurt!*" But even more painful than the hurt was the fact that she had "covered it up with so much *bitterness* . . . (Weeps). *That's* what I want to get rid of! I almost don't *care* if I hurt." Carl Rogers, her therapist, echoed her feelings: "You feel that here at the basis of it, as you experienced it, is a feeling of real tears for yourself. But that you *can't* show, mustn't show, so that's been covered by bitterness that you don't like."[1]

A clinical psychologist by training, Rogers called his response empathic: it was an attempt to get a deeper sense of the client's emotion and to "catch the flavor of the feeling." To do so, however, the therapist had to deliberately put aside judgments and diagnostic thinking. Rogers was convinced that this kind of profound participation in the client's experiential world could trigger healing. Empathy of this kind became a central plank in psychotherapy after World War II, but the roots of this approach had already emerged in social work of the 1930s.

The philosopher, social worker, and psychologist Jessie Taft developed a "controlled relationship" with a seven-year-old boy,

Jackie, in 1932 to help prepare him for placement in a foster home. Over thirty-one sessions, Jackie played, explored the room, and vented his emotions, while Taft followed his lead and reflected his feelings back to him. Taft encouraged his emotional reactions to surface without inserting judgments or delving into interpretations of the boy's past.[2] She called this controlled identification with Jackie, shorn of her projections or expectations, "relationship therapy." She drew insights for this method from George Herbert Mead's social psychology and Otto Rank's nonorthodox psychoanalysis. Rank had departed from Freudian analysis in the 1920s to highlight the supportive, empathic role of the therapist modeled after the mother or midwife. In this psychotherapeutic vein, empathy was no longer an aesthetic self-projection, but instead it demanded a disciplined bracketing of the therapist's feelings to enable an immersive understanding of another's experience.

Jessie Taft and the Uses of Emotion

At the eighty-seventh convocation at the University of Chicago in June 1913, Julia Jessie Taft graduated with a doctorate in philosophy. Her mentors were the pragmatist social philosophers George Herbert Mead and James Tufts.[3] Born in Iowa, Taft attended Drake College and then taught high school. While attending the summer session at Chicago in 1908, she met fellow student Virginia Robinson, who became her intellectual ally, lifelong partner, and later colleague at the Pennsylvania School of Social Work.[4]

In her dissertation, "The Woman Movement in the Point of View of Modern Social Consciousness," Taft tackled pressing questions of the modern age, including individualism, social consciousness, and women's place in society. She saw the self as multiple, expansive, and built from relationships with others, in line with Mead's belief that the self emerged only "as the *result* of its relations to other selves."[5] Mead had begun giving lectures on social psychology at Chicago in 1894; he argued that when we take on the standpoint of another, we see ourselves with awareness, and are able to identify the self as a role played out in the drama of social interaction.[6] Taft explained in her dissertation that a child reaching for the largest piece of cake momentarily takes on the self of his mother with her disapproving attitude, while at the same time his own impulsive self feels her disapproval. In this doubling, actions become meaningful because one imaginatively puts oneself in the place of another.[7] The self was thus constituted by its many social links, and to be socially conscious meant one was poignantly aware of one's "dependence on a social situation for the form of self" one develops.[8]

To put oneself in the place of someone who experienced injustice allowed other persons, what Mead called *alteri*, to exist within one's own consciousness.[9] A factory owner might not directly injure a child, but he could still put hundreds of children at risk if he was not consciously aware of his responsibility for them. Without this awareness, as Taft put it, he "is not constituted a self, a person, a social and moral agent, by the individuals at the other end of his system."[10] The wise man, in contrast, recognized he was a distributed self: "the man whose self includes so many and such varied 'others,' and who is so aware of his dependence on these 'others,' that it is impossible for him to act without reference to them."[11] Taft described women as possessing a "family ethics," whereas men had a sense of loyalty that extended to those in public life, law, government, and business. She urged women to widen their sympathies beyond the family unit to make their selves as "large as the world."[12]

Taft was hopeful that a heightened awareness that the self was made up by its social connections was developing in the modern age. She advocated for better working conditions for women, lessening hours of labor, a minimum wage, and improved housing and sanitation. Taft's friend Virginia Robinson was a suffragette, but Taft questioned a militant movement with a narrow sensibility: to see men as oppressors, as she put it, is "not only bad taste, but beside the mark."[13] It was more important that women be included in the chain of interconnected social selves. She believed that the cultivation of an expansive self, aware of its social makeup would itself impel social change.

Taft aimed to cultivate a new kind of social scientist who was "so socially sensitive and adaptable that they feel within themselves the impulses and points of view of all classes and both sexes."[14] This kind of reformer was more emotionally finely tuned than others: "he feels more . . . he responds more sensitively and detects values to which other people are blind."[15] Taft did not accept a natural link between women, emotion, and sentimentality as did so many writers of her day. Rather, she drew on the pragmatist tradition that viewed emotion as a useful signal that some kind of adjustment was needed. But she found sympathy to be an insufficient motivation for social intervention: "To leave relief work to the chance that suffering will make an immediate appeal to some one's sympathy is a method that does not work in such complex social situations."[16] Taft instead held up a model of an aware social self with a cultivated sensitivity to the wider realities of others' lives, a central plank of her reformist and therapeutic vision and integral to her model of empathy.

After completing her doctorate, Taft took a position as an assistant superintendent of the New York State Reformatory for Women at Bedford Hills and worked with psychiatrists and mental hygiene professionals to help prevent mental illness and raise public awareness. Robinson and Taft were separated for a year, and in 1918 Robinson moved to Philadelphia to teach at the small and developing Pennsylvania School of Social Work, becoming the associate director in 1920. The school was established in 1908 as part of the Children's Aid Society, and became affiliated with the University of Pennsylvania in 1935. Taft followed Robinson to Philadelphia, where she helped establish the Seybert School for fifteen young "problem" children.[17]

Taft soon questioned psychological efforts to control the child, writing in the school's final report, "How seldom we stop to see them as they are, rather than as objects to be changed by us into something easier to manage." Giving a child only a modicum of understanding, she reflected, how "pitifully easy it is in the majority of cases to get immediate response and magical transformations."[18] In 1920, Taft became director of the new Department of Child Study of the Children's Aid Society, and then a member of the executive committee of the Child Demonstration Clinic at the Children's Hospital at Philadelphia, established in 1925 under the direction of Frederick Allen.[19] In 1934, she joined the faculty at the Pennsylvania School of Social Work, where she developed a two-year social work curriculum and later a doctoral program.[20]

Taft and Robinson settled down for a shared domestic and intellectual life, and their public work soon became private: they adopted a young boy, Everett, after boarding him for a year when

*Figure 18. Photograph of Jessie Taft, her partner Virginia Robinson, and
their two adopted children, Martha and Everett. From left: Jessie Taft,
Martha, Everett, Virginia Robinson. Jessie Taft Papers, box 3, Rare Book
and Manuscript Library, Butler Library, Columbia University.
Used by permission of Roger C. Taft.*

his mother died. A year later they adopted five-year-old Martha.
Taft was acutely aware of the limitations of social work interventions
with no long-term guarantees of continued care, unless of course
one made the commitment to adopt.[21] They bought an old stone
house in the middle of cornfields in Flourtown, Pennsylvania, thoroughly renovated it and named it "the Pocket," because once there,
it was difficult to get out (figure 18). Robinson later saw their move
as a daring venture: "Good child placing practice today would not
have approved this placement of two children with two professional
women but I think we survived this experience without harm to any
of us."[22]

Taft took part in the shift in social work practice from an early
emphasis on simple social interventions and the determination
of social types to an in-depth psychological approach inspired by
psychoanalysis and the mental hygiene movement.[23] By the 1920s,
many social workers looked to psychoanalysis for insight, and clinical psychologists and child guidance counselors ventured beyond

testing to try out therapy. Taft spoke on the importance of psychiatry in social work at the National Conference on Social Work in Atlantic City in 1919, and the following year she declared that "case work is always fundamentally psychological, or, if you please, psychiatric, even when it is applied to the so-called normal person."[24] Social workers connected psychiatric care with aftercare, worked in outpatient clinics, assessed mental defect and deficiency, and grappled with the social problems of alcoholism and syphilis—all part of the new broader move to provide better and preventative mental health services. The first course for psychiatric social work was designed and taught at Smith College in 1918 by the collaborators, Mary Jarrett and Ernest Southard, both based at Boston Psychopathic Hospital.

With the optimism of the new mental hygiene approach came a focus on children, who were seen to be more malleable than adults and could easily "be guided into the kingdom of good adjustment."[25] But Taft found casework to be filled with moral condemnations rather than scientific descriptions of behavior or an understanding of the child's needs. Rather than report that Johnny found the penny on the mantel because he wanted a toy at the corner store, case reports judged Johnny as a boy who takes things. Taft viewed the person as "a lively organization of energies" and found it wrong to identify a person as a static character type, "neatly labeled for all time."[26] Too often, Taft complained, the child was seen as "an object which ought to be trained to behave rationally" and only a "scapegoat" for adults.[27] She told teachers at a Quaker Friends school in early 1926 that it was critical to understand a child's emotional life as part of the learning process.[28] All students, even the ones that needed special attention, were motivated by "interest"—a dynamic inner force described by progressive educators. Interest was an authentic expression of the child's emotional life, often overlooked in casework.

In 1930, at the First International Congress for Mental Hygiene in Washington, D.C., Taft declared that she was seeking "a theory of emotions which permits us to have them."[29] Emotions had generally been feared or condemned: behaviorists deemed them "conditioned reflexes," and psychoanalysts called them "infantile patterns." The training ideal for analyst and social worker alike was to dampen emotion to achieve what Taft called an "impossible objectivity." Too often the aim was to alter the emotion rather than to understand it. "Scientist and therapist, like the rest of us, are blocked in their efforts to understand any given emotional state as it actually is," she expounded in another talk, "because to them too the underlying impulse, however restrained, is to check it, divert it, or mold it into something else."[30]

Taft spoke about emotion as a valuable conduit to others. A child not only feels his own emotion, but the "emotional reactions which he arouses in the parents."[31] Emotions signaled one's felt values and thus contained rational elements. Anger, resentment, and strong emotions were natural for children who lacked a stable family; if one told the child to deny fear, hate, and other unpleasant emotions, one prevented the child from becoming a conscious self.[32] Just as in 1916 Taft had advised the reformer to cultivate an educated emotional sensibility, in 1930 she argued that a case worker should exhibit a "comparative objectivity and maturity of the emotional attitude."[33]

Taft delivered her comments at the Congress for Mental Hygiene in response to a provocative ten-minute address given by the Viennese psychoanalyst Otto Rank. In his address, Rank had decried the Freudian emphasis on "intellectual understanding as a curative factor in analysis" and instead emphasized emotional connection between therapist and patient.[34] He had struggled to obtain Freud's approval for this innovation and had finally given up. He boldly announced that he no longer had any formal allegiances: he was no "psychiatrist, no social worker, no psychoanalyst, not even an ordinary psychologist." In no uncertain terms he announced his divergence from canonical Freudian analysis.[35]

The reaction was swift. The orthodox analyst Abraham A. Brill stepped up to call Rank's ideas a sign of his "deep emotional upset" and his "own present maladjustment."[36] The analyst Franz Alexander joined in the attack. At a meeting later that day, Brill made a motion to strip Rank of his honorary membership in the American Psychoanalytic Association, which was seconded by Harry Stack Sullivan. All those who Rank had analyzed would have to be reanalyzed, as these individuals would now lack certification from the official psychoanalytic association.[37] For decades to come, orthodox psychoanalysts disparaged Rank's ideas and their popularity in social casework: one Boston analyst summarily dismissed Rankians as "un-trained women."[38] In 1939 Erich Fromm declared Rank's therapy "fascistic" in the journal *Psychiatry*, and as late as 1957 Lionel Trilling reported in the *New York Times* that Rank died insane. When Taft published her 1958 memoir on Rank, a *Time* magazine review declared that Rank was "sick, sick, sick."[39]

Otto Rank's Identification, Projection, and Empathy

But it hadn't always been this way. When Otto Rank sailed from Vienna for New York in 1924, he was the secretary of the Psychoanalytic Society and Freud's intimate friend. A slight and boyish figure, he was heartily welcomed by American psychoanalysts and was quickly elected as an honorary member of the American Psychoanalytic Association. Rank was a literary intellectual, however, not a medical doctor, and he soon found most American analysts closely wedded to medical practice. Indeed, in 1926 the New York Psychoanalytic Society voted to restrict psychoanalytic practice to medically trained psychiatrists. Along with other émigré lay analysts, Rank sought out nonmedical audiences for his analytic ideas. He told Freud in a 1925 letter that "the huge territory of the 'social workers' and the entire problem of education and instruction, social concerns, and character" promised to be a receptive field.[40]

Rank had long been a member of Freud's inner circle and had worked closely with him for more than twenty years. Born Otto Rosenfeld, Rank struggled with his Jewish identity, had considered suicide when young, and was an avid reader of Schopenhauer and Nietzsche.[41] He described creative ideas as projections or emanations from the artist's psyche.[42] After receiving his doctorate in literature from the University of Vienna, he began practicing as a lay analyst in 1919.[43] Around this time, he helped Freud compose his *Group Psychology and the Analysis of the Ego*, which briefly mentioned Einfühlung as necessary for understanding others in any fashion at all, drawing on Lipps.[44]

Rank had long been fascinated by the role of the mother, which he associated with the protective role of the totem. To the child, she was both a nurturing and forbidding figure.[45] Rank published his *Trauma of Birth* in 1923 when his only daughter was four and dedicated it to Freud, "Explorer of the Unconscious." Rank described the infant's separation from the mother at birth as the fundamental root of anxiety. If birth made individuation possible, it did so at the steep price of losing the intimate bond with the mother. Every other separation endured throughout one's life, as Rank saw it, echoed this original, traumatic birth separation.

In these years, Rank also revised psychoanalytic techniques in collaboration with the Hungarian analyst Sandor Ferenczi. They professed that emotional experiencing (*Erlebnis*) in analysis was more important than the classic emphasis on cultivating insight (*Einsicht*).[46] The therapist's ability to engage in emotional connection with the client, sometimes called empathy (*Einfühlung*) or tact (*Takt*), became indispensable to this new technique.[47]

Freud at first welcomed Rank's and Ferenczi's modifications, but he soon recognized that Rank's birth trauma upended the role of the father and the primacy of the Oedipal conflict. Rank wrote to Freud in August 1924: "Now again you're saying that I eliminated the father. That's not so, of course, and cannot be: It would be nonsense. I've only attempted to assign him the correct place."[48] Rank asserted that unearthing the traumatic separation from the mother revealed a deeper level of the psyche than did the adolescent Oedipal complex. Over the next tumultuous year Rank briefly reunited with Freud, endured the death of his brother and difficulties with his wife, and was said to be grappling with a bout of manic depression. By November 1925, Rank could no longer deny he was moving in a new direction, and wrote to Freud that he was "no longer my old self"; "the great movement in which I'm now interested seems to be developing away from the official psychoanalytic organization."[49]

Rank had by this time crafted his own technique of "will therapy," turning to the discredited psychological term "will" to champion the creative and active aspects of the ego as the "conscious bearer of a striving force."[50] He suggested that a dynamic interaction between therapist and patient could energize the individual's creative will. But the therapist had to turn his gaze from the patient's past to the immediate fluctuations in the unfolding relationship with the patient.[51] By closely attending to the present emotional interchange, the therapist encouraged the client to come to a more complete self-understanding. By the end of the therapeutic relationship, the client was ready to birth his or her authentic, individuated self. To deliberately trigger this birthing process, Rank set time limits for the analysis.

Jessie Taft had first met Rank on June 3, 1924, at a meeting of the American Psychoanalytic Association in Atlantic City. A few weeks later, Rank addressed graduating social workers in a crowded auditorium in the Social Services Building of the Pennsylvania School of Social Work.[52] Taft was taken with his approach, and two years later she began a nine-week analysis with him.[53] She attended Rank's lectures at the New York School of Social Work and those of Ferenczi at the New School of Social Research. The following winter she joined a weekly Rankian seminar composed of fifteen or twenty psychiatrists.[54] Soon Taft began the intensive undertaking of translating Rank's works, and in 1936 she published translations of his *Truth and Reality* and *Will Therapy*.

Rank was quite popular with analysts when he had first arrived in New York. "We all flocked to him," said one New York psychiatrist who found Rank to be attacking neurosis at the trunk.[55] Rank analyzed Taft's colleague Virginia Robinson; the social worker and psychiatrist Marion Kenworthy; Caroline Newton, who translated Rank and Ferenczi's *Development of Psychoanalysis*; and the psychiatrist William A. White, who published Rank's article on the birth trauma in his journal the *Psychoanalytic Review*. Philadelphia-based psychiatrists Edward Strecker and Frederick Allen, the medical director of the Philadelphia Child Guidance Clinic, also underwent Rankian analysis.[56]

Taft frequently invited Rank to lecture at the Pennsylvania School of Social Work, and on Monday evenings from October to December in 1927, Rank held forth on his genetic, or developmental, psychology. His transcribed lectures were multigraphed, bound, and placed in the social work library.[57] He described the emotional life as the crux of psychology; feelings, as he put it, "determine our whole attitude towards life and experience."[58] He then outlined the two basic polarities of emotional life: identification and projection.[59] To identify with another meant to find some similarity, which if not obvious at first, could be discovered by adjusting oneself to resemble the other. Projection, in contrast, was the ascription of the self's qualities to others. Rank likened projection to an artistic imprinting of the self and its ideals onto objects, connected to the primitive tendency to animate the world, gods, and the heavens. If moderns had rejected naive forms of projection, Rank declared that it was still alive and well in love and art.

Rank then sketched a developmental schema that began with the child's identification with the parent, which by the time of adolescence transformed into a projection into a love object. (He described the neurotic as a failed artist who never got to this stage, being unable to move past childish identification to claim his own ego.) After adolescence, the young adult came to recognize that his or her projections, far from delivering an accurate picture of others, were actually parts of the self falsely attributed to other people. Psychological maturity meant learning to "accept ourselves—that is, our true self, rather than throwing it out of ourselves, projecting it onto the other."[60]

Psychological maturity thus entailed the acceptance of one's true self, which enabled the accurate understanding of another. This capacity, as Rank described it, required the conscious practice of Einfühlung, or empathy. Empathy was not the projection of one's personality onto another, but a *conscious* practice of connection: "We are now able to accept the other as he is, that is, to adjust ourselves by means of identification."[61] Empathy comprised an active and strategic seeking of similarities with another much different from the child's unconscious identification with a parent. It was nonetheless rooted in emotional connection, a more reliable guide to understanding others than an intellectual one, which, Rank declared, usually amounted to a *"compelling of the other* to our own thought."

Rank told his audience of women social workers that the ideal educator or social worker practiced empathy through a controlled identification with the child without imposing her personality.[62] The mother-infant bond stood at the center of the woman's capacity for identification and emotional bonding. Rank explained: "In general woman is a better educator than man for the child. She has the ability to identify, especially in relation to the child with whom she is and was identical, and she has at the same time a childlike and emotional life that enables her to identify empathically."[63] Rank told his audience that women had a knack for adjusting themselves to others, which surpassed the ability of men. He contrasted the female educator to the male artist: the educator diminished herself to accentuate the needs of the other, whereas the artist excelled in projecting himself onto material forms and sometimes other people.

If Rank enshrined age-old gendered divisions between emotion and intellect, he also celebrated the insight gained through emotional understanding. Rank believed that emotion guided and informed the reasoning process. At a time when the behaviorist John B. Watson castigated the sentimentalism of mothers, or the psychiatrist David Levy warned of poor mothering, Rank celebrated the virtues of emotional connection, a form of mothering that he also saw as vital to the therapeutic bond. Of course, laying emphasis on the importance of mothers levied enormous responsibility on them, and blame was not far behind, which soon emerged in numerous theories of maternal pathology, or mal de mère.[64] Rank too pointed out the evils of "parental tyranny," which could lie at the root of a child's misbehavior. The mother stood as an ambivalent and powerful figure.

Nonetheless, the skilled educator and competent analyst should emulate mothers rather than artists: they had to refrain from imposing their conceptions onto others and instead set up the conditions to foster the individual's growth. Growth was the prerogative of the patient. Rank declared that individuals "*should be created in no one else's image but their own.*"[65] Rank's accent on empathy and emotional identification resonated with Taft's long-standing view on emotion as a conscious indicator of value. She advised parents, teachers, even the rare friend to opt for a "true identification" with another, which "permits one to enter into the work or behavior of another without resistance."[66] She called it a "priceless sympathy," even as Rank had invoked Einfühlung, or conscious empathy, for this kind of mature identification.[67] Taft depicted the errors of projection, at odds with this conscious empathy, in an unpublished poem:

> You watch the drive
> of that one talking there
> Projecting her necessity
> onto empty air
> she calls reality
> no need to speak
> she cannot hear.[68]

While working at the Children's Aid Society in foster placement, Taft began to try out short-term "experimental analyses" with patients referred to her by psychiatrists.[69] She advised a young sixth-grade teacher not to be afraid of her sexual impulses, helped the seven-year-old Jackie prepare for foster care, and worked with a child who refused to go to school.[70] As Taft saw it, social workers at children's agencies were the best positioned among mental health professionals to provide therapy of this kind: psychiatrists were not always available, and clinical psychologists were trained only to give mental tests. This practice of emotional connection soon came to be known in Philadelphia as "relationship therapy."

Experiments in Therapeutic Relationship

Seven-year-old Helen was brought to Jessie Taft by the girl's father in May 1931.[71] Helen repeatedly tore her clothes and refused to go to school. She was living with her father, grandmother, and a younger brother; her mother had left the family home four times. Helen was of average intelligence and physically normal, although somewhat underweight. Her father worked fourteen hours each night and could no longer manage her, nor could he afford to repair or replace her clothes. He told Taft, "The trouble with her is—she ain't afraid of nothing—nothing in the world. . . . It ain't natural for a seven year old girl to look the principal in the eye and tell him she won't sit on the bench."[72]

Helen agreed to come back regularly and talk to Taft, which she did twice a week for nine weeks. During their meetings, Taft let Helen draw with crayons, sit at the window, examine the typewriter, and play with ink and a doll. As Helen examined the room and its contents, Taft voiced aloud what Helen seemed to be feeling and doing in a moment-by-moment validation of her thoughts and emotions. Helen could do almost as she wished, at one point leaning so far out of an open window that Taft was afraid she would fall. Even then, Taft simply warned her that there was a possibility that she might fall. In these first therapeutic experiments, Taft and her colleagues set few limits on the child's behavior; one social worker did not stop a nine-year-old boy from stabbing her hand repeatedly with a penknife, and another child stole Taft's purse.[73] It was cer-

tainly "a strenuous affair" to conduct this kind of therapy with impulsive children who, Taft argued, inflicted anger and fear on others
as projections of their own intense emotion. The therapist had to
bear as much of the child's anger as possible, as this released the
child from his "negative will to a positive finding of himself."

Taft's method centered on emotion, not on interpretation or
analysis. She did not ask Helen about her dreams, delve into unconscious meanings, or listen to her history, all techniques of classical psychoanalysis and of the child analyses conducted by Melanie
Klein and Anna Freud. Instead, Taft closely attended to her own unfolding relationship with Helen, making a "constant effort to comprehend and respond overtly to the salient feelings and impulses
of the hour as present living realities, which a child, like an adult,
usually seeks to deny consciously."[74] It did not matter whether the
therapist and child talked about how to play with a doll or how to
use the bathroom. The therapist could make use of "the most trivial,
flimsy content drawn from the local situation and current events."[75]
Impulse and emotion radiated through all kinds of experiences.

Taft had always viewed the self as performative: it was splayed out
in the world and made real in its social encounters. To understand
the self thus meant to grasp the "actual dynamics of the relationship
as it develops from hour to hour between the two human beings
who enter upon it, the one as patient, the other as helper."[76] Robinson and Taft chose the moniker, "relationship therapy" to capture
this approach; it was preferable to "contact," which was one-sided;
"participation," which subtly indicated that the social worker knew
what was right for the client; and "transfer," which was too closely
tied to psychoanalysis.[77]

The therapist functioned as "a barometer, sensitive to the least
change in the therapeutic atmosphere," aware of her own slightest
feeling response and careful not to project judgments onto the child.[78]
The social worker had to ensure that her own emotions did not interfere with the patient's attempt to find herself, a task that required "the
most sensitive self-conscious activity of understanding and response
plus a readiness to accept and carry to the end the losing role." To
take on this losing role meant that the therapist had to renounce her
own agenda. Echoing Rank, Taft declared that the therapist had to be
"willing to leave even the 'cure' so-called, to the will of the patient."[79]

After nine weeks of relationship therapy, Helen exhibited no further behavioral problems during her summer visit to a farm, and a year later her father had not reported any difficulties. More important than this social adjustment, however, was the fact that Helen was able to live out, perhaps for the first time, her impulses and emotions. Taft was convinced that in becoming aware of her feelings, Helen was "somewhat released from the drive to defeat or dominate the other."[80] Taft sent out a report of her therapeutic experiment for publication, which included long excerpts of her moment-by-moment exchanges with Helen that Taft had scribbled down during the sessions. The eclectic-minded analyst William A. White accepted Taft's paper for the *Psychoanalytic Review*, noting that pure, "bred-in-the-bone Freudians" would not appreciate her references to Rank, but he intended his journal to be "catholic in tone." Taft thanked White and informed him that it was White's own book, *Mechanisms of Character*, that had led her to prefer Rank to Freud.[81]

Social casework was practiced at the Pennsylvania School of Social Work in accord with the "functional school" of social work, in which social workers focused on the client's presenting issue or request and sought "partialist" interventions.[82] The Boston and New York diagnostic schools, in contrast, unearthed root causes of maladjustment and administered treatment in line with a medical model. At a time when the federal government was extending its involvement in public welfare, Taft and Robinson considered social workers to be representatives of an agency attuned to practical matters of finding employment or educational opportunities and always aware of the client's own inclinations in seeking assistance.[83] The client was to go through his own "vital process," which culminated with a "purpose or plan worked out by the client and accepted as a tentative arrangement by agency."[84] Even as the functional school ostensibly lost the debate with the diagnosticians, the goal of strengthening the client's own initiative persisted into the postwar years.[85]

Relationship therapy required what Rank called "conscious empathic identification"—a studied attunement to the client's spontaneous living and feeling, conveyed with an aura of radical acceptance. Taft told an audience of Jewish social workers that "to become an assistant in an organic growth process comes more naturally to the woman." She modeled the therapist after the ideal mother or, better, a nurturing vessel or surround in which the human self could grow and unfold. Taft declared that a child in therapy should experience a "realization of wholeness and security as part of a protecting supporting medium like nothing in human experience unless it be the intrauterine existence."[86]

If Taft agreed with Rank that empathic identification came more naturally to the woman, in the next breath, she stressed that the method required strenuous training. "The fact remains that for any would-be helper, learning to carry the role of assistant requires a discipline of the self, of the will, in favor of the other, that comes only after long training and with deep purpose to enter into another's growth process helpfully."[87] Only through rigorous preparation could the social worker divest herself of moralistic judgments of the child and sharpen her perception to detect minute fluctuations of emotion. The social worker had to refrain from controlling and directing the client in order to become his or her "assistant ego." This task, Taft concluded, was "intrinsically difficult for a man and particularly for a man with medical training."

Taft designed the advanced curriculum at the Pennsylvania School of Social Work to shape the social worker's professional self. Taft and Robinson offered one of the first courses in psychotherapy for children in 1934, and they added courses on economics and the history of the labor movement during the years when New Deal policies, including the Social Security program, were implemented.[88] Taft arranged evening courses on "Theories of Personality Development" and "The Organization of the Self," with visiting lecturers Otto Rank, the cultural anthropologist Ruth Benedict, Gestalt psychologist Kurt Koffka, and psychoanalyst Karen Horney, who spoke on culture and neurosis.[89] Taft boasted to Benedict that her students were college graduates with at least two years of professional training, who "will know something about people, and they will have considerable viewpoint in their own field."[90]

Through the rigors of the advanced curriculum, students transformed themselves into finely tuned instruments for feeling and helping. At first, students naively overidentified with clients and projected their judgments onto them. One social worker believed the denials of the intelligent girl who shoplifted. As the lies increased, Robinson advised the social worker to move beyond her knee-jerk personal response of "I can't bear to have her lie to me," in order to learn what lying and stealing meant for the girl.[91] Another social worker learned to check her initial reaction to a hostile Mr. A, who seemed to be maltreating a long-suffering Mrs. A, by cultivating a radical "acceptance of difference," and "to enter into the reality of another individual's feelings."[92] After several years of training, social workers could refrain from personal negative reactions and could "identify with a variety of personality patterns."[93]

Taft taught a class on personality to help social workers acknowledge their feelings and accept their limitations in the difficult and painful process of becoming a professional helper.[94] In the first of three semesters, students dealt with the shock, surprise, and disillusionment they felt regarding attitudes and behaviors of clients. Students were free to express "the way he [the student] *feels* as well as what he *thinks* about" when there is "no norm for the feelings he should have" in a rapidly moving place where one has to "risk himself ever more deeply."[95] Taft asked her students to relay their fears and expectations of their first hour conducting therapy; one student reported she was "lit up and happy," but another student was nearly "paralyzed with fear." Taft fostered "real experiencing" and often dealt with intense emotions.[96] Taft explained to a colleague that if one struggling student "can't ever get into a real relation to a client, so she feels it and the client feels it, she can't do casework."[97]

The class grappled with the practical constraints of therapy within social casework, as well as problems of race, sex differences, and age in treatment. Students read fiction, expressed their own impulsive feelings, considered the contributions of fieldwork, and integrated experiences from their own lives. In their final papers, students described and analyzed one of their own personal or professional relationships, relaying how it had changed over time, what had held it together or drew it apart, and how to take responsibility for their role in the relationship. Students experienced an alchemy whereby learning was "transmuted into the precious metal of his own philosophy and practice."[98] The natural desire to help was transformed into skillful practice by way of deep personal engagement; it was "an understanding that must be absorbed into blood and bone."[99] One graduate of the program wrote a letter of thanks to Taft, relaying that she had changed in a profound way: "I feel it nowhere so keenly, so surely, as in my ability to learn, to take in, to see the world separate from myself."[100]

At the National Conference of Social Work in 1950, Taft trumpeted relationship therapy as the "epoch-making psychological discovery of our era that may yet be found to be more momentous for the future of civilization than the unlocking of the forces in the atom."[101] If Taft exaggerated the importance of relationship therapy, it was nonetheless true that with its close attention to the emotional dynamics of the unfolding relationship and the therapist's disciplined empathic engagement with the client's experience, it had become an influential therapeutic method. The prominent clinical psychologist Carl Rogers had already enshrined these methods into his own practice.

Carl Rogers: Empathic Mirroring and Self-Abnegation

As did Taft, Carl Rogers honed his therapeutic skills in the field of child guidance. Born in Oak Park, Illinois, to a conservative Protestant family of six children, Rogers first set his sights on the ministry. In 1924, he enrolled in Union Theological Seminary in New York City but after two years moved "across the street" to Teachers College at Columbia University, where he was soon immersed in John Dewey's ideas of progressive education.[102] Rogers worked at the Institute for Child Guidance, and after graduation he got a job in the Child Study Department at the Society for the Prevention of Cruelty to Children in Rochester, New York. Rogers soon was teaching at the University of Rochester and in 1938 became director of the Rochester Guidance Center.

In the 1930s, Rogers adopted nondirective methods in treatment interviews with children, refraining from setting his own goals and allowing the child to freely express her feelings. Rogers became intrigued by Rank's approach after one of his staff members sent him a long letter describing an analysis with Rank.[103] In 1936, Rogers invited Rank to speak at a three-day seminar, during which Rank lectured to forty-five social workers and educators and addressed a general audience.[104] Rogers later reflected that this visit had "a decided impact on our staff and helped me to crystallize some of the therapeutic methods we were groping toward."[105] He valued Rank's emphasis on time-limited therapy but was less keen on his elaboration of the birth trauma, finding it too speculative. He was impressed enough by the approach, however, to hire one of Jessie Taft's students, D. Elizabeth Davis, to work at the Rochester Guidance Center.[106] As Rogers explained much later, this "social worker who had a background of Rankian training" taught him "to listen for the feelings, the emotions whose patterns could be discerned through the client's words."[107] It was from Davis, Rogers relayed, "that I first got the notion of responding almost entirely to the feeling being expressed."[108]

In his 1942 *Counseling and Psychotherapy*, Rogers codified these "newer concepts in practice," which had emerged from student counseling, marital guidance, and, significantly, the "thinking that has come from the Philadelphia Child Guidance Clinic and the Pennsylvania School of Social Work."[109] Now at Ohio State, Rogers explained that the counselor was to "hold a mirror to the child's feelings," even if they were hateful or willful, and to recognize and accept these feelings without praise or blame.[110] Echoing Taft, Rogers explained that the therapist should develop a "controlled identification." If the therapist is too sentimental, he "becomes so wrapped up in the child's problems as to be quite incapable of helping."[111] Instead, the counselor needed a "degree of sympathetic 'identification' with the child sufficient to bring about an understanding of the feelings and problems which are disturbing the youngster, but an identification which is 'controlled,' because understood, by the therapist."[112] It was a cultivated connection, neither overly sympathetic nor too detached.

Ideally, the therapist functioned as a nonmoralizing, nonjudgmental support for the client. As Rogers saw it, the relationship furnished a "quality of social bond which differed from any the client had heretofore experienced," except perhaps that of the permissive, understanding parent.[113] The therapist refrained from diagnosing the patient or offering advice, instead seeking to recognize and clarify the feelings expressed.[114] By reflecting the client's feelings and not offering interpretation, the therapist catalyzed the client's own ability to understand himself through the encounter.[115] Rogers explained,

"Certainly this type of therapy is not a preparation for change it *is* change."[116]

Rogers sought therapeutic protocols that not only nurtured the client's deepest inclinations, but that would also stand up to rigorous scientific scrutiny. He aimed for "definite and predictable" psychotherapeutic interventions that would "show a high degree of consistency from situation to situation."[117] If Taft had provided a glimpse into her therapeutic technique by publishing the copious notes she quickly jotted down during sessions, Rogers provided verbatim accounts of therapeutic encounters for teaching and training purposes. He phonographically recorded and then transcribed therapeutic exchanges, inscribing "glass-based records" that an assistant changed every three minutes while constantly brushing off the shavings created.[118] Half of Rogers's 1942 book on counseling contained verbatim transcriptions of eight counseling sessions with Herbert Bryan, an intelligent but neurotic man in his late twenties. Rogers numbered Bryan's every utterance and those of the counselor, and in the footnotes he added his running commentary detailing which of the counselor's remarks were helpful and which were misguided.[119]

Rogers's graduate student William Snyder published transcripts in 1943 of therapy sessions with an insurance salesman who was having problems initiating conversations. Snyder underscored Rogers's dictum to recognize the feeling and not the intellectual content of his client's utterances, responding to his patient, "You feel you've figured out a reasonable answer—that nothing terrible can happen—but that you can't accept the idea emotionally?"[120] Snyder refrained from offering advice, even when the salesman repeatedly asked him for his opinion. Frustrated, the salesman demanded to know if Snyder had a PhD. Snyder sheepishly responded that he "was still working for it."[121] Although the client failed to get the advice he craved, he did have a flash of insight that it would be helpful to talk to his wife and friends. After the sessions, Snyder shared his notes with the client and recommended a psychology textbook.

Clients often demanded advice, and it was exceedingly difficult to train therapists to refrain from giving it. Rogers told therapists to speak less and to think more. A nondirective counselor spoke less than half as much as the client, and one of Rogers's students demonstrated that Rogers's method was even less directive than

Taft's.[122] When a therapist checked his own interventions, the client had greater space to express his or her feelings. Rogers instructed his students "to use words not as bludgeons but as surgical tools to release growth," a use of language that "runs so deeply counter to our ordinary ways of behaving."[123] When the therapist adeptly reflected the client's feelings, the client was able to recognize and accept them. Once the client identified with his authentic self in this way, he usually knew just what to do next. This approach allowed the client to access what Rogers believed were "the impulses toward growth and normality which exist in every individual."[124] Rogers avowed that this method allowed the client genuinely to be himself, often for the first time in his life.[125]

Rogers honed his nondirective technique during World War II and assisted the war effort by training three thousand United Service Organizations (USO) workers in New York City between 1944 and 1945. It was readily apparent that there were significant psychiatric war casualties; one psychoanalyst warned that war dislocations, familial losses, and trauma meant an "overwhelming number of acute neurotic breakdowns." Psychoanalytic treatment—often a lengthy process—would be impossible for these cases.[126] Rogers adapted his own therapeutic approach to treat patients on a large scale, penning the pamphlet "A Counseling Viewpoint for the USO Worker" for those without much clinical training.[127]

By war's end, the demand for psychotherapy had skyrocketed. In 1946, the Veterans Administration called for the training of 4,700 clinical psychologists and vocational advisors.[128] Over the next two years, Rogers trained a hundred personal counselors. He also helped to restructure the American Psychological Association (APA) in line with the growing importance of clinical psychology.[129] Clinicians had broken with the APA in 1937 to form the American Association of Applied Psychology, and Rogers served as president of this association from 1944 to 1945. After the war, he played a major role in weaving this clinical arm back into the overall APA as one of its five new divisions.[130]

Rogers had by this time relocated to the University of Chicago to set up a counseling center to teach graduate students and to conduct research. He regularly counseled seven to ten clients. The center hosted more than eleven thousand therapeutic interviews over the next seven years with students, senior citizens, young children, and professionals of many types.[131] In 1946, Rogers was elected president of the APA, signaling his growing stature among psychologists. He was well on his way to becoming one of the best-known clinical psychologists in the United States.[132]

That year also saw the founding of the National Institute of Mental Health (NIMH) to address the growing need for funding for mental health research and for the training of clinicians. Psychiatric organizations had already begun their quest to legally limit the professional remit of clinical psychologists, but soon psychologists began winning legal battles for the license to practice psychotherapy. The fourfold increase in demand for psychotherapy services from the early war years to the postwar period was more often answered by nonmedical counselors or psychologists.[133] Rogers deemed the clinical psychologist best suited to take up the intense new demand for psychotherapy. Social workers did not have the research background, experimental psychologists did not train in counseling, and psychiatrists were more attentive to organic disorders.

Rogers had renamed his counseling method "client-centered" in 1945 to signal a shift from an emphasis on the therapist's reflection of feeling to his or her immersion in the client's experience.[134] Rogers's critics had disparaged the reflection of feeling as a mechanical parroting back of the client's concerns in a "stilted and inane" manner, sometimes even delivered with a mocking air.[135] Rogers and his students pointed out that printed transcripts lacked therapists' facial expressions and voice inflections and thus gave the mistaken impression of "cold" and "wooden" remarks.[136] The caricature of Rogerian therapy as a mindless echoing of the client's utterances nonetheless persisted, immortalized in one of the first computer programs, "Eliza," designed by Joseph Weizenbaum in 1966 to automatically spit out repetitive, "therapeutic" responses.

Rogers did, however, come to question the mirroring model in therapeutic technique. In 1947, his student Oliver Bown marked up a draft of Rogers's presidential address to the American Psychological Association, writing, "The mirror does not reflect a very true image when it is much more accepting of the perceptions than the client is himself."[137] In his published remarks, Rogers omitted the term "mirror self," substituting it with the notion that the therapist "becomes almost an alternate self and looks with understanding and acceptance upon these same perceptions."[138] This alternate self was akin to Taft's portrayal of the therapist as an "assistant ego" to the client.

Rogers emphasized that client-centered therapy was not a technique but a global attitude and philosophy. The therapist counseled with "warmth" and "sensitivity to the feelings of others."[139] Even more important, the therapist empathized with the client, or ventured to inhabit the client's experienced world.[140] Rogers first used the term "empathic" to mean a way of "perceiving through the client's eyes" in a 1948 address to Psi Chi, the International Honor Society in Psychology.[141] The term was not in common use at the time and was often incorrectly printed as "emphatic" in many of Rogers's typescripts of the period.[142] Rogers may have become cognizant of the term from his colleague Rollo May's prewar writings on ministerial counseling or from his interactions with psychiatrists at the Menninger Clinic.[143] The chief psychiatrist at the clinic, Robert P. Knight, described how he established emotional contact, or empathy, with a catatonic schizophrenic patient in 1946. He stood alongside the rigid, mute patient sometimes for the entire therapeutic hour in order to "follow him with empathy in his irrational actions and attitudes." Rogers checked off "Knight's paper" in a list of references in his notes of early 1947, although did not cite Knight in his published bibliography.[144]

In his 1947 APA presidential address, however, Rogers had expounded at length on the scientific and therapeutic rewards of inhabiting the subjective world of the patient without explicitly calling it empathy. He drew on evidence from cognitive and experimental psychology and also, surprisingly, from the physiology of digestion. He began his talk by describing a medical case study that allowed for the direct observation of bodily functions. A fifty-six-year-old "small, wiry, man of Irish-American stock" had a stoma in his stomach one and a half inches in diameter because he had scalded and occluded his esophagus while eating hot clam chowder.[145] According to psychosomatic disease models popular at the time, emotions such as anxiety, hostility, and resentment caused hypersecretion and hyperermia of the stomach lining that produced ulcers.[146] While this patient felt various emotions, doctors could peer directly into this hole to observe the mucosa of his stomach lining redden, pale, and become turgid. This physiological "window onto the stomach" effectively turned the inside of the patient out.

So too did Rogers's method. With empathy one glimpsed the inner world of the client. To observe from a vantage point situated *within* the client's experience produced a direct, and even objective, view of the client's personality. For this reason, Rogers asserted that his method demonstrated less bias than other approaches. He explicated in his notes that his client-centered psychotherapy "permits better knowledge of person from internal frame of reference. Contrary to most clinc. methods in this. It is like looking into flap of stomach. Wolf's study."[147] Rogers called it a "mind-stretching experience," a way of "going backstage of the person's living where we can observe from within some of the dramas of internal change."[148]

To further support his approach, Rogers cited Donald Snygg's experiments that demonstrated rats navigated in mazes according to the path that *appeared to the rat* to be shorter, not the path that was objectively shorter. Key to understanding the rat's behavior was to understand its phenomenal field or "the world of naïve immediate experience in which each individual lives."[149] Rogers titled a page in his notes with Syngg's hypothesis: "When a change takes place in the perceptual field, a corresponding change takes place in behavior." He then proceeded to list evidence from his clients to support the theory.[150] In addition, Rogers made use of social psychologist Isidor Chein's claim that to identify with another one had "to cross a spatial gap."[151] Even as awareness possessed no actual physical or spatial dimensions, it was felt to be localized. To identify with a character in a movie, Chein explained, one imagined that one left one's seat to become immersed in the motion picture world. Likewise, to see from the perspective of the patient, the therapist had to transport his awareness into the client's position.

To take up a point of view outside of the client, in contrast, was nonempathic. A therapist might pose the following questions from an external vantage point when encountering a client: "I wonder if I should help him get started talking?" Or, "He's a veteran. Could he have been a psychiatric case?"[152] These questions were sympathetic but not empathic. To respond with empathy, Rogers explained, was to gingerly adopt the client's perspective. If a client uttered, "I feel as though my mother is always watching me and criticizing what I do. It gets me all stirred up inside," an empathic therapist might say, "If I understand you correctly, you feel pretty resentful toward her criticism. Is that right?" Or, "You're wanting to struggle toward normality, aren't you? . . . It's really hard for you to get started."[153] One first took on the client's position, then explored feelings and ventured possibilities.

Rogers listed the empathic adoption of the client's inner frame of reference in 1959 as one of three necessary conditions of the therapist's stance, the others being congruence—that the therapist was authentic and not "faking" responses—and unconditional positive regard—that the therapist possessed a warm, positive feeling for the client.[154] If Rogers spoke primarily of empathy through the modes of "seeing" or "feeling," he sometimes included other sensory modalities: "I try to perceive his experience, and the meaning and the feeling and the taste and the flavor it has for him."[155] Empathy was to Rogers a modulated emotional response, not a shared feeling: "The counselor is perceiving the hates and hopes and fears of the client through immersion in an empathic process, but without himself, as counselor, experiencing those hates and hopes and fears."[156] It was "as if one were the other person, but without ever losing the 'as if' condition."[157] Empathy was one of the necessary conditions for therapeutic personality change, but it was only successful if the client felt understood.[158] The therapist ventured empathic guesses that the client could either validate or reject. The method thus ceded authority to the client, who was encouraged "to say yes or no; you're right on or no, you've missed it."[159]

Rogers was keen to establish a scientific grounding for his approach and to show evidence of its efficacy.[160] He was awarded a Rockefeller grant in 1949 to assess therapy outcomes using newly designed Q-sort tests to assess clients' response to therapy and to measure the effectiveness of client-centered psychotherapy. By 1951 Rogers had nearly thirty psychotherapy cases fully transcribed from audiotape for research study and had plans for fifty more.[161] That year Rogers hired the psychologist Rosalind Dymond, who had in 1948 designed the first experimental studies of empathy, as we will see. She reflected, years later: "Can you imagine that I was a research director in a non-directive center [laughs]? He [Rogers] had a theory and he wanted measures developed so he could test the theory."[162] The emphasis at the Chicago Counseling Center was on research, and Rogers and Dymond published the results of the first phase of their empirical assessment of counseling in their 1954 *Psychotherapy and Personality Change*, a volume that went through six printings over twenty-five years. In 1956, Rogers received a Distinguished Scientific Contribution Award from the APA.[163]

Rogers's dictum to adopt the client's perspective meant to abandon judgments, evaluations, even diagnostic categories. Dymond observed therapist trainings and reported: "This was a really tricky set of behaviors to train. Mostly you have to train them to keep their mouth shut for awhile; you're listening not talking. . . . You may not ask a direct question, ever."[164] Rogers advised therapists to "refrain from questioning, probing, blame, interpretation, advice, suggestion, persuasion, reassurance."[165] Further, the counselor had to bracket his own professional judgments and clinical expertise. Rogers declared that one would be hard-pressed while listening to recorded therapy sessions to discover a client-centered therapist's theories of personality, diagnostic views, standards of behavior, even his or her social class.[166] The therapist was to put his own self aside to become the patient's alter ego, and in doing so he "has temporarily divested itself (so far as possible) of its own selfhood, except for the one quality of endeavoring to understand." The counselor was "only partly another person."[167] One client described the experience as a confounding of selves: "In counseling we were mostly *me* working together on my situation as I found it."[168]

On the first pages of his 1951 volume *Client-Centered Therapy*, Rogers revealed his indebtedness to relationship therapy and Rankian ideas: "I rejoice at the privilege of being a midwife to a new personality—as I stand by with awe at the emergence of a self, a person, as I see a birth process in which I have had an important and facilitating part."[169] To call client-centered therapy a birth process illustrated how nondirection and empathy, stretching back to Rank, Taft, and Robinson, amounted to the diminution of one's selfhood in service of another's.[170] If this was a feminized stance, both Rogers and Taft thought it was better carried out by clinical psychologists and social workers than psychiatrists. Medical expertise was more of a liability than an asset.

Psychiatrists and psychologists were often at odds in these years. Psychiatrists sought to legally prohibit psychologists from practicing psychotherapy and to restrict them to administering psychometric tests. Rogers confessed to fellow psychologist Robert Yerkes that "fully cooperative functioning and relationships between two professions whose work overlaps, is impossible."[171] A fractious Harvard Summer School conference in 1948 exposed these fault lines and unveiled the animosity of some psychiatrists for Rogers's methods.

The interdisciplinary conference "Ways to Mental Health" was sponsored by the Massachusetts Society for Mental Hygiene and was intended to reach a large public audience. Harvard sociologist Talcott Parsons headed the planning committee, and among the speakers were Carl Rogers, who was teaching at the summer school; the psychoanalytic psychiatrist, Lawrence Kubie; psychiatrist Karl Menninger, head of the Menninger Clinic; Harry Solomon, director of Boston Psychopathic Hospital; and Ernest Burgess, a sociologist at the University of Chicago. Menninger and Solomon had privately expressed their doubts about Rogers's participation before the conference but the organizer responded that "Rogers and Counselling are almost synonymous to many minds."[172]

To a crowd of more than nine hundred participants, Rogers gave the second to last talk and declared that reliance on expert opinion in psychological matters fostered dependency, which in extreme cases exemplified a form of social control that could tend to political totalitarianism. In matters of psychotherapy, the client should be able to assess his or her own growth process; such evaluations should not be the prerogative of the clinician. In an earlier lecture, the psychiatrist Kubie had painted the virtues of a "scientific utopia," suggesting that a small town might be studied, analyzed, and counseled by experts in psychoanalytic psychiatry over the course of ten years.[173] The two visions could not be more different.

Just as Rogers finished speaking, Menninger interjected, "I don't know what a poor fascistic psychiatrist is going to do, with psychiatric fascism threatening him!"[174] Kubie then railed against Rogers's "straw man" image of the psychiatrist, his depiction of only "the most elementary, kindergarten aspects of psychotherapy," and Rogers's omission of the fact that it was Freud himself who first developed the nondirective method in 1893 with free association techniques.[175] Rogers clarified that he had not intended to condemn psychiatrists but was speaking of expert control, whether it be on the part of the psychiatrist, clinical psychologist, or social worker.

The sociologist Burgess stepped up to defend Rogers. As a member of the Chicago School of Sociology, Burgess had already espoused the importance of empathic methods for obtaining more accurate client narratives in social case records, as we will see. Burgess explained that the Chicago area project, initiated in 1932, rejected the common and yet ineffective approach to immigrant communities in which professional social workers merely "did what they felt best." In his project, self-directed community members designed and sponsored their own programs, with counselors limited to offering suggestions. Burgess highlighted the democratic basis for this innovation.

But bad feelings lingered after the conference. A week after the event, Menninger crystallized the problem in a letter to the conference organizer: "an established medical procedure has been attacked by a non-medical man" and further, Rogers was simply not supposed to "do therapy except in conjunction with a physician." But Menninger was also chagrined at Rogers's popularity. Rogers had received so many questions from the audience that Menninger had to give him extra time to answer them after the final lecture.[176] Menninger confessed in his letter, "I think Rogers made the rest of us look ridiculous." He assumed that Rogers enjoyed the added attention because many of his own students were in the audience, but the dean summarily dismissed this idea in his reply.[177]

Publicly, Menninger had already expressed interest in Rogers's approach and even sent one of his staff members to Rogers's clinic to learn the technique. Privately, he attacked him: "For our money, Rogers is a layman."[178] Menninger found Rogers's method keenly threatening to psychiatric expertise. By transferring the locus of evaluation and power from the therapist to the client, Rogers's empathic method directly undercut expert authority. Kubie agreed and dissuaded the organizer from publishing the proceedings, in good part because Rogers should not be given the "prestige of a Harvard platform."[179] Menninger declined to edit the proceedings, and the publication was quashed even though Harvard University Press had at first been eager to publish it.[180] In an attempt to mend fences, Rogers wrote letters to both men requesting further dialogue, but perhaps only added fuel to fire by enclosing his printed lecture published by a Harvard educational journal.[181]

Rogers saw empathic psychotherapy as a nonmedical practice, a view that boosted clinical psychologists in their fight with psychiatrists.[182] But Rogers already imagined his approach to stretch beyond the bounds of any one discipline. He told his 1948 audience that he was not presenting a method of curing people, but a "principle that seems to me to be applicable to human relationships."[183] This principle could be used in teaching, administration, even at conferences. It was absurd to think that anyone would simply believe "someone who got up on platform" he continued, but nonetheless he hoped that his listeners might observe where the locus of evaluation rested in their many relationships, therapeutic and otherwise.[184]

If Rogers made a bid for the universality of his method, Jessie Taft disagreed with him on the matter of expertise. She tied relationship therapy to the "active and directive" aims of social casework and told an audience of school counselors in Philadelphia in 1947 that "never for one moment does it operate by wiping out its own essential character or refusing to stand by the responsibility it carries."[185] She critiqued Rogers's radical nondirective approach, which he had presented to the same audience only a year earlier. Taft wrote with some bitterness in her private correspondence about a colleague who had discovered Rogers: "I *am* sorry though that he has discovered Rogers who has no right to *Rank*—has *taken* it all vicariously, chiefly thru his contacts with D. Eliz. Davis when she was in Rochester—and a few visits to this clinic. He is using it pretty externally + saying anybody can do it."[186]

In 1959, John Shlein, Rogers's colleague at the Chicago Counseling Center, wrote to Taft crediting her ideas on growth and immediate experiencing as a significant influence on him. In response, Taft accentuated the "significant differences in viewpoint and therapeutic practice" between relationship therapy and client-centered therapy. She expressed admiration for Shlein's attempts to "feel your way into the confused emotions of your psychotic patient," a foray in implementing client-centered methods with deeply disturbed patients.[187] Taft declined his invitation to speak at Chicago, however, writing ruefully that the invitation would have been accepted twenty years earlier. She signaled that her contributions had not been given their due.[188] Taft died the following year. Shlein left the University of Chicago in 1967 to help establish a clinical psychology program at the Harvard School of Education based on client-centered principles.[189] As client-centered models in clinical psychology became more popular, the knowledge of relationship therapy faded. Indeed in 1959, Shlein had to ask Taft directly for a copy of her *Dynamics of Therapy* as it was out of print.[190]

Empathy beyond Therapy

If Taft tied relationship therapy to social work, Rogers imagined that empathic practices would be of benefit to many fields and to society as a whole. In 1947, he wrote to the dean of social sciences at the University of Chicago that he intended not only to "educate and develop professional leaders in the field of psychotherapy" but to develop knowledge for "significant social usefulness."[191] Time was "running out for society with such awful speed," given the recent use of the atom bomb, and it was imperative that client-centered skills be applied to political science, education, industry, and religion. Rogers invited faculty and graduate students from a number of fields to his home for a seminar devoted to sorting out the affinities between client-centered therapy, existentialism, politics, and theology. He told the group that his years of practicing therapy had resulted in "the continual rediscovery of man as positive, constructive, basically social."[192] In a memo, Rogers laid out the means whereby "we can generalize our experience and hypotheses in client-centered therapy to apply to all interpersonal relationships."[193]

Rogers believed that the very existence of the modern world was under threat by "the tragic and well-nigh fatal failures of communication," and he saw the potential for his model to resolve labor disagreements and assist in diplomacy, among other contributions.[194] Empathy, or seeing an idea "from the other person's point of view" could do more good than launching judgments and critiques.[195] Empathic understanding not only benefited face-to-face encounters, but it could also shift entrenched Cold War political positions: "If I can really understand how he hates his father, or hates the company, or hates Communists—if I can catch the flavor of his fear of insanity, or his fear of atom bombs, or of Russia—it will be of the greatest help to him in altering those hatreds and fears and in establishing realistic and harmonious relationships."[196]

The empathic stance undermined the power and control of experts and professionals and supported democracy. Submission to expert advice was not too far afield, as Rogers believed, from a political surrender to the state, a perspective he had voiced at the contentious 1948 conference on mental health. Fascism, of course, demonstrated the terrible extremes of such a path. Rogers imagined that even the small-scale implementation of empathy in a therapeutic situation might go a long way to free the human from authoritarian control.[197] The evidence that the client had "at least the latent capacity to understand and guide himself," revealed a "psychological basis for democracy."[198]

Rogerian methods spread quickly to pastoral and marital counselors, educators, parents, clinical psychologists, and social workers. Some of his students took empathic practices in new directions. Eugene Gendlin popularized the method of identifying the felt-sense of an experience in his popular 1978 book *Focusing*, still in print. Another student, Marshall Rosenberg, moved in a more political direction. He developed techniques for nonviolent communication through the empathic assessment of the underlying feelings and universal needs of those with whom one was in conflict. Rosenberg's 1983 book on nonviolent communication sold a million copies, and the International Center for Nonviolent Communication is flourishing today across the globe.[199]

The success of an empathic approach in psychotherapy, perhaps paradoxically, rested in its dissemination and consequent disappearance as a distinct method. Research conducted at Chicago in 1950 demonstrated that an "ideal therapist" was distinguished less by the school in which he or she was trained than by the quality of the rapport, defined by empathic engagement and sensitivity to the feelings of the client.[200] In the mid-1950s, psychoanalysts took a new look at empathy by reappraising the writings of Ferenczi and Rank, and empathy as "vicarious introspection" soon became integral to the Viennese-born Heinz Kohut's self-psychology.[201] The

Menninger-trained psychologist Roy Schafer wrote in 1959 that there had been little emphasis on empathy in psychoanalysis even as its importance in therapy and personal relations had been recognized.[202] By 1974, a study of eight different psychotherapeutic approaches found that eighty-three therapists gave empathy the highest ranking out of twelve treatment variables.[203]

Rogers left the academy in 1968 to establish the Center for the Studies of the Person in La Jolla, California. In the midst of the proliferation of an astonishing array of psychotherapies, Rogers continued to promote empathic and humanistic methods. He reminded his readers in 1975 that empathic skill was dependent on "neither academic brilliance nor diagnostic skill" and that it belonged "in a different realm of discourse from most clinical thinking— psychological and psychiatric."[204] To empathize meant to lay aside one's self and to temporarily live in another's life, "moving about in it delicately without making judgments."[205] Empathy was simply one of the "most delicate and powerful ways we have of using ourselves."[206] It was an unappreciated way of being that dissolved alienation, if one could put aside one's own judgments in the service of another.

CHAPTER SIX

Measuring Empathy

IN 1948, STUDENTS IN a social psychology class at Cornell formed small groups and then predicted how others in the group would describe their own and others' personality traits.[1] In making their predictions, students were supposed to employ empathy. One student explained: "My predictions of what the other was going to say about me were arrived at by placing myself in his shoes and thinking of how I acted and how he would take it." Another student reported, "I tried to see 'me' through his eyes. I wondered what he thought of me from the conversations that took place before writing the answers." And another "went almost solely on 'feel.' I relied on very tentative sensations as to what it would feel like to be that other person."[2]

This project was one of the first experiments to test for empathy, designed by the twenty-four-year-old graduate student Rosalind Dymond, who had arrived at Cornell only two years earlier. Dymond drew on sociological models of empathy as role-taking, which she had learned from the sociologist Leonard Cottrell. Cottrell and Ernest Burgess, his mentor at the University of Chicago, had promoted empathy as a useful means to conduct case study interviews. In this sociological framework, empathy was conceptualized as an accurate appraisal of another person's preferences, attitudes, or feelings as experienced within their social world.

Dymond scaled empathy as a psychological capacity, similar to the way intelligence had been first measured in the early years of the twentieth century. Her experiments sparked a profusion of attempts to test empathy over the next decades. Industrial psychologists measured empathy as an asset for sales and to improve relations between workers and management, and clinical psychologists charted counselor empathy in psychotherapy. By the mid-1950s a raft of empathy scales were in use.

Researchers soon discovered, however, that measures of empathy were marred by stereotypes and muddied by projection—the attribution to others of one's own assumptions and feelings. Even more distressing was that after more than a decade of research, psychologists found little correlation between the many empathy scales in use and even less agreement as to empathy's core definition. At best, empathy was a multidimensional ability; at worst, it was a scientific term lacking a clear referent.

Empathic Stories in Sociology

The University of Chicago hatched two doctoral students in 1913, both of whom were steeped in pragmatist philosophy and George Herbert Mead's social psychology: Jessie Taft and Ernest Burgess. As we have seen, Jessie Taft transitioned into mental hygiene and social work, but her early study of the importance of emotional understanding continued to inform her innovative psychotherapeutic approach. Ernest Burgess trained in sociology and remained within the academic fold at Chicago, where he developed a concentric model of the city and highlighted the importance of empathic engagement for conducting sociological case studies.

In these years, Chicago sociology was a vital center for the study of minority cultures, urban life, and immigrant communities undergoing Americanization. The journalist Robert E. Park, press agent for Booker T. Washington, joined the department in 1914, and drawing from German sources, he stressed an individual perspective on social relations.[3] Personal documents, such as diaries, letters, and autobiographical materials, became essential primary sources at Chicago, expertly woven into William Thomas's and Florian

Znaniecki's influential 1918 monograph *The Polish Peasant in Europe and America*. Novelist Richard Wright found inspiration in the rich personal sources contained in Louis Wirth's *The Ghetto*, Everett Stonequist's *The Marginal Man*, and Park and Burgess's *The City*, all products of the Chicago school. Wright explained that instructors were "not afraid to urge their students to trust their feelings for a situation or event," and he eschewed a "slavish devotion to figures, charts, graphs, and sterile scientific technique."[4] Burgess carried on this storytelling tradition in his courses by assigning literary autobiographical texts.[5]

Burgess and Park compiled one of the most read sociological texts of the period, the 1921 *Introduction to the Science of Sociology*, dubbed "the green bible" of sociology.[6] Burgess was a slight, harried man, who never married, lived close to the university, and was keen for collaboration. Although Park did more to shape the volume, Burgess introduced the lengthy section on theories of sympathy, imitation, and suggestion, peppered with excerpts on inner imitation in art, although without explicit mention of Einfühlung or empathy.[7] It was not long, however, before Burgess began touting empathy as an important method for writing case records.

To compose a case record, sociologists and social workers relied on various means of acquiring information. Since the turn of the twentieth century, social welfare and charity workers had engaged in "friendly visiting" to glean intimate details about the lives of families.[8] Mary Richmond, general secretary of the Baltimore Charity Organization Society told social workers to approach families with sympathy and friendliness, which "leads the family to discuss things not spoken of to others."[9] Techniques of information collection soon went beyond cursory assessments to amass detailed family, financial, and biographical material. There was little systematization of social work records, however, which featured a variety of narrative styles, from dramatic accounts to straightforward reporting.

Sociologists were keen to advise social workers on scientific data collection, and in 1926, the American Sociological Association included a section on social work.[10] Some social workers resented the intrusion; sociologists were sometimes scorned for propounding highfalutin, "meaningless verbiage."[11] But Burgess saw the sociological case study and the social work case record aligned in their appraisal of the person as part of a social group. Both had as their task "*to analyze a human situation.*"[12] Burgess himself mined social work records for his own studies, in one instance drawing from a case Jessie Taft wrote up on delinquency.[13]

Burgess found most case accounts static and lifeless; clients were so "depersonalized, they become Robots." Worse still, they were not individuals but merely undifferentiated cases epitomizing "poverty, unemployment, drunkenness, feeble-mindedness, desertion, bad housing."[14] The sociologist Charles Cooley, a potent influence on American sociology, advised that research should highlight dramatic, personal life histories imbued with the play of the imagination. "All science calls for imagination, and in our subject it largely takes the form of an insight into motives which makes possible a penetrating description of behavior."[15] Burgess, however, downplayed the role of imagination, arguing that the better method was that of direct sharing or empathy, which relied on what one social worker called "the ability of human beings to interpenetrate, and yet maintain awareness."[16] He advised the caseworker to go beyond sympathy to "put himself so far as possible in the place of the other person, to participate in his experiences, to see life, at least for the moment, as the other person sees it."[17] Empathy of this sort would produce a lively report as well as a reliable document for scientific study.

To see life as the client saw it meant to avidly attend to the client's story. Burgess's student Clifford Shaw, a research sociologist at the Institute of Juvenile Research, showcased this approach in his 1930 *The Jack-Roller: A Delinquent Boy's Own Story*, one of a series of two hundred studies of young male offenders.[18] Stanley, the jack-roller—who beat up and robbed incapacitated drunks—was given an outline of his problems, arrests, and court appearances and was then encouraged to write his own narrative. Shaw found Stanley's first draft too thin in description and over the next six years helped him to revise the document. The final 250-page account was presented as Stanley's own story, with his original, first draft appended at the end.[19]

Stanley described the day he was freed from jail: "After a year of idleness and monotony in that stagnant cesspool I was now supposed to make good on seven cents. A fine start, I'll say, with not one word of advice from anyone. They just kick you out of the place, and to hell with you." And further: "I was wearing the same old suit that I had on when I entered the place a year before. It had been crumpled into a ball for a year, and was now dirty, moldy, wrinkled, and much too small. The odor of the thing was awful. With that outfit and seven cents I was now supposed to make good. Immediately my old feeling of humiliation came back as I felt the stare of the other people burning through me."[20] Shaw intervened at this point, noting the glaring lack of aftercare for released prisoners. He took Stanley in, gave him a suit, offered him money, and found him a place to live. Stanley gained perspective on his life by telling his story, but for sociologists insight was not enough. Rehabilitation could only occur with a change in one's social circumstances. Stanley needed a new home, new job, and new friends.[21] After more than five years moving from job to job and getting into fights, Stanley was said to finally settle down in sales, to marry and have a child.

Stanley's treatment began with the case worker's empathy, which according to Burgess entailed "entering into the experience of another person by the human and democratic method of sharing experiences."[22] Listening to Stanley recount the facts as *he* understood them minimized the social worker's tendency to imaginatively embellish a client's story. Burgess declared that this method eliminated the "personal equation" and produced an objective case account. Some saw parallels between empathy and Cooley's imaginative, "sympathetic introspection," but Burgess was insistent that the imagination was not an element of direct sharing.[23] Sympathy might allow one to understand another, but empathy went further in "seeing the situation just as the subject himself saw it."[24] It was not enough to feel what another felt; one had to stand at the center of his or her social world and get a sense for the surrounding conditions. Stanley's story was not so much a portrait of an individual delinquent but of Stanley as a "person" who earned and carried status in social settings; his story opened a window onto "the social and cultural world in which the delinquent lives."[25]

Shaw's book told a sensational tale of redemption and carried authority as a social science tract. It was immediately popular. But if Shaw and Burgess argued that empathy was a means to construct a more objective case record, contemporary historians have called this objectivity into question. The happy ending may have been spurious. Shaw himself heavily shaped Stanley's story, and rather than an impartial, bare-bones narrative, it might better be classed in the literary genre of a noir, urban melodrama.[26]

Empathy, nonetheless, signaled an attempt to sharpen understanding by stepping into an individual's social and cultural world. In 1932, Shaw initiated the Chicago Area Project to implement this principle within communities. The project aimed to reduce the incidence of juvenile delinquency by creating social organizations in underprivileged areas of the city on the assumption that delinquency emerged from social failure rather than from economic lack. But rather than using social workers to develop innovative projects, local citizens were encouraged to create the new social and recreational associations that they deemed would best serve them. The aim was to empower residents on the principle, avowed by Burgess, that "wherever there are people, there are leaders."[27] Residents raised money, found deep sources of community support, and took full responsibility for the groups they formed. The program succeeded in helping delinquents before they reached the court system, and local leaders were judged to be more effective than outside experts. Burgess later described this project in his public defense of Carl Rogers's psychotherapeutic principle of empowering the client rather than the social science expert.

Social workers also called upon empathy to fine-tune their interviewing techniques. Fern Lowry, trained at the University of Chicago School of Social Services, described empathy as keeping one's own feelings apart from the situation, which she contrasted with "'sympathy' or feeling for others."[28] She viewed empathy as did Burgess, as the path to an objective grasp of another's situation. Josephine Strode defined empathy as a way to imagine oneself into another's state of mind, which necessitated emotional restraint; if the social worker became too involved, the client might feel distress, embarrassment, or even amusement.[29] In Strode's Cornell course, Skills in Case Work, she described empathy as producing a strange state of double consciousness: one simultaneously felt the other's situation as well as one's own. It was very much like an actor playing a role, a dramatic empathy that Strode learned from psychologist

Herbert Langfeld.[30] She advised social workers to train their empathy through close observation: noticing a child tugging at his mother's apron, a clenched fist, or lagging footstep could reveal feelings that a casual observer would not notice. Students could hone these skills by participating in community activities, trying out different jobs, and by reading history, biography, and novels.[31]

Social scientists saw empathy as a measured feeling response opposed to sympathy, which was deemed excessively emotional. Empathy also stood at a distance from the imagination, the spinner of wild and untrue tales. To empathize meant to hew closely to actual lived experience in order to produce reliable case reports. By the early 1930s, the term appeared in Chicago sociology texts, leading one sociologist to erroneously report that "empathy" had been invented by the Sociology Department. He defined it as a scientific means to "try and understand the behavior of someone unlike ourselves, such as a child, a criminal, or the member of another race or sex."[32] "Empathy" appeared on a 1931 list of sociological terms, and a dissertation on "Empathy as a Sociological Concept" was under way at Chicago, although it was never completed.[33]

Another student at Chicago, Leonard Cottrell, mentored by both Mead and Burgess, turned to empathy to carry out his case studies of marriage and the family. Cottrell moved from Chicago to Cornell in 1935 to teach classes in rural sociology, social psychology, and public welfare.[34] Four years later, Cottrell and Burgess published an extensive analysis of the successes and failures of marriage.[35] The sociologists distributed 7,000 questionnaires, and assessed 526 completed documents from mostly urban, native-white (parentage from North European cultures), nonneurotic, middle-class Americans, who had been married one to six years. Happiness and adjustment, as reported by the couples, were the criteria for marital success. The major findings were that "wives make the major adjustment in marriage," that a child's affectional bonds shaped their adult capacity for love, and that socialization and cultural factors were important for adjustment and attitudes toward sex.[36]

After reporting statistical findings, the sociologists turned to case studies of five marriages based on the method of empathy. While conducting extensive interviews, the "investigator attempts to assume the role position of the subject as he responds to his life *situations*, and does not stop with mere sympathetic reproduction of his acts, gestures and emotional states."[37] For these sociologists, to empathize meant to inhabit not only another's psyche but his or her social world. "Empathic introspection" of this kind, however, was difficult to carry out: the sociologist had to identify with the subject and at the same time, "a part of his personality system must be reserved to observe and note what has been going on."[38] The sociologist-self was thus divided between immersion and observation, similar to those engaged in aesthetic or dramatic empathy.

If exercising empathy was challenging, it was even more problematic to measure. "It is difficult to see how such a complex observational process can be put into mensurable form," Burgess and Cottrell lamented.[39] One had to take into account the perspectives and biases of observers; for instance, if an observer had a domineering mother (a common example of the time), he might overact to "any slight indication of aggression from a female," leading to "an almost hopeless jungle of social-psychological relativity."[40] One reviewer praised Burgess and Cottrell's book for its application of statistical tools to topics that had been reserved to "intuitive 'insights' and the 'understandings' of poets, priests, psychoanalysts, novelists, newspaper women, philosopher-aesthetes and other plumbers of the human heart."[41] The case studies, however, did not receive such high praise. The authors acknowledged that as a tool of social science, empathy lacked standardization, which they found to be both a "virtue and weakness."[42] Another decade would pass before the concept would be directly tested through experimental means.

Acting as Science

The goal of crafting a predictive and reliable science of interpersonal relations was the task not only of sociologists but also of some psychiatrists, prominent among them Jacob Moreno. Moreno pioneered the scientific analysis of interpersonal connection, group therapy techniques, and the psychodrama, getting his start in improvisational theater in Vienna in 1922.[43] In 1935, he emigrated to New York and established a small private sanitarium on the Hudson River in Beacon, New York. His new science of sociometry charted a psychological geography of social connections by asking students at the New York State Training School for Girls in Hudson, New York, to rate the desirability of rooming with other girls in cottages.[44] Moreno translated the complex mutual and one-sided attractions into an extensive sociogram, a concrete map of social ties with more than seven thousand connecting lines. Some consider his diagrams a precursor to social network theories.[45]

Moreno also used the stage to dramatize his patients' inner conflicts. He listened intently to patients, absorbed their experiences, and then enacted them. In one case he played out an estranged wife's feelings of disappointment directly to her husband, becoming the wife's "auxiliary ego." At the Beacon sanitarium, Moreno built a tiered stage on which he invited staff, visitors, and other patients to play out a patient's auxiliary egos. Audience participants would enact the roles of other persons in the patient's life, characters the subject imagined, as well as projections of the patient's personality. The concentric circles of the stage represented different levels of the psyche, allowing audience members an easier transition onto the stage and into the inner space of the patient's mind (figure 19).[46] Given his Viennese origins, Moreno was familiar with the aesthetic roots of empathy, describing "*Einfühlung* (empathy) of an actor into his part."[47] He found empathy, however, to be too closely tied to aesthetics, and it described only a one-way projection of feeling into an object or dramatic role.[48] Moreno thus invented the term "tele" to capture a two-directional "flow of feeling" or relational force that drew people together or apart in various configurations.

Moreno had a bombastic personality and was prone to theatrical excess, but his methods drew interest from a host of sociologists and anthropologists, including Leonard Cottrell, Paul Lazarsfeld, Margaret Mead, and the psychiatrist Adolf Meyer, all of whom trained at his workshops.[49] Stages for psychodrama were built at St. Elizabeth's Hospital in Washington, D.C., and at the Harvard Psychological Clinic.[50] Social psychologist Gardner Murphy wrote about Moreno's spontaneity theater in a popular article, "The Mind Is a Stage." When Jessie Taft considered inviting Moreno to lecture at the Philadelphia School of Social Work, psychoanalyst William S. White warned her that he became "so intense, 'overheated'" in his terrific effort to convey his ideas, that the audience often found his performance "risible."[51]

Figure 19. Psychodrama stage, Beacon model, built for the purpose of enacting psychodramas of patients' life and conflicts, designed by psychiatrist Jacob L. Moreno at Beacon Hill Sanitarium, Beacon, New York. From J. L. Moreno, Psychodrama *(Beacon, N.Y.: Beacon House, 1946). Used by permission of the Moreno family.*

Moreno brought scientific analysis to the murky realm of interpersonal relationships on the condition that the sociologist him- or herself participate in the drama. If an astronomer studying the skies could not transform himself into a star, the social scientist could metamorphose into another's auxiliary ego to attain knowledge.[52] Cottrell saw the benefits of role-playing as well. He took on the voice of a Mr. Jones who was having marital difficulties: "I lived through a crisis in which I mustered the courage to leave her. After I left I was lonely and 'lost.' I came back."[53] Cottrell found that using the "I" pronoun rendered Jones's experience more intelligible to him and made it easier to predict Jones's future behavior. Cottrell concluded that the sociologist should train for "the conscious and skillful use of the incorporative or role-taking processes which go on most fully in the more intimate interpersonal relationship."[54]

Role-playing, however, was a difficult skill to master. The observer played "as real a part in it as the subject," all the while taking on a "disciplined observer role."[55] It required the sharpening of one's "wits and sensitivities" and went beyond sympathy, which only asked the investigator to "imagine how *he* would feel or act if he were in the subject's situation."[56] With empathy, in contrast, the investigator actively imitated or adopted the expressions, gestures, and movements of the subject. He became an actor, ready "to speak the lines of the subject."[57] This created better rapport with the client: one researcher pointed out it was more revealing when he asked a client, "How d'ya cop the short?" instead of "How did you steal the automobile?"[58]

Without "frequent recourse to the empathic process of studying cases," Cottrell declared, knowledge would "become sterile and actually blind."[59] Empathic role-play might even provide an epistemological groundwork for diagnostic or statistical methods of analysis in sociology and medicine.[60] Case study methods of this kind, however, needed to be "as subject to testing, verification, and operational formulation as possible."[61] If social psychology could determine the precise units of interpersonal exchange, Cottrell imagined that it might become "the biochemistry of the social sciences."[62]

In 1942, Cottrell left Cornell for the Information and Education Division of the War Department, where he examined relationships between officers and enlisted men, soldiers' attitudes toward the enemy, and the struggles of African American soldiers. Cottrell became ever more convinced of the importance of empathy or role-taking—not only in intimate relationships but also for the political agenda of promoting democracy and resolving conflict.[63] It was typical to reproduce in one's own mind the expected responses of others, a social dynamic that occurred across barriers of race, class, and nation. This view, going back to George Herbert Mead, revealed that others, especially those with whom one was in conflict, were in some fashion contained within the self. Cottrell voiced the remarkable social implications of this claim: "The rebellious child is also in part the authoritarian parent; the saint is part sinner; the communist is part capitalist; the Southern White is part Negro psychologically."[64]

The awareness of one's social interconnectedness could lead to peaceful resolution of conflict. Conscious, empathic role-taking for Cottrell was therefore a civic duty. "A democratic solution of the problem requires that the citizens interacting in their roles as members of opposing groups become increasingly able to take the roles of their opponents. It is only through this ability that integrative solution of conflict rather than armed truces can be arrived at."[65] By the same token, insufficient empathy fomented war propaganda and identification with a narrow, symbolic "national" self, producing group antagonisms. Propaganda limited "group interaction in desired areas of 'we-they' relationships, and controlled the specific expectancy patterns of those relationships."[66] Employers intent on blocking labor movements, for instance, could improperly use empathic methods to exploit racial, national, or religious divisions. Even with its misuses, however, training in role-taking or empathy was imperative for what Cottrell dubbed "education for citizenship."[67]

If Cottrell and the Chicago school set their sights on a predictive science of sociology rooted in empathic methods, others were not so sanguine about such a project. Although empathy had been linked to social science methods of interpretation and understanding in distinction to causal explanation in the natural sciences, the philosopher of science Carl Hempel doubted that empathy could rise to the level of scientific evidence.[68] Rather than "feeling himself into the role of a paranoiac historic personality," Hempel argued, the historian would be better served by invoking the principles of abnormal personality.[69] History and sociology relied on systematic laws, hypothetical generalization, and theory-construction. Even if the empathic method provided plausible descriptions of behavior, it did so on the basis of "attractively worded metaphors," not scientific formulations.[70]

The historian and philosopher of science Edgar Zilsel also found "psychological empathy" suspect.[71] One might imagine that citizens in a recently bombed city felt intimidated and defeated, but they also might feel determined to resist. "Which process actually takes place cannot be decided by psychological empathy but by statistical observation only."[72] If empathy could be a useful psychological heuristic, it was highly prone to error and had to be substantiated by "observable actions."[73] Others spoke derisively of the "mysterious powers of insight, empathy and clairvoyance."[74] George Lundberg, president of the American Sociological Association in 1943, cautioned against the emphasis on the "unique particular," which could only have relevance in light of the "abstract general."[75] Another sociologist praised Cottrell for his statistical analysis but contended that to understand what an act meant for the person carrying it out had absolutely no scientific import. "Hence, the empathic element must be eliminated or at least standardized."[76] Empathy, he concluded, simply failed "to make explicit the basic difference between science and art."[77] Given that empathy connoted a form of aesthetic immersion for much of early twentieth-century psychology, this indictment of empathy was not surprising.

At war's end, Cottrell returned to Cornell and took up the chairmanship of the Department of Sociology and Anthropology. A year later, the young psychologist Rosalind Dymond, newly arrived from Toronto, would tackle the difficult task of experimentally measuring empathy under his direction. Dymond strove to fit empathy into the frame of empirical validity and statistical evidence, increasingly seen in the postwar years as essential to the social sciences.

Operationalizing Empathy

Rosalind Dymond arrived at Cornell in 1946 with a master's degree in clinical psychology from the University of Toronto. In Toronto, she had studied with the psychologist Magda Arnold, who would later propose an influential theory of emotion as a form of cognitive appraisal.[78] Dymond described Arnold as one of a number of "fabulous woman teachers" and "a very hard-headed scientist," who managed to obtain a lectureship only because many of the male professors had left for wartime obligations.[79]

Dymond may have been drawn to Cornell by its rigorous experimental program, put in place more than half a century earlier by E. B. Titchener, but she soon discovered that she was "very unhappy in the psychology department." She found the brass instrument psychology for measuring perception "dumb, uninteresting stuff."[80] As soon as she passed her psychology qualifying exams, she tried her hand at fieldwork in cultural anthropology, enrolled in Nelson Foote's sociology class and in Cottrell's seminar on social psychology. She "fell under the charm of" Cottrell, whom she called a "powerhouse," a "Franklin Roosevelt type," and "very smart, but very kindly."[81] She soon caught Cottrell's drift, as she put it, of how one "developed these interior models for role behaviors by inter-jecting the responses of the other person." Under his direction, she soon began experimenting on empathy.

Because Dymond's project stood at the intersection of experi-mental psychology and sociology, she reported that she "had a heck of a time even getting a thesis committee together . . . because Cot-trell couldn't serve as he was the Dean."[82] She ejected the educa-tional psychologist Frank Freeman because he was unable to grasp her research design. Research and teaching assistantships were not available to women at that time; an irony not lost on the three women graduate students in her class, who "got a big kick of the fact" that all of them passed the entry exams while the three men failed. Despite these difficulties, Dymond soon took up the task of defining empa-thy and then finding a way to measure it: "Throughout my whole career I know that I was often accused of attempting to put a hard science into soft areas, and it's true I did love seeing what I could do about pinning down fuzzy concepts."[83]

The concept of empathy was largely confined to the academy at that time. Dymond explained: "I can remember having to define it *every* time I used the term. People would be blank and [ask], "What does that mean?"[84] She consulted psychological and psychiatric dic-tionaries for clarification, discovering empathy to be an aesthetic projection of the self into a work of art as well as a psychoanalytic identification with another person.[85] She dedicated two introduc-tory chapters of her dissertation to Lipps's aesthetic theories and the kinesthetic theories of Titchener, Langfeld, and Gordon. But empa-thy as the projection of feelings into objects seemed to her a narrow definition in light of her exposure to Carl Rogers's psychotherapeu-tic model and to the schizophrenia researcher Roy Hoskins's 1946 definition of empathy as a coidentification in one's social group.[86] Dymond then fashioned her own definition: "The term empathy will be used throughout this work to denote the imaginative trans-posing of oneself into the thinking, feeling and acting of another, and so structuring his situations as he does."[87] She adopted the lan-guage of transposing rather than projecting and highlighted empa-thy as a way into another's *situation* as the Chicago sociologists had done.

Further, she differentiated empathy from identification, which was unconscious, long-lasting, and more emotional than empathy. Empathy was not a matter of attributing one's own wishes or attitudes to another, nor was it sympathy, the alleviation of another's distress.[88] And empathy did not have positive overtones: "No, no. no. It might be a quality of a good used car salesman, for all I know. You know, it might be used for good or for evil. . . . I had to carefully define this as neutral, not a positive implication."[89] But empathy was an individual trait that could be measured. "I really think this is an important basic ability that varies in amount between people. There are people that are good at it, and people who are not. It is like measuring intelligence, or anything else that was hard to do at that time."[90] She imagined she might do for empathy what had been done for intelligence earlier in the century.

In her first experiments, Dymond measured empathy with the Thematic Apperception Test (TAT).[91] The TAT was a series of images that depicted archetypal personalities and dramatic scenes, many of which were drawings of photographs torn from magazines. The test was designed at the Harvard Psychological Clinic by the head of the clinic, psychologist Henry Murray, with his colleague and lover, the artist Christiana Morgan.[92] Subjects gazed at the images and told stories about them. These stories often echoed their own experiences, as revealed later in interviews and free association tests. Murray called the character in an image that matched the subject in gender and age the "evocative object," which elicited empathy from the subject.[93] Murray drew on his colleague Gordon Allport's writings on empathy and personality, as well as on Jung's typology to argue in 1938 that projection was a complement to empathy: if we feel something we are prone to imagine another feels it as well. This projective process could become distorted from reality only if emotional processes were unconscious and denied.[94]

Dymond showed her subjects the TAT and rated their stories as "good" descriptions if they described the person's thoughts and feelings; "fair" if the accounts only touched upon external characteristics; and "poor" if descriptions simply named the figures.[95] Those who gave good descriptions were credited with more empathy and insight into their own relationships than those who gave fair or poor descriptions. Empathy and insight were therefore correlated: "The ability to feel and describe the thoughts and feelings of others (empathy) was accompanied by a better understanding of the relationship one has with others (insight)."[96]

Dymond's first measure of empathy was, strikingly, also a measure of projection. She acknowledged that her subjects' descriptions of the TAT cards "appear to be projections of the internalized self-other patterns."[97] Subjects projected their own conflicts, unconscious fantasies, and personality patterns into the TAT images.[98] This early gauge of empathy—of telling in-depth stories of characters—was therefore remarkably close to empathy's early projective meaning.

But Dymond had conceptualized empathy as a way to grasp another's actual situation, and to test for this ability she needed an entirely new experimental design. Her next set of tests no longer assessed rich, descriptive stories but asked subjects to empathize by predicting another's response to a questionnaire. She was now convinced that "the only practical criterion of empathy is accuracy of prediction."[99] She gathered fifty-three students in a social psychology class (twenty-nine male and twenty-four female) and divided them into small groups of six to seven members, none of whom were friends. The groups met once a week to conduct a class project. One student was deemed an observer. After the groups met three times, she asked each member (A) to ascribe six personality traits to him- or herself and then to another person (B) in the group. Then A rated B according to how B would rate himself, and A also had to rate himself as he thought B would rate him. Then B carried out the same procedure.

Could A predict whether B thought himself to be very friendly or unfriendly? The skill of empathy meant one was a good predictor of what the other would say. Dymond picked her personality traits almost at random—self-confidence, friendliness, leadership, superiority, selfishness, sense of humor—because the test measured whether A could predict the personality traits B *thought* that he possessed, not whether B actually possessed these traits or not. To make accurate predictions, A would have to take on the role of B and vice versa. Empathic ability was calculated as a quantitative deviation score that measured "how closely his [A's] predictions of B's ratings correspond with B's actual ratings."[100] Low empathizers had higher deviation scores than high empathizers. Dymond was confident that she was measuring "how well can the subject transpose himself into the thinking, feeling and acting of the others."[101]

To establish preliminary evidence for the test's reliability, she tested subjects again after the groups met eight times and found a positive correlation between the two tests. Although men and women performed similarly on the first test, women were more accurate on the second test and showed a higher learning curve.[102] Dymond also found a correlation between empathy and insight, but she now measured insight as the match between an individual's perception of him- or herself and the *average* of others' perception of that individual. Again, those with high empathy had more insight. Further, she compared her findings with results from the TAT, but she defined empathy to correlate with a subject's description of marginal figures in the picture rather than the main, evocative figure with whom the subject identified. She explained: "Essentially this method involves computing the percentage of characters *other than the self figure* introduced into the stories whose thoughts and feelings are richly described."[103] Dymond turned the TAT into an empathy test by assessing the descriptions of the characters into whom the subject did not project his or her own feelings.

In another study, Dymond divided a group of eighty social psychology students into high and low empathizers.[104] She found equal numbers of men and women in both groups and no differences in intelligence between the two groups. She gave members of each group a battery of personality tests. The high empathizers were outgoing, warm, emotional, and flexible. They cared about family and had an interest in others. Low empathic types tended to be introverts, self-centered, or solitary and often mistrusted others. She called them "lone wolves" with an intellectualized, abstract approach to life.[105] At a meeting of the Eastern Division of the American Psychological Association at Clark University, Dymond presented empathy as the "faculty" or personality trait of being able to see things from the other person's point of view."[106] She still maintained, however, that the capacity for empathy was dependent on the situation, the degree of contact and familiarity with another, and the mood and motivation of the empathizer.[107]

In 1949, Dymond completed her dissertation and left Cornell

for Mount Holyoke College, where she taught for two years. That year, Dymond and Cottrell called empathy a "neglected field" in psychology in the interdisciplinary journal *Psychiatry*, founded by Henry Stack Sullivan.[108] Dymond and Cottrell grumbled that even with Sullivan's interpersonal approach to psychiatry and Hoskins's explanation of the absence of empathy in schizophrenia, theorists had failed to make "explicit the problems posed by the empathic processes."[109] There was simply a lack of rigorous study of the topic.

Developing a measurement tool for empathy seemed imperative in the polarized Cold War political climate. In fall 1950, after fighting in Korea had already begun, Cottrell, now president of the American Sociological Association, urged his fellow sociologists to study empathy, a topic that social psychologists had "thus far succeeded in ignoring almost completely."[110] Cottrell told his audience that empathy played a key role in "our long struggle ahead for a democratic world community."[111] Unlike authoritarian regimes that produced group response with external controls, democracy necessitated "maximum participation," or the capacity to take on the role of another and to conceive of one's own activity in relation to the whole. Democratic society required citizens to extend their empathic range in a conscious and participatory way in order to establish an "experienced consensus." Cottrell called for a "reliable and sensitive index of the empathic ability" and cited Dymond's quantitative studies.[112]

The following year, Cottrell became a researcher at the Russell Sage Foundation and then served as chairman of the Advisory Group on Psychological and Unconventional Warfare at the Department of Defense.[113] Empathy, Cottrell noted, enabled one to keenly gauge one's audience. Because individuals accepted or rejected messages in line with their group membership, German soldiers fighting in fractured units had been the most receptive targets for Allied messages.[114] Cottrell advised his fellow sociologists not only to counter communism but to craft positive messages to promote democracy to the American public and to friendly audiences.[115] In a political atmosphere in which one had to be alert for "surprise nuclear attacks," he encouraged all social scientists, not just psychologists, to develop their communicative skills, foremost among them, empathy.

From Projection to Accurate Empathy

If Cottrell imagined that an empathic measure might bolster the political goal of expanding democracy during the Cold War, Dymond continued to experimentally fine-tune the empathy concept. In 1951, she became director of research at Carl Rogers's Counseling Center in Chicago, where her experimental acumen was key to developing tests of the effectiveness of client-centered therapy. She also tested rural schoolchildren with a modified TAT in 1952 to see if there were measureable changes in empathy with age.[116] The older students gave more detailed descriptions of the thoughts and feelings of the characters than the younger ones. But, again, as the authors pointed out, the TAT was a projective test—and rather than measuring empathy as a measure of accuracy, it might have reflected a child's creative imagination. Dymond also asked students to judge their likeability and that of other students, and she defined her measure of empathy as the correspondence between the likeability of a child as judged by others and as judged by himself. It was difficult to disentangle likeability from popularity, however, as popular children who were better at the test of social insight may have found it easier to say they were liked than it was for the unpopular kids to admit they were disliked.

But in Dymond's 1952 experiment on empathy and age, a subtle but significant change in her definition of empathy appeared. The definition now read: "the imaginative and *accurate* transposing of oneself into the thinking, feeling and acting of another."[117] The modifier "accurate" had not appeared in the definition in her 1948 dissertation. Empathy had therefore transformed from a creative and imaginative projection into an accurate appraisal of another. One educational psychologist of the time even attributed to Dymond the shift in empathy from inanimate objects to persons.[118]

Critics soon discovered, however, that Dymond's measure of empathy was contaminated by shared cultural norms. An analysis revealed that good empathizers better conformed to cultural norms, as well as those with whom they empathized. "In other words, conventional people get good scores on empathy tests because most of their partners (or referents) in the test are also conventional."[119] Dymond developed a partial correlation method to take into account these stereotypes. But a review of empathy experiments found that judges and subjects continued to base responses for themselves and for others on such stereotypes, resulting in a "perseverative conventionality."[120]

Dymond then conducted a more sophisticated test of fifteen married couples that assessed *assumed* similarity or projection in contrast to *actual* similarity or empathy (as measured by responses on the Minnesota Multiphasic Personality Inventory).[121] She sought to eliminate stereotypical responses by rejecting true or false questions that led to the same response more than 66 percent of the time. Controlling for these factors, Dymond asserted that happy, married couples (as determined by themselves and a researcher) were better able to empathize by correctly predicting responses of their spouse on this personality inventory.

Other researchers joined Dymond in operationally distinguishing accurate empathy from projection and conventionality. The social psychologist Irving Bender discovered in his dissertation research that after interviewing eight subjects each for an hour, he did only slightly better than chance in predicting their scores on personality tests.[122] Bender had been an executive at the B.F. Goodrich Tire Company before studying with Gordon Allport at Dartmouth and then receiving his doctorate at Syracuse.[123] Returning to Dartmouth to teach, he asked Allport for advice on a study of motives, sending him a long list of topics on identification, projection, and adjustment. He joked at the end of his letter that Allport should only tackle the topics for which he had "an *einfühling* [*sic*]."[124] Bender was clearly aware of the German roots of empathy, and in line with his mentor Allport, he sought ways to study personality holistically. One student described Bender's interest "in the individual as a total organism and not a collection of disjointed stimuli."[125]

Bender, known as "Flash" for his penchant for wearing splashy ties, began an extended collaboration with Alfred Hastorf, who had arrived at Dartmouth from Princeton in 1948. They wanted to find a way "to resolve our 'metaphysical solitude' and feel ourselves into the life of another person in order to understand what the nature of experience is for him."[126] But they soon discovered that forty-six of their male psychology students were quite impaired at predicting others' responses on a set of three personality scales, even when the students expressed confidence that they knew the others well enough to rate them.[127] Instead of understanding his college mates, a student tended "to project his own feelings into his forecasts." Projection was determined by a high correlation between the predictor's own score and his forecast for others, coupled with high correlations between forecasts for different subjects by the same predictor. The investigators concluded that undergraduates had little empathic accuracy for others, supporting rather than challenging metaphysical solipsism.[128]

Bender and Hastorf simply found projection pervasive. Projection was "the attribution to others of one's own needs, interests, and attitudes."[129] They knew that historically empathy had been defined "in the sense of projecting oneself into a work of art, or a condition of nature such as a storm, or things like airplanes or rockets." But the psychologists invoked Dymond's 1952 definition verbatim; empathy was now the accurate perception of another and opposed to self-projection.[130] They then computed deviational scores of projection and empathy: projection was the measure of how much a subject's prediction of a friend's values on the Allport-Vernon Study of Values differed from his own score, whereas empathy marked the difference between the prediction and the actual response of his friend.[131] Of fifty subjects, only twenty were closer to their associates' scores than they were to their own scores. These were the empathizers. The twenty-eight projectors made predictions that matched their own scores better than that of their comrades (the remaining two had equal empathy and projection scores). The psychologists concluded that "the phenomenon of projection was not only more frequent, but also more intense than was that of empathy."[132] Projection was personal and merely referred to the self, whereas empathy was objective, cognitive, and truly perceptive.

The psychologists then computed a more sensitive, "refined empathy" score by subtracting out projection from raw empathy scores.[133] They tested fifty students on a set of statements cataloging attitudes and feelings. Each subject selected the four others in the group whose verbal responses the subjects were confident they could predict. Again, they found more projectors (twenty-nine) than empathizers (twenty). Projection was so prevalent in the perception of others that they deemed it a persistent "handicap" that "we suffer in matters of social sensitivity."[134]

Interest in empathy, social sensitivity, and perception was growing. At the late August meeting of the APA in 1951, the social psychology division sponsored a panel on Empathy and Expressive Traits.[135] The next year, the APA offered a handful of papers on empathy in education and psychotherapy as well as on measures of social sensitivity. A study of college students presented at the 1953 APA meeting found, as did Bender and Hastorf, that projection was negatively correlated with empathy.[136]

In one remarkable end-of-season football game between Dartmouth and Princeton in 1951, profound failures of empathy and the pervasiveness of projection became undeniable. The game was a violent affair; the All-American Princeton player left the field with a broken nose and a concussion, and a Dartmouth player was carried off with a broken leg. But student newspapers from the two schools recounted very different versions of the game, perceptions that Hastorf, with the public opinion researcher Hadley Cantril, his Princeton mentor, capitalized on in their influential study "They Saw a Game."[137] Students from both schools completed questionnaires, watched the same video of the game, and then judged the number of infractions made by each team. Princeton students saw the Dartmouth team make twice as many infractions as Dartmouth students did of their own team. Although a third of Dartmouth students admitted that their side played roughly, they thought that Princeton was overly concerned with their "star player," which led to excessive complaints against Dartmouth.

The conclusion? "The 'game' actually was many different games and that each version of the events that transpired was just as 'real' to a particular person as other versions were to other people."[138] Identification with a team—which the authors did not call empathy —came with the penchant to view the other side's motivations in a negative light.[139] Social perception, far from accurately rendering the position of another, was prone to deviations based on identification and projection.

Social psychologists had come to the general consensus that many students lacked social sensitivity and were ill prepared for life tasks. Bender and Hastorf participated in an ad hoc Committee on Human Relations established at Dartmouth in 1951, which drew together various social science fields to develop a new course for students, funded by an alumnus.[140] A subcommittee spent three weeks investigating group dynamics, role-playing, and innovative methods of teaching in Bethel, Maine, at the National Training Laboratory. These group techniques, pioneered by Kurt Lewin and Alex Bavelas at MIT, had become popular in the growing science of human relations, described in the popular 1951 *Roads to Agreement* by the economist Stuart Chase, promoter of Franklin Roosevelt's New Deal.[141]

In 1952, Dartmouth offered a new course, Introduction in Human Relations, directly addressed to "the problem of living with other men and women."[142] The course aimed to increase students' "sensitivity to and respect for the attitudes and feelings and purposes of others," to help them work effectively with others, to deal with conflicts in intimate groups, and to gain insight into their own attitudes and behavior. The class had an academic component, but the core of the class consisted of laboratory sections with group experiments, role-playing, and small group tasks. These tasks, as the organizers knew from their own experience at the Bethel training laboratory, could be highly stressful. The unstructured three-hour training group session was particularly challenging. One sociology professor recounted his encounter with a Marine officer, a squadron commander off the coast of Korea who "had broken down like a child under the stress of his amorphous, unmanageable training group (T group)." The professor confessed that he too, "on temporary furlough from the ivory tower, followed suit."[143]

At Dartmouth, the committee screened students with problems and established referral protocols for troubled students in the new course. Students read Carl Rogers on client-centered therapy, Hadley Cantril on stereotypes, and Hastorf on perception, and they explored topics on the family, personality development, group loyalties, norms and identification, authoritarian and democratic leadership, power, and social control. One lecture in the course covered the individual's perception of his world, using a rotating window to demonstrate perceptual frameworks. Students predicted the responses of the instructor to a questionnaire and discussed nonverbal communication, stereotypes, projection, and empathic responses.[144]

One student called it a learning-by-experience course; the teachers called it a space where "it is possible for any individual to examine (and even to experiment with) his own behavior, ideas and motives."[145]

Empathy in Industry and Sales

Interest in measuring empathy after World War II spread to industrial psychologists, who counted it useful for smoothing worker-employer relationships, promoting business, and identifying good salesmen. This branch of psychology had been growing vigorously ever since the Harvard psychologist Hugo Münsterberg outlined the uses of psychology for applied industrial tasks in 1916.[146] Psychologists designed batteries to test vocational and mechanical abilities and considered interpersonal dynamics an important element in the factory workroom. The extensive Hawthorne experiments conducted at the General Electric plant revealed that attention to workers and good supervisory-worker relations could themselves boost productivity.[147]

Hermann H. Remmers, head of the Division of Educational Reference at Purdue University, developed tests of industrial empathy that he conducted with his students over the course of a decade. He deemed it critical to operationalize empathy in a world with endemic hostilities between groups and persons. In 1950, he called for a "quantitative index of the ability of individuals and members of groups to 'put themselves in the other fellow's shoes.'"[148] Empathic skill was important not only to industry, but also to marriage, counseling, and education, as well as for groups with racial, religious, ethnic, economic, and social status differences. He brought the ability back to poet Robert Burns's giftie, as psychiatrist E. E. Southard had done years earlier: "To see oursilves as ithers see us!"[149]

Already in 1943 Remmers had identified empathy, defined as "the ability and willingness to wear each student's 'sensorial and emotional shoes,'" to be an important trait for teachers.[150] Indicators of this trait included fairness in grading, a positive personal appearance, a sympathetic attitude toward students, and a liberal, progressive attitude. A few years later, Remmers charted empathy in an opinion poll by asking high school students how they felt about an issue, and then asking them to predict how other groups felt about the same issues.[151] Topics included the viability of a women president, whether women should work outside the home, and how much African Americans could contribute to society. He acknowledged that "empathy" was a term unknown to most high school students, and he distributed his results among high school teachers.

Remmers was not familiar with Dymond's studies, but in 1950 he defined empathy along similar lines—as accurate prediction: "having the subject or subjects predict the ordinal or cardinal position of another individual or group on one or more scales of defined psychological dimensions."[152] If the measured prediction was the same as the estimate, it was empathy, whereas a significant difference indicated projection. His studies of industrial empathy discovered that labor, supervisors, and management did poorly when predicting scores of members of other groups in a test of supervisory ability. Labor leaders underestimated the supervisory capacity of management, but they also scored higher on tests of supervision than management; management overestimated the scores of labor on the test; and supervisors in a textile factory were unable to empathize with either labor or management.[153]

Willard Kerr at the Illinois Institute of Technology developed one of the first empathy scales in these years. Kerr had earned his doctorate at Purdue University, was director of industrial music research of Radio Corporation of America, and spent the war years as an aviation psychologist. Whereas Dymond assessed interpersonal empathy with subjects who interacted with each other, Kerr and his student Boris Speroff evaluated empathy on paper and pencil tests that asked subjects to predict the preferences of the average factory worker. Kerr saw empathy as a "unique talent" possessed by "natural leaders, successful sales managers, and outstanding counselors." Far from aesthetic reverie, empathy was now linked to "selling ability," which required a mix of identification with another's feelings and an ability to anticipate reactions.[154]

Kerr and Speroff's Empathy Test Form A was a standardized instrument that asked its respondents to "answer the questions NOT AS YOU but as the average person would answer . . . try to place yourself in the position of the hypothetical average person" (figure 20).[155] The test taker had to predict what type of music

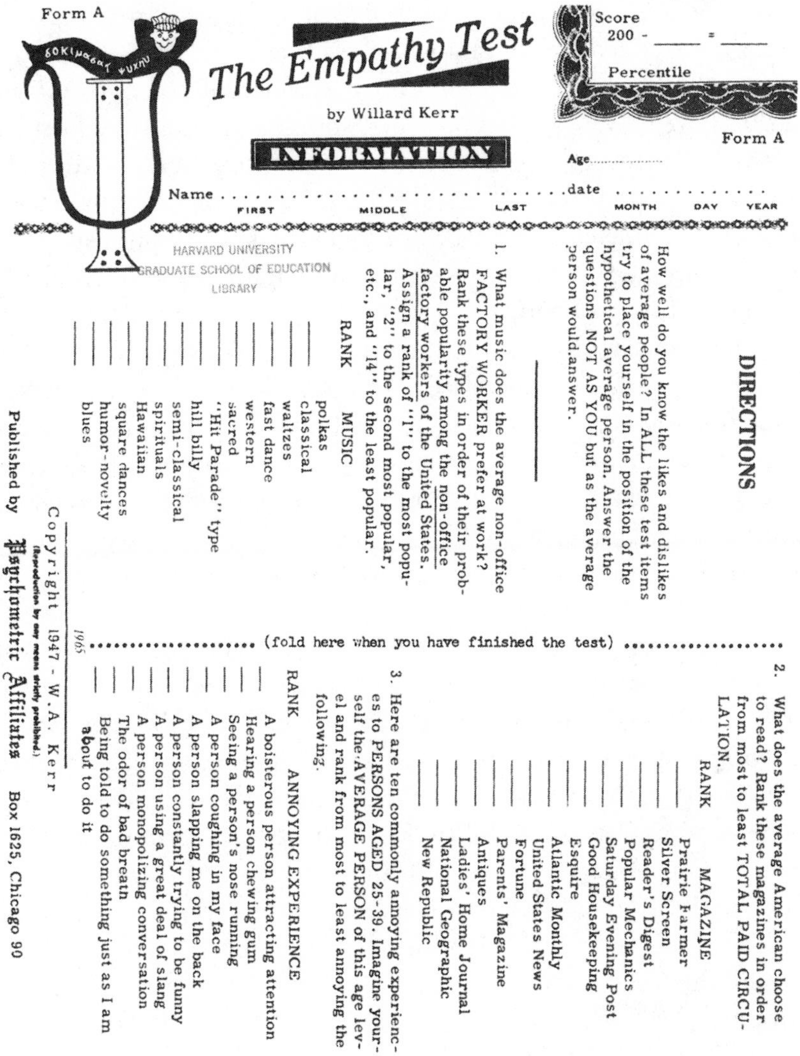

Form A

The Empathy Test

by Willard Kerr

INFORMATION

Form A

Score
200 - _____ = _____

Percentile

Age..........

Name . . . . .date . . . .
FIRST   MIDDLE   LAST   MONTH   DAY   YEAR

DIRECTIONS

How well do you know the likes and dislikes of average people? In ALL these test items try to place yourself in the position of the hypothetical average person. Answer the questions NOT AS YOU but as the average person would answer.

1. What music does the average non-office FACTORY WORKER prefer at work? Rank these types in order of their probable popularity among the non-office factory workers of the United States. Assign a rank of "1" to the most popular, "2" to the second most popular, etc., and "14" to the least popular.

RANK   MUSIC

_____ polkas
_____ classical
_____ waltzes
_____ fast dance
_____ western
_____ sacred
_____ "Hit Parade" type
_____ hill billy
_____ semi-classical
_____ spirituals
_____ Hawaiian
_____ square dances
_____ humor-novelty
_____ blues

2. What does the average American choose to read? Rank these magazines in order from most to least TOTAL PAID CIRCU-LATION.

RANK   MAGAZINE

_____ Prairie Farmer
_____ Silver Screen
_____ Reader's Digest
_____ Popular Mechanics
_____ Saturday Evening Post
_____ Good Housekeeping
_____ Esquire
_____ Atlantic Monthly
_____ United States News
_____ Fortune
_____ Parents' Magazine
_____ Antiques
_____ Ladies' Home Journal
_____ National Geographic
_____ New Republic

3. Here are ten commonly annoying experiences to PERSONS AGED 25-39. Imagine yourself the AVERAGE PERSON of this age level and rank from most to least annoying the following.

RANK   ANNOYING EXPERIENCE

_____ A boisterous person attracting attention
_____ Hearing a person chewing gum
_____ Seeing a person's nose running
_____ A person coughing in my face
_____ A person slapping me on the back
_____ A person constantly trying to be funny
_____ A person using a great deal of slang
_____ A person monopolizing conversation
_____ The odor of bad breath
_____ Being told to do something just as I am about to do it

.... (fold here when you have finished the test) ....

1965

Published by Psychometric Affiliates   Box 1625, Chicago 90

Figure 20. Empathy Test A, one of the first pencil and paper empathy tests designed to test how well subjects could predict the preferences of nonoffice factory workers. Willard A. Kerr, 1947.

a nonoffice factory worker would like at work, what magazine the average American would choose to read, and what the most common annoying experiences were for younger adults, ages twenty-six to thirty-nine. The researchers developed a second test, Form B, in which subjects predicted preferences of office workers. To judge results, Kerr and Speroff collected data from the national survey program for music, actual sales of magazines, and long lists of pet peeves compiled through questionnaires by the experimental psychologist Hulsey Cason.

The data established that the average factory worker liked "Hit Parade" type music and waltzes best, that favorite magazines were *Reader's Digest* and *Ladies Home Journal*, and that someone coughing in one's face or having bad breath were the most annoying experiences.[156] Kerr and Speroff (who moved to the Industrial Relations Center at the University of Chicago) argued their test had "universal appeal" because it evaluated preferences in music, "the common language of mankind."[157]

In 1954, the researchers concluded that after five years of testing, their empathy test was the "first, standardized empathy instrument with useful validity and reliability."[158] They validated the test for college students with an interpersonal desirability scale (a measure of popularity), measures of leadership, and success in elected office. In one test of reliability, Kerr sat near the president during the commencement exercises of Illinois Institute of Technology and watched the graduates walk forward, shake the president's hand, and smile. He then rated the breadth of the graduate's smile on a four-point scale. Graduates with the broadest smiles were more likely to score high on the empathy test!

High empathy scores were also correlated with measures of union leadership and automobile sales, but not with over-the-counter selling.[159] Kerr argued that the test had great value for the selection of managerial personnel; leaders; counselors and therapists; graduate students; and salesmen of insurance, real estate, securities, and cars. When psychologists tested salesmen at Chicago's automobile agencies, they discovered that the empathy test was correlated with sales of new but not used cars.[160] The authors attributed this finding to television advertising: the buyer was disappointed with the look of used cars and vented his frustration on the seller.

Speroff and Kerr also found a relation between likeability, empathy scores, and the tendency to have fewer industrial accidents. Ninety steel workers on the finishing end of a Chicago steel mill given high interpersonal desirability ratings by those within their "racial" group (Spanish-speaking Mexican, Puerto Rican, or black) had the fewest accidents.[161] The experimental design revealed that empathy across ethnic groups was not even considered within the realm of possibility. Low interpersonal desirability ratings were correlated with poor scores on the empathy test, which, the psychologists surmised, contributed to the workers' constitutional accident-proneness.[162] They explained that those with little empathy tended to withdraw and experienced frustration, leading to more accidents. Kerr and Speroff also viewed empathy, in the form of identification with elected officials, to be an important element of democracy.[163]

Empathy could be valuable in an office setting to assess the experience and educational history of one's interlocutor.[164] Speroff taught supervisors in a steel mill with a long history of labor unrest to role-play the position of laborers who had lodged grievances that year, culminating in a strike.[165] The exercise brought supervisors face-to-face with their own "inflexible, obdurate orientation"; one supervisor heard on a tape recording his own deprecatory manner and his repeated exclamations of "damned union." The sessions also revealed the hidden agendas of the worker. Speroff claimed that his interventions increased the rate at which grievances were resolved over the next months.

By the end of the decade, however, validity measures for empathy tests in industry, the clinic and the laboratory all came up wanting. The educational psychologist Robert Thorndike derisively reviewed Kerr's "so-called *Empathy Test*" in 1959 and questioned whether the test measured empathy at all, as it only predicted the responses of the "generalized other" and not the specific other.[166] To establish its validity, the test needed corroboration by others outside of Kerr's group. Thorndike also could not connect single items to the seven general factors measured on Kerr's new test, "Primary Empathic Abilities," which assessed "insecure people, lower middle class, [and] stable young married people." Thorndike concluded that "results from the test seem largely meaningless."[167] Other studies found only a small correlation between Kerr's test and leadership positions.[168] Scores on the empathy test surprisingly were no higher for clinical than experimental psychologists, and women liberal arts students scored lower on the test than men in the field.[169] Kerr ventured another revision, the "Diplomacy Test of Empathy," which did not fare much better. An executive officer at the APA called it "an interesting idea inadequately developed."[170] Another assessment pointed to "severe methodological errors and statistical artifacts," as it measured only the degree of similarity between the test taker and the group with whom he or she empathized. It was simply a "waste of time."[171]

Ratings of empathy were often outstripped by projection and cultural stereotypes.[172] Not surprisingly, most subjects were better at judging others of similar cultural background, age, and gender. Empathic ability correlated with age, intelligence, aesthetic interest to some degree, insight, and emotional adjustment. Gender and training in psychology did not seem to matter; clinical psychologists were discovered to be no better empathizers than students.[173]

Psychologists also found no correlation between Dymond's and Kerr's empathy tests, leading one researcher to conclude that the tests "are not measuring the same thing."[174] Kerr tested what was called "mass empathy," or the predicted responses of a group, whereas Dymond's test assessed responses of individuals known to each other. The mass empathy test was analytic, based on inference; one psychologist pointed out, "it does not lend itself so readily to empathizing with any particular person."[175] By the early 1970s, Kerr's tests disappeared from the *Mental Measurements Yearbook* and from general use. Dymond's tests fared little better: they took hours to administer, were tainted by stereotyping and projection, and never became standard instruments.[176]

After more than a decade of investigation, Dymond, now "Cartwright" after her marriage to the statistician Desmond Cartwright, confessed that "empathy has proved to be a troublesome variable to measure."[177] She reviewed a study of musical response and counted no less than three different definitions of empathy. Ranking others on their empathic ability reflected only a "reputation for empathy" not empathy itself. By this time, Dymond Cartwright gave up on creating a standardized instrument to measure empathy. She later explained: "It sort of fell apart at that point. . . . I could have developed a standardized list of questionnaires that had those kinds of instructions (your response and what your prediction of other person's responses were under these circumstances). But I really didn't want to sort of vivify those questions . . . it's not the important concept."[178] The critical factor in measuring empathy was whether one's prediction of another's response actually matched the other's response. In 1961, Dymond Cartwright left the Counseling Center and soon thereafter abandoned empathy research for the study of sleep and dreams.

Scaling Empathy

These initial attempts to measure empathy, however, were only the first of a wide variety of empathy scales, instruments, inventories and tools that psychologists continue to construct today. Because empathy was a key feature of psychotherapy at the Chicago Counseling Center, accurate empathy scales were needed to rate therapists and clients. While at Chicago, Dymond Cartwright conducted a study of the Rorschach inkblot test to measure empathy in potential clients for Rogerian psychotherapy. Subjects who projected human activity into the inkblots (high M responses) were thought to be adept at understanding what others were feeling.[179] If these subjects also showed well-controlled emotional responsiveness and adequate contact with reality, they turned out to be good candidates for client-centered therapy. In another study, Dymond Cartwright discovered that counselors were better able to match the description given by the patient of his or her experience after a successful therapy than before, demonstrating increased empathy.[180]

Carl Rogers's student Charles Truax set up a scale in 1961 that correlated high scores on therapists' empathy, warmth, and genuineness with positive outcomes for schizophrenic and neurotic patients.[181] Truax's understanding of empathy aligned with Rogers's: "the sensitivity to current feelings and the verbal facility to communicate this understanding in a language attuned to the client's current feelings."[182] Ten years later, however the scale was deemed to have little validity; the test merely measured the number of spoken words or the therapist's assertiveness in dealing with the client's emotions.[183]

The Relationship Inventory, devised by another student of Rogers's, evaluated empathic understanding with questions to clients such as "He tries to see through my eyes" and "He nearly always knows exactly what I mean."[184] But the Chapman scale, which asked subjects to watch others on videotape and try to feel as they did, was found to have no predictive validity.[185]

By the early 1960s, educators and psychologists were making clear distinctions between cognitive or predictive empathy and emotional empathy.[186] Dymond's and Kerr's tests evaluated predictive ability, whereas therapeutic empathy measured emotional response. Two major scales developed around 1970 showcased this divide: Hogan's Empathy Scale, a sixty-four-item, self-report scale of role-taking, and Mehrabian and Epstein's Questionnaire Measure of Emotional Empathy.[187] Hogan developed his scale for his Berkeley dissertation and tied empathy to a "broad moral perspective," which he correlated to socially appropriate behavior. The highly "empathic man" was socially perceptive of a wide range of interpersonal cues, was skilled at imaginative play and humor, and had insight into his own and others' motives. But the reliability of the scale was brought into question in 1982, and a later study cautioned against its use.[188]

Mehrabian and Epstein's emotional empathy scale charted empathy as a reduction in behavioral aggression based on heightened responsivity to another's emotional experience. They turned to studies conducted by the husband and wife team Seymour and Norma Feshbach in social and educational psychology at the University of California, Los Angeles. The Feshbachs used a Milgram-inspired design in which subjects shocked a confederate at increasingly high voltages when he got a wrong answer on a learning test. They speculated that those with high empathy would refrain from vigorously shocking a confederate. Their studies had mixed results.[189] Males showed greater aggression than females overall, but those with high empathy did not shock less unless they were in the same room as the confederate.

If efforts at the measurement of empathy in these decades were unreliable, they had succeeded at fracturing empathy not only into cognitive and emotional components, but into a multiplicity of dimensions.[190] One reviewer of the burgeoning literature in 1957 cited over a hundred sources on empathy but concluded that "despite the abundant theorizing, empathy remains a somewhat ambiguous hodgepodge of meanings and shades of meaning."[191] The sociologist Ralph Turner listed at least five meanings of empathy related to role-taking. He also pointed out that the motivational component of empathy had not been taken into account.[192] Because social perception was so difficult to operationalize, one critic declared that empathy had become simply "what empathy tests measure."[193] And a theater student summed up empathy research as "indecisive" with the "emergent conclusions extremely suspect." He compiled five meanings, including early aesthetic empathy, and lamented the absence of empathy research in the arts and the theater. The best option, he concluded, would be to abandon the term completely—the label, as he put it, "conceals a very real ignorance."[194]

If the initial optimism for pinning down empathy as a unified, scientific concept had waned by the early 1960s, "empathy" nonetheless had emerged as the dominant psychological term to denote the ability to understand others' experience. It had, however, lost its unique tie to situations, emphasized by sociologists at the Chicago school and in Dymond Cartwright's experiments with students in interactional groups. Empathy was a shaky scientific construct, although it was seen to be ever more essential in a postwar world hungry to reduce conflict and increase interpersonal understanding. "Empathy" in all its diversity was well on its way to becoming a household word.

PART III

Empathy in Culture and Politics

CHAPTER SEVEN

Popular Empathy

IN JANUARY 1955, AN exhibit of 503 photographs from 68 countries, *The Family of Man*, curated by photographer Edward Steichen opened at the Museum of Modern Art in New York. People flocked to see collages of black-and-white photographs of families from across the globe participating in everyday scenes of birth, childhood, work, old age, dance, and celebration. The lines snaked around the museum and the crowds shattered attendance records. The images were juxtaposed in an evocative layout and interspersed with fragments of poems. The words of poet John Masefield appeared next to photographs of children from all over the world playing ring-around-the-rosy, and spoke to the possibility of empathy: "Clasp the hands and know the thoughts of men in other lands."[1]

A critic at the *New York Times* called the "sweeping panorama" symbolic of "the universality of basic human emotions."[2] For a time, a mirror was placed on one wall of the exhibit so the viewer glimpsed him- or herself as one among the others. One reviewer called it a theme show, or a "movie of stills," with photographs of different sizes hung at varied heights and angles along the wall. The final six-by-eight-foot photograph—the only one in color—stood in its own small room. It displayed a hydrogen bomb exploding, dispersing a red-and-orange mushroom cloud.[3] These were the stakes, Steichen warned, of refusing to acknowledge "the essential oneness of mankind throughout the world."[4]

Some critics disdainfully labeled the display "folk art" and thought it a glorified photo essay that diminished the aesthetic value of individual photographs. Others lambasted the exhibit as in thrall to a Cold War mentality and in service to American imperialism and a sentimental humanism that erased cultural differences.[5] Yet one historian views it as a platform for thinking of humankind as one, which required a special imperative "for empathy, maybe even respect."[6] Another reflected that the layout encouraged individuals to cycle through the photographs according to their own inclinations, a message consonant with democratic values.[7]

In 1955, *Modern Photography* said of the exhibit, "It wants to show people of one land that people of others are really not as different as them seem"; for Steichen the images conveyed "universal elements and emotions in the everydayness of life."[8] When the photographer Barbara Morgan viewed her "co-citizens" of the world, as she put it, she felt a deeply craved "sense of human wholeness." She explained: "This woman into whose eyes I now look is perhaps today weeding her family rice paddy, or boiling a fish in coconut milk. Can you look at the polygamist family group and imagine the different norms that make them live happily in their society which is so unlike—yet like—our own? Empathy with these hundreds of human beings truly expands our sense of values."[9] Morgan invoked the power of empathy to reach across barriers of ethnicity, nationality, and religion, even as calls for empathy were still relatively new to the American public.

In the decade following World War II, the new term "empathy" began to appear more regularly in the popular press. It was introduced and defined as a manner of understanding others rather than objects. Sometimes it described an emotional immersion in another's feelings, although more often it comprised a balanced, cognitive appraisal of others. In newspapers, radio, and advice columns, it was praised as an essential technique for psychological counseling and for building greater understanding between family members. Salesmen marketed empathy for effective advertising campaigns. Media executives advocated empathy to strengthen the bonds between audiences and the characters in new comedies and quiz shows airing on television. And many journalists invoked "cultural empathy" as an aspirational value that promised intercultural harmony, a much-needed prescription in a fractured postwar world.

Empathy and Emotion

Before World War II, the word "empathy" had almost exclusively circulated in specialized psychological dictionaries directed to academic readers. There was no entry for "empathy" in the *Concise Oxford Dictionary* of 1928, nor in *Webster's Collegiate Dictionary* of 1929, nor in the 1926 *Encyclopedia Britannica*. It was not until 1944 that the term was first listed in *Webster's Collegiate Dictionary*, the same year it appeared in the *Concise Oxford Dictionary*, and then only in an addendum as a translation of *Einfühlung*.[10]

Aesthetic empathy had of course been a topic of study for psychologists in the early decades of the twentieth century, most often understood as the projection of feeling and movement into art objects. Less frequently, it was understood as a direct and powerful form of emotional transference. One unusual early instance of empathy reaching the ears of the American public came from a 1937 review of the film *You Only Live Once*, directed by the Viennese Fritz Lang. Lang's films *Metropolis*, *M*, and *Fury* had played to American audiences, and the reviewer declared that according to old Vienna, E stands for empathy, "the machine-god that rocks the movie cradle." The reviewer put the unfamiliar term in quotes, explaining that it entailed a powerful form of emotional persuasion. One evocative scene in the new film captured an actress crying as she ran down a country road. It was a simple shot but one that Lang filmed through a glass slide, stained by her very tears. Film had the power to project an emotional idea "intravenously" into the audience, the reviewer cautioned, producing sympathetic identification.[11]

This kind of "mass empathy" posed the danger of emotional manipulation that generated hypnotic effects. Rather than selectively impacting an individual, it cast a spell on the audience as a single organism. In the 1930s, German playwright Bertolt Brecht characterized empathy as a passive emotional identification with a stage personality. At a time when German society enthusiastically embraced fascism, Brecht warned that this kind of identification harbored alarming political consequences.[12] To thwart this kind of mindless absorption, Brecht promoted the alienation effect. He aimed to induce critical reflection rather than emotional identification in the theatergoer through set design, stage direction, and the manipulation of the actors' emotions.[13]

If empathy was understood in German contexts as a kind of hypnotism on a mass scale, in the United States, concerns about the powerful emotional effects of film focused on young viewers. Herbert Blumer's 1933 *Movies and Conduct* described how a viewer could identify so thoroughly with the plot or heroine as to be carried away from his or her usual conduct, although he did not explicitly call this response empathy.[14] Movies produced a surge of different emotional impulses: of fright, sadness, tears, and love, all of which involved a loss of ordinary self-control.[15] To address these concerns, sociologists, psychologists, and educators conducted a series of studies on the emotional and attitudinal effects of movies on children, sponsored by the Payne Fund. In 1930, the Hays Code was developed, the first attempt at a film rating system to designate what was morally acceptable, and the Production Code Administration was instituted in 1934 to screen all films.

There was some talk of empathy in 1948 as "the deep surrender of interest in what one is witnessing," orchestrated by the "technicians of emotions" in the theater.[16] The *New York Times* reported in 1950 that the newest thing on Broadway was theater-in-the-round—where the audience encircled the stage. It tended to place the spectator in "the stream of action," resulting in "a high degree of empathy or identification with the stage characters. Emotion is intensified."[17] The Theatre de Lys opened in Greenwich Village with an apron stage extending into the audience to foster intimacy and audience empathy.[18] But if empathy was sometimes understood as a form of unbridled emotional contagion, the postwar American press more often showcased empathy as a conscious strategy undertaken to enhance human relationships.

Introducing a New Word

In the postwar period, popular audiences were eager to draw on the expertise of psychologists, who enjoyed remarkable influence and visibility. The treatment needs of thousands of traumatized war veterans helped usher in an explosion in the field of clinical psychology and a dissemination of new psychotherapeutic methods. Governmental commissions turned to social science and psychologists for expert advice.[19] A popular article explained that the new term "empathy" had "prestige value" as one of a handful of fashionable words borrowed from psychoanalysis and psychology.[20]

If empathy was an elite psychological term, it nonetheless did not have a uniform meaning, and popular interpretations of the term differed widely. The brother of the famed vaccination expert Dr. Jonas Salk, developed tranquilizers for animals and said he borrowed the technique of empathy from psychiatry. He explained: "A vet has to feel what the dog feels."[21] Most articles assumed that readers did not know the new term; it was often put in quotes, with an explanation of how it differed from the more common sympathy. It was usually given a verbatim dictionary definition, and it was frequently misspelled. In 1949, an excerpt from the popular book *Live a New Life* sponsored by the Dale Carnegie Institute, printed it as "emphathy" and called it creative listening—a way to feel the "emotional intensity stirring others."[22]

That year a reporter for the *New York Times* was startled to hear a former model use the word "empathy" to explain an audience's awareness of what the actor was doing on the stage. The reporter agreed with her remarks, only to go home and look up the word in Webster's dictionary! He then defined the "$64 word" for his readers as the "imaginative projection of one's own consciousness into another being."[23] A year later "empathy" was described as a "four-bit word," of more value than the everyday two-bit word worth twenty-five cents.[24] Another article claimed that empathy was used by "the candlelight and wine set" to understand music by getting a sense of the composer's experience. One could "achieve empathy by projection into the artist's frame of reference."[25] By 1945 the word "empathy" began to appear more frequently in print according to a Google n-gram charting the number of appearances of "empathy" in print sources.[26] The use of "empathy" shows a steady uptick from 1945 through the subsequent decades (figure 21).

The *Los Angeles Times* column "Take My Word" asked readers in 1952 if they were familiar with the word "EMPATHY," capitalizing

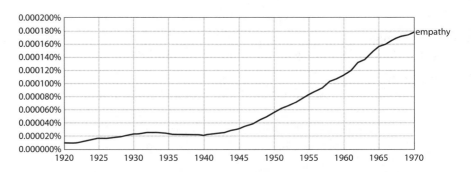

Figure 21. Google n-gram charting the number of appearances of "empathy" in print sources from 1920 to 1970.

it for effect.[27] The author defined it as a process of "mentally entering into the feelings of a person or thing; appreciative perception and understanding." Empathy for another's grief means that the "other's grief is as real to us as it is to him." The author suggested that the word would be a valuable addition to the "average vocabulary" and instructed readers how to pronounce it. The column "What's Your Question" posted this question from a reader: "What do you call the ability to project one's self into the shoes of another and thus try to feel as he does?" Professor Fax, who regularly answered these queries, responded: "Empathy (golden rule)."[28] A critic at the *Washington Post* joked about his reluctance to use the new word in his review of the TV special *Tales of Tomorrow*. He admitted that science fiction was a branch of literature "for which I have no empathy (which is a word I have no sympathy for which is a dangling participle. I like to dangle participles.)"[29]

Some of empathy's earliest appearances in popular sources of the late 1940s retained its early kinesthetic meaning: empathy explained why fans "blow their tops" at sports events a 1946 article explained, putting the term in quotes and adding that it was the reason "very interested spectators twitch, grunt, strain, and practically throw and hit every pitch."[30] One columnist described watching her husband on a ski trip "schussing away." Thrilled, and "filled with empathy," she tried to follow suit but discovered one foot followed in quite a different direction than the first.[31] One could feel empathy for a ball in a pinball machine by tilting the machine to help it move. And as late as 1955 observers watching the fifty-foot steeple of Old North Church in Boston as it was hoisted up to its place were portrayed as "swaying their bodies in empathy as the spire swayed to or from its mark."[32]

In August 1949, the *New York Times* reviewed the Book of the Month Club selection, *The Mature Mind* by philosopher Harry Overstreet. Overstreet delivered a digestible synthesis of Freudian ideas and behavioral conditioning, leavened with a Christian sensibility. The reviewer declared that Overstreet wants Americans to grow up, and one way of doing so was to develop empathy, defined as the "sympathetic social imagination."[33] Riding the wave of psychology's popularity, Overstreet told his readers: "Today, at last, the time clock of science strikes the hour of psychology, and a new enlightenment begins."[34] He defined empathy as "the imaginative projection of one's consciousness into an object or person outside oneself." It was essential to the mature mind. This "psychic identification" with another was more powerful than sympathy and enabled one "to stop being an outsider and become an insider."[35] Overstreet interlaced the kinesthetic and emotional meanings of the term: to watch the pole vaulter meant to "rise with him as he vaults," just as to witness another's embarrassment was to "'borrow' his humiliation and feel it within themselves."[36] Empathy still wove together bodily movement and psychological understanding, but this conception became less frequent over the subsequent decades.

Overstreet lamented that most people were stunted in their empathic potential. Faulty parenting was partly to blame, but "empathic provincialism" was more often the problem. This refusal of empathy toward an "outsider," or someone of a different race, class, or religion was all too common in American society. American culture rewarded competition and even the projection of hostility onto others, only intermittently encouraging inclusive feelings toward others. To develop a wide-ranging empathy, individuals first had to make an effort to better understand themselves: "Nowhere are adults, in sizable numbers and in a community of relationship, *seeking to understand themselves*."[37] Given the "desperate plight of our world," including the threat of atomic weapons and the looming menace of Russia, Overstreet believed it was imperative to develop one's empathic potential.[38] To do so one had to push past provincialisms of all kinds to embrace the "oneness of the human race." In an opinion piece, "Through Others' Eyes," Overstreet and his wife, Bonaro, explained that empathy generated an awareness of the oneness of humanity that could prompt social reform. Readers could cultivate empathy by attending adult education classes, trying role-playing exercises, and by creating more connections to others.[39]

Already in 1943, this vision of "One World" had been promulgated by Wendell Wilkie's book of that title. Wilkie, the 1940 Republican candidate for president, decried imperialism abroad and impugned "race imperialism" within the borders of the United States. He avowed that "it is not racial classifications nor ethnological considerations which bind men together; it is shared concepts and kindred objectives."[40] A universalizing impulse appeared as well in Joseph Campbell's popular *The Hero with a Thousand Faces* of 1949. Campbell overlooked what he considered to be superficial differences in modern and ancient religious myths from the East and West to uncover the "basic truths by which man has lived throughout the millennia of his residence of the planet." If the anatomist found biological commonalities across various peoples, the psychologist unearthed universal myths that proved that "differences will be found to be much less great than is popularly (and politically) supposed."[41]

If empathy might generate social reform, at a more everyday level it could also improve interpersonal relationships. A psychologist and physician explained in the *Boston Globe* that the diplomatic and tactful person had "a high empathy score." One could join the compliment club to nurture empathy and thwart egoism by giving three compliments each day to three different people.[42] The popular radio personality Uncle Dudley advised college graduates in one of his 1956 lunchtime shows to sharpen their sensitivities and to develop *empathy* (which he italicized) as way to decisively contribute to their success in business, the professions, marriage, and parenthood.[43]

Insufficient empathy marked the immature, according to newspaper columnists, but its absence could signal the delinquent or even the pathological. A news report of two young men who attempted to extort five thousand dollars from a woman whose baby had been kidnapped, noted that their absence of feeling supported the findings of psychologists that "much of modern mankind is rapidly losing the faculties of empathy and compassion."[44] Without the imagination necessary for empathy, warned a Baltimore psychoanalyst, atavistic primitive impulses could be triggered. Psychologists also declared that a lack of normal empathy explained why an eleven-year-old boy pushed another child into the Hudson River.[45]

Empathy in the Family

In a postwar world where sociologists charted growing problems in the family, empathy was promoted as an important new value in advice columns and popular psychological forums. The sociologist Ernest Burgess identified a postwar crisis in the family: families were now smaller and living in urban areas, more unstable, and had higher rates of divorce.[46] In response to these changes, family and marriage counseling surged, a new family-life education movement was established, and the National Conference on Family Life was inaugurated.[47]

Sociologists Nelson Foote and Leonard Cottrell promoted the new ideals of interpersonal competence and optimal development in both academic and public settings. The postwar emphasis on competence, they believed, was a major improvement on the prewar focus on adjustment. Their 1955 book *Identity and Interpersonal Competence* listed empathy as one of six elements necessary for strong social relationships, along with health, intelligence, autonomy, judgment, and creativity. Despite its lengthy appendix of sources, the book was addressed to a general, educated audience.[48] The *New York Times* review of the book explained the importance of empathy: "being able to put yourself in the other fellow's shoes, to understand his attitudes and intentions, to appreciate his feelings, is essential to getting along well with others."[49]

Foote directed the Family Study Center at the University of Chicago, which fostered empathy in family relationships and assisted families with democratic planning, emotional training, sexual health and hygiene, economy in spending and saving, child development, education, and recreation.[50] Foote happily declared in 1954 that many were keen to hone their social skills because "as a nation Americans are becoming social-science-minded."[51] The center held family-life education workshops for teachers and counselors, and it counseled couples who came for "participant experiments." Couples role-played their conflicts over a ten-week period and examined their talents for empathy, autonomy, and creativity. Participants suggested the situations and enthusiastically played them out. "People get going and don't want to quit, some having to be sent home at 3 am."[52] In one test for empathy, a husband and wife were each given private instructions in a role-play: "The wife is trying to get her husband out of the house to arrange a surprise party for him, but is afraid to directly suggest his leaving his comfortable chair. The husband wants to leave to buy his wife the present he forgot but knows she hates to be left alone at night. Some subjects show an un-canny ability to detect the spouse's unspoken intentions. Others remain puzzled even when stumbling over blatant cues."[53] Successful empathy meant getting to the underlying, sometimes secret agendas of one's spouse.

Popular articles in newspapers and magazines advised husbands to empathize with their wives, wives with their husbands, and mothers and fathers with their children. Children were celebrated for having a natural empathy that should be nurtured, and good teachers had empathy for their students.[54] One article suggested "Pack Empathy for Family Trip," which meant to make a special effort to engage children. "Although a hippo is a hippo, whether in Karlsruhe or Basel, empathy helped us realize that children might regard museum relics in the same light."[55] A child would view different museum exhibits as all too similar to one other. One column featuring women attending social events called empathy the "secret of getting along with people" and the "best way to increase your social popularity." Even if you broke all the rules of etiquette, empathy would still win you friends.[56] The skill of empathy in this case went deeper than good manners; it meant to forget oneself in concern for a friend.

Advice columns sang the virtues of empathy.[57] "Health for All," advised couples to practice empathy after the honeymoon. This meant not feeling *with* one's spouse but instead making the conscious effort to put *aside* one's own emotions to be able to say, "I understand how you feel."[58] The advice columnist Mary Haworth chastised a mother for not bringing up a girl with enough empathy, which seemed evident to Haworth after hearing how the nineteen year old, who was engaged to be married, still slept with her mother at night. The girl had evidently never been properly understood and had not been given enough empathy.[59] Haworth drew from the literature of infantile attachment and the importance of a close tie with the mother.[60] Psychiatrists of a psychoanalytic bent, adopting Harry Stack Sullivan's interpersonal analysis, saw empathy as a form of emotional transfer closely associated with mothers and infants. According to Sullivan, as explained in the *New York Times*, the mother transmitted security or anxiety through empathy to the infant.[61]

Too much empathy, however, could create another set of problems. The Gesell Institute of Child Study at Yale University offered advice on child behavior in the *Washington Post*, counseling a forty-year-old mother to refrain from empathizing with her daughter. It was simply not right that her heart was broken every time her child's relationship didn't work out. Daughters need "not so much empathy, as sympathy and support. . . . Support, but not full participation."[62] This kind of empathy entailed an emotional immersion in the child's life, which caused the mother pain and was unhelpful to the child. Some associated empathy with the feminine instincts, as did the president of Sarah Lawrence College, along with "caring qualities, concern for beauty and form, reverence for life, and a demand that men be better than they are," but this was only one strand of postwar empathy.[63]

Empathy in Counseling

Empathy most often in these years entailed a controlled, conscious, even rational appraisal of another's feelings and circumstances. *Reader's Digest* told its readers in 1955 that the new word "empathy" (italicized in the article) had "only recently made its way out of the psychological laboratories" as the "ability to appreciate the other person's feelings without yourself becoming so emotionally involved that your judgment is affected."[64] Empathy was, in this case, *not* an immersive emotional bond but a deliberate bracketing of one's own emotions in order to more fully and accurately grasp another's feelings.

Reader's Digest was in the business of republishing significant articles from other journals, and it had reprinted "How's Your Empathy" from the progressive magazine *Christian Century*.[65] The author, John Kord Lagemann, drew from play therapy with children and marriage therapy with couples to describe empathy as "detached insight" into others. The task of empathy was to consciously "tune in on the feelings behind their words and acts" while remaining detached and "acknowledging the other person's feelings but never sharing them." To truly comprehend a child's "I hate you" was to sense the anger behind the words. More ominously, empathy could make a wife comfortable being a "scapegoat" to her husband's anger, which she could see as misdirected at her because her husband could not express it to his boss. Because "empathy enables us to use our heads rather than our hearts," it often required that one abandon one's own feelings. A salesgirl responded to an aggravated customer by thinking, "You poor thing, you are probably frustrated in some way and you're taking it out on me." The customer smiled and apologized. "Using empathy to enter the mind and heart of another human being," the article concluded, "can become a great adventure." *Reader's Digest's* definition of empathy was echoed just a month later by the advice columnist "Eleanor" in the *Atlanta Daily World*.[66]

Empathy in counseling meant that one had to be careful not to project one's judgments and inclinations but at the same time not to lose one's own grounding. One popular piece explained that when good psychiatrists and psychologists demonstrated "empathic objectivity," they could more accurately gauge their own feelings as well as those of others.[67] A family counselor advocated for empathy as partaking in the feelings of others without becoming submerged in them.[68] The theologian and clinical pastoral counselor Seward Hiltner advised his pastors against emotional entanglement in the new journal *Pastoral Psychology:* "We can feel our way into the experience of another only to the extent that we have felt ourselves at home with our own experience."[69] In 1951, Hiltner conversed with Carl Rogers on many of the tenets of client-centered therapy in a radio discussion, "New Approach to Solving Personal Problems."[70] Rogers was seen at this time as a "virtual guru for the pastoral counseling movement."[71]

In 1956, Carl Rogers held a public dialogue with the German-Jewish theologian Martin Buber at the University of Michigan. In preparation, Rogers read Buber's 1925 remarks on empathy, translated into English only in 1947. Buber described Lipps's notion of empathy as a way to "glide with one's own feeling into the dynamic structure of an object, a pillar or a crystal, of the branch of a tree, or even of an animal or a man."[72] The ministerial counselor Rollo May also drew directly from Theodor Lipps's early model of empathy, calling it a fusion of the self in the other in his informal lectures to ministers at local YMCAs in 1939.[73]

But Buber believed that to empathize in this fashion erased the lived, concrete situation of the empathizer. He ventured an alternative model that he called inclusion (*Umfassung*). One imagined the experiences of another person while at the same time, one held onto one's own felt reality. It was a matter of adding or including the standpoint of the other to one's own. Buber explained, "I call it experiencing the other side."[74] Rogers reviewed Buber's conception of inclusion and wrote in his notes that empathy was being "able to live in internal fr[ame] of ref[erence] of another, to see and sense his world, without ever losing own personhood."[75]

As Rogers refined his conception of empathy, he emphasized that one engaged in another's experience without losing one's own identity. In 1957, he was profiled in *Time* magazine as practicing a psychotherapy that "emphasizes empathy" in distinction to psychoanalysis.[76] The article quoted Rogers at length: "To sense the client's private world as if it were your own, but without ever losing the 'as if quality'—this is empathy, and this seems essential to therapy." The counselor's job was not to provide guidance but to establish empathy, which would "enable the client, through greater insight, to accept experiences as they are." Rogers's method of empathic listening was integral to those training to answer telephone emergency hotlines, according to a 1971 article in the *Los Angeles Times*. At a conference held in Monterey, the "old and the young, freaks and squares, professionals and antiprofessionals" were taught that with empathy they could see the world as it appeared to the caller, with "no trace of judgement or evaluation."[77] Rogers's ability to cultivate an "empathic stance" toward others was one of his major accomplishments as attested by memorials at his death in 1987.[78]

There were also a handful of psychoanalysts, trained, not surprisingly, in Vienna, who ventured to explain empathy to a popular audience. Analyst and writer Theodor Reik published *Listening with the Third Ear* in 1948, an accessible account of psychoanalysis animated by numerous case examples. Reik worked closely with Freud as the secretary of the Psychoanalytic Society, and in 1938 he fled Berlin and The Hague for New York. Because he was not medically trained, he was not accepted in the New York Psychoanalytic Society, and thus he established the National Psychological Association for Psychoanalysis. By the late 1940s, he had become something of a literary celebrity. In his popular books he unveiled the detective-like nature of psychoanalytic work; discoursed on love, literature, and religion; and spoke about the unconscious and the "magic" of psychoanalysis.[79]

Reik explained empathy as a process whereby the unconscious meanings of the patient's words and gestures resonated in the analyst's own unconscious to awaken deep-seated memories and experiences. Through this awakening, the analyst actually shared the experiences of the patient. It was a fleeting but transformative part of the process in which, Reik declared, "we must, at least for a moment, change ourselves into and become that person."[80] Empathy worked like wireless telegraphy to allow one to tune in to the inchoate messages of another's unconscious, a reservoir of instinct and animistic tendencies, and a powerful and "incorruptible psychological organ of perception."[81] But if empathy began as a "natural, unconscious condition of psychological comprehension" it was transformed through the analytic process into "a special effort and conscious endeavor."[82] A reviewer of *Listening with the Third Ear* described the art of analysis as "a fundamental capacity to feel his way into a patient" but opined that Reik would have been better served had he recognized the "direct, extra-sensory contact between mind and mind."[83] Another reviewer pointed out that the third ear was an "intuitive sensibility," a necessary talent of the gifted analyst.[84]

Pastoral counselors and social workers found Reik's model of empathy useful. Robert Langdon Katz, a rabbi and professor of human relations at Hebrew Union College in Cincinnati, outlined Reik's four-phase empathic process in his 1963 book *Empathy: Its Nature and Uses*.[85] In the first phase, the counselor became so en-

grossed with the other personality to temporarily "lose consciousness of the self."[86] The other's personality became incorporated into
the therapist's personality in the second phase, and in the third, the
other's experience reverberated with that of the therapist's. For Katz,
this "*dialectic* between the actual me and the me which is identified
with the other person becomes the source of new insight."[87] The
counselor is divided and vibrates in two rhythms. In the final detachment phase, the therapist employs reason and analysis to arrive
at a more complete understanding of the client.

The social worker Pauline Lide operationalized Reik's model
with a set of fifteen descriptive sentences to guide students through
these four stages of empathy. Most social workers were adept at
identifying with the client's emotions in the first phase, but those
who completed the forty-five-minute questionnaire and proceeded
through all four stages achieved a fuller empathic understanding of
the client. By directing the social worker to "devote affective and
cognitive attention to the client's inner life and external world,"
the tool enabled more accurate predictions of the client's behavior.[88]

If Reik's model of empathy was popular with pastoral counselors and social workers, psychoanalysts turned to Vienna-born analyst Heinz Kohut's formulation.[89] Kohut described empathy in 1959
as a "value-neutral model of observation" and a form of "vicarious
introspection."[90] Empathy allowed the analyst to think him- or herself in the patient's place in order to grasp the patient's actual intents
and motives. Kohut was familiar with anthropomorphic empathy
that imputed psychological motives to animals and plants, for example, seeing water running downhill as seeking or avoidant behavior.
He discarded these forms of empathy, however, as beyond the bounds
of psychology as science.[91] Empathy was above all an observational
act that led the analyst to a scientific, even objective appraisal of the
other. Kohut maintained that empathy was an epistemological undertaking that delineated an observational field rather than one of
the "sentimentalizing perversions of psychotherapy" or the idea that
empathy cures.[92] The claim that empathy could cure, of course, was
exactly what Carl Rogers had asserted as early as 1947 when he argued that a judgment-free immersion in the client's situation could
itself produce positive change in the client.

Empathy on Television and in Advertising

By the early 1950s, empathy had become a buzzword in radio, television, and advertising, billed as a technique to reach new media audiences. The radio announcer Arthur Godfrey was featured on the February 1950 cover of *Time* magazine with the caption "He has empathy."[93] The description would have intrigued readers, many of whom would have been puzzled by the new word. In the accompanying article, "Oceans of Empathy," the manager at the CBS radio station crowed: "Arthur creates a two-way conversation all by himself. It's more than a soliloquy; it's a great art. What do you call it—? Empathy.* You know, the ability to get inside other people, to understand exactly how they're feeling."[94] The word was starred and footnoted, clearly still an unknown quantity. After reading through the lengthy description of Godfrey's personal and professional history, one learned that the author of the piece had only newly discovered the term "empathy" himself "in the far reaches of Webster." He found it necessary to print the definition verbatim—the "imaginative projection of one's own consciousness into another being."[95]

Empathy explained to TV moguls why the new situation comedies were more successful than earlier stand-up comedies. The vice president of NBC contended that the domestic-situation comedy appealed to most people on the basis of age, region, and education and had "the broadest base in terms of empathy."[96] Television stars were declared successful because of their empathy: Jack Benny would have never used the word, an article in the *Chicago Daily Tribune* acknowledged, but he used empathy to project his personality into the public and not into the object of contemplation, as the dictionary had it.[97] Empathy signaled the ability to make a strong connection—sometimes between the characters in the comedy, but more frequently between the performer and the audience. Comedian Lucille Ball groped for the new term in 1960, asking, "'What's that word, Peter?' 'Empathy,' said Mr. Hayes who has been through all this with the people in the advertising dodge who use talk like that. 'If you got empathy, you got it made. That's what they told us at Four Star. You don't have to be funny as long as the audience knows you love each other.'"[98]

Television quiz shows made use of audience empathy with contestants to reach larger audiences. The creator of the successful quiz show *The $64,000 Question* explained that a winning show was dramatic, suspenseful, and produced empathy.[99] Executives recognized that the hangover contestant or continuing hero who kept returning to a show held the public's interest longer. The quiz show *Twenty One* maintained audience empathy with the contestant Charles Van Doren by giving him answers to keep him on the show, erupting in the notorious quiz show scandals of the late 1950s. In its investigation of rigged TV shows in 1959, the House Special Subcommittee on Legislative Oversight collected documents showing that advertisers frequently consulted with TV producers regarding what worked and what didn't in these quiz shows. One adman wrote of a contestant, "Her egoism has turned to egotism and the audience no longer had the empathy with her which had been so strong in her earlier appearances."[100] Another reviewer exclaimed, "The device appealed to Madison Avenue, where the word 'empathy' once reserved to psychologists, has long spitballed across the council tables."[101]

Advertisers too were keen to profit on empathy: it was effective in encouraging women to buy face cream, as well as to "exploit[ing]" the Negro market by "using Negro models to create empathy."[102] "Empathy" formed a centerpiece of the Revlon marketing campaign of the Madison Avenue advertising firm of Norman, Craig & Kummel. Advertisers had discovered that women wanted to look more beautiful naturally, and consequently some firms had begun to use the phrase "natural beauty" to sell their makeup products. One advertiser, palindromically named Norman B. Norman, created illustrations that showed women looking beautiful naturally in candlelight, accompanied by the headline "The fabulous flattery of candlelight in a face make-up." Norman explained that his "advertisements are aimed at having the reader find himself inside the advertisements. . . . We call it empathy and we are serious about it. We like to think of it as emotional advertising or emotional reason-why."[103] Advertising empathy banked on the self-projective techniques that encouraged the consumer to place herself in the scene itself.

In 1953, the insurance magazine the *National Underwriter* asked its readers, "How's Your Empathy?" holding it up as an important quality for executives. For readers who didn't understand the concept, the writer relayed the old story of the village idiot who found a lost horse by imagining he was the horse and going where it would have wandered. It was an important, albeit elusive quality. Psychological consultants advised executives to develop empathy so they could more readily "understand, predict and control the thinking, feeling and actions of other people."[104] A salesman could make use of the skill by sensing whether or not he got his message across to the customer. Psychologists advocated for empathy in the *Harvard Business Review* as the "ability to feel as the other fellow feels—without becoming sympathetic."[105] And an advertisement for a management development consultant sought an applicant with "flexibility, empathy, and basic respect for others."[106] To be a "better boss," as a number of articles advised, executives would do well to take up methods of psychodrama and role-playing that created insight through empathy.[107]

Empathy in Theater and Novels

By the postwar period, empathy most often demarcated a consciously undertaken relationship between persons. A few critics familiar with the older empathy tradition, however, still spoke of empathy for objects via self-projection of one's feelings or movements. One critic reviewed the novel *The Sun and the Moon* in 1944 and explained that the heroine experienced various "empathetic" identifications, including empathy with rocks. Her empathy with her betrothed was shifting and problematic: at first it meant an ability to lose herself in him, but eventually it transformed into a "spiritual vampirism," whereby she absorbed his personality. This bidirectional empathy confused the boundaries between self and other.[108] Another critic declared that writer Liam O'Flaherty had the gift of empathy, or an "ability to project himself into a man, a mouse, a wave, and imagine how that man or mouse or wave feels."[109] Keats was described as a chameleon poet who submerged himself in his subject through "empathy," printed in scare quotes and defined as "the projecting of one's self into the feelings of others, even such slight creatures as sparrows scrabbling for crumbs in the street, or a field mouse peeping out of a field's withered grass."[110]

The Hungarian-born writer and journalist Arthur Koestler drew on the German empathy literature in his 1949 *Insight and Outlook* to explain the literary process, excerpts of which appeared in the popular *Saturday Review of Literature*.[111] He described the "feeling-in process or empathy" as the "projection of part of our own personality into the shell of the other."[112] A writer might use projective empathy to create a fictional character, through which one could experience, often unconsciously, a partial identity, making it possible to participate in the character's emotions. We often perceived others around us in this way: "Images of *real people* in our memory are not as different from our images of *fictional characters* as we generally believe."[113]

Aesthetic empathy also remained in the lexicon of the German abstract expressionist painter Hans Hofmann. He invoked empathy in a psychoplastic and rhythmic sense in his New York gallery exhibit featured in the 1951 *Time* article "Trapezoids and Empathy."[114] Hofmann taught painting in Munich in the early twentieth century before relocating in 1932 to New York and Provincetown, Massachusetts. Throughout his career, Hofmann celebrated the power of empathy to interweave the visual and kinesthetic in the tradition of aesthetic Einfühlung. The faculty of empathy enabled one to see the intrinsic life of things: "the inner eye sees to the core and grasps the opposing forces and the coherence of things."[115] Hofmann's recurrent trope of "push-pull" describing the tension and dynamism inherent in painterly abstraction was directly indebted to Einfühlung. One of his students described Hofmann's hand gestures of push and pull as if he were dancing in a ballet class: "People were trying to feel into it—it was empathy. Empathy was the big word."[116]

Yet this kind of aesthetic empathy for objects and works of art had gone underground in the postwar years to become only a shadow of the earlier vibrant tradition. Empathy now took place predominantly between persons or sentient beings. These persons, however, could exist in one's imagination, on the pages of a book, or on a theatrical stage. Empathy mediated a variety of effects between audience and performer, author and reader, and writer and character. These effects ranged from the uplifting to the disagreeable, from the calming to the destabilizing. One letter writer described the characters of a French woman and Japanese man in the film *Hiroshima Mon Amour:* "Both are so strong and appealing, and our empathy therefore so complete, that we leave the theatre with the feeling of humility and, at the same time, of having been somehow ennobled."[117] Upon seeing Dylan Thomas's *Under Milkwood*, another critic declared, "Seldom does one feel such lilting empathy between stage and audience."[118] A theatergoer wrote to the drama editor of the *New York Times* to say she couldn't understand how two reviews of Archibald MacLeish's play, based on the story of Job, could come to such differing assessments. One critic reported that there was an utter absence of emotion, whereas another wrote, "The most blasé audience submits to the spell of an almost unbearable experience of empathy." The letter writer agreed with the latter assessment, remarking it was "an evening in the theatre I will remember the rest of my life."[119]

Empathy was not only about the ennobling emotions, however. The actor, Norm Shelley, who played the dog Nana in *Peter Pan* was described facetiously in 1955 as "crawling with what is known as empathy for dogs, having had some emotional involvement with them at an early age."[120] Sir John Gielgud thrilled audiences with his "consummate empathy" by giving them Shakespeare and "only incidentally himself."[121] One columnist, Jack Smith, jokingly attributed his failed acting career in high school to his lack of empathy. He defined empathy as "the ability to project yourself into the consciousness of the audience so that they don't think of you as Jack Smith at all." He explained the failure of his early theatrical debut: "I really lost empathy when I first walked on . . . because a girl I knew hollered, 'Hooray for Jack!' and I turned to the footlights and said in a sophisticated way, 'Thank you, Agnes.'"[122] He ended up a scullion in a ship's galley, where as he put it, "nobody cared if I had empathy or not."

One psychologist writing on emotion judged empathy to be unscientific but good for the movies![123] Others saw the term reserved for "fancy literary critics."[124] The *Los Angeles Times* book editor, Robert Kirsch made frequent use of the word to describe a host of successful characters created by the writers Rebecca West, Boris Pasternak, and Arthur Marx, son of Groucho Marx. Kirsch considered "total empathy with a character, the ability to see and experience life beyond the borders of our own existence" to be the writer's most important contribution.[125]

Empathy could stretch one's experience in a transformative but also destabilizing way. To prepare for the role of Al Jolson in the film

The Jolson Story, the actor Larry Parks accompanied Jolson for days, talking with him and going to ball games together. This constant association produced an empathy or transubstantiation in which "Parks became Jolson to a point of which he was a little frightened. He could not stop being Jolson, he says, even when he was alone."[126] Joyce Cary described the process of writing dialogue as intuition or empathy, reflecting, "Perhaps it is not far from the truth to say that for the moment one is that character."[127] Empathy encompassed the strange, exhilarating, and sometimes disturbing possibility of becoming someone other than oneself.

Empathy, however, had its limits. One reviewer wrote of Frank Norris's *Vandover and the Brute*, "One's empathy might snap when the brute takes over, but, then, how many readers have really hurled themselves with Anna Karenina in front of a fast freight?"[128] W. H. Auden gestured to empathy's failings in his 1970 poem "The Aliens":

But between us and the Insects,
   namely nine-tenths of the living, there grins a prohibitive
      fracture
empathy cannot transgress.[129]

And yet in Philip K. Dick's 1968 novel *Do Androids Dream of Electric Sheep?* empathy was celebrated as the signature ability of the human. In an era of proliferating empathy tests, Dick designed the fictional Voight-Kampff machine to measure empathy through eye movements and heart rate, the only way to reliably distinguish the human from the machine.

Cultural Empathy

If "empathy" became the term of choice for an emotional and reasoned understanding of others in the postwar years, it was also seen as a powerful means to bridge racial, national, and cultural divides.[130] One reporter declared that teachers did not naturally possess empathy for students in the new Head Start program, which beginning in 1965 set up nursery schools for the nation's poorest children.[131] Because the teachers' backgrounds were completely foreign to the children's experience, to foster empathy the teachers had to dig up childhood memories that bore at least some similarity to those of their students. An opinion piece in 1963 sarcastically faulted President John F. Kennedy for taking a vacation just after the Birmingham protests: "Our Glorious Leader showed how much empathy and sympathy he has for the colored people who put him in office."[132] Empathy was cited as important in American-Korean relations, and an ethnologist was praised for her empathy with Native Americans.[133]

It was repeatedly acknowledged that empathy beyond one's own circle was difficult to accomplish. At a Mayor's Commission on Human Relations in Pittsburgh, Leland Hazard, vice president of the Pittsburgh Plate Glass Company, pointed out that "it was difficult for the dominant (white) majority to gain in-feeling with the excluded minority. He used the word 'empathy' to sharpen this point."[134] A black exchange student from Cameroon at the University of Pittsburgh's Graduate School of Business asked a series of tough questions in 1970 to executives and "forced the white executives to admit that what is really needed for solution of the race problem in business was empathy for blacks."[135] Some saw empathy as only possible between those of similar ethnic or racial groups: the *Chicago Defender* reported a white priest's comment in 1970 that black Catholic parishes should have black priests because they have more empathy and understanding.[136] Similarly, a black or Chicano psychologist was said to better empathize with problems of black or Chicano children.[137] Empathy explained what one reporter in 1964 called "the extraordinary King mystique." Martin Luther King, Jr., he continued, "has an indescribable capacity for empathy that is the touchstone of leadership. . . . He articulates the longings, the hopes, the aspirations of his people in a most earnest and profound manner."[138]

Popular articles urged readers to expand their empathy beyond their own racial identity, culture, or religion. The new phrase "cultural empathy" captured this aspiration. A Liberian United Nations correspondent, coordinating Africa Day, worked toward demonstrating "cultural empathy between American blacks and Afros."[139] The United Presbyterian Church sponsored a meeting of forty ministers and laymen in Stony Point, New York, for a weeklong "Institute on Overseas Churchmanship." Christian emissaries were

educated as to the mission work of the church, the meaning of industrial revolution in Asia for Christianity, population problems, and
cultural empathy.[140] To develop a positive relationship with Latin
Americans, one 1959 article advocated that North Americans should
serve as a "an export of cultural empathy and political understanding."[141] The American Council of Education reported that a liberal
education meant understanding how to live in a world community,
which meant to instill "world awareness and cultural empathy" in all
students.[142] And one reporter grumbled about the limited appeal of
Hollywood films to foreign audiences in 1961, asking, "Has Hollywood lost cultural empathy?"[143]

If there remained any doubt that empathy had lodged in the
public imagination by the late 1960s, Robert Hogan, a graduate student at Berkeley put the question to experiment. Could a layperson
recognize the meaning of the term, or was "empathy" still, as he put
it, only a "creature of Academia"?[144] Hogan asked fourteen teachers, clerks, and other non-psychologists to affix a set of attributes to
the concept using descriptions from a Q sort test. He also gave his
subjects the term's dictionary definition: "intellectual or imaginative
apprehension of another's condition without actually experiencing
that person's feelings." He found that subjects possessed "a common
behavioral referent" for empathy, which was that of the moral or
good man. Of course, he may have skewed this finding by offering
his subjects a definition. Hogan emphasized empathy's moral va-
lence: it was accomplished through the recognition of the rights and
integrity of others.[145]

Empathy had become an aspirational value in postwar American culture. Few voices aired concerns about empathy's emotional
excesses or its imaginative distance from reality. It was instead celebrated as a means to light up a path to a clear-eyed, objective perception of others, one that held out the promise of social harmony.
And as the movement to desegregate schools and the struggle for
civil rights intensified, calls for empathy became more urgent.

CHAPTER EIGHT

Empathy, Race, and Politics

The social psychologist Kenneth B. Clark prefaced his 1965 book *Dark Ghetto* with the voices of Harlem residents: "A lot of times when I'm working, I become as despondent as hell and I feel like crying. I'm not a man, none of us are men!" Clark attributed this quote to a "man, about age 30." A woman said: "I have been uncomfortable being a Negro. I came from the South—Kentucky on the Ohio River line—and I have had white people spit on me in my Sunday suit." Another man, identified only as thirty-eight years old, relayed, "No one with a mop can expect respect from a banker, or an attorney or men who create jobs, and all you have is a mop. Are you crazy? Who ever heard of integration between a mop and a banker?" And a boy, age about seventeen said, "I would like to be the first Negro president."[1]

Clark wrote his book to appeal to a wide audience. He deliberately intended to stir the empathy of white liberals so they might play a more significant role in the struggle for civil rights. Clark was a public intellectual, civil rights leader, and community activist as well as a professor of social psychology at City College in New York City. He decried the focus in academic psychology on "isolated, trivial and convenient problems rather than with those problems directly related to urgent social realities."[2] He and his wife, Mamie Clark, carried out studies of race and prejudice, and they established community programs offering clinical and social services to disadvantaged youth in Harlem. Notably, Clark and his colleagues crafted the social science statement appended to the 1954 Supreme Court decision to desegregate schools.

Clark was among a small group of psychologists dedicated to the amelioration of social problems. Gordon Allport, the personality and social psychologist who taught at Harvard for most of his career, encouraged students to examine their own prejudicial leanings, assessed discrimination in local neighborhoods, supported equitable legislation, and published the classic *The Nature of Prejudice* in 1954. Clark and Allport were both members of the Society for the Psychological Study of Social Issues (SPSSI), which tackled topics of prejudice and social betterment and supported "action research" to find empirically tested approaches to improving pressing social problems.[3] Racism and prejudice, Allport and Clark believed, were products of a too competitive and too insecure American society that warped positive human inclinations. And if American culture caused people to hate, psychologists were duty bound to alleviate prejudice and to nurture tolerance.

Allport and Clark were convinced that empathy could play a key role in the fight against racism. Allport drew from the literature on Einfühlung to describe empathy as a means to holistically grasp the uniqueness of another's personality. By the time of World War II, he deemed the empathic, nonstereotyped perception of an individual to be a fundamental capacity of the tolerant person. For Clark, empathy was not a matter of sentimentality or pity, but a conduit to an objective understanding of the experiences of those with little power and on the receiving end of discrimination. Empathy thus served as a psycho-political basis for equality under the law, making it possible, as Clark put it, "to see in one man all men; and in all men the self."[4]

Gordon Allport: From Personality to Prejudice

In one of his first published articles, Gordon Allport described empathy as a means for understanding "the undivided personality."[5] Allport arrived at Harvard as an undergraduate from Montezuma,

Indiana, on a full scholarship, and he completed his graduate training at Harvard under the direction of Hugo Münsterberg and Herbert Langfeld, both avid proponents of aesthetic empathy. In his dissertation, Allport employed a plethora of experimental techniques for analyzing, measuring, and correlating personality traits. After carrying out postdoctoral studies in Gestalt and personalistic psychology, Allport investigated methods to assess the whole personality.[6] He found Lipps's concept of empathy useful to capture another's expression in a "more lively" manner than usual acts of perception. He soon declared that empathy possessed a "supremacy in determining our apprehension of personality," although he was not convinced by Lipps's claim that empathy was instinctual.[7] When he returned to Harvard in 1924 to teach one of the first courses in personality psychology he outlined empathy as key to the science: "When we fail to empathize with a person we fail to understand him; conversely, the greater our emphatic [*sic*] ability the greater is our capacity for understanding."[8]

Save for four years teaching at Dartmouth College, Allport remained at Harvard until his death in 1967. He is known for his hierarchical trait theory of personality and his conception of functional autonomy: infantile drives did not determine adult motives, but these early impulses were interwoven into the ongoing process of becoming. In his influential 1955 book of that name—*Becoming*—he described the scope of science to include general laws as well as a focus on the individual case. In botanical science, for instance, one could study the laws of metabolism or of cell growth, but one could also scrutinize the shape of an individual leaf. This latter approach was an aesthetic one, and for Allport delivered the best understanding of the individual personality. As he put it, "It is only in our aesthetic moments that we are interested in the precise shape, size, form, or individuality of a given leaf, plant, or animal."[9] Allport expressed this view of the personality as late as 1961, scribbling on a notepad after teaching his personality class, "Each person like a novel, metaphor."[10] Empathy enlivened the perception of others, even if the method might not always be reliable. He reflected: "There is danger in this empathic act, but without it we end up with a wooden and often erroneous account of their behavior. The problem is, can we check ourselve, [*sic*] i.e. validate our subjective act, and yet make full use of it?"[11]

Allport's conviction that with empathy one could perceive individual uniqueness came to inform his growing interest in prejudice and discrimination. During World War II, he began teaching a seminar on national morale. He soon discovered that morale was directly incumbent upon what he called "the most urgent problem of national unity, namely, group conflict and prejudice." He quickly redesigned his seminar to focus exclusively on prejudice, renaming it Prejudice and Group Conflict.[12] Students read case studies, conducted community investigations and interviews, and wrote personal essays. Each student also took part in one of a number of committees—to study scapegoating, to grapple with police and minority relationships, to compile data on class members' personal histories of prejudice, or to carry out research on group relations in the city of Cambridge.

For the personal essay assignment, each student described experiences of prejudice as both victim and perpetrator. Allport instructed: "*Be Frank*. What groups of people do you dislike (or have you disliked), and why? How does it feel to be on the receiving end of prejudice and what consequence has it had in your life?"[13] His students were for the most part white, male, and Protestant, but Allport thought that some would have felt ridicule as a member of a religious, racial, occupational, or economic group. After tallying his students responses, he discovered that 81 percent admitted to harboring prejudice, most commonly against "Jews, Negros, Catholics" but also against "Co-eds, foreigners, Labor, Episcopalians." Students who claimed to be victims of prejudice were often more prejudicial than non-victims, and a quarter of the students described undergoing some kind of trauma, unspecified in the reports.[14] Those with feelings of inferiority sometimes identified with victims of prejudice, but as Allport indicated, they could also "take it out on others."

His students read the monumental 1944 report *The American Dilemma: The Negro Problem and Modern Democracy*, funded by the Carnegie Corporation and compiled by Swedish sociologist and economist Gunnar Myrdal with a bevy of research assistants.[15] On the basis of ethnographic data and extensive fieldwork, Myrdal documented the stark realities of prejudice and discrimination in American life. Because such practices were antithetical to the American creed of justice for all and dissonant with religious principles, the report predicted that when white Americans came face-to-face with these realities they would quickly see the ills of discrimination and embrace legal remedies. Allport shared this belief, evidenced by his letter of support for a bill for fair employment practices written to the Massachusetts state legislature. He asserted to the chairman of the governor's committee that even though many Americans were indeed prejudiced, "They know it is incompatible with their religions and with the American creed."[16]

Allport had made it a practice to engage in community action. He penned pamphlets on scapegoating, participated in local workshops, and lectured in community forums on racial and religious prejudice.[17] Already in 1938, as incoming president of the American Psychological Association, Allport had established a committee to help find positions for refugee psychologists fleeing Germany, among them Gestalt art psychologist Rudolf Arnheim.[18] And during the war, he wrote the feature "Rumor Clinic" in the *Boston Traveler* to call into question wartime rumors, ranging from "bogies" and "pipe-dreams" to "wedge-drivers," that used prejudice as a wedge to drive apart different sectors of society.[19]

At the urging of community leaders in 1944, Allport taught a mandatory eight-hour course to Boston police officers to help quell racial tensions. The officers were extremely angry that they were forced to participate, and Allport endured what he called an "abusive torrent of released hostility" from the forty participants, directed at him, African Americans, the press, and society at large.[20] He did not mince words when describing the event ten years later: "Whenever an objective point was made concerning Negroes in the community, some police officer would be sure to respond with a story of some vicious Negro who bit him while being arrested."[21] Allport allowed the officers to air their frustrations, which took up many hours of the course, while he employed the technique of nondirective or "unemotional listening," borrowed from clinical psychologist Carl Rogers. Allport reported that some catharsis had been achieved by the end of session as the officers became bored by their own complaints. One who had "at first railed against the Jews tried in later remarks to make amends."[22] In his concluding note, Allport warned educators to expect this kind of "catharsis," but he cautioned that overt expressions of anger could be habit forming and might actually increase aggression.

Allport urged others to take an active role in the life of the neighborhood, community, and, more broadly, the nation. He drew out the implications of this "psychology of participation," which assessed personality by cataloging traits as well as by documenting an individual's activity and involvements. He pointed out that "in studying participation, the psychologist has an approach to the complete person."[23] For those living in a democracy, participation in community life came as an obligation. As the war came to an end in 1945, Allport admonished his fellow citizens, "But unless he is in some areas ego-engaged and participant his life is crippled and his existence a blemish on democracy."[24] New tools and technologies in psychology—from polling, content analysis, and group decision-making processes to leadership training and interventions for alleviating racial tensions—made citizen involvement all the more possible and necessary.[25]

In 1946, Allport threw his support behind the creation of a Department of Social Relations at Harvard that enveloped the departments of sociology, social psychology, social anthropology, and clinical psychology. The department was an immediate success. Allport's course in social relations received nine hundred subscribers, and the department soon had six hundred concentrators.[26] Allport had also vigorously advocated for the establishment of a research center at Harvard for the Gestalt psychologist Kurt Lewin; it was instead set up at MIT, just down Massachusetts Avenue, called the Center of Group Dynamics. Interest was growing in group training procedures, and in 1947, the National Training Laboratory to study group dynamics was established in Bethel, Maine.[27] Allport reported that the field of social psychology and the study of social relations underwent "spectacular expansion of its researches and influence during and after World War II."[28]

Almost a decade after the war, Allport described a culture reeling from "the spread of communism, the rise of Hitler, the genocide of the Jews, race riots, the Second World War and its consequent anomie." He topped off this distressing list with the threat of nuclear annihilation. Given these dire circumstances, he urged a deeper examination of social and interpersonal relations so as to find some remedy for the overwhelming evidence of "man's inhumanity to man."[29] Not only had the social sciences fallen far behind the rapid developments in the natural sciences, but it was clear that the failure to understand social relationships posed an existential threat: "Our human relations is poor; our education is poor; our chances for survival are poor—unless we can improve mankind's understanding and control of social and personal factors."[30] If Allport's vision of social psychology encompassed "the ways thought, feeling, and behavior of individuals are influenced by the actual, imagined, or implied presence of other human beings," he emphasized that its most important element was the strengthening of "a philosophy and ethics of democracy."[31]

Allport published *The Nature of Prejudice* in 1954, a compilation of cutting-edge social scientific research on prejudice interwoven with insights gleaned from many years of teaching. Allport believed that prejudice and authoritarian thinking were socialized behaviors and therefore mutable. He rejected biological determinism and disagreed with those biologists and anthropologists who stressed the innate aggressivity of "man."[32] Instead, he espoused the human "capacity to learn," which rested on "something inherently plastic in his neuropsychic nature."[33] Allport allied himself with sociologist Pitirim Sorokin and anthropologist Ashley Montagu in asserting that the intrinsic human ability to love and to forge affiliations could become deformed through education and social training.[34] Only when these primary affiliative tendencies failed did aggression and hatred emerge as reactive protests. There always remained then, the hopeful possibility that interventions could lessen socialized aggression.

Child-rearing and socialization practices played an important role in shaping adults into tolerant or authoritarian personality types.[35] Allport drew from the culture and personality literature to argue that the tolerant adult had matured as a secure child in a permissive atmosphere without experiencing threats or fear. The child could be critical of the parent, learned to tolerate ambiguity, saw that there was more than one right way to do something, and refrained from projecting conflict onto others.[36] Tolerant personalities were inward leaning, imaginative, theoretical, and often politically liberal. Those with prejudicial and bigoted ideas, in contrast, were raised in restrictive home settings and developed a rigid sense of right and wrong, an inability to tolerate ambiguity, and a cognitive style that misrepresented reality.[37]

The tolerant person, Allport declared in *The Nature of Prejudice*, possessed the key psychological attribute of empathy. Empathy enabled one to make intelligent and fine-tuned distinctions between individuals and to avoid blanket stereotyping.[38] To view another only as representative of an ethnic or minority group was by definition prejudicial. Empathy counteracted prejudice by individualizing; one perceived a unique person rather than a member of a group. Allport believed that some people had a natural endowment of empathy, but that it could also be fostered in a home setting where social values and aesthetic sensitivity were cultivated.[39]

Allport was keenly aware, however, that this 1954 conception of empathy had significantly departed from its origins in Einfühlung. He was well versed in the German debates on the merits of Einfühlung for knowing others, having read Lipps as well as philosopher Max Scheler's delineation of eight different terms to mark slight differences in the capacity to connect with others.[40] Allport concluded that postwar "empathy" was now closer to "the expressive German term *Menschenkenntnis*"—the skilled knowledge of others, or a realistic appraisal of another's feelings—than to Einfühlung. Postwar empathy encompassed the "gift of understanding people," or "'the ability to size up people,' 'social intelligence,' 'social sensitivity.'"[41] In Allport's history of social psychology, he called it "that clear and normal condition where one person appreciates accurately another's feelings, and usually (though not necessarily) values them positively."[42]

Empathy thus comprised a realistic, objective appraisal of others rather than an inaccurate prejudicial assessment. Studies demonstrated that those with authoritarian tendencies erroneously projected their own attributes onto others.[43] Using the slang of the day, Allport told Dartmouth undergraduates, "If you're down on them, you're not up on them."[44] Empathy was linked to the aptitude for taking-the-role-of-the-other and was correlated with equalitarianism, a view of the other as an equal. Allport cited experiments revealing that subjects who scored low on authoritarian and ethnocentrism scales were better at taking on a role—even an authoritarian one—than subjects who earned higher ethnocentrism scores.[45] He compiled research data and advocated for empathic methods of accurate observation in order to lessen racial prejudice, as he put it, "on the grounds of conscience and science."[46]

Educating Empathy

If prejudice emerged from personality defects, it was also shaped by faulty socialization. Functional prejudice, Allport claimed, was a product of the rigid, authoritarian-leaning personality type, whereas conformity prejudice developed through broader patterns of socialization. Allport could not pin the very high rate of prejudice on personality pathology alone as there was twice as much antiblack sentiment in southern as in northern states, but the incidence of the authoritarian personality was no higher in the South than in the North. Allport concluded that even if prejudice was "at bottom a personal state of mind it requires social forces to bring it into a kinetic state."[47]

Allport discovered that contact between different groups might lessen prejudice, but it could just as well increase it.[48] The key to reducing prejudice was to level power and status differences between people so that they could associate on an equal basis. Those living in an integrated setting in South Africa, for instance, were more likely to say that other ethnicities were similar to themselves (80 percent) than those who lived in a segregated area (57 percent). Healthy forms of contact connected in- and out-groups through shared values and beliefs, and through the pursuit of common goals with the support of social institutions.[49] Allport's theory of intergroup contact remained influential for the next few decades, even as further research demonstrated that positive interactions were never more powerful than existing social and economic structures.[50]

Allport supported as well as participated in interventions to alleviate prejudice, among them the intercultural education projects of the Quaker social studies teacher Rachel Davis DuBois. Davis DuBois founded the service bureau for Intercultural Education in

New York City in 1934, which tutored teachers and promoted diversity through assembly programs and curriculum units on race and culture at fifty schools in New York, Philadelphia, San Francisco, and Washington, D.C.[51] During the war years, she cooperated with the U.S. Office of Education with a mission "to give children of minority groups the feeling of security, of belonging to and of accepting the life of the country."[52] She developed a twenty-six-week radio show with CBS, called *Americans All, Immigrants All* (figure 22), to promote acceptance of immigrant cultures and to highlight the need for tolerance.

Drama was an especially powerful method for intercultural work because "vicarious experiences tended to modify emotional attitudes."[53] Davis DuBois reported that "Gentile students who acted with their Jewish fellow-students in a Jewish play long remembered their experiences during the time when they were a part of the ways of thinking, feeling, acting of that culture group."[54] Under the direction of a social studies teacher, community members in Yonkers wrote and enacted a play entitled *American Is You and Me*. One student revealed the impact of the program on his entrenched stereotypes: "I thought the program about the Italian contribution was the most important because up to that time I had no idea Italians and other races had helped America. I had thought it was Americans who helped and protected the 'dumb foreigners' as I called them."[55]

The intercultural workshop sponsored the Philadelphia Early Childhood Research Project, which trained teachers in two different curricula over fourteen weeks. One curriculum emphasized intercultural tolerance, whereas the traditional curriculum allowed stereotypes to stand uncorrected, and teachers reinforced the idea that certain groups had "funny customs." Teachers enacted these different pedagogic styles as dramatic roles. At first, many teachers found the traditional role more comfortable. They easily slipped out of the tolerant role when forced to identify with different religious groups and returned to stereotyped "we-they" distinctions. One teacher, however, felt growing discomfort in enforcing conformity in the traditional curriculum: "I could see Marie squirm when I said, 'but pumpkin pie is good; everyone should like it!'" A few moments later, this teacher "shamefacedly" volunteered, "I used to teach like that a few weeks ago."[56] At the end of the fourteen

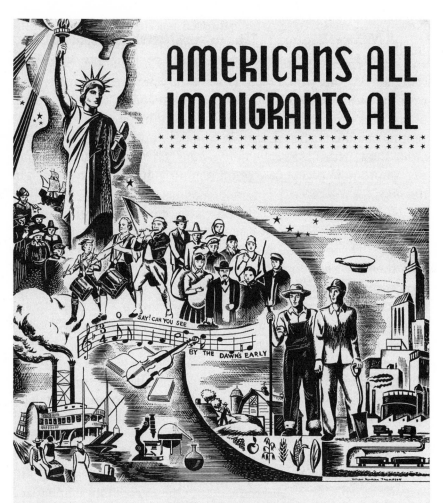

Figure 22. Image on cover of pamphlet describing Rachel Davis DuBois's radio show with CBS, "Americans All, Immigrants All," developed with the U.S. Office of Education. Rachel Davis DuBois Papers, Immigration History Research Center Archives, University of Minnesota.

weeks, the children in the cultural pluralism group not surprisingly showed a reduction in prejudice, whereas those in the traditional group had increased their stereotyped responses. The researchers credited the dramatic role-playing technique as "a crucial factor in the success achieved."[57] Teachers felt more freedom and experienced less resistance to the project because they were enacting a role rather than expressing their true beliefs.

Allport stated that role-playing and sociodrama made "empathizing with two points of view" possible and was powerful enough to change attitudes.[58] One study of role-playing allowed children to explore their own "feeling-level" first, giving them greater insight into a problem.[59] The social psychologist Gerhart Saenger advised teachers to help students develop empathy by first sensitizing students to their own needs and feelings, which then made it possible to understand others' needs and to "learn to identify with them."[60] If a child considered the difficulties his or her own parents faced in their immigration experience, the child's empathy with other immigrants would be augmented. For Saenger, "the class room should be made a laboratory in democratic living."[61]

Allport also championed Davis DuBois's "contact and acquaintance" programs that sought to build bonds between adults of different backgrounds and religious orientations through Unity Home Festivals and the method of Group Conversation. Davis DuBois organized a unity festival in Plainfield, New Jersey, with forty-seven persons of "Danish, Negro, English, German, Chinese, Jewish, Yankee and Dutch backgrounds" sharing and celebrating diverse rituals, including Puritan hymns, Jewish Succoth, an Indian corn dance, Negro spirituals, and Quaker silence. Enacting all these traditions, Davis DuBois believed, dramatized the "oneness of humanity."[62]

Group Conversations took place with people from a variety of ethnic, racial, and religious traditions in PTAs, churches, synagogues, settlement houses, labor union halls, YMCAs, and YWCAs. Davis DuBois orchestrated these conversations, held in a circle, with the help of an artist and a musician. She described it as a symphony with recurrent major and minor themes. A participant would share a simple childhood experience that evoked strong emotions. Others in the group soon discovered resonant similarities in their own experience, often leading the group to break into spontaneous song and dance. In one conversation, attended by the anthropologist Margaret Mead, "a white New Englander could not remember all the words of a hymn precious to her. A black American from South Carolina lined out the words, while the two sang it together. The joy was inexpressible. The group silence held it for a few precious moments."[63]

Allport believed that participating in conversations on the basis of equal status could build more tolerance, even if the exchange did not result in lasting relationships.[64] He participated in at least one Group Conversation, reporting to Davis DuBois afterward that the experience "penetrates below the verbal level."[65] He spelled out the impact of these experiences in her Group Conversation manual: "Unless we get this acceptance of others into our very muscles, glands and bones, we do not have it."[66]

Small-scale actions of this kind were initiated by community groups as part of a "civic unity" movement formed after the Harlem riots of 1943.[67] By 1951, there were over five hundred local, state, and national organizations working on "intergroup" relations, some of which had emerged even earlier from New Deal–era appointments of "race relations advisors." In 1944, the Commission on Community Interrelations (CCI) was founded as an arm of the Jewish Congress. The commission developed action-oriented programs to foster intercultural understanding and cooperation. Their innovative self-survey method rallied communities to investigate their own discriminatory practices rather than relying on social science outsiders to conduct traditional surveys. Allport wrote letters of support for the commission and introduced the method in their promotional pamphlet. He bolstered the scientific legitimacy of the self-survey method, which employed "the delicate tools of interviewing, coding, sampling, statistics to the immediate objective of social therapy."[68] The findings of the self-surveys were more likely to be accepted by the community than an outsider's verdict.

Self-surveys were conducted in Montclair, New Jersey, Minneapolis, Minnesota, and a city called "Northtown" near New York City.[69] Community and civic groups were enlisted and citizens collated data and conducted interviews to evaluate discriminatory practices in their churches, businesses, and organizations. Interviewers gained insight into the home life of others living in their community. According to one researcher, "He learns to empathize with the Negro white collar girl, who tells him of her struggles to get an office job, the Italian who has difficulty in getting decent living quarters."[70] Widespread discrimination was discovered in Northtown, "an eye opener for most people." The local committee developed an action plan that spurred some changes: the public school hired its first black teacher, and a department store employed a black salesclerk for the first time.

The CCI also conducted research to determine the best way to respond to a bigoted remark in a public setting. The most effective response, the researchers discovered, was a calm and unemotional one that conveyed the importance of fairness and American democracy.[71] Activists used this information to stage short experimental plays for audiences at YMCAs, union groups, even for passers-by who were pulled off the street to participate in what they thought was an opinion survey. Professional actors dramatized "incident situations": one actor uttered an anti-Semitic or other prejudicial remark in a scene on a bus or in an office waiting room, and an onlooker offered a response. The incident was played out a number of times with the bystander making different comments to the bigot. Audience members were then asked to participate in the drama and to suggest their own responses. Group discussions and interviews followed.[72] Allport supported the project and participated in at least one such "incident-control" demonstration with a small local cast organized by a Civic Unity Committee of Cambridge in November 1949.[73] The CCI trained several hundred volunteers to initiate their own programs in churches and community organizations and claimed to have reached more than 25,000 people by 1951.[74]

Allport promoted the techniques of role-play and dramatic enactment as among the "boldest advances of modern social science." They effectively produced what he called "a kind of forced empathy."[75] By acting out the roles "of employees, of students, of Negro servants," as Allport explained, one "learns through such 'psychodrama' what it feels like to be in another's shoes."[76] Role-play could also provide a glimpse into one's own motives, insights, and projections. It was found to be useful in play therapy to help children deal with racial conflict.[77] Human relations groups adopted role-play techniques to train leaders in education, local communities, and industry. One group at the University of California, Los Angeles, employed lectures, buzz groups, role-playing, case studies, and whole-group activities to provide trainees with better awareness of themselves, their impact on others, and their feelings and prejudices.[78]

In his conclusion to *The Nature of Prejudice*, Allport underscored the challenges of combating prejudice in American society. He recognized the persistent structural discrimination in social institutions as well as the deep-rooted patterns of prejudice in the personality. He nonetheless continued to support small-scale interventions to cultivate empathy, believing that even these slight contributions might alter one small part of an unstable social and psychological system. These minor shifts, he hoped, might ramify more widely through society. Yet he surmised that battling segregation in the law would likely be more successful than directly attacking prejudicial attitudes, which were deeply entrenched. Allport advised finding areas of least resistance in which to act for the cause of civil rights, supporting both militant reformers and executive action that could enact antidiscriminatory policies by fiat. Above all, Allport promoted a social science activism that required engaged, empathic participation: "When he *does* something, he *becomes* something."[79]

Allport had always promoted tolerance as the antidote to prejudice, but in 1956 he ventured a more ambitious goal. While perusing a slim volume of Mahatma Gandhi's letters, Allport discovered Gandhi's notion of "equimindedness." Gandhi explained that tolerance of those of different religions merely reflected an absence of ill will, whereas "equimindedness" accepted that each religion approached God and truth in its own way.[80] Allport explained in a Chicago lecture, "Conquest of Bigotry," that equimindedness constituted "that blend of fairness, reasonableness and inclusive sympathy that stand in opposition to bigotry, safeguarding all productive human relationships."[81] Equimindedness harbored an "inclusive sympathy" and relied on "a freer use of intelligence, and a wider human compassion" than did tolerance.[82] It entailed a recognition of the "profound similarity among people" and the "common core of human existence and destiny."[83] Allport asked his audience: "Who does not want food, shelter, and a measure of physical comfort? Is there any normal person who rejects family felicity or wishes to see children suffer?"[84] Equimindedness traded in equality and universality and was closely aligned with the expansive empathy that Allport's friend and colleague Kenneth Clark came to passionately espouse.

Kenneth B. Clark: Psychologizing Politics

On July 30, 1953, Kenneth Clark wrote to Gordon Allport, asking his help in preparing a document for the upcoming Supreme Court deliberations on desegregation in the *Brown v. Board of Education* case. He requested evidence that "non-segregation can be accomplished without severe or permanent disruption of a community."[85] It was not the first time Clark had called upon Allport for advice; he had done so in 1944 when he was developing a proposal to study black-white conflict, funded by the Council for Democracy. Clark planned to interview 2,500 black and white youth to gather information on family attitudes, economic conditions, community structures, "psychological patterns of feelings," and "how the respondent views himself and his social environment in light of his immediate experience."[86] Although Allport had not signed on as Clark's official advisor, he had strongly supported the project and agreed to provide feedback through correspondence.

Allport responded quickly to Clark's 1953 call for material in light of the "present emergency," acknowledging the weightiness of the task. He sent Clark selections from his chapter on interracial contact and gave him a list of social scientists working on discrimination but could offer no specific evidence on the response to desegregation in schools or in the South.[87] He nonetheless voiced his assurances: "People really know that segregation is un-American, even the masses in the South know it. . . . The decision will be accepted with only a flurry of anger, and soon subside. People do accept legislation that fortifies their inner conscience."[88]

Allport's confidence in the quick and unproblematic implementation of the decision to desegregate schools was common to what has been called the "liberal orthodoxy" on race, articulated in 1944 by Gunnar Myrdal's *American Dilemma*. The blatant contradiction between the American creed of justice for all and the existence of glaring discrimination was thought to weigh heavily on the white psyche. If whites could be made to face their guilt, reform would come quickly. Clark too held this view, at least while a research assistant on Myrdal's project. He later explained that he had identified with his liberal mentors because "it offered a general ideological and political approach to obtaining justice with which I felt comfortable."[89] Clark would soon, however, come to find a reliance on white guilt to effect political change exceedingly problematic.

Born in the Panama Canal Zone, Clark moved to Harlem at the age of five with his mother. He attended Howard University, where he studied with political scientist Ralph Bunche and psychologist Francis Cecil Sumner, the first African American to receive a doctorate in psychology from Clark University, with a dissertation on Freud and Alfred Adler.[90] Clark found psychoanalyst Adler's connection of the inner psyche to social dynamics so compelling that he shifted his intended major from neurophysiology to psychology. Soon he was learning about the child's feelings of insecurity that transmuted into a desire for superiority and power, which if unchecked by community feeling and social connection, could become pathological.[91] Clark also steeped himself in Franz Boas's and Ruth Benedict's anthropological theories that debunked ideas of inherent black racial inferiority.

Clark had always been a vocal protestor against discrimination. While an undergraduate, he picketed the Capitol Hill restaurant that refused to serve African Americans and was almost thrown out of Howard University.[92] When visiting the offices of *Time* magazine in 1939, an employee slurred him, and Clark penned a vehement letter of complaint: "Anyone who is unable to pass a young Negro, who happens to be using a pen rather than a slop mop, without giving vent to an obviously emotionally motivated insult should hardly be associated with a magazine pretending the objectivity and unbiased reporting claimed by *Time*." Offering a mix of psychological analysis and an appeal for justice, he identified the office in which the perpetrator had disappeared in order to "aid in determining who this gallant defender-to-the-death of mediocre individual's ego satisfying superstition of Nordic superiority is."[93]

Clark transitioned to Columbia University for graduate study and enlisted the social psychologist Otto Klineberg as his mentor. Klineberg had discredited theories of racial inferiority in black schoolchildren, arguing that the "dislike of the unlike is not a natural

Figure 23. Social psychologist Kenneth B. Clark, professor at City College of New York. Archives, City College of New York, CUNY.

but an acquired trait" as it is "entirely absent in young children."[94] Clark graduated in 1940 as the first African American psychologist to be trained at the university; two years later he began teaching at the City College of New York (figure 23).[95] His wife, Mamie Clark, also received her PhD from Columbia, and together they established the Northside Treatment Center in Harlem in 1946 to improve education, counseling, and psychological services for Harlem youth. It was the first of their community activism projects: in 1962, they founded Harlem Youth Opportunities Unlimited (HARYOU); in 1964, the Metropolitan Applied Research Center, which developed research projects on school desegregation and civil rights.[96]

While working for her master's degree in the late 1930s, Mamie Clark set out to investigate black children's consciousness of race, and Kenneth soon joined in her research project. Together, they showed young black children drawings of white and black children, asked them to perform coloring tasks, and inquired whether they preferred white or black dolls. Because some subjects were disturbed by the task, and many preferred white dolls to black dolls, the Clarks concluded that their young black subjects experienced damage to their self-esteem and self-image.[97] They mined the literature on the struggles of the black family by E. Franklin Frazier, Clark's mentor at Howard, and Kurt Lewin's writings on Jewish self-hate to conclude that children do not merely learn to identify themselves as a particular race, but they learn "the larger pattern of emotions, conflicts, and desires which are part of his growing knowledge of what society thinks about his race."[98] These ideas dovetailed with Adler's views on learned inferiority acquired by individuals through social imbalances in power and status.

In 1950, Clark began collecting a wide range of materials on racial prejudice and its effects on personality for the mid-century White House Conference on Children and Youth. When the legal defense fund of the NAACP began designing a brief against segregation it asked for Clark's help. In 1954, with the collaboration of Isidor Chein and Stuart Cook, Clark wrote the appendix to the Supreme Court decision on *Brown v. Board of Education*, entitled "The Effects of Segregation and the Consequences of Desegregation: A Social Science Statement." It became instrumental evidence for the case, signed by thirty-two social scientists, among them, Gordon Allport.[99]

While preparing this brief, Clark had called upon Allport for assistance. Clark had a soft spot for his colleague, telling him in a letter just two years before Allport died, "At the risk of being awkward and sentimental I want you to know how deeply I appreciate the quality and depth of your friendship."[100] And in 1979, when the twenty-five-year anniversary edition of Allport's *The Nature of Prejudice* was published, Clark introduced the volume. He affirmed that Allport was not only a prominent social philosopher but "an empathic and warm human being."[101] This was high praise for Clark: empathy was the key quality that enabled the powerful white person to recognize and defend the shared humanity that lay deeper than differences of culture, ethnicity, national origin, and race.

Clark published his popular book *Prejudice and Your Child* in 1955, largely drawn from his White House report on Children and

Youth. He asked, "Who teaches a child to hate and fear—or to respect as his equal—a member of another race?"[102] The answer was: social institutions, segregated residential areas, inferior schools and segregated transportation, parents, teachers, television, and the media. Drawing on Myrdal's findings, he pointed to suggestive evidence showing that white children "are insidiously and negatively disturbed by these contradictions in the American democratic creed."[103] Yet Clark did not point to guilt as evidence of a white conscience; instead he highlighted white insecurity as the engine of prejudice. Insecurity was part of the American way of life, manifesting in the exploitation of the land and its natural resources, and in the competitive struggle for personal achievement, which for whites often depended on the denial of status to the African American. For Clark, "This basic motivation of insecurity was inherent in the very foundations of the American nation."[104]

Racism was a by-product of the cultural pattern of striving for status and success, coupled with a need for conformity. Prejudicial ideas afforded its proponents privileges and benefits, helping them to get ahead in American society.[105] Clark insisted that prejudice was not opposed to the American way of life but inherent in it. He provided evidence from a poll of five hundred social scientists, 90 percent of whom believed that those in a segregated group experienced negative psychological effects ranging from frustration, feelings of inferiority, submissiveness, and martyrdom to aggressiveness, withdrawal, and conflicts about self-worth. But 83 percent of these social scientists also believed that the privileged group experienced adverse psychological effects, including maladjustment, hostility, deterioration of moral values, hardening of social sensitivity, rationalization, inner conflicts, guilt feelings, and sometimes a disturbance in the sense of reality.[106] Prejudice was therefore a social disease that inflicted conflict and distress to some degree in all its members.

Clark's diagnosis of American society was informed by Adlerian and Freudian psychoanalysis. He had undergone a yearlong analysis with the Columbia analyst Aaron Karush, who had an interest in psychosomatic medicine. Although Clark found it difficult to get over his initial self-consciousness, he believed the analysis had reduced his frustration and anxiety levels, giving him "a bit more realistic appraisal of myself—my abilities and goals and how best to distribute my energies"[107] Given this experience and his extensive psychological knowledge, Clark was not hesitant to diagnose the insecurities and callow psychological attitudes in whites that produced racism. He excoriated a drama critic who panned the play *On Whitman Ave.* on the topic of prejudice against blacks because it "failed as human drama." Clark's 1946 letter to *PM* magazine professed, "Anyone who has not personally experienced the seering [*sic*] humiliation of being rejected and despised because of color would not be likely to perceive the intense human drama involved in this play."[108] He found the critic simply unable "to project oneself into the unpleasant experiences of another." The critic's inability to empathize, as he would later call it, could be attributed to his "deep, unconscious repressions and blockages." Just a few years later, Clark raged against the psychological roots of prejudice in a letter to the magazine *Reporter:* "The problem is fundamentally a problem of the lack of maturity, the lack of integrity, the absence of intelligence, the greed and frustrations of the perpetrators of prejudice. It is they who must become assimilated into the forward-moving currents of mankind."[109]

Clark's early indictment of status-conscious, psychologically unstable white American society looked prescient by the 1960s. The initial gains of the civil rights movement had not induced guilt in whites but rather had fomented greater resistance to desegregation and other civil rights measures. These issues came to head in a forum on "Liberalism and the Negro," held at New York's Town Hall in 1964 and sponsored by *Commentary* magazine, a left liberal forum for politics, Judaism, and cultural issues. The philosopher Sidney Hook, the sociologist Nathan Glazer, and Gunnar Myrdal participated, along with writer James Baldwin; the editor Norman Podhoretz was the moderator.

Baldwin inveighed against the failings of white liberals: "What I mean by a liberal is . . . someone, furthermore, whose real attitudes are revealed when the chips are down—someone who thinks you're pushing too hard when you rock the boat, who thinks you are bitter when you are vehement, who has a set of attitudes so deep they're almost unconscious and which blind him to the fact that in talking to a black man, he is talking to another man like himself."[110] Stepping up from the audience to agree with Baldwin, Clark recounted how, at an academic meeting earlier that day in that very room, his colleagues had declined to hire a psychologist studying race relations despite having funding earmarked to do so. The vote went instead to an experimentalist of visual perception. Clark's unspoken thought was that his fellow psychologists did not want to hire an African American. He explained, "If I had said this, I would have been accused of bigotry, my liberal white friends would have been unable to understand why I had violated the code of affability."[111]

Clark then called out the simmering undercurrents in the conversation at hand: "Mr. Baldwin has been put on the defensive all throughout this discussion by people who don't want to be made uncomfortable by him." And turning to Hook, Clark continued, "All you've been saying to Mr. Baldwin is: 'Don't make me have to look behind my own façade. Don't let me have to find out that my Negro friends aren't really giving it to me straight.'"[112] He extended his critique to liberal institutions that had failed to alter their discriminatory practices: "There is a peculiar kind of ambivalence in American liberalism, a persistent verbal liberalism that is never capable of overcoming an equally persistent illiberalism of action."[113]

In spring 1965, Clark continued his exposé of the flaws of white liberalism in his opinion piece "Delusions of the White Liberal," published in the *New York Times*. Liberals were often harder to deal with than bigots, Clark declared, given their guilt, conflicting loyalties, and acquiescence in the flagrant system of racial injustice.[114] He took them to task for their refusal to fully support civil rights and for their lack of understanding of the motivations of African Americans. He was not alone in this perception. Martin Luther King, Jr., wrote of white moderates from the Birmingham jail: "Perhaps I was too optimistic; perhaps I expected too much. I suppose I should have realized that few members of the oppressor race can understand the deep groans and passionate yearnings of the oppressed race, and still fewer have the vision to see that injustice must be rooted out by strong, persistent and determined action."[115]

In November 1965, Assistant Secretary of Labor Daniel Patrick Moynihan's report was released by the U.S. Department of Labor. Many thought the Moynihan Report indicted black families as matriarchies enmeshed in a "tangle of pathology" and the major culprit in urban decay. Fervent critiques contended that Moynihan had failed to offer palpable policy initiatives or to locate black experience within the frame of larger white society. Moynihan had been Clark's student at City College, and Clark had himself employed the language of pathology to describe the black community. Clark initially came to Moynihan's defense. Moynihan thanked Clark in December 1965 for "the way you have stood by me in recent weeks" and cited a recent study that showed a decline in IQ scores among black youth from age five to ten that he believed pointed to "the broken family differential." He told Clark that he "must have derived much 'quiet, scholarly' satisfaction at seeing your Youth in the Ghetto findings so elegantly confirmed."[116]

Clark was unlikely to have felt any distanced scholarly satisfaction in these findings, which only confirmed the dreadful state of ghetto schools. When a few years later Moynihan espoused the explicit policy of benign neglect in matters of race and the inner cities, Clark vociferously denounced him, writing that Moynihan had left out "the truth of American racism, of which he now unfortunately is a symptom."[117]

Empathy as Antidote

In 1965, Clark assessed the civil rights movement as having produced only minimal practical gains. It had primarily succeeded in releasing the emotions of despair, hopelessness, and anger on the part of black Americans. As Clark put it: "His own wounds have been unhealed for what seems like forever. He now feels free—or rather, more free—to reveal the extent of his hurt. The great tragedy will be if the white does not see or listen, with his heart as well as his mind."[118] In order to avert this tragedy that would stall further progress and even spark a regression, Clark exhorted his white liberal colleagues to find the ground of mutual respect that crossed racial lines, rooted in an underlying similarity of the human condition—what he called "empathy."

Empathy was neither sentimentality nor pity. Sentiment was the underside of the racist lie, what Clark called the "sentimental lie," or the tendency of whites to attribute virtue to the oppressed. Neither sentiment nor pity would suffice because both emanated from a distanced, superior position. "In contemporary society, no one, Negro or white, can be totally without prejudice. No one should expect purity of himself or others. Any genuine relationship between Negro and white must face honestly all of the ambivalences both feel for each other. Each must identify with the other without sentiment."[119]

James Baldwin had also railed against sentimentality, enshrined in *Uncle Tom's Cabin* with its dominant theology of white purity arrayed against the evils of blackness. Tom had to be "robbed of his humanity" in order to function as a theological caricature rather than a human being.[120] Sentimentality evoked "spurious emotion" and obscured the truth. For Baldwin the truth lay in "a devotion to the individual human being, his freedom and fulfillment," which was "not to be confused with a devotion to Humanity."[121] As the black studies scholar Darryl Michael Scott has pointed out, the flip side of pity is contempt, and therefore a flimsy, and dangerous basis on which to base political intervention.[122] Martin Luther King, Jr., asked in 1967 not for white pity, but for empathy—"fellow feeling for the person in need—his pain, agony and burdens."[123]

If sentimentalism could empty itself out into an excess of emotion, empathy was intelligent, measured, and reasonable. Clark believed that the deep identification achieved through empathy leveled power imbalances and formed a conduit to the recognition of the "common predicament" of human beings. Accordingly, it could serve as the psychological basis for equal protection and treatment under the law. Clark's empathy was similar to Baldwin's truth in that it was rooted in the most basic appreciation of another as a human being. Baldwin fluently explained: "White Americans have never, in all their long history, been able to look on him as a man like themselves. This point need not be labored; it is proved over and over again by the Negro's continuing position here, and his indescribable struggle to defeat the stratagems that white Americans have used, and use, to deny him his humanity."[124]

Clark's highlighting of the white liberal's delusions not surprisingly sparked controversy. Clark reported, "Some of my white friends insist that they are 'perplexed,' or 'confused,' or in downright disagreement with everything from the tone to the specifics of the article."[125] But he had intended to be provocative, hoping to move white liberals, who had been nominally on board with the political agenda of civil rights, to greater commitment. He was angling for a transformation of white values. The white had to dispense with "the fantasy of aristocracy or superiority," and the white liberal, in particular, "the fantasy of purity," or the idea of being free of bias and prejudice. In short, the white liberal had to "reconcile his affirmation of racial justice with his visceral racism" and face the fact that his or her own privileged status was threatened.[126] It was easy to write a letter to one's congressman, but it was much more difficult to grapple with one's own racial bias. If whites could "transcend the barriers of their own minds" and to listen with the heart, it might be possible, Clark imagined, to "respond insofar as he is able with a pure kind of empathy that is raceless, that accepts and understands the frailties and anxieties and weaknesses that all men share, the common predicament of mankind."[127]

Clark intended to provoke a "therapeutic crisis of truth, which is essential for that next step of genuine activeness."[128] This kind of psychological shift might make engaged action possible. Clark's bid for empathy did not aim to smooth jagged conversations and difficult friendships but to shape a political reality that affirmed the rights of all. When Clark was asked in 1964 to sign a petition put forth by members of the Psychologists' Committee on International Relations advocating for "positive interracial attitudes consistent with an equalitarian society," he refused. The undersigned acknowledged that progress toward the goal of equal rights had been unfortunately too gradual, but signees were to refrain from negative statements and hostile acts, a thinly veiled reference to black militancy. Clark responded sharply: "Personally, I am not now interested in an effort 'to engender positive racial attitudes.' I am only interested in the ways and means by which an alleged democratic government protects the rights of its citizens."[129]

In 1965, Clark published *Dark Ghetto*, an urban ethology of Harlem, which drew from *Youth in the Ghetto: A Study of the Consequences of Powerlessness and a Blueprint for Change*, an intensive social science study of the city carried out by Clark's organization, HARYOU. His book stood as both a social science treatise and an accessible narrative designed to inform, to engender feeling, and to galvanize social action. He strategically designed his volume to wake up liberal and moderate whites because he believed that "many flagrant forms of racial injustice North and South could not exist without their acquiescence" and liberal support was essential for the ultimate success of the civil rights movement.[130] Myrdal called Clark's book a demand for "human empathy and even compassion on the part of as many as possible of those who can read, think, and feel in free prosperous, white America.[131] *Dark Ghetto* went on to sell almost 40,000 copies in hardcover and nearly 140,000 in paperback. It became a required text in many of the first black studies courses at universities.[132]

Clark was well aware of its hybrid nature: "*Dark Ghetto* is, in a sense, no report at all, but rather the anguished cry of its author. But it is the cry of a social psychologist, controlled in part by the concepts and language of social science, and as such can never express the pure authenticity of folk spontaneity or the poetic symbolism of the artists."[133] Clark called himself an "involved observer" of Harlem life and touched on his own experience growing up in Harlem. He composed the prologue, "The Cry of the Ghetto," of short utterances from city residents—identified only as "Man," "Woman," "Boy," "Girl," "Drug Addict," sometimes including their age. The topics ranged from poverty, robberies, not owning real estate, stereotypes, the sadism of the police, hope and despair, and getting spit upon in the street.

Clark saw Harlem as a colony within American society inhabited by a subjected people. His book begins with the sociology of the city and then considers psychological and pathological topics, mirroring the broader social context in which individual struggles took place. He discussed schools, power in the ghetto, politics, the press, social services, church and religious leaders, and strategies for change. Clark depicted intense daily struggles but also identified pockets of resilience. Even with the ghetto's high delinquency rates, more than 90 percent of youth did not come into direct conflict with the law, a mark of the "power of human resiliency."[134] And he spoke of the reservoirs of energy in Chicago, Boston, and New York that promised a "more forceful pattern of personal and community action," stirred by hope.[135] In other writings, he celebrated the strength and resolve of black children who were pushing through jeering white crowds to attend school at Little Rock: "centuries of oppression have immunized them and given them the necessary protective defenses for survival."[136]

Clark revealed difficult truths in order to make the suffering of

Harlem's inhabitants palpable to a population that had never entered its confines. He fought against what he called the powerful psychological impulse of denial made palpable by commuters on a New York train: "This human tendency to block out the undesirable may account for why Westchester suburban commuters bury their heads in their newspapers as their trains pass through the dilapidation of Harlem's Park Avenue."[137] W. E. B. Du Bois too had bemoaned the fact that in matters of race, "the passing throng does not even turn its head."[138] Clark concluded, "But the chances for any major transformation in the ghetto's predicament are slim until the anguish of the ghetto is in some way shared not only by its victims but by the committed empathy of those who now consider themselves privileged and immune to the ghetto's flagrant pathologies."[139]

Clark wrote against psychological denial as well as academic indifference. Narrow scientific research stood in thrall to the fetish of objectivity and conveniently bracketed difficult moral insights so as to exclude questions of feeling and value. "It may be that where essential human psychology and moral issues are at stake, noninvolvement and noncommitment and the exclusion of feeling are neither sophisticated nor objective, but naïve and violative of the scientific spirit at its best."[140] He asked, "How is it possible to study a slum objectively?"[141] The detached professionalism of social workers with their "cool objectivity," Clark proclaimed, "feels more like insensitivity."[142] Social workers promoted middle-class norms and focused on individual needs while overlooking the blatant social injustices all around them. Clark's alternative to this "patronizing, social work colonialism" required the involvement of "empathic professionals" who without condescension could define, energize, and maximize "whatever power does reside within the people."[143]

Clark's airing of the struggles of the ghetto became a touchstone for controversy. Some argued that he perpetuated a discourse of victimization and a pathologization of black culture. Others faulted him for failing to even touch upon the vibrant intellectual and musical life of Harlem and women's complex roles in the community.[144] Further, the Clarks' doll studies purporting black children's experiences of low self-esteem and psychological damage have undergone intense critique for, among other things, a lack of scientific rigor, misinterpretation of results, and a failure to disentangle subjects' personal sense of selfhood from their racial identity.[145] Scholars have since reexamined the data to discover that the preference for the white doll was strong in the northern children but not in the southern sample of six-year-olds (who preferred brown by 67 percent). The trend reversed for seven-year-olds in the northern sample (60 percent preferred brown dolls).[146]

More positively, historian Damon Freeman has grounded Clark's view of social superiority and inferiority in Adlerian theories, and others have celebrated his commitment to action research and his redrawing of the boundaries of objective social science.[147] Some have found his conception of "damage" to be rooted in the structural inequalities in society and not conceived in biological or racial terms. One historian credits Clark, unlike many of his colleagues who traded in damage imagery, with portraying the struggles of those at the bottom of society with "empathy and respect," born out of his own experience growing up in Harlem.[148]

If Clark tended to pathologize life in Harlem, it is important to recognize that he extended his diagnosis of disease to American society as a whole. He even claimed a special status for doing so: "As a Negro social psychologist, I feel a certain degree of alienation and detachment from the larger American culture, which I believe make it possible for me to observe and understand certain aspects of American society which it would be more difficult, if not impossible, for a white American of similar background, training, and intelligence to understand with the same degree of clarity or emphasis."[149]

What then was his diagnosis? White American society was built around capitalist greed and was competitive, insecure, and anxiety-producing at its core. Clark indicted the urban renewal and large public housing projects in the city of Newark in no uncertain terms in his unpublished writings. These projects "left a no man's land or buffer zone between ghetto residential and business areas and the revitalized commercial and civic core."[150] Rather than providing benefits to residents, they had only succeeded in delivering profits to the real estate industry, financial sector, and public officials. Clark found most Americans profoundly materialistic; they glorified work and technology and hollowly professed an egalitarian creed, yet they functioned on the basis of powerful insecurities that led them to deny equality to others in order to feel superior. Clark told readers of *Ebony* magazine in 1965 that if blacks were indeed to obtain equal rights, it would be a "psychological calamity for the average American white," as they would have to "find other scapegoats, or to face again, the intolerable state of their own emptiness."[151]

Empathic Reason

By the time Clark published *Dark Ghetto* the tide of liberalism had ebbed. Progress toward black emancipation beginning with the 1954 *Brown v. Board of Education* decision, successful boycotts and sit-ins, and the 1963 March on Washington gave way to increased white backlash. Because many of the legislative civil rights victories had not translated into palpable changes, Clark believed they had produced a "devastating negative effect."[152] Northern riots occurred immediately after the passage of the 1964 Civil Rights Act, and Watts exploded after the 1965 Voting Rights Act was enacted. Clark lamented that the apparent civil rights victories were "ashes," which "have not affected a single child in a ghetto school as far as his ability to read is concerned and have not changed a single rat in the deteriorated slums of New York, Boston, Philadelphia, Chicago, Detroit, Los Angeles."[153] Twenty years later, Clark explained this political shift: "When the 1964 Civil Rights Act and the Civil Rights Movement in seeking equality and decency in Northern urban centers came too close to the liberals of the North, it brought an end to liberalism. It was all right of them to be liberal when justice was being sought thousands of miles away. When justice was being sought in your neighborhood, neo-conservatism took its place."[154]

Clark also tied the embrace of neo-conservatism to an erosion of empathy. He complained in 1973 that most of his white liberal colleagues had "lost all empathy with low income people and black people."[155] Liberals in their ivory towers engaged in a sophisticated white backlash by repudiating their earlier positions and blaming those receiving benefits for the failure of social programs. Conservatism was masked by calls for a "tough minded realism, objectivity, moral relativism and other varieties of intellectual laissez-faire."[156] At an APA panel scheduled on the twenty-fifth anniversary of the *Brown* decision, psychologists who signed on to the social science statement were now accused of using social science to blithely advance their political aims as liberal reformers.[157]

But Clark also directed his critique to the black power movement, which "like their white segregationist counterparts, demand the subjugation of rational and realistic thought and planning to dogmatism and fanaticism."[158] Clark conceded that the movement had injected life into the civil rights struggle, but he found the slogan "Black Power" to be an oxymoron that "cannot be defined with precision because it has no objective reference point other than the common predicament of Negro Americans who share only their lack of power and their resentment and anger at being denied equality and justice in the American democratic system."[159] Black nationalism promoted a separatist agenda and a "grandiose ideology" that did not translate into substantive and pragmatic approaches to improve housing or education.[160] Clark stridently rejected its emotional palette: "Nor can one build a solid pride on the quicksands of emotion, anger, rage, hatred—no matter how justifiable."[161]

Further, the movement distracted from an analysis of power dynamics as they played out in the real world. Power, as Clark defined it, drawing from British philosopher Bertrand Russell, entailed "energy or force or a combination of forces required to bring about, to sustain, or to prevent social, political, or economic change."[162] Verbal promises of change, legislative and judicial victories, even executive commitments were empty and lacking in power when they resulted in no "observable changes in the actual conditions of the life of the lower status, rejected peoples."[163]

If power was necessary to forge concrete change, Clark warned that the exercise of power without empathy formed the root evil of many social ills, foremost among them a racist society. One historian explains that for Clark "power in America was dominance without empathy."[164] The solution to the immense problems of poverty and discrimination required the melding of power with intelligence and empathy. "Whites and Negros must join together in an experiment to determine whether systematic and empathic use of human intelligence and training can be a form of power which can be used constructively in the quest for solutions of long standing urban and racial problems."[165]

Over the next decades, Clark championed the importance of "empathic reason"—the entwining of feeling and intelligence—for the design and implementation of political reform.[166] He was convinced that social justice could be achieved only through "sensitivity and empathic reason and intelligence."[167] Clark made use of "Adler's emphasis upon the potential social sensitivity and empathy in man," which he thought could provide "the important motivational base for an affirmative social technology."[168] He consulted a 1963 translation of Adler's writings and ascribed to his description of intelligence as inherently social and empathic. Adler had explained in 1930 that the key to intelligence was "getting close to others by identifying with them, by seeing with their eyes, by hearing with their ears, by feeling with their hearts."[169]

Clark insisted that a narrow, instrumental view of intelligence was profoundly ignorant about human nature and thus posed a grave danger to the survival of the human species.[170] A truer "multidimensional and complex intelligence," he argued, was "pervaded by an inescapable human and social concern," or "moral and empathetic components."[171] If the constricted human ego expanded, it would yield not only a greater sensitivity to others but also a new form of intelligence. He exclaimed in a 1976 interview: "There's not a damn thing on any of the intelligence tests that we now have that addresses itself to a sense of social responsibility. All of our intelligence tests talk about intelligence as if it were an isolated cognitive capacity, and intelligence tests are constructed and used as if the only function of intelligence is competitive, you know."[172] Clark faulted the American educational system for these failures. Education had become "ruthlessly competitive and anxiety-producing—in which the possibility of empathy, concern for one's classmate and the use of superior intelligence as a social trust are precluded."[173] Clark skewered higher education for failing miserably to "instill moral sensitivity as an integral part of the complex pattern of functional human intelligence."[174]

In 1970, Clark was elected president of the APA, and he soon formed a subcommittee and a new board to examine the profession's social responsibilities.[175] A year later he delivered his parting address as president, which ventured beyond racial politics to plead for empathy once again. The exercise of empathy necessitated the repudiation of power. The failures of federally funded antipoverty programs could be attributed to those who were "deeply unwilling or unable to share even a modicum of real power with those who have been powerless."[176] Empathy required an actual shift of power to the dispossessed, one step toward equality.

Power was not so willingly given up, however, and Clark then made a radical suggestion. He weighed the possibility of developing a psycho-pharmaceutical intervention to be administered to world leaders to increase their levels of empathy and compassion. An empathy pill, perhaps? He described it as "a scientific biochemical intervention that could stabilize and make dominant the moral and ethical propensities of man and subordinate, if not eliminate, his negative and primitive behavioral tendencies."[177] This suggestion was born out of desperation, but perhaps it was in keeping with the contemporary fascination with psychedelic drug experimentation and the behaviorist vision of an engineered society. Clark nonetheless received swift condemnation.[178]

Religious figures and psychologists reacted negatively: one chaplain wrote to the *New York Times* to dub Clark the devil himself. Clark thought his colleagues viewed him as a traitor.[179] Looking back on his address five years later, Clark considered his remarks to be incendiary not so much because he suggested a biochemical substance to directly alter behavior, but because it would be administered to powerful world leaders rather than to children or criminals, already a common practice. He told his interviewer, "Look, our primary danger is not criminals, not hyperactive children, but mere human beings with unprecedented power to determine the survival or the extinction of the human species."[180]

Over the next decade or more, Clark often repeated his refrain that American society suffered from a pervasive "lack of compassion, an absence of empathy—a lack of that positive identification which is essential for the broader perspective of man."[181] He continued to fulminate against a competitive, anxiety-prone American culture that rewarded the rampant pursuit of one's own interest. He offered a contrasting vision of racial communication and "real community." It was imperative for educators to work to strengthen "man's empathic capacity—man's ability to be identified functionally with the human needs of his fellow man."[182]

In 1979, Clark received the Distinguished Contribution to Psychology in the Public Interest Award, and in his acceptance address he highlighted the importance of empathy once again. Published the following year as "Empathy, a Neglected Topic in Psychological Research," the article's title echoed one published thirty years earlier. Then, the social psychologists Cottrell and Dymond had deemed empathy to be an overlooked field of research in the social sciences.[183] Clark confessed in 1979 that while searching the literature he had found more studies than he had anticipated, although these narrowly took up "questions of measuring, testing or observing empathic behavior." Because empathy was "a fundamental concept in social science" and, moreover, was "most relevant to the public interest," Clark was dismayed that it still lacked a "clear definition and a comprehensive theoretical approach."[184]

To pin down empathy's meaning, Clark turned to the dictionary, as did so many of his psychologist forebears. In Webster's unabridged *Third New International Dictionary*, the first definition of "empathy" still listed aesthetic imaginative projection into an object. Clark skipped this outdated meaning in favor of the second: the "capacity for participating in, or vicarious experience of, another's feelings, volitions or ideas." He then cobbled together his own definition: "The essential aspect of empathy is the capacity of an individual to feel into the needs, the aspirations, the frustrations, the joys, the sorrows, the anxieties, the hurt, indeed, the hunger of others as if they were his own."[185] One respondent to his published essay faulted Clark for consulting the dictionary when empirical tests had already defined empathy as a form of perspectival thinking or as a vicarious affective response to another that decentered one's own aims.[186] Another respondent questioned Clark's emphasis on empathy as a force at odds with power.

But Clark had indeed pitted power against empathy: the powerful in society clearly lacked this ability, or they would not structure and support the kinds of brutal inequalities that continued to exist in American society. And empathy short-circuited the egocentric drive for individual power.[187] Empathy was directly at odds with the biological imperative for individual survival and for the satisfaction of egocentric needs. Clark concluded that empathy was uniquely human; it required abstract thought and emerged from the most recently evolved portion of the human brain—the anterior frontal lobes. Clark generated this hypothesis on evidence from lobotomized patients who lacked both the ability to think abstractly and to empathize with others.

Clark speculated that differences in the structure of the human brain resulted in varying degrees of empathy. The egocentric possessed little empathy, and tyrants, sadists, and psychopaths had no empathy at all. Those with a greater degree of empathy were "compelled to assume risks and to jeopardize personal status and position in the compulsive need to identify with those who are less privileged."[188] The highest expression of empathy manifested in the embrace of all individual beings. Most people possessed at least a "chauvinistic empathy" with those similar in "color, religion, nationality, sex and status."[189] This form of empathy was a liability, however, as it produced intergroup hostilities, war, and international tensions. Chauvinistic empathy, Clark warned, could bring about the extinction of the human species.

As Clark's pessimism grew concerning the progress of civil rights, his calls for empathy became more insistent. His desperation echoes in the unpublished draft of his 1979 speech: "The only thing that will save us is a universal increase in empathy."[190] That same year he called American racism no less than a form of "psychological genocide."[191] His placed his last hope in the unique human capacity to respond to suffering with intelligence, social sensitivity, and the recognition that beneath cultural and racial differences something was shared. Empathic reason offered a psycho-political foundation for equal rights, a way to level power differentials and to embrace the "interdependence, the oneness of mankind."[192] Empathy and justice went hand in hand; as Clark voiced in 1983 at St. Mercy's College, "Justice and empathy are possible through the commonality of human experience—and the ability to understand and identify with these common human experiences."[193]

Clark has not been alone in seeing empathy as critical to social justice, human rights, and even to the procedures of a deliberative democracy.[194] One recent theorist envisions empathy as Clark did—in both affective and cognitive terms—and as integral to "the kind of equal consideration necessary to make democratic decisions legitimate."[195] Others support empathy's political importance but warn against a neo-liberal, market-oriented vision of empathy, which judges it as just another skill to be developed by the self-enterprising.[196] How far can empathy take us politically? Poet Claudia Rankine avows that there is "no mode of empathy that can replicate the daily strain of knowing that as a black person you can be killed for simply being black."[197] Empathy, by itself, may not be enough.

But more than fifty years ago now, Clark held up the antiracist potential of empathic reason as the psycho-political capacity to feel and to cognize the principle of the equality of all. The question remains as to how to translate this moral and psychological vision of empathy into a realistic and workable politics. Such a task is parallel to that of the international movement for human rights according to historian Samuel Moyn, who sees the challenge in converting a "set of global moral principles and sentiments" into political action.[198]

Clark never abandoned the idea that with experience and education more expansive forms of empathy could be nurtured, even as he postulated in 1980 that empathy was in part a hard-wired neurological capacity. It would take another decade, however, for neuroscientists to vigorously investigate empathy's neural underpinnings.

CHAPTER NINE

Empathic Brains

IN SPRING 2013, I attended a teaching workshop sponsored by a performance coach from a local theater. The coach instructed forty of us how to use our voice, gestures, and physical stance to capture and maintain student interest. If one slouched while teaching at the lectern, the instructor warned us, students would unconsciously mimic such movements. They did so, she explained, due to the activity of mirror neurons in their brains. No longer was it enough for a teacher to gauge interest through eye-contact or by watching the way students shifted in their seats. Now one had to imagine their neurons firing!

Mirror neurons were first named in 1996, four years after they were discovered in a neurophysiological laboratory in Parma, Italy. In these experiments, electrodes were placed in individual neurons in the prefrontal lobes of macaque monkey brains. These neurons fired when the monkey performed an action. The researchers were surprised to learn that these same neurons also fired when the monkey simply *perceived* someone else performing the action. The activation was taken to be a neural simulation of the other's action.

The Parma studies spurred a wave of experiments, some of which employed neuroimaging technologies to assess human brains. Neuroscientists soon mapped out a putative mirror neuron system in the human brain, linking the prefrontal lobe with the superior temporal sulcus, the posterior parietal lobe, and the insula.[1] Neuroscientists theorized that mirror neurons fire in a simulation of another's action, a mechanism that allows us to directly grasp the meaning and sometimes even the intention of a perceived action. By the early 2000s, mirror neurons were purported to be the key neural mechanism for empathy and social understanding. Popular newspapers and magazines touted these findings as a revolutionary new understanding of the brain's social capacity.

Mirror neuron studies, however, constitute only one of many neuroscientific mappings of empathy and social behavior. Over the past twenty years, neuroscientists have charted the neural mechanisms of empathy in collaboration with social and cognitive psychologists in the rapidly growing interdisciplinary field of social neuroscience. If the mirror neuron literature views empathy as an automatic neural simulation, other neuroscientific models characterize empathy as an emotionally regulated feeling response, sensitive to social context and dependent on an awareness of the difference between the self and the other. Different empathies have been found to possess different neural correlates: emotional contagion has neural patterns distinct from perspective taking, for instance. Some contend, however, that emotional contagion, as well as self-oriented perspective taking, is only pseudo-empathy and should not be called empathy at all.[2]

Truth be told, there is little agreement today among psychologists, neuroscientists, and philosophers on empathy's contours. For a time, mirror neurons dominated popular media accounts as the key agents of empathy. However, the expansive claims that mirror neurons subserve the understanding of actions, the capacity to empathize, and even the use of language have recently come under critique. The fact that neuroscientists do not agree as to the neural basis of empathy is not surprising when one acknowledges the existence of many forms of empathy, ranging from emotional resonance and contagion, to cognitive appraisal and perspective taking, and to an empathic concern with another that prompts helpful interventions.

Physiological Empathy

Back in 1979, Kenneth B. Clark told his audience at the American Psychological Association meeting that empathy was a neglected topic of psychology research. He admitted, however, that while preparing his remarks, he had discovered eighty-six entries on empathy in social science indices.[3] The counseling psychologist Gerald Gladstein faulted Clark for not clearly differentiating empathy from sympathy, and went on to publish a short history of empathy four years later.[4] Another commentator admonished Clark for consulting a dictionary to ascertain empathy's meaning. She urged psychologists to use experimental protocols to define and measure the ability, so that "all [could] agree on a definition that is psychological rather than lexicological."[5]

That was easier said than done. In fact, the lack of agreement on empirical models to assess empathy formed the hub of the problem. The psychological literature of the 1970s and 1980s catalogued empathy variously as the sharing of feelings, cognitively taking on another's perspective, acting to help another, engaging in fantasy, and as a type of physiological arousal when seeing another in pain. Among these studies were Martin Hoffman's research on empathic distress, which discovered that witnessing another's pain might not lead to helpful or prosocial behavior but could actually thwart it.[6] Experimenters at Syracuse University defined empathy to contain an initial stage of affective reverberation and then a stage of cognitive analysis. They sought to train empathy in children and psychotherapists.[7] In 1983, the psychologist Mark Davis presented an influential, multidimensional approach to empathy, which encompassed the interrelated but dissociable components of perspective taking, fantasy, personal distress, and empathic concern, all subscales of his Interpersonal Reactivity Index.[8]

For those interested in identifying biological indicators of empathy, physiological arousal was an important avenue of inquiry. Already in the 1960s, researchers had tested skin conductance and heart rates of subjects as they viewed crude films of surgical operations or watched another person receive a shock and then pull his hand back in pain.[9] Psychologist Ezra Stotland at the University of Washington hooked one subject up to a diathermy machine that produced heat in the body through electromagnetic currents. The subject would experience pleasurable, neutral, or painful stimuli while observers watched his or her reactions and movements.[10] Observers witnessing the subject feel pain demonstrated greater arousal—measured as palmar sweating, rise in basal skin conductance, and vasoconstriction—but only when they were given explicit instructions to "imagine him" or to "imagine the self" experiencing the stimulus. When instructed merely to "watch him," arousal did not occur. Stotland discovered that only three questions in his empathy battery correlated with physiological arousal. These questions explored whether subjects tended to become involved with characters in a book or with actors on a stage.[11] Stotland called this subset of questions the fantasy subscale, a capacity he concluded was necessary to trigger physiological and emotional arousal.

Another experiment measured physiological responses to a performer who received shocks and rewards, described at the outset of the experiment as either similar to or different from the subject.[12] Subjects demonstrated greater physiological response—defined as greater empathy—to those who were similar to them. Empathizers also tended to help the performer on a task at the end of the experiment. In another study, married couples were hooked up to machines to measure heart rate, skin conductance, general somatic activity, and pulse transmission. Subjects could better empathize with their spouse when they shared a similar physiological state.[13] Those with lower cardiovascular arousal, however, were better detectors of the spouse's positive emotion.

The prominent physiological psychiatrist Paul MacLean suggested in 1967 that empathy was a product of the human neo-cortex, the most evolutionarily advanced part of the brain.[14] A decade earlier, MacLean had identified the "limbic system" as the brain structure responsible for emotional and visceral experiences. He went on to develop an influential evolutionary model of the "triune" brain, which depicted the human brain as essentially three brains wrapped into one. The reptilian brain constituted the oldest evolutionary segment, which included the brain stem, reticular system, midbrain, and basal ganglia. Encircling this ancient brain was the second brain or limbic system, common to all mammals, including humans. The highest brain or neocortex emerged late in evolution only in humans, and was responsible for intellectual functions and the advanced visual faculties of foresight and insight. MacLean amended Lipps's account of empathy as "feeling into" to incorporate these advanced faculties of foresight and insight. He described it as "'see-

ing with feeling' into another person's situation" that relied on the
ability of the human neocortex "to 'look inward' for obtaining *insight* required for *foresight* in promoting the welfare of others."[15] As
we have seen, Kenneth Clark as well attributed the capacity for empathy to the higher levels of the human brain.

Over the next decade, however, new research demonstrated that
the brain was affected by social factors, and that empathic response
might originate in the limbic system. In 1985, the conception of a
"social brain" emerged with the studies of psychologist John Cacioppo. Cacioppo studied the effects of solitude and perceived loneliness on the brain and documented neuroendocrine and immune
responses to social stress.[16] In 1989, the psychiatrist Leslie Brothers
published an influential account of the biological basis of empathy.
She drew on evolutionary models as well as on neurophysiological
data in primates that showed the firing of a single neuron to the
perception of faces. She speculated that the amygdala, part of the
limbic system, played a role in empathy and outlined a template for
future research based on her conviction that empathy is "a biological concept par excellence."[17]

As imaging technologies grew more sophisticated, neuroscientists began to localize social emotions in the brain, a venture that
gave rise to the new field of social neuroscience. The field relies on
a confluence of methods drawn from neuroscience as well as from
evolutionary, cognitive, and social psychology. Cacioppo became
the director of the Center for Cognitive and Social Neuroscience at
the University of Chicago in 2004, and two years later the new journal *Social Neuroscience* appeared in print. The editor, the University
of Chicago neuroscientist Jean Decety, defined social neuroscience
in the inaugural issue as the exploration of the biological dimensions of social interaction, namely, the identification of neurological mechanisms for social psychological abilities. He extended the
scope of the "social" from the most complex human relationship to
the simplest animal connection. "Empathy" or "morality" were to
be closely analyzed, decomposed to their basic elements, and then
mapped onto neural processes.

Decety argued that new neuroscientific concepts would change
common notions of blame and responsibility and eventually impact
social policies. At the same time, he cautioned researchers not to be

overly influenced by politics or external pressures.[18] This caution came at a moment when journalists and neuroscientists writing for popular audiences had already begun to broadcast the successes of imaging studies in unlocking the secrets of social understanding and empathy. The discovery of mirror neurons was one such triumph about which journalists spilled a great deal of ink.

Mirror Neurons

"Cells That Read Minds" was the banner headline, in extra-large print, on the first page of the Science Times section of the *New York Times* on January 10, 2006.[19] The subtitle of the two-page article informed readers that the "secrets of mirror neurons" enable "the brain to perform its highest tasks—learning, imitating, empathizing." Four color diagrams were spread over a full page to illustrate the action of mirror neurons. Researchers were "flabbergasted" by the finding that humans possessed mirror neurons that were "far smarter, more flexible and more highly evolved than any of those found in monkeys."[20] In humans, mirror neurons comprised a complex system that enabled the understanding of intentions and emotions as well as many "sophisticated social abilities." In breathless prose, the article proclaimed that the discovery was "shaking up numerous scientific disciplines," and that studies of mirror neurons now answered questions about a wide variety of social behaviors including: "how children learn, why people respond to certain types of sports, dance, music and art, why watching media violence may be harmful and why many men like pornography." Mirror neurons themselves were the agents of empathy: "mirror neurons seem to analyze scenes and to read minds."

The author explained that it was sometime in 1991 or 1992 that a graduate student licking an ice cream cone walked into the neurophysiology laboratory in Parma, Italy, where macaque monkeys sat with electrodes inserted into neurons in the frontal area of their brains. These motor neurons were located in the F5 area of the monkey's inferior frontal cortex and were known to fire when a monkey made a grasping movement. What so astonished the researchers was that when the student entered the room with a cone in hand and moved it to his mouth, the monkey neurons also began to fire. These "mirror neurons" responded not only when a monkey made a grasping action but also when the monkey *watched* another make a grasping action.

Mirror neurons were theorized to have visuo-motor properties.[21] This meant that the perceptual system, primed to see action, shared a similar neural mechanism as the execution system that performed the action. When the neuron became active, the perceived action was directly paired with a motor simulation of that action.[22] The Parma neuroscientists proffered a "perception-action theory" to explain that the functions of perceiving and simulating were linked to a single cell. Mirror neurons were soon viewed as a rudimentary neural basis for the capacity to simulate others' movements as well as to imitate and to learn through social modeling.[23] Researchers found the system so powerful that it even responded to actions that were not fully carried out, as revealed in experiments where a subject stretched to pick up a book but did not actually grasp it.[24] The Parma researchers explained in 2001 in *Nature Reviews Neuroscience* that "an action is understood when its observation causes the motor system of the observer to 'resonate.'"[25]

These initial findings were based on the firing of electrodes placed in single cells of the monkey and therefore were not possible to duplicate in humans. But neuroscientists quickly adopted a variety of imaging technologies to uncover what they deemed to be a complex mirror neuron system (MNS) in humans. The first attempt to locate this system in humans took place with a transcranial magnetic stimulation (TMS) in 1995.[26] When neuroscientists stimulated Broca's area—the motor language area in human subjects and homologous to F5 in monkeys—they found greater evoked potentials when the subject observed another person moving as compared to a person at rest. By the late 1990s, Positron Emission Tomography (PET) and functional Magnetic Resonance Imaging (fMRI) studies documented activation in frontal areas near Broca's area as well as in the anterior parietal cortex when subjects watched human actions.

Mirror neurons have since been postulated to exist in several areas of the brain, including the superior temporal sulcus (STS) (sensitive to the observation of biological motion in monkeys and humans), the premotor cortex, the posterior parietal lobe, and the insula.[27] In 2010, Mukamel and his colleagues directly identified human mirror neurons in the frontal and temporal lobes in a study of twenty-one epileptic patients undergoing surgery.[28] The researchers concluded that multiple systems in the brain possess mirroring properties for perceptual and motor aspects of actions performed by others. Some neuroscientists contended that mirror neuron activity underlay the human ability to imitate, to empathize, to learn through socialization, even to use language. Further, a dysfunction of the mirror neuron system might account for autism.[29]

Popular science periodicals and newspapers enthusiastically reported these findings. *Science News* told its readers in 2005 that "neurons may track action as a prelude to empathy," citing a study that had appeared in *Science* showing mirror neurons fired not only for actions but for the intentions of actions as well.[30] *Science* displayed an image from the James Bond film *Dr. No* of a tarantula crawling up the horrified and sweaty Bond as he lay in bed.[31] The scene from the film had been screened by the Dutch neuroscientist Christian Keysers during his lecture to the annual meeting of the American Association for the Advancement of Science in Washington, D.C. As audience members shivered and felt their own arms tingle while watching the tarantula inch its way up Bond's arm, Keysers told them that these sensations were produced by "mirror" mechanisms in their brains.

Mirror neurons could also explain the public's empathic reaction to politicians, an article on the front page of the *New York Times* announced in April 2004. "Using MRIs to See Politics on the Brain" presented preliminary results of an experiment funded by a political consultant firm and carried out by UCLA neuroscientist Marco Iacoboni. Early results showed that eleven politically sophisticated subjects had higher activity in mirror neuron areas (medial-orbitofrontal cortex) when subjects were watching videos of their preferred presidential candidate.[32] Iacoboni posited that subjects emotionally identified with their favored politicians and simulated the actions of these candidates through mirror neuron activity. The subjects did not actually move, however, because the concomitant firing of "super" mirror neurons signaled mirror neurons to inhibit actual movement.[33] When subjects viewed politicians with whom they disagreed, in contrast, the area of the dorsolateral prefrontal cortex, subserving rational thinking, showed elevated activity. Iacoboni concluded that these subjects were considering logical arguments to counter these candidates. He asserted that this brain scanning technique was superior to voter focus groups and psychological methods of polling; it was simply better suited "to figure out what is actually going on inside their heads."

When the study was completed that fall, however, subjects failed to show elevated activity in the medial-orbitofrontal areas while watching their own candidates. This finding threw the reliability of his results into question. Iacoboni speculated that the absence of activity may have been due to the increase in negative advertising over the summer, dulling the positive response.[34] He was hesitant however to put much weight on this ad hoc hypothesis. The *Toronto Star* nonetheless showcased his study in an article, "Politics on the Brain," pointing out a different but more reliable finding showing no differences between Democrats and Republicans in their emotional reaction to the use of force in political advertisements.[35]

The start of the next presidential election cycle generated yet another political scanning study. This time, the article that appeared on November 11, 2007, in the *New York Times* was written by Iacoboni and the political consultants themselves. Democrats and Republicans showed more empathy, measured as mirror neuron activity, for candidate Fred Thompson than for Rudy Giuliani, and both John McCain and Barack Obama failed to make significant impressions on the brains of their subjects.[36] The following year, psychologist George Lakoff explained in a radio interview that mirror neurons could register positive (and negative) feelings about a political figure. He relayed to the interviewer: "That tall, supple, smiling Obama figure, standing tall, fires up good feelings through the 'mirror neurons' in our brains. 'Up and forward' is *the effect we feel*."[37] Because mirror neurons detected and then simulated movement, one actually felt the "up and forward" effect of someone standing tall. The projection of one's own simulated movements of striving upward into a tall figure echoed the early understanding of aesthetic and kinesthetic empathy. Now, however, this feeling of movement was allied to the firing of mirror neurons.

The science journalist and psychologist Daniel Goleman explained in a 2006 newspaper article that mirror neurons "operate like neural WiFi" to produce emotional contagion and physiological rapport.[38] That year, he published a ten-year anniversary edition of his best seller *Social Intelligence* and described mirror neurons as ensuring "that the moment someone sees an emotion expressed on our face, they will at once sense that same feeling within themselves. And so our emotions are experienced not merely by ourselves in isolation but also by those around us—both covertly and openly."[39] A year later, he told readers of the *New York Times* that social neuroscience could explain why it was so easy to flame another on the internet. The social cues present in face-to-face interaction were processed in brain "circuitry centered on the orbitofrontal cortex, a center for empathy" that was simply not operative via email.[40]

Scientific American ran an extensive series of articles on mirror neurons, titled "Mirror Neurons and Autism," on the cover of its November 2006 issue. Inside, the reader discovered a lengthy article explaining the origins and workings of mirror neurons written by the Parma researchers, Rizzolatti, Fogassi, and Gallese, replete with images of brains, graphs of physiological activation, illustrations of dancers mirroring each other, and young guitar players imitating each other. The neuroscientist Vilayanur S. Ramachandran and his student Lindsay M. Oberman wrote the adjoining article, "Broken Mirrors," to explain that autism resulted from a malfunctioning mirror neuron system.[41] Ramachandran had already made the bold claim that the discovery of mirror neurons was as significant to neuroscience as the discovery of DNA had been for biology, a claim that circulated widely in the popular press.[42] An inset in the *Scientific American* piece declared that "when people use the expression 'I feel your pain,' they may not realize how literally it could be true."[43] "Literally" meant, of course, according to brain imaging that measures blood oxygenation from which mirror neuron activation is inferred. To merely *report* feeling pain or distress now no longer earned the moniker "literally" in the world of popular brain science.

Mirror neurons could also account for why people shop, as the article "Consumed with Guilt" explained, drawing on findings from the new field of neuroeconomics. When people viewed Cartier jewelry and Gucci handbags while undergoing brain scans, mirror neurons fired in supposed interest and excitement. In this 2009 study, however, researchers found to their surprise that activation in other areas of the brain—the insula and prefrontal cortex—signaled the presence of negative feelings as well. Researchers speculated that the economic recession had caused subjects not only to be excited about these luxury goods but also to feel disgusted by their extravagance. The monkey mirror neuron model was nonetheless still instructive for human consumers, the article concluded. "So if monkeys could shop, then Monkey A seeing Monkey B walking out of a store with a brand-new Bottega Veneta bag and a huge smile on its face could very well fire up Monkey A's neurons for a splurge."[44] Mirror neuron studies were also called upon in the *Wall Street Journal* to elucidate "How Your Brain Allows You to Walk in Another's Shoes."[45] And a Canadian reporter concluded that mirror neurons firing in the brains of excited sports fans meant that "you are right there in the game, swinging at every pitch and bracing for every bodycheck."[46] The article was titled "Go Neurons Go!"

Empathy as Simulation

Journalists have not been the only promoters of mirror neuron models of empathy to popular audiences. Neuroscientists have published an array of books aimed at general audiences, among them: *Mirrors in the Brain, Mirroring People: A Science of Empathy, The Empathic Brain,* and *The Tell-Tale Brain.*[47] These books seek to explain how mirror neurons simulate another person's actions, leading us to understand the meanings and even intentions of these actions. The underlying theory is that we empathically understand others by simulating their emotional states rather than by concocting an abstract conception of their thinking processes—the theory of mind, or mentalizing explanation for understanding others.[48] Proponents of simulation theory argue that the mirror perception-action system developed through evolution, with the neurons of the macaque monkey premotor cortex functioning as a neural correlate to human mirror neurons, some of which are also located in frontal areas. Mirror neurons, these neuroscientists claim, provide the brain mechanism for imitation, mimicry, and simulation as well as for language, empathy, and social learning.[49]

In his popular book *Mirroring People,* Marco Iacoboni showcased what he claims are the remarkable features of mirror neurons with his teacup experiment. Using PET scans, he tested subjects' neural activations while they perceived videotapes of three scenes of a hand reaching for a teacup with different intentions embedded in each scene. In the first scene, the actor picked up a teacup in an empty setting; in another, the teacup was lifted up from a table covered with dirty dishes; and in a third, the teacup was grasped from a table full of uneaten treats. The intentions in these different contexts were simply to grasp a cup, to clean a dirty cup, or to drink from a full cup. Results showed mirror neurons were most active while watching the scene in which the intention was simply to drink—supporting the conclusion that the basic biological function of drinking constituted a more fundamental intention than the others. According to Iacoboni, the pattern of mirror neuron activation showed that subjects understood the action as well as the intention or meaning behind the action. He concluded that "our brains are capable of mirroring the deepest aspects of the minds of others—intention is definitely one such aspect—at the fine-grained level of a *single brain cell.* This is utterly remarkable." We thus have no need to use inference or to draw on algorithms to grasp the intentions of others' actions. "Instead, we use mirror neurons, " Iacoboni asserts.[50]

Some neuroscientists have made the case for mirror neuron perception-action theories by culling the insights of pragmatic, or action-oriented, theories of mind, some of which date back to the early twentieth century. Giacomo Rizzolatti describes mirror neurons in his book, *Mirrors in the Brain* as pragmatic mediators of the relation between perception and action. Humans see possibilities of movement in their environments, an inclination that he illustrates throughout his book with the recurring gesture of picking up a cup of coffee. It is like "seeing with the hand," an expression Rizzolatti adopts from the social philosopher George Herbert Mead, mentor to Jessie Taft and Ernest Burgess, the early advocates of empathy. Rizzolatti cites Mead to explain how perception and simulation of action intertwine in the firing of mirror neurons: "We look because we handle, and we are able to handle because we look."[51]

Rizzolatti also finds J. J. Gibson's 1970s ecological model of perception illuminative of the way we immediately pick up the meanings of another's actions as "goal-centered movements."[52] Gibson argued that we perceive objects in our environments with a sense for the possibilities of interaction that such objects "afford" us. These affordances identify the latent interactive properties of objects and environments that make actions possible.[53] So, for instance, the affordance of a doorknob is for twisting, the affordance of a chair is for sitting. We simply see things in ways that allow us to do things with them. Mirror neurons may not convey the full meaning of an object, according to Rizzolatti, but they register these kinds of motor affordances. He explains that mirror neurons "respond only to certain aspects of the object (shape, size, orientation, etc.) and therefore their selectivity is important as these aspects are treated as systems of visual affordances and potential motor acts."[54]

Vittorio Gallese, another member of the original Parma group, has turned to the philosophers Edith Stein, Edmund Husserl, and Merleau-Ponty to support mirror neuron simulation theories. Gallese defines simulation as an "action-related sensori-motor process of knowing others and the world."[55] He finds Merleau-Ponty's conception of the bodily basis of perception illuminative of the action of mirror neurons: "It is as if the other person's intention inhabited my body and mine his."[56] Empathy is possible, Gallese argues, because of the existence of a "shared manifold of intersubjectivity," which exists at the level of everyday experience, at the level of observable behavior, and also at the subpersonal level at which mirror neurons fire.[57] A patient with Huntington's disease, for example, with damage to his insula and putamen, possessed a faulty subpersonal manifold. This neuronal deficit manifests not only in the patient's inability to experience disgust but also in his difficulty recognizing the expression of disgust in others.[58] Gallese expressed confidence that these century-old philosophical insights on the nature of intersubjectivity could now be applied to the level of brain function with the discovery of mirror neurons.

Neuroscientists Hannah and Antonio Damasio have also drawn on mirror models to explain why patients with damage to the somatosensory and prefrontal cortices fail to imagine emotions while viewing facial expressions.[59] Ethologist Frans de Waal and Stephanie Preston, director of an ecological neuroscience laboratory at the University of Michigan, have integrated a perception-action model into their comprehensive account of empathy. The researchers argue that the perception-action mechanism forms the basis not only for motor behavior but for emotional response and empathy as well.[60] The broad framework of perception-action encloses the myriad phenomena of emotional contagion, sympathy, cognitive empathy, helping behavior, and "true empathy," all of which, the researchers explain, "cannot be totally disentangled."

Relying on evidence from ethology, behavioral studies, and neurophysiology, de Waal and Preston explain the workings of mirror neurons. They corroborate their model of empathy by returning to Theodor Lipps's projection model of Einfühlung. They declare that empathy and projection are simply not in opposition: "There is no empathy that is not projection, since you always use your own representations to understand the state of another."[61] The subject assumes that his or her state is the same as that of the other, and success is determined by the presence of an actual similarity between the two. One study backed up these claims: subjects who first experienced a shock demonstrated greater empathic response to others' receiving shock at a later time. The authors concluded that developing one's cognitive abilities, broadening one's experience, and gaining greater affective congruence would increase one's ability to empathize with another.

Many current simulation theorists, surprisingly, invoke elements of early twentieth-century kinesthetic empathy. In 1909, psychologist Edward Titchener pinpointed the kinesthetic image, or the interlacing of perception with inner images of movement, as the basis for empathy. The intertwining of perception and action is central to many contemporary simulation models. In a 2004 study, for instance, subjects were asked to visually imagine rotating an image, and neural activity was charted in premotor areas of the brain.[62] Mentally imagining the movement, it turned out, produced neural activity in motor areas, interpreted to comprise a neuronal simulation of the movement. One theorist argues that images that elicit motor and visual responses capture the way an organism moves and engages with the environment.[63]

Interlaced visual and motor neural responses have also been documented in the viewing of art. Gallese collaborated with art historian David Freedberg to show that when subjects looked at abstract art, they imagined the gestures that might have produced the designs, for instance the hand's sweeping movement with a paintbrush.[64] One neuroaesthetic theorist declares the "imagery of motion to be at the heart of our capacities for both simulation and aesthetic experience."[65] Neuroscientist and Nobel Prize winner Eric Kandel explains in a popular piece that we are indebted to the activity of mirror neurons while viewing modern expressionist portraiture: "The sense of stimulation we often experience when we look at a portrait is thought to be due in part to the activity of 'mirror neurons.' Signaling by these cells in the motor areas of the brain can make us perceive the actions of others as if they were our own."[66] Kandel accords the brain with an ability to "form a representation of the face and of the body, analyze the body's motion, experience emotion, and perhaps, empathy."

If some neuroscientists have revived the early conception of empathy as a kind of simulation accomplished through the linking of visual and motor images, they now root the ability in mirror neuron activity. Some of the same debates, however, still resonate today, particularly the question: How much meaning can one attribute to a perceived movement? Back in 1905, psychologist Ethel Puffer saw Einfühlung as a way to capture the feeling of a moving line but insufficient to convey the full meaning of the aesthetic object. Just a few years later, Vernon Lee speculated that the empathic sense of a mountain rising felt as an emotional lifting up was never a pure appraisal of movement. To empathically project the feeling of movement always carried with it a rich set of associations and memories of this type of movement. The question as to how much meaning can be conveyed through an unadorned perception of movement is still with us today, especially in regard to the scope of simulation.

The Limits of Simulation

Even as the simulation theory of empathy has received great attention in neuroscience and has been disseminated widely in the popular media, the model has been subject to increasing scrutiny. Critics argue that neuronal simulation might make it possible to grasp the intention of a movement, but it does not allow for the immediate apprehension of social and communicative intentions.[67] Empathy, according to many psychologists and neuroscientists, is more complex than motor resonance or simulation: it entails the understanding of the other person's perspective as well as the ability to clearly distinguish the self from the other.

The philosopher Pierre Jacob and cognitive scientist Marc Jeannerod have pointed out the flaws in simulation theories by imagining the differences between perceiving Dr. Jekyll holding a scalpel and Mr. Hyde wielding one.[68] The mirror neuron simulations might be identical, but they cannot code for the understanding of Hyde's ill intentions in contrast to Jekyll's benevolent ones. To make this judgment, the critics argue, one needs an additional, higher level of processing. Jacob argues that the human mirror neuron system is much more complex than the monkey models in which single neurons are activated. For instance, mirror neurons that fire when observing an act of grasping can also fire for a related motor act—that of drinking, for example. The chains of neurons in the human mirror neuron system do much more than simply simulate or replicate another's movement, Jacob contends. They can also predict the next movement on the basis of the motor act and contextual cues.[69]

Further, Jacob and Jeannerod question whether it is indeed necessary to enact motor simulations to gauge others' intentions. They cite a well-known study of "apparent behavior" dating back to the 1940s.[70] Subjects watched animated geometric shapes moving around and into an opening in a box. In describing the movements, subjects commonly ascribed intentions to the moving triangles and squares: the triangle was deliberately getting in the way of the square, and the square was chasing after the triangle. The regular attribution of human or animal-like movements to geometric shapes revealed that a simulation of actual human movements was not necessary to impute intentions to human actions. Rizzolatti has conceded that simulation is not necessary to understand others' movements, but he asserts that the activation of the parietal-frontal mirror neuron circuit allows us to understand action from the "inside," or as a possibility of movement for us.[71]

Others have been more strident in their critiques. The Berkeley psychologist Alison Gopnik called the penchant to invoke mirror neurons to explain helping behavior "a new scientific myth" in *Slate* magazine.[72] She cautioned against the simple transfer of function from studies of monkeys to that of humans and questioned the idea that one type of cell underlies one type of experience: mirror neuron systems in humans tell us about large portions of the brain, not individual neurons. Her conclusion: "It is little more than a lovely metaphor to say that our mirror neurons bring us together."

In 2014, the cognitive psychologist Gregory Hickok published a book-length analysis and critique of the claims that mirror neurons underlie language, the understanding of others, theory of mind, and empathy. In *The Myth of Mirror Neurons*, he closely examined the original 1992 study of mirror neurons to discover that there were only a small number of perceptual-motor neurons that fired when monkeys watched an action similar to one they had performed. Other neurons in the macaque F5 area fired when different, complementary actions were enacted, neurons not investigated by the Parma team.[73] Hickok does not contest evidence that the mirror system processes motor action concepts but argues that the hub where such processing would likely take place is not in primary motor cortex or Broca's area, asserted by mirror neuron advocates, but rather the posterior superior temporal sulcus (STS).[74] Because the mirror neuron system in the human brain extends across a number of brain areas, Hickok finds problematic the idea that the motor cortex is the primary locus for action understanding.

Hickok deems simulation to be simply inadequate to generate meaning, which he finds dependent on higher-level processing. Mirror neurons allow a direct matching between the observation and the execution of an action, which, he allows, could explain the simple resonance we feel to another's action. But this fact fails to explain how mirror neurons decide how to mirror at the outset of the task.[75] In Hickok's view, mirror neurons rely on the complicated architecture of a cognitive system, which then significantly reduces the power of mirror neurons themselves. As he repeatedly intones throughout his book, "the meaning simply is not in the movement," a remarkable echo of early debates on aesthetic empathy.[76]

The impact of these critiques has been sifting into popular accounts. A neurobiologist at the University of Chicago questioned whether mirror neurons could capture the intentions of actions in a 2015 article in *Scientific American* attached to de Waal's photograph-rich feature article "Do Animals Feel Empathy?" She decried the "paint by numbers" interpretation of brain scans and posited instead that complex brain circuits underlie empathic processes.[77]

Beyond Mirror Neurons

Mirror neuron empathy has received the bulk of the attention in popular sources, but empathy has also been examined within other neuroscientific frameworks. One 2006 headline in the *New York Times* provocatively proclaimed "When Bad People Are Punished, Men Smile (but Women Don't)," describing neuroscientist Tania Singer's findings that while playing a game, men showed little empathy for cheaters as measured by brain scans.[78] When male subjects watched those who had previously cheated get shocked, fMRI scans showed no activation in areas of the brain that were linked to empathy for another's pain (fronto-insular and anterior cingulate cortices). Women showed some activation for cheaters, but less than for the honest players. The researchers also found activation in reward areas of the men's brains, which they correlated with an expressed desire for revenge.[79] Because the perceived fairness of the game significantly reduced the empathy response for men, the report concluded that women were more empathic than men.

The cognitive neuroscientist Cordelia Fine describes repeated attempts to delineate neural differences between men and women as falling into a familiar "neurosexism."[80] She skewers the idea that there is an "E-type" or empathic female brain in contrast to the male "S-type" or systematizing brain. British psychologist Simon Baron-Cohen, director of the Autism Research Center at the University of Cambridge, suggests that the female brain is shaped by low levels of testosterone and is more attuned to another's mental state than the male brain, which is trained on perceiving lawful regularities. He bases this theory on the tendency for autism to afflict more males than females and on experiments that showed that boy babies preferred to look at mobiles, whereas girl babies favored faces. For Baron-Cohen, empathy is the preeminent sign of femininity.

Baron-Cohen and Sally Wheelwright developed the Empathy Quotient Scale (EQ) to assess these differences.[81] Subjects were asked to agree or disagree to sixty questions (twenty of which are fillers) that included: "I can easily work out what another person might want to talk about"; "I am very blunt, which some people take to be rudeness, even though this is unintentional"; "Friendships and relationships are just too difficult so I tend not to bother with them."[82] Subjects with autism scored lower than matched controls on the EQ, and women showed slightly higher scores than men. The authors took these results as indicative of the reliability of the instrument, even as they offered this caveat: "Whether this reflects women's greater willingness to report empathic behavior or their higher levels of underlying empathy cannot be determined by this study."[83] Self-report questionnaires, as they point out, are dependent not only on individuals' beliefs but also on subjects' states of mind when they take the test. The researchers nonetheless mailed these questionnaires to subjects and were therefore not in a position to determine the mental state of any subject when completing the battery.

Cognitive and emotional empathy are now commonly differentiated in the neuroscience literature. One study finds that these two types of empathy are dissociated in the disorders of autism and psychopathy (a term with a very different meaning than in the first half of the twentieth century). The psychopathic type, now deemed a callous impulsive person with limited capacity for remorse, leans toward a deficiency in emotional empathy, whereas those with autism suffer from impairments in cognitive empathy.[84] Those with Asperger's syndrome demonstrated deficits in cognitive empathy but not in emotional empathy using subscales of the Interpersonal Reactivity Index. These subjects, however, scored higher on the empathic distress subscale.[85] Patients with schizophrenia were also found to score higher on this subscale, while showing deficits in cognitive empathy or mentalizing. Given the wide range of schizophrenic conditions, however, the researchers urged caution, noting that paranoid patients tended to over-mentalize.[86]

Neuroscientist Jean Decety has investigated both the emotional and cognitive elements of empathic response when subjects view others in pain. In his neuroimaging studies, he adopted a test for empathy developed by social psychologist C. Daniel Batson, who has researched the finer dimensions of empathy and altruism for more than four decades. In 1997, Batson and collaborators Shannon Early and Giovanni Salvarini asked subjects to listen to "Katie's" story, which narrated her struggle to take care of her younger siblings after the death of their parents.[87] The researchers asked subjects to first imagine her- or himself in Katie's position, and in the second condition to imagine Katie undergoing the experience. Not surprisingly, subjects felt more distress when they imagined *themselves* losing their own parents and caring for siblings than when they imagined Katie experiencing the loss.

Ten years later, Decety took up Batson's research design to test these psychological distinctions in a neuroimaging study conducted with Claus Lamm, director of the Social, Cognitive, and Affective Neuroscience Unit at the University of Vienna.[88] Subjects imagined themselves undergoing a painful medical procedure in one condition, and they imagined others enduring the same procedure in the second condition. When subjects imagined *themselves* in the situation, they reported higher personal distress than when imagining others. Their distress was accompanied by stronger activation in brain areas responsible for motivational-affective dimensions of pain (the anterior medial cingulate cortex, or ACC). The researchers concluded that the two conditions of "imagining the self" and "imagining the other" were not only phenomenologically different but also neurally distinct.

Decety has examined a variety of situational factors that influence the neuronal signatures of empathy. The disposition of the empathizer, the nature of the relationship, and the context in which the exchange takes place all modulate brain activation. In one study, subjects watched patients undergo a painful treatment and were told that the treatment was either effective or ineffective. Subjects observed the exact same medical procedure but showed differing patterns of neural activation depending on whether the intervention produced positive or negative results. The different cognitive appraisals produced different patterns of neural activation in two subregions of the orbitofrontal cortex and in the rostral part of the medial cingulate cortex (MCC).[89] Decety reports that even as automatic neural activation occurs when subjects view others in pain, subjects modulate their neuronal responses with input from social and informational contexts and by shifting their attention.[90] Results from some of these experiments have been aired in popular venues: one 2008 article reported that children seem to respond similarly to adults when observing scenes of others experiencing pain.[91] But when children watched scenes of someone intentionally being hurt, brain areas governing moral reasoning also became active, indicating that children engaged a complex cognitive response.

Decety and the cognitive neuroscientist Philip Jackson presented an ambitious overview of the functional architecture of human empathy in 2004.[92] Their multidimensional account begins with a simulation-based perception-action system that may be based on mirror neuron activity. But simulation, either unconscious or conscious, they contend, is not yet empathy. Empathy means that one never loses sight of the other: "without self-awareness and emotional-regulation processing, there is no true empathy."[93] Perceiving another's pain activates only a portion of one's own pain networks, thus producing measurable neural differences between actually experiencing pain and empathizing with another's pain.[94] The contribution of right inferior parietal lobe activation (at the temporoparietal junction, or TPJ) signals the capacity to discriminate whether it is the self or another that is feeling pain.[95] To empathize thus requires the mental flexibility to adopt another's position to override one's default egoistic stance. The neuroscientists conclude that empathy entails multiple dissociable neural mechanisms that underpin the main components of empathy, which include: "shared neural representations, self-awareness, mental flexibility, and emotional regulation."[96] Because empathy entails multiactivation across different brain areas, Decety and Jackson conclude, "We do not assume that there is a unitary empathy system (or module) in the brain."[97]

Social psychologists, philosophers, and neuroscientists have all grappled with empathy's complexities.[98] Stephanie Preston and collaborators asked subjects to "actively project oneself into the shoes of another person" while testing subjects on psychophysiological measures and PET scans.[99] Subjects imagined a time when they experienced fear or anger and were asked to choose one of seven different scenarios that they found most familiar to them. The following story was judged to be highly relatable: "You are riding in the car with your friend, crossing over a train track. You see that a train is coming closer and closer. You are not driving and have no control over the wheel and cannot run away. Your heart is pumping and you are scared. You see the train approaching. The train actually hits the car and it is smashing in your side of the car. Picture yourself in that situation and feel as scared as you can." Subjects showed similar patterns of neuro-activation when they remembered their own emotional experience of fear and anger and when they imagined another person in one of the situations they deemed familiar, such as the above scenario. But subjects demonstrated different patterns of neuro-activation in the left hemisphere and higher order visual association areas when attempting to imagine or empathize with others in the unfamiliar scenarios.

To effectively empathize with others, the authors concluded, we rely on our own representations of similar kinds of experience to simulate or "try on" another's experience. Of course, if I am similarly neurologically active when I imagine my own experience and when I imagine another's relatable experience, perhaps I am just "projecting" my own experiences into another. The authors concede that this was indeed possible, as they could not determine whether subjects were in fact responding to another's experience while trying to empathize or were simply activating their own memories of a similar experience.[100] This experiment reveals, once again, how difficult it is to sharpen the blurry line between projection and empathy.

One recent review of studies on the neuroscience of empathy stresses the importance of correlating behavioral or self-report findings with measures of neural activation. Jamil Zaki and Daniel Ochsner find that many studies use an artificial testing situation to link neural signatures to empathy without concomitant behavioral input or reports from subjects that they indeed felt empathy.[101] The authors note that activation in the anterior insula while viewing another in pain, for instance, may not mean sharing in the perceived pain, because the insula performs many other cognitive tasks. One might be instead remembering one's own experiences of pain or simply feeling personal distress. Simply equating a particular emotion with neuro-activation and overlooking a subject's self-reports of his or her own feeling states may be misleading.[102]

Tania Singer has separated out the processes of mentalizing (theory of mind) from empathizing (sharing of emotions) but understands both functions to be commonly used by normal adults. In a neuroeconomic study, she defined empathy as the motivational basis for behaviors that take the other into account.[103] When playing a game such as prisoner's dilemma, for example, one relies on a belief about an opponent's personality to determine whether he or she will cooperate or not, but to make correct predictions one also needs to be aware of the other player's feelings and motivational state. We typically predict the behavior of others with input from both mentalizing and empathizing systems. Evidence shows that cognitive and emotional empathy have distinct but also common neuronal activation patterns; a number of researchers agree that "cognitive and affective empathy are not mutually exclusive processes."[104]

To define empathy then only as a narrow emotional resonance with those of one's kin is a minority position.[105] Although numerous studies show that empathy is strongest with those of one's social group, many researchers now define empathy more broadly to include emotional regulation and top-down processing that link subcortical sites like the amygdala to the prefrontal cortex. Rigidly separating emotional from cognitive processing may oversimplify brain connectivity. According to one historian, the stark divide often made between emotion and cognition is a historical artifact of an outdated moralism.[106] Some theorists view cognitive appraisal as inherent to emotion; philosopher Martha Nussbaum goes as far as to label emotions "upheavals of thought."[107] Psychologists have also come to question the existence of universal, basic emotions relatively immune to cultural and situational factors. Humanities scholar Daniel Gross and neuroscientist Stephanie Preston argue that generic empathy may be, in fact, a different emotion than empathy for Holocaust victims. They also suggest that racial fear would likely register differently in the brain from other forms of fear. Situated emotions of this kind, the authors surmise, may indeed have different neurological signatures.[108]

The view of empathy as a flexible process, drawing on different subsystems, with voluntary, conscious components as well as unconscious elements evokes a rich, multiphasic model of the ability, malleable to training and to social and cognitive interventions. In natural settings, empathy relies on a variety of subsystems depending on the demands of the task, the situation, and the empathizer. The best neuroscientific models, in Zaki and Ochsner's estimation, go beyond an "either/or" model to a "when/how" model of empathy that "posits that perceivers flexibly deploy multiple, interactive processes when they are relevant to current social goals and cues."[109] With regard to the question as to whether a simulationist or a mentalizing conception of empathy leads to helpful or prosocial behavior, these authors conclude that the answer is beholden to the experimental design!

If neuroscientific findings have been enthusiastically and often uncritically embraced in public forums in the past decades, critics have recently raised the specter of neurocentrism or, even more acerbically, "neurononsense."[110] The *New York Times* columnist David Brooks underscored his claim that the "brain is not the mind" in a recent review of books on the brain sciences. He advises readers to be a little skeptical about what a brain scan says.[111] Critics from a host of fields have advocated for a more measured application of neuroscientific findings to human social psychology and cognition and have questioned the impulse to think through every social problem in neurological terms.[112] The developmental neuropsychologist Dorothy Bishop at Oxford finds it problematic to assume that brain scans are more authoritative than behavioral data. If you want to know if people like music better with their eyes closed, she counsels, the best way to find out is to set up experimental and control conditions and ask them, rather than assuming a brain scan of blood flow offers a more direct window onto emotional satisfaction.[113]

Popular audiences are nonetheless fascinated to hear about the brain mechanisms of empathy, which have revealed, among other findings, an ability to connect with animals, and the understanding of prejudice as a muting of brain activation. One lengthy *New York Times* article featured veterans suffering from PTSD who experienced empathy with abused parrots. The article called empathy a "long-ago, neuronally ingrained bioevolutionary tool for survival."[114] The veterans received comfort and healing from these parrots, which one badly injured helicopter squad member described as follows: "They look at you, and they don't judge. . . . It's pure." In 2015, the *New York Times Magazine* featured the research of two MIT neuroscientists, Emile Bruneau and Rebecca Saxe, who found an "empathy gap" in the brain characterized by muted empathic activation for those in conflict groups or outgroups.[115] *Slate* magazine showcased studies on implicit, nonempathic, even racist responses when white subjects viewed black subjects in pain.[116] A study conducted in Milan, Italy, revealed that Caucasians who watched Africans get touched by a needle on the hand exhibited lower skin conductance rates produced by the brain's pain network (anterior cingulate cortex) than when watching Caucasians get poked.[117] Another study found that white subjects—from college students to nurses—assumed that African Americans feel less pain than whites, although further testing revealed that this belief was attributed to perceptions of enduring difficulty and social status, not race per se.[118] And white subjects in a Canadian experiment did not show the same mirror neuron activation (the suppression of EEG oscillations in the 8–13 Hz mu frequency) when watching people of different ethnic groups pick up a glass of water and take a sip. Subjects showed the least activation when watching South Asians, moderate levels for blacks, and the highest for East Asians. Researchers translated these activation levels into intensities of prejudice.[119]

Investigators have not only documented prejudice as reduced neural activation, but have also probed whether experimental manipulations might alter prejudicial responses. White subjects were instructed to mimic the actions of the South Asians and black subjects by actually picking up a glass of water. Those who mimicked the action exhibited less implicit racism on tests conducted after the exercise than those who did not.[120] The researchers concluded that "mimicry reduces racial prejudice." The malleability of prejudice was also demonstrated in a brain imaging study of Israelis and Arabs who read political statements of those on the opposite side of the conflict. The neuroscientist Emile Bruneau identified three outliers whose brain activation did not conform to the expected biases and later discovered they were peace activists.[121]

If we look to neuroscience for evidence that empathy is hardwired and built into our biological systems, we discover that not only can its neural underpinnings be modulated but that they are also still up for debate. Bruneau declares that recordings of fMRI scans of subjects watching another get jabbed with a needle is "not empathy," which he considers to be something one does, not merely something one feels.[122] To make sense of neural patterns, neuroscientists have to agree on empathy's parameters. It is easy to forget that measures of brain activation are directly dependent on the capacity to describe, to illuminate, and to think through the meanings of empathy, a task that has occupied a diverse array of scholars over the past hundred years.

In 2007, the Tibetan Buddhist monk and theoretical biologist Mathieu Ricard entered an MRI scanner to evaluate his capacity for empathy and compassion. He had just viewed a BBC documentary depicting physically and mentally disabled children, many of them skeletal, living in a hospital in Romania. In the scanner he was instructed to feel empathy, and his brain activity was monitored in real time (fMRI-rt). He "pictured as intensely as possible these nameless sufferings" but soon found it intolerable. He then shifted the focus of his meditation, and the neuroscientist conducting the study, Tania Singer, asked him, "What are you doing? It doesn't look at all like what we usually observe when people feel empathy for someone else's suffering." Studies had shown that when non-meditators saw someone receive a painful electrical shock, they demonstrated activity in the anterior insula and cingulate, a response characterized as empathy. Ricard explained that he had begun to meditate on unconditional compassion in order to feel love and kindness for the children's suffering. His shift in attention transformed his mental landscape, and according to Singer, brain areas associated with the positive emotions became engaged.[123]

Empathy, defined in this study as intensely feeling the pain of Romanian orphans, produced a different brain signature than that of compassion, the expression of loving and positive feelings for the children. But feeling another's pain in such an unmitigated fashion is only one among many definitions of empathy. Ricard himself defines empathy in his popular 2013 book *Altruism* as both an "*affective resonance* with the others' feelings and *to become cognitively aware of his situation.*"[124] Empathy entails more than feeling another's pain; it is also the capacity to engage in an "extended altruism" that transcends "the ties of family and tribal proximity."[125] Ricard calls empathy the catalytic reaction that transforms altruistic love into compassion.

Whether we automatically empathize with our mirror neurons and/or activate a complex set of neural patterns to imagine taking on the position of another, Ricard observes that this is an ability we can educate. We have been keen to cultivate our intelligence and individualism in Western culture, but we have not similarly trained our empathy, altruism, or compassion. Through initiatives to promote "an enlightened education," he suggests, we might just do that.[126]

Conclusion

The psychologist delights in the use of recording instruments—galvanometers, kymographs, and scales of all kinds. Yet strange to say he discredits the most delicate of all recording instruments—himself.

—GORDON W. ALLPORT

EMPATHY AS A MEANS to step inside another's experience to grasp it more fully has been popular ever since World War II.[1] But as we have seen, the historical origins of empathy lie in the arts. Empathy used to mean placing ourselves in the world about us: in the curve of a rolling hill, in the towering height of a column, in the swirls of a modernist design, even in the shape of grape. This imaginative stretch is accomplished through what one philosopher recently called "aesthetic semblances," a term the psychologist J. Mark Baldwin suggested more than a hundred years ago as the best translation for Einfühlung. Semblance or empathy in this guise is an act of the aesthetic imagination—not as artful window dressing but as a key capacity for connection.

In 1974, the philosopher Thomas Nagel famously called on empathy to answer the question: "What is it like to be a bat?"[2] If speculating on the bat's experience might constitute an anthropomorphic error, animal experts have recently argued that the greater mistake is anthropocentrism, or the belief that only human intelligence, feeling, and experience count.[3] Frans de Waal tells the story of the female bonobo Kuni who picked up a starling it had captured, climbed to the highest limb on a tree, carefully unfolded the wings of the bird, and then threw it into the air.[4] A tendency toward anthropocentrism, according to contemporary theorists of materiality, blocks the recognition that animals, other beings, and even things, possess their own nature.[5]

If the sensibilities of a bat, a bird, or even of a rock or tree lie beyond human empathy, it may still be the case that inner "experience" of some sort exists for these creatures and objects.[6] Can we envision the possible experiences of a rock? Or the hidden life of trees, living in forest communities with a language all their own?[7] To imagine extending the mind into things was common to early twentieth-century proponents of aesthetic empathy, many of whom also thought that matter and mind were not wholly distinct. There may be benefits to developing this kind of eco-empathy today as we rush headlong toward climate catastrophe.

Over the past one hundred years, empathy has conveyed notions of fusion, identity, and similarity as well as projection, separation, and difference. Empathy matches one's experience to something or someone else, but it also marks difference. We might feel "empathic unsettlement" when we hear about Holocaust experiences that we cannot fully grasp. To empathize with art born of trauma can produce an "encounter with something irreducible and different, often inaccessible," explains art theorist Jill Bennett.[8] Some neuroscientists posit that empathy hinges on the ability to distinguish the self from the other. The philosopher Edith Stein declared in 1916 that empathy grasps an experience which is, by definition, <u>not</u> our own but another's.[9] E. B. Titchener, one translator of the term, described the workings of empathy in 1915 in this way: "Everything is strange, but it is to us that the strange experience has come."[10] An empathic stretch toward the different, the strange, or even the unfathomable awakens us to the actuality of the unique, singular lives of others. In the words of a contemporary philosopher, "We recognize each other *in our difference* as equals."[11] Novelist Colum McCann calls empathy a way "to inhabit an otherness beyond ourselves."[12] Empathy draws us into what can be known in others and in things, but also into what cannot be known.

How far then can empathy take us? Alfred Koestler wrote presciently in 1944 that "our awareness seems to shrink in direct ratio as communications expand; the world is open to us as never before, and we walk about as prisoners, each in his private portable cage." He continued: "A dog run over by a car upsets our emotional balance and digestion, three million Jews killed in Poland cause but a moderate uneasiness. Statistics don't bleed; it is the detail which counts. We are unable to embrace the total process with our awareness; we can only focus on little lumps of reality."[13]

If focusing only on little lumps of reality is, for some, the problem of empathy, a host of theorists over the past century have imagined empathy to be precisely that effortful task to expand our awareness and to widen the compass of the self through the inclusion of many different others. Kenneth Clark lamented the fact that empathy was not cultivated in American culture; schools and universities were keen to whip up competition but did not teach empathy. He knew all too well that "chauvinistic empathy" for one's own ilk was so easy to come by that it posed a danger to the human species. Today, neuroscientists call it "parochial empathy" and find that it can be mitigated when subjects listen to narrative descriptions of individuals from social and ethnic groups unfamiliar to them.[14]

In 1954, Gordon Allport defined empathy as the ability to perceive individuality rather than a blunt stereotype. To detect the uniqueness of another person, however, the self needed to be honed as a fine-tuned psychological instrument. In 1916 Jessie Taft admonished the factory owner to recognize how his actions ramified throughout the entire system. Wisdom, she declared, entailed the conscious knowledge that the self was distributed: it included many different others. And to engage empathy for Clark was to challenge the unquestioned association of whiteness with power and privilege.

Across the historical arc of empathy's meanings from projection to self-abnegation, from imaginative flight to empirical validity, empathy continues to be a technology of the self. In its earliest meanings, the self artfully expanded or projected into shapes, objects, or designs to make the world in its own image. In its later renditions, however, empathy shrank the self so as to better appreciate another's experience. Empathy, in its many varieties, offers an oblique and sometimes direct challenge to the idea that we are enclosed selves, sharply defined against the world and others.

I have come to see empathic connection more often than I once did: in the pink sky spreading behind the dark knotty trees at twilight, and at moments when habitual judgments and usual opinions give way and another's experience takes the stage. The ways in which we imagine empathy are important, for these imaginings themselves can open out new possibilities for connection. History tells us that empathy comprises a complex, artful but also effortful practice that enrolls feeling, intellect, and imagination. Empathy dares us to move beyond the habitual borders of the self to reach toward another human being, animal, art object, or the natural world. We need the self to empathize, but we also have to leave it behind. This is one of empathy's mysteries, but it is also its promise.

Notes

Introduction

1. Andy Clark and David Chalmers, "The Extended Mind," *Analysis* 58, no. 1 (1998): 7–19. Brian Rotman writes that we are "being-beside ourselves" in the modern world and our dissolving I "bleeds outwards into the collective which in turn introjects, insinuates, and internalized itself within the 'me.'" Brian Rotman, *Becoming beside Ourselves: The Alphabet, Ghosts, and Distributed Human Being* (Durham: Duke University Press, 2008), 99.

2. Frans de Waal, *The Age of Empathy: Nature's Lessons for a Kinder Society* (New York: Harmony Books, 2009); Jeremy Rifkin, *The Empathic Civilization: The Race to Global Consciousness in a World in Crisis* (New York: J. P. Tarcher/Penguin, 2009); Nicholas Kristof and Sheryl Wudunn, *A Path Appears: Transforming Lives, Creating Opportunity* (New York: Alfred A. Knopf, 2014).

3. Rifkin, *Empathic Civilization*, 544–546; Daniel Goleman, Richard E. Boyatzis, and Annie McKee, *The New Leaders: Transforming the Art of Leadership into the Science of Results* (London: Sphere, 2002).

4. Rifkin, *Empathic Civilization*, 546, 554–555. Rifkin presents a telescoped history of empathy, however, jumping from Goethe to psychoanalyst Heinz Kohut.

5. *Emotional Intelligence: Empathy* (Boston: Harvard Business Review Press, 2017).

6. Keith O'Brien, "Empathy Is So Yesterday," Ideas, *Boston Sunday Globe*, October 17, 2010; Jamil Zaki, "What Me Care? A Recent Study Finds a Decline in Empathy among Young People in the U.S.," *Scientific American* 21 (2010): 14–15.

7. Gary Olson, *Empathy Imperiled: Capitalism, Culture and the Brain* (New York: Springer, 2013).

8. Nicholas Kristof, "Where Is the Empathy?" *New York Times*, January 24

2015; See also Kristof, "How Do We Increase Empathy?" *New York Times*, January 29, 2015.

9. Susan Lanzoni, Robert Brain, and Allan Young, eds., "Varieties of Empathy in Science, Art and History" *Science in Context* 25, no. 3 (2012).

10. Casey Kelbauth, "I Know How You're Feeling, I Read Chekhov," *New York Times*, October 3, 2011; David Comer Kidd and Emanuele Castano, "Reading Literary Fiction Improves Theory of Mind," *Science* 342, no. 6156 (October 18, 2013): 377–380.

11. Tom Kelley and David Kelley, *Creative Confidence: Unleashing the Creative Potential within Us All* (New York: Crown, 2013), 85–89, 222–224.

12. Natasha Singer, "The Fountain of Old Age," *New York Times*, February 6, 2011; http://www.empathybelly.org/.

13. See http://grist.org/climate-energy/newtown-tragedy-empathy-and-grow ing-our-circle-of-concern/; http://dotearth.blogs.nytimes.com/2012/12 /20/empathy-as-a-path-to-climate-and-energy-progress/; http://www.wbur .org/cognoscenti/2017/02/22/empathy-as-resistance-adversaries-shouldnt -see-trump-as-monster-steven-wineman?utm_source=cc&utm_medium =email&utm_campaign=nwsltr-17-02-24.

14. J. D. Trout, *The Empathy Gap: Building Bridges to the Good Life and the Good Society* (New York: Viking, 2009), 36–38. Trout argues that empathy should be combined with disciplined action and rational analysis. Daniel Goleman has written on the empathy gap between rich and poor: http:// opinionator.blogs.nytimes.com/2013/10/05/rich-people-just-care-less/.

15. Jeneen Interlandi, "The Brain's Empathy Gap," *New York Times*, March 19, 2015; Emile G. Bruneau, Nicholas Dufour, and Rebecca Saxe, "Social Cognition in Members of Conflict Groups: Behavioural and Neural Responses in Arabs, Israelis and South Americans to Each Other's Misfortunes," *Philosophical Transactions of the Royal Society B* 367, no. 1589 (2012): 717–730.

16. Michael Kraus, Stéphane Côté, and Dacher Keltner, "Social Class, Contextualism and Empathic Accuracy," *Psychological Science* 21, no. 11 (November 2010): 1716–1723. http://www.nytimes.com/2014/07/27/opinion /sunday/powerful-and-coldhearted.html.

17. http://www.huffingtonpost.com/george-lakoff/empathy-sotomayor -and-dem_b_209406.html.

18. Mark Honigsbaum, "Barack Obama and the 'Empathy Deficit,'" *Guardian/Observer*, January 4, 2013, http://www.theguardian.com/science /2013/jan/04/barack-obama-empathy-deficit. This article is drawn from Honigsbaum's blog, "The Politics of Empathy," *The History of Emotions*, December 3, 2012, which cites my research on the translation of "empathy": Susan Lanzoni, "Empathy in Translation: Movement and Image in the Psychological Laboratory," *Science in Context* 25, no. 3 (2012): 301–327.

19. Orrin Hatch was cited on ABC's *This Week*; Josh Gerstein, "Obama's

Search for 'Empathy' Shapes Supreme Court Replacement Debate," *Politico*, May 4, 2009.

20. William Safire, "Empathy for Empty Pockets," On Language, *New York Times*, May, 17, 2009; David Brooks, "The Empathy Issue," *New York Times*, May 28, 2009.

21. Susan Lanzoni, "Sympathy in Mind, 1876–1900," *Journal of the History of Ideas* 70, no. 2 (2009): 265–287.

22. Lauren Wispé, *The Psychology of Sympathy* (New York: Plenum Press, 1991), 79.

23. Nicholas Wade, "Scientist Finds the Beginnings of Morality in Primate Behavior," *New York Times*, March 20, 2007.

24. de Waal, *Age of Empathy*, 89, also 102–103.

25. Ibid., 2, 43. See also Franz de Waal, *Primates and Philosophers: How Morality Evolved* (Princeton: Princeton University Press, 2006).

26. de Waal, *Age of Empathy*, 116–117.

27. Rita Charon, *Narrative Medicine: Honoring the Stories of Illness* (Oxford: Oxford University Press, 2006); Charon, "Narrative Medicine: A Model for Empathy, Reflection, Profession, and Trust," *JAMA* 286 (October 17, 2001): 1897–1902; Ellen Singer More and Maureen A. Milligan, *The Empathic Practitioner: Empathy, Gender and Medicine* (New Brunswick: Rutgers University Press, 1994); Howard Spiro, ed., *Empathy and the Practice of Medicine: Beyond Pills and the Scalpel* (New Haven: Yale University Press, 1993).

28. Charon cites psychoanalyst Roy Schafer who described empathy in 1959 as giving up one's own ego and trying on the ego of another. Charon, *Narrative Medicine*, 132–133.

29. Jodi Halpern, *From Detached Concern to Empathy: Humanizing Medical Practice* (Oxford: Oxford University Press, 2001).

30. Suzanne Koven, "Actors Help Medical Professionals Learn to Convey Empathy," *Boston Globe*, March 25, 2013, 12–14.

31. Giuseppe Di Pellegrino, Luciano Fadiga, Leonardo Fogassi, Vittorio Gallese, and Giacomo Rizzolatti, "Understanding Motor Events: A Neurophysiological Study," *Experimental Brain Research* 91 (1992): 176–180; Giacomo Rizzolatti, Luciano Fadiga, Vittorio Gallese, and Leonardo Fogassi, "Premotor Cortex and the Recognition of Motor Actions," *Cognitive Brain Research* 3, no. 2 (1996): 131–141.

32. Jean Decety and Claus Lamm, "Human Empathy through the Lens of Social Neuroscience," *Scientific World Journal* 6 (2006): 1146–1163.

33. Paul Bloom, "The Perils of Empathy," *Wall Street Journal*, December 2, 2016; Paul Bloom, *Against Empathy: The Case for Rational Compassion* (New York: Ecco, 2016).

34. See http://www.zocalopublicsquare.org/2017/07/17/sorry-reading-jane -austen-doesnt-make-better-person/ideas/nexus/; http://www.zocalopublic

square.org/2017/07/17/culture-empathy-perpetuating-inequality/ideas
/nexus/, both accessed July 17, 2017.

35. C. Daniel Batson, "These Things Called Empathy: Eight Related but
    Distinct Phenomena," in *The Social Neuroscience of Empathy*, ed. Jean De-
    cety and William Ickes (Cambridge: MIT Press, 2009).

36. Halpern, *From Detached Concern to Empathy*, 77.

37. J. Decety, ed. *Empathy: From Bench to Bedside* (Cambridge: MIT Press,
    2011); Amy Coplan and Peter Goldie, eds., *Empathy: Philosophical and Psy-
    chological Perspectives* (Oxford: Oxford University Press, 2011); Robin
    Curtis and Gertrud Koch, eds., *Einfühlung* (Munich: Wilhelm Fink,
    2009).

38. Theodor Reik, *Surprise and the Psycho-Analyst: On the Conjecture and Com-
    prehension of Unconscious Processes* (London: Kegan Paul, 1936), 192.

39. Mark H. Davis, *Empathy: A Social Psychological Approach* (Boulder: West-
    view Press, 1996), 11.

40. Wispé, *Psychology of Sympathy*, 79.

41. Ute Frevert, *Emotions in History—Lost and Found* (Budapest: Central Eu-
    ropean University Press, 2011), 12.

42. See Edith Stein's 1916 dissertation, published as *On the Problem of Empa-
    thy*, trans. Waltraut Stein (The Hague: Nijhoff, 1964); Edmund Husserl's
    Fifth Cartesian Meditation in *Cartesian Meditations*, trans. Dorion Cairns
    (The Hague: Nijhoff, 1960); Edmund Husserl, *Ideas Pertaining to a Pure
    Phenomenology and to a Phenomenological Philosophy*, trans. F. Kersten (Dor-
    drecht: Kluwer [1913], 1982); Max Scheler, *The Nature of Sympathy*, trans.
    Peter Heath (New Haven: Yale University Press, 1954); Wilhelm Dil-
    they, "Ideas Concerning a Descriptive and Analytic Psychology," in *De-
    scriptive Psychology and Historical Understanding*, trans. Zaner and Heiges
    (The Hague: Nijhoff, [1894], 1977), 41–81; Rudolf Makkreel, "From
    Simulation to Structural Transposition: A Diltheyean Critique of Empa-
    thy and Defense of Verstehen," in *Empathy and Agency: The Problem of
    Understanding in the Human Sciences*, ed. Hans Herbert Kögler and
    Karsten Stueber (Boulder: Westview Press, 2000), 181–193; Lou Agosta,
    Empathy in the Context of Philosophy (New York: Palgrave Macmillan,
    2010).

43. Kurt Danziger, *Constructing the Subject: Historical Origins of Psychological
    Research* (Cambridge: Cambridge University Press, 1990); William R.
    Woodward and Mitchell G. Ash, eds., *The Problematic Science: Psychology
    in Nineteenth-Century Thought* (New York: Praeger, 1982).

44. Susan Lanzoni, "Empathy's Translations: Three Paths from *Einfühlung*
    into Anglo-American Psychology," in *Empathy: Epistemic Problems and
    Cultural-Historical Perspectives of a Cross-Disciplinary Concept*, ed. Sigrid
    Weigel and Vanessa Lux (London: Palgrave-Macmillan, 2017).

45. Edwin Boring, H. S. Langfeld, and Harry P. Weld, *Introduction to Psychol-
    ogy* (New York: J. Wiley and Sons, 1939), 274. See Janet Beavin Bavelas,

Alex Black, Charles Lemery, and Jennifer Mullett, "Motor Mimicry as Primitive Empathy," in *Empathy and Its Development*, ed. Nancy Eisenberg and Janet Strayer (Cambridge: Cambridge University Press, 1987), 317–338.

46. Heinz Kohut, "Introspection, Empathy and Psychoanalysis," *Journal of the American Psychoanalytic Association* 7 (1959): 459–483; Elizabeth Lunbeck, "Empathy as a Psychoanalytic Mode of Observation: Between Sentiment and Science," in *Histories of Scientific Observation*, ed. L. Daston and E. Lunbeck (Chicago: University of Chicago Press, 2011).

47. William Maria Malisoff, "What Is Insight," *Philosophy of Science* 7, no. 2 (1940): 135–139, 137.

48. Ellen Herman, *The Romance of American Psychology: Political Culture in the Age of Experts* (Berkeley: University of California Press, 1995); James H. Capshew, *Psychologists on the March: Science, Practice, and Professional Identity in America, 1929–1969* (Cambridge: Cambridge University Press, 1999).

49. "How's Your Empathy?," *Reader's Digest* 66 (April 1955): 62–64.

50. Lux discovered that the German *Empathie* first appeared in the 1950s and was adopted by 1961. Vanessa Lux, "Measuring the Emotional Quality: Empathy and Sympathy in Empirical Psychology," in *Empathy*, ed. Weigel and Lux, 121–122.

51. Greg Hickok, *The Myth of Mirror Neurons: The Real Neuroscience of Communication and Cognition* (New York: W. W. Norton, 2014).

52. Empathy is a key topic in literature and the arts; these are only two among many publications: *Rethinking Empathy through Literature*, ed. Meghan Marie Hammond and Sue J. Kim (New York: Routledge, 2014); Suzanne Keen, *Empathy and the Novel* (Oxford: Oxford University Press, 2010).

53. Bellah speaks of an expressive individualism giving way to a postwar therapeutic ethos, which emphasized individual rights and the social virtues of "empathic communication, truth-telling and equitable negotiation." Robert N. Bellah, Richard Madsen, William M. Sullivan, Ann Swidler, and Steven M. Tipton, *Habits of the Heart: Individualism and Commitment in American Life* (Berkeley: University of California Press, 1996), 127.

54. In this article, low empathy skills in teens are attributed to brain development, not to parenting: Sue Shellenbarger, "Teens Are Still Developing Empathy Skills," *Wall Street Journal*, October 15, 2013.

55. Arnold Buchheimer, "The Development of Ideas about Empathy," *Journal of Counseling Psychology* 10, no. 1 (1963): 61–69; Gerald Gladstein, "The Historical Roots of Contemporary Empathy Research," *Journal of the History of the Behavioral Sciences* 20 (1984): 38–59; Lauren Wispé, "History of the Concept of Empathy," in *Empathy and Its Development*, ed. Nancy Eisenberg and Janet Strayer (Cambridge: Cambridge University Press, 1987), 17–37.

56. Daniel Goleman, *Emotional Intelligence: Why It Can Matter More Than IQ* (New York: Bantam, 2005); Antonio Damasio, *Descartes' Error: Emotion,*

Reason and the Human Brain (New York: G. P. Putnam, 1994); Otniel Dror, "The Affect of Experiment: The Turn to Emotions in Anglo-American Physiology, 1900–1940," *Isis* 90, no. 2 (1999): 205–237; Peter N. Stearns and Jan Lewis, eds., *Emotional History of the United States* (New York: New York University Press, 1998). See also Daniel Wickberg, "What Is the History of Sensibilities? On Cultural Histories, Old and New," *American Historical Review* 112, no. 3 (2007): 661–684; Susan Lanzoni, book review "Frank Biess; Daniel M. Gross, eds., *Science and Emotions after 1945: A Transatlantic Perspective;* David Cantor; Edmund Ramsden, eds., *Stress, Shock, and Adaptation in the Twentieth Century,*" *Isis* 107, no. 1 (March 2016): 208–210.

57. Martha Nussbaum, *Upheavals of Thought: The Intelligence of Emotions* (Cambridge: Cambridge University Press, 2003). Affect theory privileges the flow of emotions as distinct from structures of language and draws on the psychological theories of Silvan Tomkins; see Brian Massumi, *Parables for the Virtual: Movement, Affect, Sensation* (Durham: Duke University Press, 2002); Eve Kosofsky Sedgwick and Adam Frank, *Touching Feeling: Affect, Pedagogy, Performativity* (Durham: Duke University Press, 2003); Melissa Gregg and Gregory Seigworth, eds., *The Affect Theory Reader* (Durham: Duke University Press, 2010).

58. Bertolt Brecht, "Indirect Impact of the Epic Theatre (Extracts from the Notes to *Die Mutter*)," *Brecht on Theatre: The Development of an Aesthetic,* ed. John Willet (New York: Hill and Wang, [1932], 1992), 57–62; Koss sees empathy as a "traditional, passive model of bourgeois spectatorship." Juliet Koss, "Bauhaus Theater of Human Dolls," *Art Bulletin* 85, no. 4 (2003): 724–744.

59. Ian Hacking writes, "A concept is nothing other than a word in its sites." Ian Hacking, *Historical Ontology* (Cambridge: Harvard University Press, 2002), 17.

60. Lauren Wispé, "Sympathy and Empathy," in *International Encyclopedia of the Social Sciences,* ed. David L. Sills, vol. 5 (1968), 441–447, 441.

61. A recent conceptual history of Einfühlung roots the concept in Herder's writings in eighteenth-century Germany but fails to mention the many scientific contexts in which empathy was studied as an aesthetic concept in early twentieth-century American psychology. Laura Hyatt Edwards, "A Brief Conceptual History of *Einfühlung*: 18th Century Germany to Post–World War II U.S. Psychology," *History of Psychology* 16, no. 4 (2013): 269–281.

62. David Armitage's method "links discrete contexts, moments and periods while maintaining the synchronic specificity of those contexts." David Armitage, "What's the Big Idea? Intellectual History of the Longue Durée," *History of European Ideas* 38, no. 4 (2012): 493–507, 498. My narrative of the "emergence of empathy" is also indebted to historical epistemology and historical ontology: Lorraine Daston and Peter Galison,

Objectivity (New York: Zone, 2010); Arnold Davidson, *The Emergence of Sexuality: Historical Epistemology and the Formation of Concepts* (Cambridge: Harvard University Press, 2001); Ian Hacking, *Rewriting the Soul: Multiple Personality and the Sciences of Memory* (Princeton: Princeton University Press, 1995); Lorraine Daston, "The History of Emergences," *Isis* 98 (2007): 801–808; Ruth Leys, *Trauma: A Genealogy* (Chicago: University of Chicago Press, 2010); Allan Young, *The Harmony of Illusions: Inventing Post-Traumatic Stress Disorder* (Princeton: Princeton University Press, 1997). An excellent example of tracking a concept across different historical moments is Alison Winter, *Memory: Fragments of a Modern History* (Chicago: University of Chicago Press, 2012).

63. Genealogy "must record the singularity of events outside of any monotonous finality; it must seek them in the most unpromising places, in what we tend to feel is without history in sentiments, love, conscience, instincts." Michel Foucault, "Nietzsche, Genealogy, History," in James D. Faubion, ed., *Aesthetics, Method, and Epistemology: Essential Works of Foucault*, vol. 2 (New York: New Press 1998), 369–391, 369.

64. Susan Verducci, "A Conceptual History of Empathy and a Question It Raises for Moral Education," *Educational Theory* 50, no. 1 (2000): 63–80, 78.

65. Ted Cohen, *Thinking of Others: On the Talent for Metaphor* (Princeton: Princeton University Press, 2009), 11. On empathy as a form of heteropathic identification drawing from the philosopher Max Scheler, see Kaja Silverman, *The Threshold of the Visible World* (New York: Routledge, 1996), 23.

66. *Technologies of the Self: A Seminar with Michel Foucault*, ed. Luther H. Martin, Huck Gutman, and Patrick H. Hutton (Amherst: University of Massachusetts Press, 1988).

Chapter 1. The Roots of Einfühlung or Empathy in the Arts

1. Vernon Lee and C. Anstruther-Thomson, "Beauty and Ugliness," *Contemporary Review* 72 (1897): 544–569, 669–688, 548.

2. Aesthetics as the study of the beautiful dates back only to about 1750 with Alexander Baumgarten's *Aesthetica*. Mary J. Gregor, "Baumgarten's Aesthetica," *Review of Metaphysics* 37, no. 2 (1983): 357–385, 360. See Elizabeth Wilkinson, ed., introduction to *Aesthetics: Lectures and Essays*, by Edward Bullough (Stanford: Stanford University Press, 1957), xix; Christian G. Allesch, *Geschichte der psychologischen Ästhetik: Untersuchungen zur historischen Entwicklung eines psychologischen Verständnisses ästhetischer Phänomene* (Göttingen: C. J. Hogrefe, 1987); Martin Jay, *Songs of Experience: Modern American and European Variations on a Universal Theme* (Berkeley: University of California Press, 2005). Eighteenth-century aesthetic works include: Anthony Ashley Cooper, Third Earl of Shaftesbury, *Characteristics*

of Men, Manners, Opinions, Times, ed. Lawrence E. Klein (Cambridge: Cambridge University Press, 1999 [1711]); Edmund Burke, *A Philosophical Enquiry into the Origin of Our Ideas of the Sublime and the Beautiful* (Notre Dame: University of Notre Dame Press, 1968, [1757]); Immanuel Kant, *Critique of Judgment*, trans. Werner S. Pluhar (Indianapolis: Hackett, 1987), part 1, book 1, Analytic of the Beautiful, § 2–5.

3. Katherine Gilbert and Helmut Kuhn, *A History of Esthetics* (New York: Macmillan, 1939), 524–549.

4. Gustav Fechner, *Vorschule der Aesthetik* (Leipzig: Breitkopf und Haertel, 1876); Thomas H. Haines and Arthur Ernest Davies, "The Psychology of Aesthetic Reaction to Rectangular Forms," *Psychological Review* 11, no. 4 (1904): 249–281.

5. James Sully, *Sensation and Intuition: Studies in Psychology and Aesthetics* (London: Henry S. King, 1874); Grant Allen, *Physiological Aesthetics* (New York: Appleton, 1877); Robert Michael Brain, *The Pulse of Modernism: Physiological Aesthetics in Fin-de-Siècle Europe* (Seattle: University of Washington Press, 2015); Mitchell B. Frank and Daniel Adler, eds., *German Art History and Scientific Thought: Beyond Formalism* (Surrey, Eng.: Ashgate, 2012); Frederic Schwartz, *Blind Spots: Critical Theory and the History of Art in Twentieth-Century Germany* (New Haven: Yale University Press, 2005).

6. James Sully, "Illusions of Introspection," *Mind* 6, no. 21 (1881): 1–18.

7. Mark Jarzombek, *The Psychologizing of Modernity: Art, Architecture and History* (Cambridge: Cambridge University Press, 2000), 71–72. Jonathan Crary, *Suspensions of Perception: Attention, Spectacle and Modern Culture* (Cambridge: MIT Press, 1999).

8. Cited in Wilhelm Perpeet, "Historisches und Systematische zur Einfühlungsaesthetik," *Zeitschrift für Aesthetik und allgemeine Kunstwissenschaft* 11, no. 2 (1965): 193–216, 198, note 15, taken from Friedrich Theodor Vischer, "Kritische Gänge," 2nd ed., ed. Robert Vischer, vol. 4 (1922), 383; Ethel Puffer Howes, "Aesthetics," *Psychological Bulletin* 11, no. 7 (1914): 256–262.

9. "Einfühlungsaesthetik" was first used by Theobald Ziegler in 1894. Perpeet, "Historisches und Systematische zur Einfühlungsaesthetik," 196, note 7. On Einfühlung theories, see Robin Curtis and Gertrud Koch, eds., *Einfühlung: Zu Geschichte und Gegenwart eines ästhetischen Konzepts* (Munich: Wilhelm Fink Verlag, 2009). For the roots of Einfühlung in nineteenth-century projection theories, see Jutta Müller-Tamm, *Abstraktion als Einfühlung: Zur Denkfigur der Projektion in Psychophysiologie, Kulturtheorie, Ästhetik und Literatur der frühen Moderne* (Freiburg im Breisgau: Rombach Verlag, 2005). For a rejection of hydraulic models of empathy in favor of a circular model of metaphoric transfer, see Andrea Pinotti, "Stimmung and Einfühlung: Hydraulic Model and Analogic Model in the Theories of Empathy," *Axiomathes* 1–2 (1998) 253–264, 263.

10. Philip Hobsbaum, "Current Aesthetic Fallacies," *British Journal of Aesthetics* 7, no. 2 (1967): 107–131, 113.

11. Mary Whiton Calkins, review of Paul Stern, *Einfühlung und Association in der Neueren Aesthetik*, *Philosophical Review* 8, no. 1 (1899): 92–93. Calkins saw Stern's associative view as close to that of Lipps, as both relied on unconscious associations of similarity.

12. Vineta Colby, *Vernon Lee: A Literary Biography* (Charlottesville: University of Virginia Press, 2003), 60; see also Carolyn Burdett, "'The Subjective Inside Us Can Turn into the Objective Outside': Vernon Lee's Psychological Aesthetics," *Interdisciplinary Studies in the Long Nineteenth Century* 19, no. 12 (2011). DOI: http://doi.org/10.16995/ntn.610.

13. Henry James to William James, January 20, 1893, cited in Carl J. Weber, "Henry James and His Tiger-Cat," *PMLA* 68, no. 4 (1953): 672–687, 683.

14. Vernon Lee, "Lake Charlemagne: An Apology of Association," *Juvenilia: Being a Second Series of Essays on Sundry Aesthetical Questions* (Boston: Roberts Brothers, 1887), 25–76, 72. Colby, *Vernon Lee*, 138–139.

15. "The International Congress of Experimental Psychology," Notes and News, *Mind* 1, no. 4 (1892): 580–588.

16. Vernon Lee to Mrs. Paget, August 2, 1892, #644; Vernon Lee to Mrs. Paget, August 5, 1892, #645, Vernon Lee Archive, Colby College Special Collections, Miller Library, Waterville, Maine (hereafter VLA). On Lee's relation to her half-brother, see Catherine Maxwell, "Vernon Lee and Eugene Lee-Hamilton," *Vernon Lee: Decadence, Ethics, Aesthetics* (Basingstoke and New York: Palgrave Macmillan, 2006), 21–39; Colby, *Vernon Lee*, 147.

17. Vernon Lee to Mrs. Paget, April 15, 1893, #697, VLA.

18. William James, "What Is an Emotion?" *Mind* 9, no. 34 (1884): 188–205, 190.

19. Violet Paget to William James, April 29, 1909, Il Palmerino San Gervasio, Florence, in William James Papers (1842–1910), BMS Am 1092 (641), Houghton Library, Harvard University.

20. Vernon Lee (Florence) to K. Anstruther-Thomson (London), August 26, 1895, #791, VLA.

21. Lee cited Alfred Fouillée's 1893 work, *La Psychologie des Idées Forces*. Vernon Lee, "Beauty and Ugliness, Holograph Notes," VLA. On Fouillée, see Deborah Silverman, *Art Nouveau in Fin-de-Siècle France: Politics, Psychology and Style* (Berkeley: University of California Press, 1989), 90–91.

22. Vernon Lee Commonplace Books, XII, Easter Day, 1895, VLA. Italics added. Lee cited S. Stricker, *Studien über die Sprachvorstellungen* (Vienna: Braunmüller, 1880). See also J. M. Baldwin, *Mental Development in the Child and the Race: Methods and Process* (New York: Macmillan, 1895), 433.

23. H. C. Bastian, *The Brain as an Organ of Mind* (New York: Appleton, 1880), 543.

24. William James, "Notes: The Congress of Physiological Psychology at Paris," *Mind* 14, no. 56 (1889): 614–616. L. Montoro et al., "Brief History of International Congresses of Psychology, 1889–1960," in M. Richelle and H. Carpintero, eds., *Contributions to the History of the International Congresses of Psychology* (Valencia: Universidad de Valencia, 1992), 75–89.

25. William James, *The Principles of Psychology* (Cambridge: Harvard University Press, 1983 [1890]), 1174. W. B. Pillsbury, "The Place of Movement in Consciousness," *Psychological Review* 18, no. 2 (1911): 83–99, 86. J. Mark Baldwin, *History of Psychology: A Sketch and an Interpretation*, vol. 2 (London: Watts, 1913), 112–122.

26. James, *Principles of Psychology*, 1104–1130.

27. A. Hildebrand, "The Problem of Form in the Fine Arts," in H. F. Mallgrave and E. Ikonomou, eds., *Empathy, Form and Space: Problems in German Aesthetics, 1873–1893* (Santa Monica: Getty Center for the History of Art and the Humanities, 1994), 228–279, 247. On Hildebrand's use of Helmholtz's optics, see Timothy Lenoir, "Politics of Vision: Optics, Painting, and Ideology in Germany, 1845–1895," in *Instituting Science: The Cultural Production of Scientific Disciplines* (Stanford: Stanford University Press, 1997), 131–178, 176.

28. Lee and Anstruther-Thomson, "Beauty and Ugliness" (1897), 683–686.

29. Bernard Berenson, *The Florentine Painters of the Renaissance* (New York: G. P. Putnam's Sons, 1896), 4. Lee reviewed Berenson's book for the journal *Mind*.

30. Lee, "Beauty and Ugliness, Holograph Notes," December 9, 1894, VLA.

31. Vernon Lee, Commonplace Book, XII, December 7, 1895, VLA.

32. Lee expressed concern to her mother that Kit's illness might interfere with their work in the galleries that spring. Vernon Lee to Matilda Paget, May 5, 1895, #762, VLA.

33. Lee, "Beauty and Ugliness, Holograph Notes," VLA. Lee wrote these notes after Berenson's accusation of plagiarism. Lee noted that Anstruther-Thomson had written three-quarters of their 1897 manuscript and saw the accusation as having a strong negative impact on Kit's health. Colby, *Vernon Lee*, 161–173.

34. Vernon Lee and C. Anstruther-Thomson, *Beauty and Ugliness and Other Studies in Psychological Aesthetics* (London: John Lane, Bodley Head, 1912), 35–36. (The 1897 paper was reprinted in the 1912 volume.)

35. Irene Cooper Willis, "Biographical Essay on Vernon Lee," 14–15, VLA.

36. Lee "Beauty and Ugliness, Holograph Notes," VLA. On Lee's distinction between aesthetic contemplation and emotional suggestion in music, see Carlo Caballero, "'A Wicked Voice': On Vernon Lee, Wagner, and the Effects of Music," *Victorian Studies* 35 (1992): 385–408.

37. Lee and Anstruther-Thomson, "Beauty and Ugliness" (1897). Excerpt drawn from 548–550.

38. Ibid., 552.
39. Ibid., 680.
40. Ibid. Italics in original.
41. Ibid., 554.
42. Vernon Lee, Commonplace Book, XIII, January 14, 1897, VLA.
43. Lee and Anstruther-Thomson, "Beauty and Ugliness" (1897), 550–551.
44. Ibid., 545.
45. Ibid., 669.
46. Ibid., 564. Lee cited the art historian August Schmarsow on the "spatial enclosure of the subject" in the appendix to her 1912 text. See Schmarsow, "The Essence of Architectural Creation," in Mallgrave and Ikonomou, eds., *Empathy, Form and Space*, 289.
47. Lee and Anstruther-Thomson, "Beauty and Ugliness" (1897), 677.
48. Ibid., 678.
49. Theodor Lipps, *Raumaesthetik und Geometrisch-Optische Täuschungen* (Leipzig: Ambrisius Barth, 1893–1897); William F. H. Listowel, *A Critical History of Modern Aesthetics* (London: George Allen and Unwin, 1933), 69–71.
50. Wilhelm Wundt attributed optical illusions to actual or anticipated eye movements in spatial perception, a view that Lipps rejected. See S. Alexander, "Review of *Raumaesthetik und Geometrisch-Optische Täuschungen*," *Mind*, n.s. 8, no. 29 (1899): 84–91. Alexander translated *Einfühlung* as "sympathy."
51. "Ich fühle, allgemeiner gesagt, mich in einem Wahrgenommenen strebend nach Ausführung einer Bewegung. Diese Tatsache bezeichnen wir wiederum mit dem Namen 'Einfühlung.' In dieser besteht zugleich das ästhetische Verständnis des optisch Wahrgenommenen." Theodor Lipps, *Ästhetik: Psychologie des Schönen und der Kunst*, 2 vols. (Leipzig: Leopold Voss, 1903–1906), vol. 1 (1903), 120.
52. On Lipps's changing notions of Einfühlung, see Gustav Jahoda, "Theodor Lipps and the Shift from 'Sympathy' to 'Empathy,'" *Journal of the History of the Behavioral Sciences* 41, no. 2 (2005): 151–163. Sawicki argues that Lipps held two different conceptions of Einfühlung: a mirroring of oneself in another or "lived inner coincidence," and a projection of feeling into another that appeared in his 1906 aesthetics. Mariane Sawicki, *Body: Text and Science* (Dordrecht: Kluwer, 1997), 9–18.
53. This citation from Lipps's *Psychologischen Studien* appears in Liliana Albertzazzi, "The Aesthetics of Particulars: A Case of Intuitive Mechanics," *Axiomathes* 1–2 (1998): 169–196, 176. This notion was not only central to Einfühlung but also to Husserl's realist phenomenology.
54. Freud mentions Lipps in the seventh chapter of his *Interpretation of Dreams*. See Mark Kanzer, "Freud, Lipps and Scientific Psychology," *Psychoanalytic Quarterly* 50 (1981): 393–410, 397. On the link between Helmholtzian perceptual theories and Freud's view of a motivated transfer-

ence, see George J. Makari, "In the Eye of the Beholder: Helmholtzian Perception and the Origins of Freud's 1900 Theory of Transference," *Journal of the American Psychoanalytic Association* 42, no. 2 (1994): 549–580.

55. Herman Lotze, *Microcosmus: An Essay Concerning Man and His Relation to the World*, vol. 1, trans. Elizabeth Hamilton and E. E. Constance Jones (Edinburgh: T. and T. Clark, 1885), chap. 2; Friedrich Vischer's 1866 "Kritik meiner Aesthetik" called aesthetic experience "the symbolic interjection of emotions into objective forms." Mallgrave and Ikonomou, introduction to *Empathy, Form and Space*, 20.

56. Robert Vischer, "On the Optical Sense of Form: A Contribution to Aesthetics," in Mallgrave and Ikonomou, eds., *Empathy, Form and Space*, 89–123, 104.

57. Ibid., 108.

58. Ibid.

59. Allesch, *Geschichte der psychologischen Aesthetik*, 335; David Morgan, "The Enchantment of Art: Abstraction and Empathy from German Romanticism to Expressionism," *Journal of the History of Ideas* 57, no. 2 (1996): 317–341, 321.

60. Theodor Lipps, "Dritter aesthetischer Litteraturbericht," III, *Archiv für Systematische Philosophie* 6, no. 3 (1900): 377–409, 385.

61. "Ich bin nach Aussage meines unmittelbaren Bewusstseins in ihm; ich bin also da oben. Ich bin dahin versetzt. Nicht neben den Akrobaten, sondern genau dahin, wo er sich befindet. Dies nun ist der volle Sinn der 'Einfühlung.' Diese Einfühlung nannte ich die Innenseite der Nachahmung." Lipps, *Ästhetik*, vol. 1, 122.

62. Mary Whiton Calkins, Helen Buttrick, and Mabel Young, "An Attempted Experiment in Psychological Aesthetics," *Psychological Review* 7, no. 6 (1900): 580–591, 580.

63. J. M. Baldwin and W. J. Shaw, "Types of Reaction," *Psychological Review* 2, no. 3 (1895): 259–272; E. B. Titchener, "The Type-Theory of the Simple Reaction," *Mind*, n.s. 4, no. 16 (1895): 506–514.

64. Lee and Anstruther-Thomson, *Beauty and Ugliness* (1912), 24.

65. Vernon Lee and C. Anstruther-Thomson, "Le Rôle de l'élément moteur dans la perception esthétique visuelle: Mémoire et questionnaire," Des Actes du 4me Congrès de Psychologie (Imola: Coopérative Typographique Édit, 1901), in VLA.

66. Vernon Lee, "Weiteres über Einfühlung und ästhetisches Miterleben," *Zeitschrift für Ästhetik und allgemeine Kunstwissenschaft* 5 (1910): 145–161, 161. This article was revised as "The Central Problem of Aesthetics" in Lee and Anstruther-Thomson, *Beauty and Ugliness* (1912), 77–152.

67. Lee, "Weiteres über Einfühlung," 149.

68. This was question 6 of the questionnaire, Lee and Anstruther-Thomson, "Le Rôle de l'élément moteur," 11, VLA.

69. Karl Groos, *Einleitung in die Aesthetik* (Giessen: J. Ricker, 1892); Karl Groos, *Der aesthetische Genuss* (Giessen: J. Ricker, 1902); Herbert Sydney Langfeld, *The Aesthetic Attitude* (Port Washington, N.Y.: Kennikat Press, 1920), 254–56.

70. Groos called it a "Spiel der inneren Nachahmung." Groos, *Der aesthetische Genuss*, 179; Karl Groos, *The Play of Man*, trans. Elizabeth L. Baldwin, preface by James Mark Baldwin (New York: Appleton, 1901). Karl Groos, "Das ästhetische Miterleben und die Empfindungen aus dem Körperinnern," *Zeitschrift für Ästhetik und allgemeine Kunstwissenschaft* 4, no. 2 (1909): 161–182. Groos demoted the imitative instinct to an impulse in his later work, which allowed for more flexible responses. See J. L. MacIntyre's review of *The Play of Man* by Karl Groos in *Mind*, n.s. 11, no. 34 (1902): 398–401.

71. Lee and Anstruther-Thomson, *Beauty and Ugliness* (1912), 120–122.

72. Karl Groos to Violet Paget (Vernon Lee), Basel, February 15, 1901, #1, Vernon Lee Collection, Somerville College, Oxford University (hereafter VLC).

73. Karl Groos to Fräulein (Vernon Lee), July 30, 1901, #3, VLC.

74. Colby, *Vernon Lee*, 167.

75. Lee and Anstruther-Thomson, *Beauty and Ugliness* (1912), 325; E. B. Titchener, *Lectures on the Elementary Psychology of Feeling and Attention* (New York: Macmillan, 1908), 179.

76. Lee and Anstruther-Thomson, "Extracts from the Gallery Diaries," *Beauty and Ugliness* (1912), 281. Also published as Vernon Lee "Essais d'esthéthique: L'Individu devant l'oeuvre d'art," *Revue Philosophique* 30, no. 1 (1905): 46–60, and no. 2 (1905): 134–146.

77. Irene Cooper Willis, Biographical Essay, 4, VLA. The last line was crossed out in the typescript.

78. Lee and Anstruther-Thomson, *Beauty and Ugliness* (1912), 333.

79. Vernon Lee, "Art and Usefulness," *Laurus Nobilis* (London: Bodley Head, 1909), 239–240. This essay first appeared in the *Contemporary Review* 80 (September 1901): 362–74; 80 (October 1901); and in *Living Age* 231 (December 14, 1901): 696–706; 231 (December 8, 1901): 804–816. On the uses of "sympathy" in psychological circles in the late nineteenth century, see Susan Lanzoni, "Sympathy in *Mind*, 1873–1900," *Journal of the History of Ideas* 70, no. 2 (2009): 265–287.

80. Lee and Anstruther-Thomson, *Beauty and Ugliness* (1912), 47; Vernon Lee, "La Sympathie Esthétique," *Revue Philosophique* 44 (1907): 614–631. Lee cites Vischer and Lotze in her 1913 *The Beautiful*, 27.

81. Theodor Lipps, "Die Wege der Psychologie," *Att del. V. Congresso Internazionnale di Psicologia* (Roma: Forzani E.C. Tipografi del Senato, Editori, 1905), 57–71, 67. The German reads: "Ich verlege, was ich unmittelbar nur in mir finden kann, in einen sinnlich wahrgenommenen Gegenstand, order versetze es in einer nicht näher beschreibbaren Weise

da hinein, 'projiziere' es und objektivere es damit zugleich." See also Lipps, "Das Wissen von fremden Ichen," *Psychologische Untersuchungen* 1, no. 4 (1907): 694–722.

82. Theodor Lipps, *Leitfaden der Psychologie* (Leipzig: Wilhelm Engelmann, 1903), 187–202.

83. Moritz Geiger, "Über das Wesen und die Bedeutung der Einfühlung," *Bericht uber den Kongress der Deutschen Gesellschaft für Psychologie* 4 (1911): 29–73.

84. Husserl argued that empathic viewing of the other was an act of intuition but was not originary. Husserl, *Ideas Pertaining to a Pure Phenomenology and to a Phenomenological Philosophy*, trans. F. Kersten (Dordrecht: Kluwer, 1982 [1913]), § 1, 6. Edith Stein, an assistant to Husserl, disputed Lipps's claims that one could achieve a seamless unity with the experience of another person, arguing that we possess our own and the other's standpoint simultaneously: Edith Stein, *On the Problem of Empathy*, trans. Waltraut Stein (The Hague: Nijhoff, 1964 [1917]). Scheler critiqued Lipps's projection theory on the basis that inner perception allowed one to directly perceive another's psychological reality. Scheler, *Zur Phänomenologie und Theorie der Sympathiegefühle und von Liebe und Hass* (Halle: Max Niemeyer, 1913), trans. as *The Nature of Sympathy* (New Haven: Yale University Press, 1954). For Martin Buber, Einfühlung was a narrowly aesthetic concept that did not embrace the full concrete life situation. Martin Buber, "Education" [1926], in *Between Man and Man* (New York: Collier Books, 1965).

85. Susan Lanzoni, "An Epistemology of the Clinic: Ludwig Binswanger's Phenomenology of the Other," *Critical Inquiry* 30 (2003): 160–186; Wilhelm Dilthey, "Ideen über eine beschreibende und zergliedernde Psychologie," *Gesammelte Schriften*, ed. Karlfried Gründer and Frithjof Rodi, vol. 5 (Stuttgart: Teubner, 1961), 139–240; Michael Ermarth, *Wilhelm Dilthey: The Critique of Historical Reason* (Chicago: Chicago University Press, 1978), 171–176.

86. Miss Paget (Firenze), "Problèms et methods de l'aesthétique contemporaine," *Att del. V. Congresso Internazionnale di Psicologia* (Roma: Forzani E.C. Tipografi del Senato, Editori, 1905), 462–466.

87. Ibid.

88. Lee and Anstruther-Thomson, *Beauty and Ugliness* (1912), 67.

89. Oswald Külpe, "Ein Beitrag zur Experimentellen Aesthetik," *American Journal of Psychology* 14, no. 3/4 (1903): 215–231. Oswald Külpe, "Über die Methoden der psychologischen Forschung," *Internationale Monatschrift für Wissenschaft, Kultur & Technik* 8 (1914): 1053–70; 1218–32; R. M. Ogden, "Oswald Külpe and the Würzburg School," *American Journal of Psychology* 64, no. 1 (1951): 4–19. On Külpe's experimental aesthetics, see Paul Ziche "Aesthetik 'von unten' von oben: Experimentelle Aesthetik von Gustav Theodor Fechner bis Oswald Külpe," in *Aesthetik von Unten: Em-*

pirie und aesthetisches Wissen, ed. Marie Guthmüller and Wolfgang Klein (Tübingen: A. Francke Verlag, 2006), 325–350.

90. Külpe, "Ein Beitrag zur Experimentellen Aesthetik," 230.

91. Oswald Külpe, "Der gegenwärtige Stand der experimentellen Ästhetik" (Leipzig: Verlag von Joahnn Ambrosius Barth, 1907), 1–57.

92. Ibid., 57.

93. Jacob Segal, "Über die Wohlgefälligkeit einfacher räumlicher Formen: Eine psychologische-ästhetische Untersuchung," *Archiv für die gesamte Psychologie* 7 (1906): 53–124.

94. Charles W. Valentine, *An Introduction to the Experimental Psychology of Beauty* (Long: T. C. and E. C. Jack, 1913), 50.

95. Charles W. Valentine, "Psychological Theories of the Horizontal-Vertical Illusion," *British Journal of Psychology* 5, no. 1 (1912): 8–35, 35.

96. Ethel Puffer Howes, *The Psychology of Beauty* (Boston: Houghton, Mifflin, 1906), 103.

97. George Stratton, "Eye-Movements and the Aesthetics of Visual Form," *Philosophische Studien* 20 (1902): 336–359, 349.

98. Ibid., 358.

99. Ibid., 356.

100. Charles Judd, review of Stratton's "Eye-Movements and the Aesthetics of Visual Form," *Psychological Review* 10, no. 3 (1903): 336–337.

101. Hugo Münsterberg, *The Principles of Art Education: A Philosophical, Aesthetical and Psychological Discussion of Art Education* (New York: Prang Education, 1904), 82.

102. Ibid., 87. Bruno argues that Munsterberg's 1916 cinematic theory entailed empathic transport or a movement from inside to outside inspired by Lipps: Giuliana Bruno "Film, Aesthetics, Science: Hugo Münsterberg's Laboratory of Moving Images," *Grey Room* 36 (2009): 88–113, 91.

103. Münsterberg, *Principles of Art Education*, 87.

104. Thomas H. Haines and Arthur Ernest Davies, "The Psychology of Aesthetic Reaction to Rectangular Forms," *Psychological Review* 11, no. 4 (1904): 249–281, 274.

105. Elizabeth Scarborough and Laurel Furumoto, *Untold Lives: The First Generation of American Women Psychologists* (New York: Columbia University Press, 1987), 77.

106. Puffer Howes, *Psychology of Beauty*, 77.

107. Ibid., 77–79.

108. Ethel D. Puffer, "Studies in Symmetry," *Psychological Review Monograph Supplements* 4, no. 1(1903): 467–539, 467.

109. Puffer Howes, *Psychology of Beauty*, 121.

110. Ibid., 116.

111. Ibid., 118.

112. Ethel Puffer Howes, "Accepting the Universe," *Atlantic Monthly* 129 (1922): 444.

113. Ethel Puffer Howes, "Aesthetics," *Psychological Bulletin* 10, no. 5 (1913): 196–201.

114. Puffer Howes, *Psychology of Beauty*, 104. Theodor A. Meyer, "Kritik d. Einfühlung," *Zeitschrift für Aesthetik* 7 (1912): 529–567; Viktor Basch, "Les Grands Courants de L'esthétique Allemande Contemporaine," *Revue Philosophique* 73 (1912): 22–43, 167–190.

115. August Endell, "Formenschönheit und Dekorative Kunst," *Dekorative Kunst: Illustrierte Zeitschrift für Angewandte Kunst*, vol. 1 (Munich: H. Bruckmann, 1898), 75–77; Zeynep Çelik, "Kinaesthesia," in *Sensorium: Embodied Experience, Technology and Contemporary Art*, ed. Caroline Jones (Cambridge: MIT Press, 2006), 159–162; Zeynep Çelik Alexander, "Metrics of Experience: August Endell's Phenomenology of Architecture," *Grey Room* 40 (2010): 50–83.

116. Wilhelm Worringer, *Abstraktion und Einfühlung: Ein Beitrag zur Stilpsychologie* (Munich: R. Piper, 1908), trans. as *Abstraction and Empathy: A Contribution to the Psychology of Style* (New York: International Universities Press, 1953).

117. For the parallels between Kandinsky's work and empathy theory, and an account of how the viewer imaginatively enters into the pictorial space of Kandinsky's and Mondrian's paintings, see Dee Reynolds, *Symbolist Aesthetics and Early Abstract Art: Sites of Imaginary Space* (Cambridge: Cambridge University Press,1995), 116–194; David Morgan, "The Idea of Abstraction in German Theories of the Ornament from Kant to Kandinsky," *Journal of Aesthetics and Art Criticism* 50, no. 3 (1992): 231–242; Barbara Rose, "Hans Hofmann: From Expressionism to Abstraction," *Arts Magazine* 53, no. 3 (1978): 110–114. Art historian Heinrich Wölfflin's 1886 dissertation described how architecture evoked a sense of one's body, with ties to Einfühlung theory. See Mark Jarzombek, "De-Scribing the Language of Looking: Wölfflin and the History of Aesthetic Experientialism," *Assemblage* 23 (1994): 28–69, 34; Christopher S. Wood, "Theories of Reference," *Art Bulletin* 78, no. 1 (1996): 6–25, 24; Aby Warburg's notion of the symbol bridged the mind and the phenomenal world with a "kinetic potentiality" indebted to Friedrich Vischer, according to Giorgio Agamben, *Nymphs* (London: Seagull Books, 2013), 22.

118. E. F. Carritt, *The Theory of Beauty* (London: Methuen, 1914), 273.

119. Listowel, *A Critical History of Modern Aesthetics*, 46; Barasch argues the tradition lasted up to 1910. Moshe Barasch, *Modern Theories of Art, 2: From Impressionism to Kandinsky* (New York: New York University Press, 1998), 113–114.

120. O. Külpe to Vernon Lee, Bonn, July 11, 1911; O. Külpe to V. Paget, Bonn, August 15, 1911; O. Külpe to Lee, Bonn, December 16, 1911, VLC.

121. "What Is Beauty: Vernon Lee Seeks an Answer in Distinctly Verbose Terms," *New York Times*, April 28, 1912.

122. Puffer Howes, "Aesthetics," 197.

123. Ibid.

124. Vernon Lee, "The Tower of Mirrors," *Genius Loci, Notes on Places* (London, Grant-Richards, 1899).

125. V. Lee, "The Motorcar and the Genius of Places," *The Enchanted Woods* (London, J. Lane, 1905), 97.

126. Ibid., 99.

127. Vernon Lee, *The Beautiful: An Introduction to Psychological Aesthetics* (Folcraft, Pa.: Folcraft Library Ed., 1970 [1913]), 38.

128. Ibid., 15.

129. Ibid., 60. Italics in original.

130. Ibid., 63.

131. Ibid., 59–60. Italics in original.

132. Ibid., 69.

Chapter 2. From Einfühlung to Empathy

1. Alice Helen Sullivan, "An Experimental Study of Kinaesthetic Imagery," *American Journal of Psychology* 32, no. 1 (1921): 54–80.

2. Lauren Wispé, "History of the Concept of Empathy," in *Empathy and Its Development*, ed. Nancy Eisenberg and Janet Strayer (Cambridge: Cambridge University Press, 1987), 17–37; Gerald Gladstein, "The Historical Roots of Contemporary Empathy Research," *Journal of the History of the Behavioral Sciences* 20 (1984): 38–59; Jørgen B. Hunsdahl, "Concerning *Einfühlung* (Empathy): A Concept Analysis of Its Origin and Early Development," *Journal of the History of the Behavioral Sciences* 3, no. 2 (1967): 180–191.

3. The term "empathy" did appear in 1895, not as a translation of *Einfühlung* but as an energy concept. "For the capacity factor of psychophysical energy the name 'empathy' is proposed. Empathy is then a physical quantity, a physiological brain-function, and is defined as the relation of the whole energy at any change of the central organ to the intensity." E. L. Hinman review of K. Lasswitz, "Ueber psychophysische Energie und ihre Factoren," in "Summaries of Articles," *Philosophical Review* 4, no. 6 (1895): 673.

4. J. Mark Baldwin, "Imitation: A Chapter in the Natural History of Consciousness," *Mind* 3, no. 9 (1895): 26–55; J. Mark Baldwin, *Mental Development: The Child and the Race* (New York: Macmillan, 1903). On Baldwin's views of sympathy, see Susan Lanzoni, "Sympathy in Mind, 1876–1900" *Journal of the History of Ideas* 70, no. 2 (2009): 265–287, 274–276.

5. Michael M. Sokal, "Baldwin, Cattell and the *Psychological Review*: A Collaboration and Its Discontents," *History of the Human Sciences* 10, no. 1 (1997): 57–89; Robert H. Wozniak, "Lost Classics and Forgotten Contributors: James Mark Baldwin as a Case Study in the Disappearance and

Rediscovery of Ideas," in T. C. Dalton and R. B. Evans, eds., *The Life Cycle of Psychological Ideas* (New York: Kluwer Academic/Plenum, 2004), 33–58; Robert Wozniak, "Consciousness, Social Heredity and Development," *American Psychologist* 64, no. 2 (2009): 93–101; Robert Richards, "James Mark Baldwin: Evolutionary Biopsychology and the Politics of Scientific Ideas," in *Darwin and the Emergence of Evolutionary Theories of Mind and Behavior* (Chicago: University of Chicago Press, 1987), 480–496.

6. James Mark Baldwin, "James Mark Baldwin," *A History of Psychology in Autobiography*, vol. 1 (Washington D.C.: American Psychological Association, 1930), 1–30, 26.

7. Ibid.

8. James Mark Baldwin, *Thoughts and Things: A Study of the Development and Meaning of Thought or Genetic Logic*, vols. 1 and 2 (New York: Arno Press, 1975 [1906, 1908]), vol. 1, 122.

9. J. Mark Baldwin, ed., *Dictionary of Philosophy and Psychology*, 3 vols. (New York: Macmillan, 1901–1905), 2:679.

10. Volume 1 is entitled *Functional Logic, or Genetic Theory of Knowledge* (1906); volume 2, *Experimental Logic, or Genetic Theory of Thought* (1908); volume 3, *Interest and Art, Being Real Logic: I Genetic Epistemology* (1911); and volume 4, *The Genetic Theory of Reality* (1915).

11. Baldwin, *Thoughts and Things*, vol. 1, 124.

12. Ibid., 122.

13. Baldwin called the play instinct the "lower semblant." James Mark Baldwin, *Thoughts and Things: A Study of the Development and Meaning of Thought or Genetic Logic*, vols. 3 and 4 (New York: Arno Press, 1975 [1911, 1915]), vol. 3, 157.

14. Karl Groos, *The Play of Man*, trans. Elizabeth L. Baldwin (in collaboration with Groos), preface by James Mark Baldwin (New York: D. Appleton, 1901).

15. Baldwin, *Thoughts and Things*, vol. 1, 122.

16. Ibid., note 1.

17. Baldwin, *Dictionary of Philosophy and Psychology*, vol. 2, 549.

18. Baldwin, *Thoughts and Things*, vol. 3, 162.

19. Ibid., 159.

20. Wilbur M. Urban, *Valuation: Its Nature and Laws, Being an Introduction to a General Theory of Value* (London: Sonnenschein, 1909), 235, note 1. Urban preferred Einfühlung: "We shall accordingly use the term to designate the entire process (projection, imitation, and ejection) involved in the activities of characterisation and participation, and shall consider it, more over, in its aspect of affective-conative process" (235). Urban used his own translation of "sympathetic participation" or "affective projection." Wilbur Urban, "The Knowledge of Other Minds and Problem of Meaning and Value," *Philosophical Review* 26, no. 3 (1917): 274–296, 281.

21. Robert H. Wozniak and Jorge A. Santiago-Blay, "Trouble at Tyson Alley: James Mark Baldwin's Arrest at a Baltimore Bordello," *History of Psychology* 16, no. 4 (2013): 227–248.

22. Emily D. Cahan, "The Genetic Psychologies of James Mark Baldwin and Jean Piaget," *Developmental Psychology* 20, no 1 (1984): 128–135. For the use of Einfühlung as akin to "identification" in Piaget's developmental schema, see Eugene Lerner, "The Problem of Perspective in Moral Reasoning," *American Journal of Sociology* 43, no. 2 (1937): 249–269. It would be fascinating to track the possible connection between Baldwin's semblant object and Winnicott's transitional object.

23. Baldwin, *Thoughts and Things*, vol. 3, 167, note 2; James Mark Baldwin, *History of Psychology: A Sketch and an Interpretation*, vol. 2 (New York: G. P. Putnam's Sons, 1913), 151.

24. The review mentioned an article by Frl. von Renauld that appeared in *Archiv für die gesamte Psychologie* on David Hume's reflexive sympathy. The text explained that we are aware of the existence of others, "analogous to ourselves by way of empathy, which is based mainly upon the impulse to imitation." Philosophical Periodicals, *Mind*, n.s. 17, no. 68 (October 1908): 593. Baldwin to Titchener, March 10, 1910, box 2, Edward Bradford Titchener Papers, 1887–1940, #14–23–545, Division of Rare and Manuscript Collections, Cornell University Library (hereafter EBT).

25. The editor, G. F. Stout, thanked Titchener for writing "fresh Notices of Periodicals," for which he had sent payment: G. F. Stout to Titchener, May 17, 1894, EBT.

26. Edward Bullough, "The 'Perceptive Problem' in the Aesthetic Appreciation of Single Colours," *British Journal of Psychology* 2, no. 4 (1908): 406–463, 444, note 2. The journal was founded by Charles S. Myers, William McDougall, Alexander Shand, and psychiatrist W. H. R. Rivers. The proposal for the journal declared that "the time has come for starting an English Journal devoted exclusively to psychology in all its branches." Ward to Myers, "Copy," April 6, 1903, KENNA/2/4/4, Wellcome Library, Wellcome Trust, London.

27. "Notes," *Philosophical Review* 17, no. 6 (1908): 694.

28. Oscar Ewald, "German Philosophy in 1907," *Philosophical Review* 17, no. 4 (1908): 400–426, 407.

29. James Ward to Titchener, October 3, 1904; C. S. Myers to Titchener, August 17, 1903, EBT.

30. Baldwin, *History of Psychology*, vol. 2, 152.

31. He derived this "pancalist" view from Theodor Lipps as well as from Kant and Schelling. James Hastings, ed., "James Mark Baldwin, 'Pancalism,'" *Encyclopedia of Religion and Ethics*, vol. 9 (New York: Charles Scribner's Sons, 1917), 599.

32. Baldwin, *Thoughts and Things*, vol. 4, 240.

33. Ibid.

34. On Ward's faith and panpsychism, see Frank M. Turner, *Between Science and Religion: The Reaction to Scientific Naturalism in Late Victorian England* (New Haven: Yale University Press, 1974), 201–246.

35. Ward published a portion of his dissertation, "An Attempt to Interpret Fechner's Law," in the journal *Mind* in 1876. Olwen Ward Campbell, "Memoir," in James Ward, *Essays in Philosophy* (Cambridge: Cambridge University Press, 1927), 53, 68–72.

36. Robert Brain, *The Pulse of Modernism: Physiological Aesthetics in Fin-de-Siècle Europe* (Seattle: University of Washington Press, 2015), 52–53; Gerald L. Geison, *Michael Foster and the Cambridge School of Physiology: The Scientific Enterprise in Late Victorian Society* (Princeton: Princeton University Press, 1978).

37. James Ward to Henry Sidgwick, March 22, 1899, Trinity College Manuscripts, Add. MS c/95/187, Trinity College Archive and Manuscript Collection, Cambridge University (hereafter TCA). Beatrice Edgell, "The British Psychological Society," *British Journal of Psychology* 37, no. 3 (1947): 113–132, 114; Colin Crampton, "The Cambridge School the Life, Work and Influence of James Ward, W. H. R. Rivers, C. S. Myers and Sir Frederic Bartlett" (PhD diss., University of Edinburgh, 1978), 148–166.

38. Charles S. Myers, *Text-Book of Experimental Psychology* (London: Edward Arnold, 1909), 331. Others who attributed the translation to Ward include: Charles Spearman, review of C. S. Myers, *Text-Book of Experimental Psychology*, "New Books," *Mind*, n.s. 18, no. 72 (1909): 617–618; R. F. Hoernle, review of A. C. Macmillan, *The Crowning Phase of the Critical Philosophy: A Study in Kant's Critique of Judgment* (London: Macmillan, 1912), in *Mind*, n.s. 23, no. 92 (1914): 597–604, 600.

39. Charles W. Valentine, "Psychological Theories of the Horizontal-Vertical Illusion," *British Journal of Psychology* 5, no. 1 (1912): 8–35, 26. Charles Valentine, *An Introduction to the Experimental Psychology of Beauty* (London: T. C. and E. C. Jack, 1913), 50–51; T. H. Pear, "Charles Wilfred Valentine, 1879–1964," *British Journal of Psychology* 55, no. 4 (1964): 385–390.

40. James Ward, "The Present Problems of General Psychology," in *International Congress of Arts and Sciences*, vol. 5, ed. Howard J. Rogers (London: University Alliance, 1906), 637.

41. Crampton, "Cambridge School," 82; Frederic Bartlett, *Remembering: A Study in Experimental and Social Psychology* (Cambridge: Cambridge University Press, 1995 [1932]); On Bartlett, see Alison Winter, *Memory: A Fragment of a Modern History* (Chicago: Chicago University Press, 2012).

42. James Ward, "Mechanism and Morals," in *Essays in Philosophy with a Memoir of the Author*, by Olwen Ward Campbell (Cambridge: Cambridge University Press, 1927 [1905]), 243.

43. James Ward, *Psychological Principles* (Cambridge: Cambridge University Press, 1919), 335–336.

44. David Skrbina, *Panpsychism in the West* (Cambridge: MIT Press, 2005), 141–156; Turner, *Between Science and Religion*, 237–239.

45. Ward, "Mechanism and Morals," 244.

46. Ibid., 247.

47. Ibid., 245.

48. Ward, *Psychological Principles*, 335–336; Hugh Joseph Tallon, *The Concept of Self in British and American Idealism: A Dissertation* (Washington, D.C.: Catholic University of America Press, 1939), 118–121.

49. Ward, "Heredity and Memory," in *Essays in Philosophy*, 276; W. R. Sorley, "James Ward," *Mind*, n.s. 34, no. 135 (1925): 273–279, 276.

50. James Ward to James Frazer, November 11, 1915, Add. MS b/37/331, TCA.

51. Robert Ackerman, *J. G. Frazer: His Life and Work* (Cambridge: Cambridge University Press, 1987), 228.

52. Ibid., 229; Olwen Ward Campbell, "Memoir," 73, 75.

53. Ackerman, *J. G. Frazer*, 89.

54. Henry Jackson to James Ward, January 28, 1904, Add. MS c/101/120, TCA.

55. James G. Frazer, *The Golden Bough: The King of the Wood, The Perils of the Soul* (London: Macmillan, 1900), 2nd ed., vol. 1, 212.

56. James Ward, "Introduction to Philosophy," in *Essays in Philosophy*, 212–213.

57. Ward to James Frazer, November 19, 1915, Add. MS b/37/331, TCA.

58. See Freya Matthews, *For Love of Matter: A Contemporary Panpsychism* (Albany: SUNY Press, 2003); Godehard Brüntrup and Ludwig Jaskolla, eds., *Panpsychism: Contemporary Perspectives* (Oxford: Oxford University Press, 2017).

59. Rand B. Evans, "The Scientific and Psychological Positions of E. B. Titchener," in *Defining American Psychology: The Correspondence between Adolf Meyer and E. B. Titchener*, ed. Ruth Leys and Rand B. Evans (Baltimore: Johns Hopkins University Press, 1990), 1–39; Edna Heidbreder, *Seven Psychologies* (New York: Appleton-Century-Crofts, 1933), 113–151.

60. Titchener coedited the journal with G. Stanley Hall and E. C. Sanford, taking over sole editorship in 1921. Evans, "Scientific and Psychological Positions of E. B. Titchener," 30–32; Michael J. Hindeland, "Edward Bradford Titchener: A Pioneer in Perception," *Journal of the History of the Behavioral Sciences* 7, no. 1 (1971): 23–28.

61. Titchener to T. A. Hunter, January 1, 1908; Titchener to T. A. Hunter, May 17, 1908, EBT. Hunter was one of the first experimental psychologists to establish a laboratory in New Zealand.

62. Wilhelm Wundt, *Völkerpsychologie, III Die Kunst* (Leipzig: Verlag W. Engellman, 1908), 5. Wundt's sixth edition of volume 3 of his *Principles of Physiological Psychology*, published in 1911, discoursed at length on aesthetic Einfühlung, even as he found it an imprecise term with many mean-

ings. Wundt, *Grundzüge der physiologischen Psychologie* (Leipzig: W. Engelmann, 1911), 161–174.

63. E. B. Titchener, "A Psychophysical Vocabulary," *American Journal of Psychology* 7, no. 1 (1895): 78–85, 79. E. C. Sanford, coeditor of the *American Journal of Psychology*, wrote: "I prefer a good English word to a literal translation of the German-French terms, and where that is for any reason poor, a decent classical term made new for the thing." E. C. Sanford to Titchener, June 16, 1895; see also E. C. Sanford to Titchener, May 23, 1895, EBT.

64. On the imageless thought debates, see Martin Kusch, *Psychological Knowledge: A Social History and Philosophy* (London: Routledge, 1999); Adrian Brock, "Imageless Thought or Stimulus Error? The Social Construction of Private Experience," in W. R. Woodward and R. S. Cohen, eds., *World Views and Scientific Discipline Formation* (Dordrecht: Kluwer, 1991), 97–106; E. B. Titchener, *Lectures on the Elementary Psychology of Feeling and Attention* (New York: MacMillan, 1908), 8.

65. Lipps argued that in imitation (*Nachahmung*), the optical image of an action of an acrobat was directly identified with the viewer's kinesthetic image (*kinästhetisches Bild*). With Einfühlung, one felt kinesthetic images within the object. Theodor Lipps, *Ästhetik: Psychologie des Schönen und der Kunst*, 2 vols. (Leipzig: Leopold Voss, 1903–1906), vol. 1, *Grundlegung der Ästhetik* (1903), 115–120.

66. Topics of the Times, *New York Times*, January 1, 1907; John B. Watson, "Kinesthetic and Organic Sensations: Their Role in the Reactions of the White Rat to the Maze," *Psychological Review Monograph Supplements* 8, no. 2 (1907): 1–100. For the history of the sixth sense, see Nicholas J. Wade, "The Search for a Sixth Sense: The Cases for Vestibular, Muscle, and Temperature Senses," in *The Sixth Sense Reader*, ed. David Howes (Oxford: Berg, 2009), 55–85.

67. E. B. Titchener to Hunter, January 24, 1907; E. B. Titchener to Hunter, July 15, 1907, EBT; Laurence Binet Brown and Alfred Herman Fuchs, eds., *The Letters between Sir Thomas Hunter and E. B. Titchener* (Wellington, N.Z.: Department of Psychology, Victoria University, 1969), 12. The frame was devised by Ernst Mach in 1875. Howard Warren, *Dictionary of Psychology* (Boston: Houghton Mifflin, 1934), 156.

68. E. B. Titchener, *Experimental Psychology of the Thought-Processes* (New York: MacMillan, 1909), 13.

69. Titchener wrote that he possessed "a sort of logical and aesthetic *Einfühlung* for music and immediate (or very rapid) grasp of the sense and fitness of the musical structure." Titchener, *Experimental Psychology of the Thought-Processes*, 205.

70. Ibid., 11–12.

71. Ibid., 18.

72. Ibid., 19.

73. Ibid.

74. Titchener had earlier expressed doubt whether a kinesthetic image could exist without reviving accompanying sensations, but by 1904 he began speaking of organic and kinesthetic images. E. B. Titchener, "Organic Images," *Journal of Philosophy, Psychology and Scientific Methods* 1, no. 2 (1904): 36–40.

75. E. B. Titchener, *A Text-Book of Psychology* (New York: Macmillan, 1909), part 1, 198–199, 283; Titchener, *Lectures on the Elementary Psychology of Feeling*, 102. See A. E. Davies, "Discussion: Professor Titchener's Theory of Memory and Imagination," *Psychological Review* 19, no. 2 (1912): 147–157.

76. E. B. Titchener, *A Text-Book of Psychology* (New York: Macmillan, 1910), 48; see also Fred Kuhlmann, "The Place of Mental Imagery and Memory among Mental Functions," *American Journal of Psychology* 16, no. 3 (1905): 337–356, 346.

77. Titchener, *Experimental Psychology of the Thought-Processes*, 21.

78. Ibid., 182; Heidbreder, *Seven Psychologies*, 145–46.

79. Titchener, *Experimental Psychology of the Thought-Processes*, 13.

80. Ibid., 21. Titchener alluded to aesthetic Einfühlung in 1899 when he spoke of aesthetic sentiments as "one's own emotions, projected into other people or into external nature, and refound there by one's active attention." Titchener, *An Outline of Psychology* (New York: MacMillan, 1916 [1899]), 330.

81. Titchener *Experimental Psychology of the Thought-Processes*, 21.

82. Ibid., 292, also 185–86.

83. Stephen S. Colvin, "A Marked Case of Mimetic Ideation," *Psychological Review* 17, no. 4 (1910): 260–268, 266; Titchener, *Experimental Psychology of the Thought-Processes*, 291.

84. Colvin, "Marked Case of Mimetic Ideation," 260.

85. Wilfrid Lay, "Organic Images," *Journal of Philosophy, Psychology and Scientific Methods* 1, no. 3 (1904): 68–71, 70.

86. Karl M. Dallenbach, "Karl M. Dallenbach," in *A History of Psychology in Autobiography*, vol. 5 (New York: Appleton-Century-Crofts, 1967), 57–93, 74.

87. Ibid., 83.

88. Ibid.

89. Ibid., 84.

90. Karl M. Dallenbach, "The Psychology of Blindfold Chess," in *Studies in Psychology*, contributed by colleagues and former students of Edward Bradford Titchener (Worcester, Mass.: Louis N. Wilson, 1917), 214–230.

91. Ibid., 223.

92. Ibid., 218.

93. June Downey, *Creative Imagination: Studies in the Psychology of Literature* (New York: Harcourt, Brace, 1929), 37.

94. Kurt Danziger, *Constructing the Subject: Historical Origins of Psychological Research* (Cambridge: Cambridge University Press, 1990).

95. Burt Miner, "The Changing Attitude of American Universities toward Psychology," *Science*, n.s. 20, no. 505 (1904): 299–307, 302.

96. Titchener, *Experimental Psychology of the Thought-Processes*, 145–146; Mary Henle, "Did Titchener Commit the Stimulus Error? The Problem of Meaning in Structural Psychology," *Journal of the History of the Behavioral Sciences* 7, no. 3 (1971): 279–282; Kenton Kroker, "The Progress of Introspection in America, 1896–1938," *Studies in History and Philosophy of Biological and Biomedical Sciences* 34 (2003): 77–108.

97. E. B. Titchener, "The Past Decade in Experimental Psychology," *American Journal of Psychology* 21, no. 3 (1910): 404–421, 405. On Titchener's persona, see Francesca Bordogna "Scientific Personae in American Psychology: Three Case Studies," *Studies in History and Philosophy of Biological and Biomedical Sciences* 36 (2005): 95–134; and for his method, see Christopher D. Green, "Scientific Objectivity and E. B. Titchener's Experimental Psychology," *Isis* 101, no. 4 (2010): 697–721.

98. Titchener, *Experimental Psychology of the Thought-Processes*, 25.

99. Tamekichi Okabe, "Experimental Study of Belief," *American Journal of Psychology* 21, no. 4 (1910): 563–596, 568–69.

100. Helen Maud Clarke, "Conscious Attitudes," *American Journal of Psychology* 22, no. 2 (1911): 214–249, 216; Alma De Vries Schaub, "On the Intensity of Images," *American Journal of Psychology* 22, no. 3 (1911): 346–368.

101. The instructor was L. R. Geissler. Okabe, "Experimental Study of Belief," 589.

102. Titchener, *Text-Book of Psychology* (1910), part 1, 198.

103. Cheves Perky, "An Experimental Study of Imagination," *American Journal of Psychology* 21, no. 3 (1910): 422–452, 448.

104. Ibid., 448–449.

105. E. B. Titchener, *A Beginner's Psychology* (New York: Macmillan, 1915), 200.

106. Anna Rogers, "An Analytic Study of Visual Perceptions," *American Journal of Psychology* 28, no. 4 (1917): 519–577, 551. Anna Rogers was appointed graduate assistant in 1914. See "Notes and News," *Journal of Philosophy, Psychology and Scientific Methods* 11 (1914): 721.

107. Rogers, "Analytic Study of Visual Perceptions," 558.

108. "Meaning is, originally, kinaesthesis; the organism faces the situation by some bodily attitude, and the characteristic sensations which the attitude involves give meaning to the process that stands at the conscious focus." Titchener, *Experimental Psychology of the Thought-Processes*, 176.

109. Hermann Rorschach, *Psychodiagnostik* (Vern: Hans Huber, 1983 [1921]), 26, 95; According to Rorschach, to perceive movement in the blots evidenced an introversive type with a creative inner life, a departure from Jung's typology. See Naamah Akavia, *Subjectivity in Motion: Life, Art and Movement in the Work of Hermann Rorschach* (New York: Brunner-Routledge,

2013), 13–35; Ernest Schachtel, "The Dynamic Perception and the Symbolism of Form," *Psychiatry* 4, no. 1 (1941): 79–96, 92–95; Damion Searls, *The Inkblots* (New York: Random House, 2017), 133–134.

110. Michael Zigler, "An Experimental Study of Visual Form," *American Journal of Psychology* 31 no. 3 (1920): 273–300, 287.

111. An observer at the Clark University laboratory noted a feeling of "being stretched out like a starfish" while visualizing a triangular shape, defined as kinesthetic empathy: Sara Carolyn Fisher, "An Analysis of a Phase of the Process of Classifying," *American Journal of Psychology* 28, no. 1 (1917): 57–116, 71.

112. J. P. Guilford, "Spatial Symbols in the Apprehension of Time," *American Journal of Psychology* 37, no. 3 (1926): 420–423, 423.

113. Charles Warren Fox, "An Experimental Study of Naming," *American Journal of Psychology* 47, no. 4 (1935): 545–579.

114. Callie Hull, "Doctorates, Conferred in the Sciences by American Universities in 1920," *Science*, n.s. 52, no. 1352 (1920): 514–517, 516. Sullivan became an associate in the Psychology Department at the University of Illinois at Urbana, and Titchener assured her that she had the same degree and the same good judgment as her male counterparts. Titchener to Sullivan, February 1, 1923, March 14, 1923, May 18, 1923, EBT.

115. Sullivan, "Experimental Study of Kinaesthetic Imagery," 69.

116. Ibid., 69–70.

117. Ibid., 70.

118. Ibid., 80.

119. Titchener, *Beginner's Psychology*, 198. A decade later, however, a researcher at the University of Illinois argued pictures with familiar elements were recognized through "an empathic kinaesthesis." E. Murray, "A Note on Recognition," *American Journal of Psychology* 39, no. 1/4 (1927): 259–63.

120. Titchener, *Beginner's Psychology*, 198, emphasis in original.

121. Ibid.; Titchener, *Text-Book of Psychology* (1910), 417, footnote.

122. Titchener, *Beginner's Psychology*, 198.

123. Titchener, *Beginner's Psychology*, 200.

124. Titchener, *Experimental Psychology of the Thought-Processes*, 206.

125. Vernon Lee and Clementina Anstruther-Thomson, *Beauty and Ugliness and Other Studies in Psychological Aesthetics* (London: John Lane, Bodley Head, 1912), 148.

126. John T. Metcalf, "Empathy and the Actor's Emotion," *Journal of Social Psychology* 2, no. 2 (1931): 235–238.

127. Cited in George W. Pigman, "Freud and the History of Empathy," *International Journal of Psychoanalysis* 76 (1995): 237–256, 244.

128. William L. Storey, "Empathy," *Notes and Queries* 150, no. 14 (April 3, 1926): 243.

129. Edward Bensly, "Empathy," *Notes and Queries* 150, no. 18 (May 1, 1926): 321.

130. Cited in A. W. Pollard, review of "Francis Jenkinson, Fellow of Trinity College, Cambridge and University Librarian, a Memoir by H. F. Stewart," *Review of English Studies* 3, no. 9 (1927): 117–119, 118. Ducasse called empathy a "misleading name for what it is" and defined it as "the psychological process through which action (not mere motion) is perceived where it is, or imaginatively ascribed where it is not." C. J. Ducasse, "What Has Beauty to Do with Art?" *Journal of Philosophy* 25, no. 7 (1928): 181–186, 185; Ernest Mundt, "Three Aspects of German Aesthetic Theory," *Journal of Aesthetics and Art Criticism* 17, no. 3 (1959): 287–310, 291.

131. In 1934, empathy's primary definition was the "imaginal or mental projection of oneself into the elements of a work of art or into a natural object." Howard C. Warren, *Dictionary of Psychology* (Boston: Houghton Mifflin 1934), 92.

Chapter 3. Empathy in Art and Modern Dance

Epigraph: June Etta Downey, *The Heavenly Dykes* (Boston: Gorham Press, 1904), 51.

1. Rebecca West, "Explanation," in *The Strange Necessity* (Garden City, N.Y.: Doubleday, Doran, 1928), 1.

2. Mark Jarzombek, *The Psychologizing of Modernity: Art, Architecture, and History* (Cambridge: Cambridge University Press, 2000); Jonathan Crary, *Suspensions of Perception: Attention, Spectacle and Modern Culture* (Cambridge: MIT Press, 2001).

3. Siobhan Burke, "Rejecting Artifice, Advancing Art: The Dance Criticism of John Martin," *Columbia Journal of American Studies* 9 (2009): 289–305.

4. On the overlooked modernist values of movement and kinesthetics, see Robin Veder, *The Living Line: Modern Art and the Economy of Energy* (Hanover, N.H.: Dartmouth College Press, 2015); see also Robert Brain, *The Pulse of Modernism: Physiological Aesthetics in Fin-de-Siècle Europe* (Seattle: University of Washington Press, 2015).

5. June Downey, *Creative Imagination: Studies in the Psychology of Literature* (London: Harcourt Brace, 1929), viii, 2.

6. June Downey, "Emotional Poetry and the Preference Judgment," *Psychological Review* 22, no. 4 (1915): 259–278; June Downey, "A Program for a Psychology of Literature," *Journal of Applied Psychology* 2, no. 4 (1918): 366–377; June Downey, *The Kingdom of the Mind* (New York: Macmillan, 1927); Edwin Emery Slosson and June Downey, *Plots and Personalities: A New Method of Testing and Training the Creative Imagination* (New York: Century, 1922).

7. Downey's dissertation, "Control Processes in Modified Handwriting," was completed under the supervision of James Rowland Angell and the behaviorist John B. Watson.

8. Richard S. Uhrbrock "June Etta Downey," in *In Memoriam: June Etta*

Downey, 1875–1932 (Laramie: Faculty of the University of Wyoming, June 1934), foreword; James. E. Angell to Dean P. T. Miller, November 29, 1932, *In Memoriam*, 24.

9. Downey's interest in the Imagist poets is detailed in Susan Lanzoni, "Empathy Aesthetics: Experimenting between Psychology and Poetry," in *Rethinking Empathy through Literature*, ed. Meghan Marie Hammond and Sue J. Kim (New York: Routledge, 2014), 34–46.

10. June Downey, "A Case of Colored Gustation," *American Journal of Psychology* 22, no. 4 (1911): 528–539. Tim Armstrong, *Modernism, Technology and the Body: A Cultural Study* (Cambridge: Cambridge University Press, 1998); Wilma Koutstaal, "Skirting the Abyss: A History of Experimental Explorations of Automatic Writing in Psychology," *Journal of the History of the Behavioral Sciences* 28 (January 1992): 5–26.

11. June Downey, *The Will-Temperament and Its Testing* (Yonkers-on Hudson, N.Y.: World Book, 1923), 3.

12. Leila Zenderland, *Measuring Minds: Henry Herbert Goddard and the Origins of American Intelligence Testing* (Cambridge: Cambridge University Press, 1998).

13. June Downey, "The Will-Profile: A Tentative Scale for Measurement of the Volitional Pattern," *University of Wyoming Bulletin* 16, no. 4b (1919): 1–40.

14. Downey, *Will-Temperament and Its Testing*, 56–57. June Downey, *Graphology and the Psychology of Handwriting* (Baltimore: Warwick and York, 1919). Emily Davis, "Debunking the Handwriting Experts: Graphology Found to Have Some Truth, Much Error," *Science News-Letter* 17, no. 479 (1930): 230–234.

15. Downey, *Will-Temperament and Its Testing*, 295.

16. Downey, *Creative Imagination*, 6–7.

17. Ibid., 175.

18. Ibid., 185.

19. Ibid., 82.

20. June Downey, "Literary Self-Projection," *Psychological Review* 19, no. 4 (1912): 299–311, 301.

21. Ibid., 308; Downey, *Creative Imagination*, 187.

22. Downey, *Creative Imagination*, 188.

23. Ibid., 176.

24. Downey, "Literary Self-Projection," 309.

25. Downey, *Creative Imagination*, 189.

26. Ibid.

27. Ibid.

28. Ibid., 186.

29. Ibid., 177–178.

30. Walter S. Hunter, *General Psychology* (Chicago: University of Chicago Press, 1919), 194–196.

31. Downey, "Individual Differences in Reaction to the Word-in-Itself," *American Journal of Psychology* 39, no. 1 (1927): 323–342, 324.

32. Ibid., 337.

33. Edward Bullough, "The 'Perceptive Problem' in the Aesthetic Appreciation of Single Colours," *British Journal of Psychology* 2, no. 4 (1908): 406–463, 418; Edward Bullough, *Aesthetics, Lectures and Essays,* ed. Elizabeth M. Wilkinson (Stanford: Stanford University Press, 1957).

34. Bullough, "The 'Perceptive Problem' in the Aesthetic Appreciation of Single Colours," 436–437.

35. Edward Bullough, "'Psychical Distance' as a Factor in Art and an Aesthetic Principle," *British Journal of Psychology* 5, no. 2 (1912): 87–118; Edward Bullough, "The 'Perceptive Problem' in the Aesthetic Appreciation of Simple Colour-Combinations," *British Journal of Psychology* 3, no. 4 (1910): 406–447; C. S. Myers, "Individual Differences in Listening to Music," *British Journal of Psychology* 13 (1922): 52–71.

36. Edward Bullough, "On the Apparent Heaviness of Colours," *British Journal of Psychology* 2, no. 2 (1907): 111–152, 152.

37. Bullough, "'Perceptive Problem' in the Aesthetic Appreciation of Single Colours," 457, 446–447. He considered empathy to be animation (*Beseelung*) and cited Johannes Volkelt.

38. Downey, *Creative Imagination,* 192.

39. Downey, "Individual Differences," 325. Downey cited Richard Müller-Freienfels, a student of art historian Heinrich Wölfflin, who argued that one could engage with art as spectator, participant, or ecstatic viewer who disappeared into the object.

40. Herbert Sydney Langfeld, *The Aesthetic Attitude* (Port Washington, N.Y.: Kennikat Press, 1920), vi; Langfeld, "A Response Interpretation of Consciousness," *Psychological Review* 38, no. 2 (1931): 87–108, 98.

41. John Dewey, "The Reflex Arc Concept in Psychology," *Psychological Review* 2 (1896): 357–370.

42. Herbert Langfeld, "Consciousness and Motor Response," *Psychological Review* 34, no. 1 (1927): 1–9.

43. Helen Huss Parkhurst, review of *The Aesthetic Attitude,* by Herbert Sydney Langfeld, *Journal of Philosophy* 19, no. 26 (1922): 717–718.

44. Carl Stumpf, Stanford Encyclopedia of Philosophy, revision February 2, 2015, https://plato.stanford.edu/entries/stumpf/.

45. F. C. Bartlett, "Herbert Sidney Langfeld, 1879–1958," *American Journal of Psychology* 71, no. 3 (1958): 616–619.

46. "Albert H. Hastorf, an interview conducted by Susan Ward Schofield: Transcript 2007–2008," Stanford Historical Society Oral History Collections (Stanford, Calif.: Stanford Oral History Project, 2010), 29.

47. Langfeld, *Aesthetic Attitude,* 112–113, see also 64.

48. Ibid., 279–280.

49. Ibid., 280.

50. Ibid., 60. He elaborated on empathy and drama in Herbert S. Langfeld, "The Ninth International Congress of Psychology," *Science*, n.s. 70, no. 1816 (1929): 364–368.

51. Edwin Boring, H. S. Langfeld, and Harry P. Weld, *Introduction to Psychology* (New York: J. Wiley and Sons, 1939), 274.

52. Gardner Murphy, *General Psychology* (New York: Harper and Brothers, 1933), 238–239.

53. Ibid., 239.

54. Boring, Langfeld, and Weld, *Introduction to Psychology*, 274.

55. Kate Gordon, "A Device for Demonstrating Empathy," *Journal of Experimental Psychology* 17, no. 6 (1934): 892–893.

56. Kate Gordon, *Esthetics* (New York: Henry Holt, 1909), 172.

57. Gordon Allport, "Muscle Tension/Empathy Pictures," HUG 4118.50, box 2, folder 31, Gordon Allport Papers, Harvard University Archive (hereafter GWA Papers); Gordon Allport, "Psychology of Participation," *Psychological Review* 53, no. 3 (1945): 118. The full quote reads: "*Empathy* arrived in a portmanteau packed in Munich. It was embedded in a whole self-psychology and in an epistemology of *Wissen von fremden Ichen*. Everything went into the ash can save only a greatly oversimplified version of what Lipps originally intended. *Motor mimicry* was all we wanted. What would we be doing with a 'mental act that held a guarantee of the objectivity of our knowledge'?" Italics in original.

58. The others were the *New York Herald Tribune* and *New York World*. Lynne Conner, *Spreading the Gospel of the Modern Dance: Newspaper Dance Criticism in the United States, 1850–1934* (Pittsburgh: University of Pittsburgh Press, 1997), 1, 7.

59. Conner, *Spreading the Gospel*, 90–93.

60. John Martin, *Introduction to the Dance* (New York: W. W. Norton, 1939), 241; Martin, *The Modern Dance* (Princeton, N.J.: Dance Horizons Book, 1989 [1933]), 55.

61. Graham wrote, "Dance is an absolute." Quoted in Mark Franko, *Dancing Modernism/Performing Politics* (Bloomington: Indiana University Press, 1995), 38. Lucile Marsh, the dance critic for *New York World*, used the designation "absolute" from Martin before "modern" became widely accepted. See Conner, *Spreading the Gospel*, 121. On the modernism of Graham's dance, see "Letters from Sally Banes and Susan Manning," *Drama Review* 33, no. 1 (1989); Franko, *Dancing Modernism/Performing Politics*, 38–74.

62. Dee Reynolds, *Rhythmic Subjects: Uses of Energy in the Dances of Mary Wigman, Martha Graham and Merce Cunningham* (Alton, Hampshire: Dance Books, 2007), 95.

63. John Martin, "The Dance: Its March from Decadence to a Modern 'Golden Age,'" *New York Times*, December 12, 1937, 152; John Martin, "The Dance Is Attuned to the Machine: As a Living Art It has Found a

New and Profitable Inspiration in the Modern Mechanistic Age," *New York Times*, February 24, 1929, 79.

64. John Martin, "The Dance: The Emphasis on Modernism," *New York Times*, October 13, 1929. See also Martin, "The Dance: Two Training Systems," *New York Times*, July 19, 1931.

65. John Martin, *America Dancing: The Background and Personalities of the Modern Dance* (New York: Dodge Publishing, 1936), 119, 146; Martin, *Introduction to the Dance*, 161.

66. Martin, *Introduction to the Dance*, 49.

67. Ibid., 48.

68. Ibid., 50.

69. Ibid., 51.

70. Martin, *Modern Dance*, 8.

71. Herbert Ellsworth Cory, "The Interactions of Beauty and Truth," *Journal of Philosophy* 22, no. 15 (1925): 393–402, 394.

72. Siobhan Burke, "Rejecting Artifice, Advancing Art: The Dance Criticism of John Martin," *Columbia Journal of American Studies* 9 (2009): 289–305.

73. Martin, *Modern Dance*, 59.

74. John Martin, "The Dance: One Artist," *New York Times*, March 10, 1929.

75. Martin, *Modern Dance*, 85.

76. Ibid., 53. On kinesthetic empathy as both imitation and creative innovation, see Reynolds, *Rhythmic Subjects*, 14.

77. Langfeld, *Aesthetic Attitude*, 117.

78. Martin, *Modern Dance*, 52.

79. Susan Leigh Foster, *Choreographing Empathy: Kinesthesia in Performance* (New York: Routledge, 2011); *Touching and Being Touched: Kinaesthesia and Empathy in Dance and Movement*, ed. Gabriele Brandstetter, Gerko Egert, and Sabine Zubarik (Berlin: de Gruyter, 2013); C. F. Berrol, "Neuroscience Meets Dance/Movement Therapy: Mirror Neurons, the Therapeutic Process and Empathy," *Arts in Psychotherapy* 33, no. 4 (2006): 302–315. See also Watching Dance: Kinesthetic Empathy project website and 2010 conference proceedings, http://www.watchingdance.org/.

80. Helge Lundholm, "The Affective Tone of Lines: Experimental Researches," *Psychological Review* 28, no. 1 (1921): 43–60.

81. Lundholm went on to a position in psychopathology at McLean Hospital in Belmont, Massachusetts, and taught psychology at Duke University. Biographical material, Helge Lundholm, box 36, News Service Biographical Files, circa 1930s–2004, University Archives, Duke University, Durham, N.C. Lundholm called empathy "that act of expanding the ego into the art-object." Helge Lundholm, *The Aesthetic Sentiment* (Cambridge Mass.: Sci-Art Publishers, 1941), 115–118.

82. Lundholm, "Affective Tone of Lines," 43–60.

83. Ibid., 56.

84. A. T. Poffenberger and B. E. Barrows, "The Feeling Value of Lines,"

Journal of Applied Psychology 8 (1924): 187–205. The phrase "feeling value of lines" was drawn from the work of Hugo Münsterberg.

85. Ibid., 200.

86. Ibid., 203.

87. Ibid.

88. Mark Johnson, *The Meaning of the Body: Aesthetics of Human Understanding* (Chicago: University of Chicago Press, 2007), 224–226. Johnson relies on Nancy Aiken, *The Biological Origins of Art* (Westport: Praeger, 1998).

89. W. E. Walton, "Empathic Responses in Children," *Psychological Monographs* 48, no. 213 (1936): 40–67.

90. Ibid., 65.

91. Carl Jung, "Psychological Types," in "Appendix: Four Papers on Psychological Typology," *The Collected Works of C. G. Jung*, ed. Herbert Read, Michael Fordham, and Gerhard Adler (Princeton: Princeton University Press, 1966), vol. 6, 510–523, 517. Jung's four basic functions—sensing, thinking, feeling, intuiting—were connected to one of the attitude types (extroversion or introversion) to produce eight different types.

92. Wilhelm Worringer, *Abstraktion und Einfuhlung: Ein Beitrag zur Stilpsychologie* (Munich: R. Piper, 1908), trans. as *Abstraction and Empathy: A Contribution to the Psychology of Style* (Chicago: Ivan R. Dee, 1997).

93. Worringer, *Abstraction and Empathy*, 5.

94. Ibid., 15.

95. Ibid., 9–10; Alois Riegl, *Spätrömische Kunstindustrie* (Vienna: Österr. staatsdruckerei, 1927 [1901]). On Riegl's notion of attentiveness, which drew from empathy theory, see Margaret Olin, "Forms of Respect: Alois Riegl's Concept of Attentiveness," *Art Bulletin* 66, no. 2 (2005): 285–299, 290. See also Frederic J. Schwartz, *Blind Spots: Critical Theory of and the History of Art in Twentieth-Century Germany* (New Haven: Yale University Press, 2005), 1–7.

96. Worringer, *Abstraction and Empathy*, 112–113.

97. Ibid., 137, note 7, see also 48.

98. Carl Jung, "A Contribution to the Study of Psychological Types," *Collected Works of C. G. Jung*, vol. 6, 497–509, 500. This lecture was translated into French in 1913 and into English in 1916 and published in Jung's *Collected Papers on Analytical Psychology*.

99. Jung, "Contribution to the Study of Psychological Types," 504–505.

100. Carl Jung, *Psychologische Typen* (Zurich: Rascher, 1921); *Psychological Types or the Psychology of Individuation*, trans. H. G. Baynes (New York: Harcourt, Brace, 1923).

101. Carl Jung, "Psychological Types," *Collected Works of C. G. Jung*, vol. 6, 290. He attributed the definition of *Einfühlung* as assimilation to Wilhelm Wundt.

102. Jung, *Psychological Types or the Psychology of Individuation*, 289–299; Jung, *Psychologische Typen*, 407–421.

103. Jung, "A Psychological Theory of Types," in "Appendix: Four Papers on Psychological Typology," *Collected Works of C. G. Jung*, vol. 6, 524–541, 534. This lecture was delivered in 1928, and appeared in English as "A Psychological Theory of Types," trans. W. S. Dell and Cary F. Baynes, in *Modern Man in Search of a Soul* (New York: Harcourt, Brace and World, 1933).

104. Herbert Read, *Art Now: An Introduction to the Theory of Modern Painting and Sculpture* (New York: Harcourt, Brace, 1936 [1933]), 49–50.

105. Herbert Read, *Education through Art* (New York: Pantheon Books, 1974 [1943]), 84–89.

106. Gordon W. Allport, "The Study of the Undivided Personality," *Journal of Abnormal and Social Psychology* 19, no. 2 (1924): 132–141.

107. Gordon Allport, "An Experimental Study of the Traits of Personality: With Application to the Problem of Social Diagnosis" (PhD diss., Harvard University, 1922), HU 90.1429, GWA Papers.

108. Allport, "Experimental Study of the Traits of Personality," 182.

109. Ibid., 202.

110. Gordon Allport, *Personality: A Psychological Interpretation* (New York: Holt, 1937), 18; Ian Nicholson, *Inventing Personality: Gordon Allport and the Science of Selfhood* (American Psychological Association, 2003), 103–132.

111. Allport, "Study of the Undivided Personality," 140. Floyd Allport, a social psychologist and Gordon's brother, called empathy a conditioned and circular behavioral response.

112. Allport, *Personality*, 531.

113. Gordon W. Allport, review of *Creative Imagination* by June Downey, *Psychological Bulletin* 27, no. 5 (1930): 408–410, 410. Gordon Allport to June Downey, February 26, 1930, 400025, box 11, folder 2, Downey Papers, American Heritage Center, University of Wyoming, Laramie (hereafter AHC).

114. June Downey to Allport, January 28, 1932, HUG 4118.10, box 2, Misc. Correspondence, 1930–1945, folder D, GWA Papers.

115. June Downey to Gordon Allport, February 6, 1931, 400025, box 5, folder 14, AHC.

116. Allport to Downey, April 5, 1931, 400025, box 5, folder 14, AHC.

117. Philip Vernon to June Downey, April 2, 1931, 400025, box 5, folder 14, AHC.

118. June Downey, "The Handwriting of Introverts and Extraverts," in *A Decade of Progress in Eugenics, Scientific Papers of the Third International Congress of Eugenics* (Baltimore: William and Wilkins, 1934), 67–75.

119. Downey, *Will-Temperament and Its Testing*, 299.

120. Uhrbrock, "June Etta Downey," 3.

121. Gordon W. Allport and Philip E. Vernon, *Studies in Expressive Movement* (New York: Macmillan, 1933), 171.

122. Allport, "Study of the Undivided Personality," 134. Italics in original.

123. Gordon W. Allport, *The Use of Personal Documents in Psychological Science* (New York: Social Science Research Council, 1942), chaps. 2, 4. He praised the case studies elaborated in John Dollard, *Criteria for the Life History: With Analyses of Six Notable Documents* (New Haven: Yale University Press, 1935).

124. Allport, *Personality*, 515–516; Allport, "The Study of Personality by the Intuitive Method: An Experiment in Teaching from the Locomotive God," *Journal of Abnormal and Social Psychology* 24 (1929): 14–27, 26. After 1929, Allport used the term "intuition" more frequently than "empathy," although he was not always consistent in this choice. See Nicolson, *Inventing Personality*, 157–158.

125. Llewellyn N. Wiley, "A Résumé of Major Experiments in Abstract Design Ending with the Year 1941," *Psychological Bulletin* 38, no. 10 (1941): 976–990, 976.

126. Daniel Catton Rich, "Aesthetic Theory for Museum Curators," *College Art Journal* 6, no. 3 (1947): 171–172, 172.

127. Van Meter Ames, "On Empathy," *Philosophical Review* 52, no. 5 (1943): 490–494, 490.

128. Ernest Mundt, "New Program for an Art School," *College Art Journal* 14, no. 3 (1955): 236–240, 238; Mundt, "Scientific and Artistic Knowledge in Art Education," *College Art Journal* 10, no. 4 (1951): 333–336. Raymond Bayer, "Method in Aesthetics," *Journal of Aesthetics and Art Criticism* 7, no. 4 (1949): 308–324, 313.

129. Thomas Munro, "The Psychology of Art: Past, Present, Future," *Journal of Aesthetics and Art Criticism* 21, no. 3 (1963): 263–282, 266. Munro was an assistant to Albert Barnes, art collector and critic of empathy theories, even as he retained a kinesthetic interpretation of art. See Veder, *Living Line*, 311–313. Clarence DeWitt Thorpe, "Some Notices of 'Empathy' Before Lipps," *Papers of the Michigan Academy of Science, Arts and Letters* 23 (1937): 525–533, 525. I. A. Richards, *Coleridge on Imagination* (London: Kegan Paul, 1934).

130. Clement Greenberg, "Modernist Painting," Forum Lectures (Washington, D.C.: Voice of America, 1960). For an account of how Greenberg expunged the German roots of modernism, adapting and excluding Hans Hofmann's spiritualist leanings and highlighting its French cubist heritage, see Caroline Jones, *Eyesight Alone: Clement Greenberg's Modernism and the Bureaucratization of the Senses* (Chicago: University of Chicago Press, 2005), 114, 145–203. Dee Reynolds critiques Greenberg's claim regarding the opticality of modernist painting, arguing that a viewer responded with projected movement; Kandinsky said one could enter into and "'stroll' within the picture." Reynolds, *Rhythmic Subjects*, 96.

131. Max Dessoir, "Aesthetics and the Philosophy of Art in Contemporary Germany," *Monist* 36 (1926): 299–310, 301.

132. See Balcomb Greene, "The Doctrine of Pure Aesthetic: Views and Comments of a Contemporary Artist," *College Art Journal* 19, no. 2 (1959–1960): 122–133, 122; Alden F. Megrew, "College Fine Arts Today," *College Art Journal* 9, no. 2 (1949–1950): 168–175, 172; Walter Quirt, "Art's Theoretical Basis," *College Art Journal* 12, no. 1 (1952): 12–15, quote on 13.

133. Jarzombek argues that empathy theory had an immense impact on twentieth-century modernist discourses as well as on "the depths of popular culture." Jarzombek, *Psychologizing Modernity*, 59–60.

134. Lester D. Longman, "The Fine Arts in Higher Education: Advice for Curriculum Planners," *College Art Journal* 19, no. 2 (1959–1960): 154–157, 155.

135. Richard H. Fogle, "Empathic Imagery in Keats and Shelley," *PMLA* 61, no. 1 (1946): 163–191.

136. Kurt Koffka, "Problems in the Psychology of Art," in *Art: A Bryn Mawr Symposium*, R. Bernheimer, R. Carpenter, K. Koffka, and M. C. Nahm (New York: Oriole Editions, 1972), 180–273.

137. R. M. Ogden "Review of Art: A Bryn Mawr Symposium," *American Journal of Psychology* 55, no. 2 (1942): 297–298, 298.

138. Rudolf Arnheim, "Expression," in *Art and Visual Perception* (Berkeley: University of California Press, 1965 [1954]), 360–376.

139. Rudolf Arnheim, "The Gestalt Theory of Expression," *Psychological Review* 56, no. 3 (1949): 156–171, 163.

140. Ibid., 164.

141. Caroll C. Pratt, *The Meaning of Music: A Study in Psychological Aesthetics* (New York: McGraw-Hill, 1931), 185–186.

142. Ibid., 184.

143. John Dewey, *Art as Experience* (New York: Penguin, 2005 [1934]), 103.

144. Ibid., 105.

145. Ibid., 106. The citation is from Vernon Lee, *The Beautiful* (Cambridge: Cambridge University Press, 1913), 33.

146. Dewey, *Art as Experience*, 108.

147. Wolfgang Köhler, "Psychological Remarks on Some Questions of Anthropology," *American Journal of Psychology* 50, no. 1/4 (1937): 271–288.

148. H. S. Langfeld, "Concerning Empathy," 4, Herbert S. Langfeld Papers, box M586, folder 2, Archives of the History of American Psychology, Center for the History of Psychology, University of Akron; published as Langfeld, "Concerning Empathy," *Miscellanea Psychologica Albert Michotte* (Louvain: Editions de l'Institut Supérieur de Philosophie, 1947), 106–110.

149. Ibid.

150. Ibid., 5. One theorist called the new television camera an empathic perceiver for "lending motion to motionless things." Nancy Newhall, "Television and the Arts," *Parnassus* 12, no. 1 (1940): 37–38, 38.

151. Rudolf Arnheim, "Art among the Objects," *Critical Inquiry* 13, no. 4

(1987): 677–685, 680. Arnheim's views still circulate; see Bill Brown, "Thing Theory," *Critical Inquiry* 28, no. 1 (2001): 1–22.

152. Langfeld, "Concerning Empathy," 1.

153. Geddes MacGregor, *Aesthetic Experience in Religion* (London: Macmillan, 1947), 84.

154. Edward Sankowski, "Emotion and the Appreciation of Art," *Journal of Aesthetic Education* 10, no. 2 (1976): 45–67, 56. The psychologist Gardner Murphy, however, continued to describe empathy in 1947 as motor engagement with objects: "He puts himself in the place of the pillar that is too slender to support the shaft, and he judges it inappropriate; he is pulled awry by the Picasso painting which tilts the house upon its foundation." Gardner Murphy, *Personality: A Biosocial Approach to Origins and Structure* (New York: Harper and Brothers, 1947), 494.

155. Clarence DeWitt Thorpe, "Empathy," *Dictionary of World Literature*, ed. Joseph T. Shipley (New York: Philosophical Library, 1943), 186–188, 187.

Chapter 4. The Limits of Empathy in Schizophrenia

1. E. E. Southard and Mary Jarrett, *The Kingdom of Evils: Psychiatric Social Work Presented in One Hundred Case Histories Together with a Classification of Social Divisions of Evil* (New York: Arno Press, 1973 [1922]), 302.

2. E. E. Southard, "The Empathic Index in the Diagnosis of Mental Diseases," *Journal of Abnormal Psychology* 13, no. 4 (1918): 199–214, 207–208.

3. The relevant two lines of Robert Burns's "To a Louse" are: "O wad some Power the giftie gie us / To see ToursLs as ithers see us!"

4. Southard and Jarrett, *Kingdom of Evils*, 475.

5. Roy G. Hoskins, *The Biology of Schizophrenia* (New York: W. W. Norton, 1946), 70.

6. Susan D. Lamb, *Pathologist of the Mind: Adolf Meyer and the Origins of American Psychiatry* (Baltimore: Johns Hopkins University Press, 2014); Elizabeth Lunbeck, *The Psychiatric Persuasion: Knowledge, Gender and Power in Modern America* (Princeton: Princeton University Press, 1994), 65; Hans Pols, "Divergences in American Psychiatry during the Depression: Somatic Psychiatry, Community Mental Hygiene, and Social Reconstruction," *Journal of the History of the Behavioral Sciences* 37, no. 4 (2001): 369–388. Southard lectured on "The Major Divisions of Mental Hygiene: Public, Social, Individual" at the Massachusetts Society for Mental Hygiene on November 17, 1915, printed in *Boston Medical and Surgical Journal* 175, no. 12 (1916): 404–406.

7. See L. Vernon Briggs, *History of the Psychopathic Hospital, Boston Massachusetts* (Boston: Wright and Potter, 1922).

8. "Reports of the President and the Treasurer of Harvard College, 1913–1914," *Official Register of Harvard University* 12, no. 1, part 7 (Cambridge:

Harvard University, 1915), 152. Richard C. Cabot, "Elmer Ernest South-ard, 1876–1920," *Harvard Graduates Magazine* 28 (1919–1920): 611–626. E. E. Southard and H. C. Solomon, *Neurosyphilis: Modern Systematic Diagnosis and Treatment Presented in One Hundred and Thirty-Seven Case Histories* (Boston: W. M. Leonard, 1917); E. E. Southard, *Shell-Shock and Other Neuropsychiatric Problems Presented in Five Hundred and Eighty-Nine Case Histories from the War Literature, 1914–1918* (Boston: W. M Leonard, 1919).

9. Harvard class reports as cited in Frederick P. Gay, *The Open Mind: Elmer Ernest Southard, 1876–1920* (Chicago: Normandie House, 1938), 43.

10. Research materials of Ada P. McCormick, Interviews, box 19 out of 20, Richard Clarke Cabot Papers, Harvard University Archive, HUG 4255.80.

11. Gay, *Open Mind*, 24, 26. Southard's brain was examined by his colleague Myrtelle Canavan, who discovered an anomaly in cerebral circulation, which she said accorded with the mental overexertion Southard displayed throughout his life. Gay, *Open Mind*, 26–27.

12. Walter Arensberg to Frederick P. Gay, February 4, 1935, box 11, Elmer Earnest Southard 1876–1920 Papers, Center for the History of Medicine, Francis A. Countway Library of Medicine, Harvard University (hereafter EES Papers).

13. Gay, *Open Mind*, 252–253. Southard was friendly with art collector Walter Conrad Arensberg, whom he visited frequently in New York City and who arranged the talk. Walter Pach to F. Gay, January 11, 1935, box 11, EES Papers.

14. Gay, *Open Mind*, 64.

15. R. C. Cabot, "Elmer Ernest Southard, 1876–1920," *Harvard Graduates Magazine* 28 (1919–1920): 611–626, 621. E. E. Southard, "Has Pathology a LOGIC of Its Own?" Syracuse address, May 6, 1916, 9, box 9, folder 15, EES papers.

16. Harvey Cushing, Yale University School of Medicine, to Frederick P. Gay, November 23, 1934, box 11, EES Papers.

17. E. E. Southard, "On Descriptive Analysis of Manifest Delusions from the Subject's Point of View," *Journal of Abnormal Psychology* 11 (1916): 189–202; Josiah Royce, "The External World and the Social Consciousness," *Philosophical Review* 3, no. 5 (1894): 513–545, 539. On Royce, see Bruce Kuklick, *The Rise of American Philosophy* (New Haven: Yale University Press, 1977), 307–308. Royce also delved into abnormal psychology: Josiah Royce, "Some Observations on the Anomalies of Self-Consciousness," *Psychological Review* 2, no. 6 (1895): 574–584.

18. E. E. Southard, "On the Application of Grammatical Categories to the Analysis of Delusions," *Philosophical Review* 25, no. 3 (1916): 424–455.

19. Southard and Jarrett, *Kingdom of Evils*, 369.

20. Southard, "Empathic Index," 201.

21. E. E. Southard, "Psychological Wants of Psychiatrists: A Psychopathic Hospital Point of View," paper presented at American Psychological Association, Pittsburgh, December 28, 1917, box 8, folder 3, EES Papers; Southard, "Brief Statement of Progress in the Development of Methods for the Psychological Examination of Psychopathic Patients," box 8, folder 4, EES Papers.

22. "Examples of Southard's Chess Play and His Use of Introspection for Chess Imagery (His Own Notes)," Appendix C, in Gay, *Open Mind*, 297–299.

23. Gay, *Open Mind*, 56.

24. Robert M. Yerkes, *Introduction to Psychology* (New York: Holt, 1911), 190.

25. Ibid., 191.

26. Ibid., 192.

27. Southard, "Empathic Index," 205.

28. Ibid. Southard was not an adherent of psychoanalysis. See E. E. Southard, "Sigmund Freud, Pessimist," *Journal of Abnormal Psychology* 14, no. 3 (1919): 197–216.

29. Southard, "Empathic Index," 200.

30. Ibid., 200, 203.

31. Ibid., 203.

32. Ibid., 206.

33. Ibid.

34. Southard and Jarrett, *Kingdom of Evils*, ix. Richard C. Cabot wrote the introduction. For more on Cabot's medical practice, see Christopher Crenner, *Private Practice: In the Early Twentieth-Century Medical Office of Dr. Richard Cabot* (Baltimore: Johns Hopkins University Press, 2005).

35. Southard and Jarrett, *Kingdom of Evils*, 123.

36. Ibid., 269.

37. Ibid.

38. There is a large critical historical literature on psychiatry as a form of social control, initiated in good part by Michel Foucault's 1961 *Histoire de la folie*, with notable contributions by Andrew Scull, Elizabeth Lunbeck, and Jonathan Metzel, among many others.

39. Southard, "Empathic Index," 211.

40. Clarence I. Lewis, *Mind and World-Order: Outline of a Theory of Knowledge* (New York: Charles Scribner's Sons, 1929), 409. On the pathetic fallacy, see John Ruskin, *Modern Painters* (Boston: Estes and Lauriat, 1894), vol. 3, 172–188.

41. William James, *Principles of Psychology* (Cambridge: Harvard University Press, 1983 [1890]), vol. 1, 195; Edward Reed, "The Psychologist's Fallacy as a Persistent Framework in William James's Psychological Reasoning," *History of the Human Sciences* 8, no. 1 (1995): 61–72.

42. Jimena Canales, *A Tenth of a Second: A History* (Chicago: University of Chicago Press, 2009), 21–58.

43. E. E. Southard, "Recent American Classification of Mental Diseases," *American Journal of Insanity* 75, no. 3 (1919): 331–349, 342.

44. Southard, "Empathic Index," 212.

45. William A. White, "Suggestion, Empathy and Bad Thinking," in *Problems of Personality* (New York: Harcourt, Brace, 1925), 29–36, 32.

46. William A. White, *Principles of Mental Hygiene* (New York: Macmillan, 1917). On White, see Nathan Hale, Jr., *Freud and the Americans* (Oxford, 1971), 379–383. Nathan Hale, *The Rise and Crisis of Psychoanalysis in the United States: Freud and the Americans, 1917–1985* (Oxford: Oxford University Press, 1995), 23.

47. White, "Suggestion, Empathy and Bad Thinking," 33.

48. Theodore Schroeder, "The Psychoanalytic Method of Observation," *International Journal of Psychoanalysis* 6 (1925): 155–170, 162. Schroeder defined Einfühlung as a delusive process of animating and investing inanimate objects with our feelings and mental processes, whereas he described empathy as a conscious process necessary for psychoanalysis.

49. A. A. Brill, "The Empathic Index and Personality," *Medical Record: A Weekly Journal of Medicine and Surgery* 97, no. 4 (1920): 131–134. One respondent wrote that empathy should sport the adjective "empathetic" and not "empathic" but that dictionaries were silent on the issue. Harry Dexter Kitson, "Notes and News," *Journal of Philosophy, Psychology and Scientific Methods* 17, no. 23 (1920): 644. A. A. Brill, "Thoughts on Life and Death," *Psychiatric Quarterly* 21, no. 2 (1947): 199–211.

50. A. A. Brill, *Fundamental Conceptions of Psychoanalysis* (New York: Harcourt, Brace, 1921), 170; A. A. Brill, *Lectures on Psychoanalytic Psychiatry* (New York: Alfred A. Knopf, 1946).

51. Foster Ware, "The Answer to Those Who Ask Another," *New York Times*, May 1, 1927, SM4.

52. Ibid.

53. Brill, "Empathic Index," 134.

54. K. L. Chatelaine, *Harry Stack Sullivan: The Formative Years* (Washington, D.C.: University Press of America, 1981).

55. Harry Stack Sullivan, "Conceptions of Modern Psychiatry: The First William Alanson White Memorial Lectures," *Psychiatry* 3, no. 1 (1940): 1–117, 8; Harry Stack Sullivan, "A Note on the Implications of Psychiatry, the Study of Interpersonal Relations, for Investigations in the Social Sciences," *American Journal of Sociology* (1937): 848–861, 852.

56. Ernest Beaglehole, "Notes on the Theory of Interpersonal Relations," *Psychiatry* 3, no. 1 (1940): 511–526, 513.

57. Ibid., 514.

58. Harry Stack Sullivan, *The Interpersonal Theory of Psychiatry*, ed. Helen Swick Perry and Mary Lad Gawel (New York: W. W. Norton, 1953), 41–42.

59. E. E. Southard, "Non-Dementia Non-Praecox: Note on the Advantages to Mental Hygiene of Extirpating a Term" [1919], with an introduction

by Richard Noll, *History of Psychiatry* 18, no. 4 (2007): 483–502. On the history of dementia praecox, see Richard Noll, *American Madness: The Rise and Fall of Dementia Praecox* (Cambridge: Harvard University Press, 2011).

60. Southard and Jarrett, *Kingdom of Evils*, 313; E. E. Southard, "The Range of the General Practitioner in Psychiatric Diagnosis," *JAMA* 73, no. 17 (1919): 1253–1256, 1255.

61. E. E. Southard, "A Key to the Practical Grouping of Mental Diseases," *Journal of Nervous and Mental Disease* 47, no. 1 (1918): 1–19, 15.

62. Southard concluded that brains of patients with dementia praecox had convolutional abnormalities and microscopic evidence of structural abnormalities. Gay, *Open Mind*, 244. E. E. Southard, "The Stratigraphical Analysis of Finer Cortex Changes in Certain Normal-Looking Brains in Dementia Praecox," *Journal of Nervous and Mental Disease* 45, no. 2 (1917): 97–129.

63. Lawson G. Lowrey, "An Analysis of the Accuracy of Psychopathic Hospital Diagnoses," *American Journal of Insanity* 75, no. 3 (1919): 351–370, 332; Lawson G. Lowrey, "A Study of the Diagnoses in Cases Seen at the Psychopathic Department and Hospital Department of the Boston State Hospital," *American Journal of Insanity* 77 (1921): 438–449.

64. Lowrey, "Analysis of the Accuracy of Psychopathic Hospital Diagnoses," 367.

65. Gay, *Open Mind*, 116; L. G. Lowrey, "Differential Diagnosis in Psychiatry: A Comparison of Symptoms in Various Disease States," *Boston Medical and Surgical Journal* 178, no. 21 (1918): 703–708, 703.

66. Southard and Jarrett, *Kingdom of Evils*, 388. Lunbeck, *Psychiatric Persuasion*, 43; Gay, *Open Mind*, 135.

67. The first diagnostic manual was *The Statistical Manual for the Use of Institutions for the Insane* (American Medico-Psychological Association and National Committee for Mental Hygiene, 1918). Southard, "Non-Dementia Non-Praecox."

68. E. E. Southard, "A Key to the Practical Grouping of Mental Diseases," *Journal of Nervous and Mental Disease* 47, no. 1 (1918): 1–19.

69. He called it "telesmatics." Southard to Gay, May 8, 1919; Southard to Gay, April 10, 1919, box 11, EES Papers. E. E. Southard, "Applications of the Pragmatic Method to Psychiatry," *Journal of Laboratory and Clinical Medicine* 5, no. 3 (1919): 139–145. See also Southard and Harry Solomon, "Morbi Neurales: An Attempt to Apply a Key Principle the Differentiation of the Major Groups," *Archives of Neurology and Psychiatry* 3, no. 3 (1920): 219–229; Southard, "Recent American Classification of Mental Diseases," *American Journal of Insanity* 75, no. 3 (1919): 331–349, 342.

70. He allowed that internists might want to exclude somatic forms of disease (group 6) before focal brain disease (group 5) but thought this order should stand for psychiatrists. Southard, "Applications of the Pragmatic Method to Psychiatry," 143.

71. Ibid., 144. Southard, "Key to the Practical Grouping," 15.

72. Southard, "Key for History Reading" (abbrev. folder title), Arch. GA 81, box 2, EES Papers.

73. Cases of Dementia Praecox, Danvers State Hospital, box 6, folder 5, EES Papers.

74. Southard, "Key to the Practical Grouping," 15; Lowrey, "Differential Diagnosis in Psychiatry," 707.

75. E. E. Southard, "Last Lecture to Third Year Class in Psychiatry, November 28, 1916," Arch. GA 81, box 10, "Lectures, 1916," 7, EES papers.

76. Southard, "Empathic Index," 206; Southard and Jarrett, *Kingdom of Evils*, 474.

77. Mary Isham, "The Paraphrenic's Inaccessibility," *Psychoanalytic Review* 7, no. 2 (1920): 246–256, 231.

78. Ibid., 256.

79. Louis Sass, "Introspection, Schizophrenia, and the Fragmentation of Self," *Representations*, no. 19 (1987): 1–34, 27.

80. Southard, "Empathic Index," 213.

81. Gay states that his death was due to "general septicemia and meningitis with brain hemorrhage (apoplexy) due to *Staphylococus aureus.*" Gay, *Open Mind*, 288.

82. Jaspers distinguished between "Einfühlbares und Nichteinfühlbares (Natürlichenes und Schizophrenes) Seelenleben," *Allgemeine Psychopathologie* (Berlin: Julius Springer, 1913), 89, translated as *General Psychopathology* (Chicago: University of Chicago Press, 1968); Eugen Bleuler, *Dementia Praecox oder Gruppe der Schizophrenien* (Tübingen: Ed. Discord, 1988 [1911]).

83. Susan Lanzoni, "Diagnosing with Feeling: The Clinical Assessment of Schizophrenia in Early Twentieth-Century European Psychiatry," in *Emotions, Medicine and Disease, 1750–1950*, ed. Fay Bound Alberti (London: Palgrave Macmillan, 2006), 169–190; Sass, "Introspection, Schizophrenia, and the Fragmentation of Self," 4.

84. Sander Gilman, "Seeing the Schizophrenic: On the 'Bizarre' in Psychiatry and Art," *Disease and Representation: Images of Illness from Madness to AIDS* (Ithaca: Cornell University Press, 1988), 231–244.

85. George W. Pigman, "Freud and the History of Empathy," *International Journal of Psychoanalysis* 76 (1995): 237–252, 248.

86. James Sully, *Studies of Childhood* (London: Longmans, 1895); L. W. Stern, *Psychologie des frühen Kindheit bis zum sechsten Lebensjahr* (Leipzig: Wuelle und Meyer, 1914); Alfred Storch, "The Primitive Archaic Forms of Inner Experience and Thought in Schizophrenia," *Nervous and Mental Disease Monograph*, no. 36 (1924); George Devereux, "A Sociological Theory of Schizophrenia," *Psychoanalytic Review* 26 (1939): 315–342, 332; Gustav Jahoda, "Piaget and Lévy-Bruhl," *History of Psychology* 3, no. 3 (2000): 218–238.

87. White, "Suggestion, Empathy and Bad Thinking," 32.

88. W. A. White, "Symbolism," *Psychoanalytic Review* 3, no. 1 (1916): 1–25, 20.

89. Ibid., 14. Victor Tausk, a member of Freud's circle, described the schizophrenic as suffering from a "loss of ego boundaries," see Sass, "Introspection, Schizophrenia, and the Fragmentation of Self," 5.

90. William A. White, "Individuality and Introversion," *Psychoanalytic Review* 4, no. 1 (1916): 455–457, 456.

91. Hal Foster, *Prosthetic Gods* (Cambridge: MIT Press, 2004), 197. A later study of "schizophrenic art" drew on Prinzhorn to argue that subjects using empathy could distinguish paintings by schizophrenics from those painted by controls. A. N. Main, "A New Look at Empathy," *British Journal of Aesthetics* 9, no. 1 (1969): 60–72.

92. Foster, *Prosthetic Gods*, 199.

93. Doris Kaufmann, "'Pushing the Limits of Understanding': The Discourse on Primitivism in German *Kulturwissenschaften*, 1880–1930," *Studies in History and Philosophy of Science* 39, no. 3 (2008): 434–443, 442.

94. Nolan D. C. Lewis, preface to *Language and Thought in Schizophrenia: Collected Papers Presented at the Meeting of the American Psychiatric Association, May 12, 1939, Chicago, Illinois* (New York: W. W. Norton, 1944), xi.

95. Bleuler, *Dementia Praecox*, 1911; J. Parnas and P. Bover, "Autism in Schizophrenia Revisited," *Comprehensive Psychiatry* 31, no. 1 (1991): 7–21.

96. Hoskins, *Biology of Schizophrenia*, 165.

97. For a history of Worcester State Hospital before Hoskins's time, see Gerald Grob, *The State and the Mentally Ill: A History of Worcester State Hospital in Massachusetts, 1830–1920* (Chapel Hill: University of North Carolina Press, 1966).

98. Hoskins to C. Charles Burlingame, January 9, 1945, 2, Salmon Committee on Psychiatry and Mental Hygiene Records, Lecturer Files, box 8-9, New York Academy of Medicine Library, New York, New York.

99. Walter B. Cannon, "Roy Graham Hoskins: An Appreciation," *Endocrinology* 30, no. 6 (1942): 839–845, 840, reprint located in Biographical and Personal Papers, 1942–1959, H MS c 210, box 2, folder 8, Roy G. Hoskins Papers, 1908–1965, Center for the History of Medicine, Francis A. Countway Library of Medicine, Harvard University (hereafter RGH Papers); Walter B. Cannon, *Body Changes in Pain, Hunger, Fear and Rage: An Account of Recent Researches into the Functions of Emotional Excitement* (New York: D. Appleton, 1920). See also Otniel Dror, "The Affect of Experiment: The Turn to Emotions in Anglo-American Physiology, 1900–1940," *Isis* 90, no. 2 (1999): 205–237.

100. Personal Communication, Robert G. Hoskins (son of Roy G. Hoskins), May 18, 2017.

101. For a fictionalized account of McCormick's plight, see T. Coraghessan Boyle, *Riven Rock* (New York: Viking, 1998).

102. For excerpts of the case notes made by these psychiatrists, see Richard Noll, "Styles of Psychiatric Practice, 1906–1925: Clinical Evaluations of

the Same Patient by James Jackson Putnam, Adolph Meyer, August Hoch, Emil Kraepelin, and Smith Ely Jelliffe," *History of Psychiatry* 10 (1999): 145–189.

103. Kraepelin, 1908, cited in Noll, "Styles of Psychiatric Practice, 1906–1925," 171.

104. Katherine McCormick to R. G. Hoskins, July 16, 1932, "Administrata: Memorial Foundation Correspondence, 1932–1957," H MS c 210, box 2, folder 4, RGH Papers.

105. Miriam Kleiman, "Rich, Famous, and Questionably Sane: When a Wealthy Heir's Family Sought Help from a Hospital for the Insane," *Prologue Magazine* 39, no. 2 (Summer 2007), http://www.archives.gov/publications /prologue/2007/summer/mccormick.html. Accessed November 19, 2014.

106. Joseph P. Morrissey and Howard H. Goldman "The Ambiguous Legacy," in *The Enduring Asylum: Cycles of Institutional Reform at Worcester State Hospital* (New York: Grune and Stratton, 1980), 45–97, 75–78.

107. Roy G. Hoskins, Fourth Annual Report of the Director of Research, January 1, 1931, 9, 11, "Administrata: Reports and Memos for the Memorial Foundation, 1931–1965," H MS c 210, box 2, folder 5, RGH Papers.

108. R. G. Hoskins, "Dementia Praecox: A Simplified Formulation," *JAMA* 96, no. 15 (1931): 1209–1211.

109. Hoskins to Mrs. McCormick, February 3, 1932, "Administrata: Memorial Foundation Correspondence, 1932–1957," 1, H MS c 210, box 2, folder 4, RGH Papers.

110. R. G. Hoskins and F. H. Sleeper, "A Case of Hebephrenic Dementia Praecox with Marked Improvement under Thyroid Treatment," *Endocrinology* 13, no. 5 (1929): 459–466; David Shakow, "The Worcester State Hospital Research on Schizophrenia, 1927–1946," *Journal of Abnormal Psychology* 80, no. 1 (1972): 67–110.

111. R. G. Hoskins, "The Manganese Treatment of 'Schizophrenic Disorders,'" *Journal of Nervous and Mental Disease* 79, no. 1 (1934): 59–62.

112. "Memorandum on the 5th Annual Meeting of the Memorial Foundation for Neuro-Endocrine Research, held on March 2, 1932," "Administrata: Memorial Foundation Correspondence, 1932–1957," H MS c 210, box 2, folder 6, RGH Papers.

113. Ibid., 7.

114. "Special Interim Report of the Director of Research to Board of Trustees of the Memorial Foundation for Neuro-Endocrine, November, 1, 1935," 11, H MS c 210, box, 2 folder 6, RGH Papers.

115. "Memorandum . . . 1932," 3, "Administrata: Memorial Foundation Correspondence, 1932–1957," H MS c 210, box 2, folder 6, RGH Papers.

116. R. G. Hoskins, "An Analysis of the Schizophrenia Problem from the Standpoint of the Investigator," *JAMA* 97, no. 10 (1931): 682–685, 684.

117. The results of the poll were distributed to the staff: "The Nature of Schizophrenia," box M1304, folder "Dementia Praecox, 1933," 3, David

Shakow Papers, Drs. Nicholas and Dorothy Cummings Center for the History of Psychology, University of Akron (hereafter Shakow Papers).

118. Mrs. Stanley McCormick to R. G. Hoskins, June 23, 1932, "Administrata: Memorial Foundation Correspondence, 1932–1957," H MS c 210, box 2, folder 4, RGH Papers; Shakow, "Worcester State Hospital Research on Schizophrenia," 83. Morrissey and Goldman, "Ambiguous Legacy," 78.

119. In the 1939 annual report, the research staff included Roy G. Hoskins, PhD, MD, director; Andras Angyal, PhD, MD, resident director of research; Joseph M. Looney, MD, director of laboratories; Harry Freeman, MD, internist; Conrad Wall, MD, psychiatrist; Otto Kant, MD, psychiatrist; Nathan Blackman, MD, psychiatrist; Mortin A. Rubin, MD, neurophysiologist; David Shakow, MA, chief psychologist; George L. Banay, PhD, medical librarian. Public Document #23, Annual Report Trustees, Worcester State Hospital, for the year ending November 30, 1939. http://archive.org/stream/annualreportoftr142worc/annualreportoftr142worc_djvu.txt. Accessed November 15, 2014.

120. Shakow, "Worcester State Hospital Research on Schizophrenia," 80.

121. Ibid., 81, 87–88.

122. Hoskins, *Biology of Schizophrenia*, 11.

123. Shakow, "Worcester State Hospital Research on Schizophrenia," 74.

124. Ibid., 74–75.

125. Morrissey and Goldman, "Ambiguous Legacy," 65–69.

126. Memo, August 23, 1933, box M1304, folder "Dementia Praecox, 1933," 2, Shakow Papers.

127. David Shakow, "Clinical Psychology Seen Some Fifty Years Later," in *Evolving Perspectives on the History of Psychology*, ed. Wade Pickren and Donald A. Dewsbury (Washington, D.C.: American Psychological Association, 2002), 434; L. Shaffer, "Frederic Lyman Wells, 1884–1964," *American Journal of Psychology* 77, no. 4 (1964): 679–682.

128. David Shakow, *The Nature of the Deterioration in Schizophrenic Conditions*, Nervous and Mental Disease Monographs (New York: Coolidge Foundation, 1946), 61. Shakow's first attempt at a dissertation under Professor Boring on subliminal psychology was deemed inconclusive. He was awarded the PhD for his work with schizophrenics in 1942.

129. Ibid., 59.

130. David Shakow, "The Worcester Internship Program," *Journal of Consulting Psychology* 10 (1946): 191–200. On the Conference for the Training of Clinical Psychologists and Shakow's role, see James H. Capshew, *Psychologists on the March: Science, Practice, and Professional Identity in America, 1929–1969* (Cambridge: Cambridge University Press, 1999), 134–137.

131. Anton T. Boisen, *The Exploration of the Inner World: A Study of Mental Disorder and Religious Experience* (Philadelphia: University of Pennsylvania Press, 1936), 3.

132. Ibid., 11.

133. Ibid., 28.

134. Allison Stokes, *Ministry after Freud* (New York: Pilgrim Press, 1985), chap. 4; E. Brooks Holifield, *A History of Pastoral Care in America: From Salvation to Self-Realization* (Eugene, Ore.: Wipf and Stock, 1983), 234. On Boisen, see 244–249.

135. Hoskins, *Biology of Schizophrenia*, 61.

136. R. G. Hoskins and E. Morton Jellinek, "The Schizophrenic Personality with Special Regard to Psychologic and Organic Concomitants," *Proceedings of the Association for Research in Nervous and Mental Disease* 14 (1933): 211–233; Shakow, "Worcester State Hospital Research on Schizophrenia," 76.

137. "Official Interim Report of the Director of Research to the Board of Trustees of the Memorial Foundation for Neuro-Endocrine Research, November 1, 1935," 9, "Administrata: Reports and Memos for Memorial Foundation, 1931–1965," H MS c 210, box 2, folder 6, RGH Papers.

138. Hoskins, *Biology of Schizophrenia*, 121. He cites Hans Selye, "Role of the Hypophysis in the Pathogenesis of Diseases of Adaptation," *Canadian Medical Association Journal* 50, no. 5 (1944): 426–433.

139. Hoskins and Jellinek, "Schizophrenic Personality with Special Regard to Psychologic and Organic Concomitants," 231.

140. Hoskins, *Biology of Schizophrenia*, 102. Schizophrenics were described as lacking empathy in the 1968 Diagnostic and Statistical Manual of Mental Disorders II. Jonathan Metzl, *The Protest Psychosis: How Schizophrenia Became a Black Disease* (Boston: Beacon Press, 2009), 96.

141. Hoskins, *Biology of Schizophrenia*, 77.

142. Ibid., 80.

143. Ibid., 53.

144. Ibid., 51. Hoskins referenced Peter Kropotkin's 1902 *Mutual Aid*, which counted cooperation as an important evolutionary principle; Walter Bradford, "Roy Graham Hoskins: An Appreciation," *Endocrinology* 30, no. 6 (1942): 839–845.

145. Andras Angyal, *Foundations for a Science of Personality* (New York: Commonwealth Fund, 1941), 224–225.

146. Ibid., 181, 222.

147. Hoskins, *Biology of Schizophrenia*, 52–53.

148. The first definition was: "the imaginal or mental projection of oneself into the elements of a work of art or into a natural object." Howard C. Warren, ed., *Dictionary of Psychology* (Boston: Houghton Mifflin, 1934), 92.

149. Hoskins, *Biology of Schizophrenia*, 54.

150. Ibid., 55.

151. Milton H. Erikson and R. G. Hoskins, "Grading of Patients in Mental Hospitals as a Therapeutic Measure," *American Journal of Psychiatry* 88, no. 1 (1931): 103–109.

152. Ibid., 107–108.
153. Hoskins, *Biology of Schizophrenia*, 57.
154. Howard A. Rusk "The Vexing Problem of Schizophrenia," *New York Times*, August 11, 1946.
155. Hoskins, *Biology of Schizophrenia*, 169.
156. Nathan Blackman, "Experiences of a Literary Club in the Group Treatment of Schizophrenia," *Occupational Therapy and Rehabilitation* 19 (1940): 293–305. Another attempt at group psychotherapy took place at the Eloise State Hospital in Michigan, where empathy was described as a patient's tapping along to a rhythm in a group musical activity: Ira Altschuler, "One Year's Experience with Group Psychotherapy," *Mental Hygiene* 24 (1940): 190–196.
157. Nathan Blackman, "Ward Therapy: A New Method of Group Psychotherapy," *Psychiatric Quarterly* 16, no. 4 (1942): 660–667.
158. Hoskins read Blackman's manuscript in 1954, but the paper was not published until 1958. See Hoskins, "Empathy—Defined by Nathan Blackman ms. Read 2 July 54," in Biographical and Personal Papers, 1942–1959, H MS c 210, box 2, folder 8, RGH Papers. Nathan Blackman, "The Development of Empathy in Male Schizophrenics," *Psychiatric Quarterly* 2, no. 3 (1958): 546–553, 548.
159. Blackman, "Development of Empathy in Male Schizophrenics," 549.
160. Andras Angyal, H. Freeman, and R. G. Hoskins, "Physiologic Aspects of Schizophrenic Withdrawal," *Archives of Neurology and Psychiatry* 44, no. 3 (1940): 621–626, 625; Joesph C. Aub, "In Memoriam, Roy G. Hoskins, M.D., 1880–1964," *Psychosomatic Medicine* 27, no. 2 (1965): 101; Hoskins, *Biology of Schizophrenia*, 49; Anne Harrington, *The Cure Within: A History of Mind-Body Medicine* (New York: W. W. Norton, 2008), 80–94.
161. Hoskins to friend, Alan, March 15, 1947, H MS c 210, box 2, folder 4, RGH Papers. In a letter to Shakow on February 7, 1947, Hoskins describes "my own little coronary aberration" and notes that he is a "Special Consultant" for the Gerontology Section of the U.S. Public Health Research Grants Division, box M1316, folder 1947, 1950 1951, 1953, 1962, Shakow Papers.
162. Blackman, "Development of Empathy in Male Schizophrenics," 547, 550.

Chapter 5. Empathy in Social Work and Psychotherapy

1. Carl Rogers and Rosalind Dymond, eds., "The Case of Mrs. Oak: A Research Analysis," in *Psychotherapy and Personality Change* (Chicago: University of Chicago Press, 1954), 326. In 1975, Rogers substituted "Softly, and with an empathic tenderness toward the hurt she is experiencing" for "Gently." Carl Rogers, "Empathic: An Unappreciated Way of Being," *Counseling Psychologist* 5, no. 2 (1975): 2–10.

2. Jessie Taft, *The Dynamics of Therapy in a Controlled Relationship* (New York: Dover, 1962 [1933]), 120.

3. Herman describes Taft as a pragmatist with a progressive social ethic. Ellen Herman, *Kinship by Design: A History of Adoption in the Modern United States* (Chicago: University of Chicago Press, 2008), 92–94.

4. Virginia P. Robinson, "The Influence of Otto Rank in Social Work: A Journey into a Past," in *A Century of Social Work and Social Welfare at Penn*, ed. Ram A. Cnaan, Melissa E. Dichter, and Jeffery Draine (Philadelphia: University of Pennsylvania Press, 2008), 82–101.

5. Jessie Taft, *The Woman Movement from the Point of View of Social Consciousness* (Chicago: Chicago University Press, 1916), x, 37.

6. Ellsworth Faris, "The Social Psychology of George Herbert Mead," *American Journal of Sociology* 43, no. 3 (1937): 391–403, 399–400. Mead's lecture notes were published posthumously in George Herbert Mead, *Mind, Self and Society* (Chicago: Chicago University Press, 1934).

7. Taft, *Woman Movement*, 38.

8. Ibid., 35.

9. George Herbert Mead, "1914 Class Lectures in Social Psychology," *The Individual and the Social Self: Unpublished Work of George Herbert Mead* (Chicago: University of Chicago Press, 1982), 27–106. He wrote, "Our need for imagery is fundamental, for it is by that means we can put ourselves in other people's places" (97).

10. Taft, *Woman Movement*, 26. Livingston's analysis of Taft's account of the social self does not take into her notion of self-reflexivity: the self had to become conscious of its own social interests to be truly progressive. James Livingston, "The Strange Career of the 'Social Self,'" *Radical History Review* 2000, no. 76 (2000): 53–79.

11. Taft, *Woman Movement*, 45

12. Ibid., 34, 9.

13. Ibid., 52–53.

14. Ibid., 57.

15. Ibid., 16.

16. Ibid., 26.

17. *Jessie Taft: Therapist and Social Work Educator: A Professional Biography*, ed. Virginia P. Robinson (Philadelphia: University of Penn. Press, 1962); Rosalind Rosenberg, *Beyond Separate Spheres: The Intellectual Roots of Modern Feminism* (New Haven: Yale University Press, 1982), chap. 5. On Taft, see John Reuland, "The Social Worker's License: Reconstructing Social Selves in the Work of Jessie Taft and Charlotte Perkins Gilman," *Modernism/Modernity* 22, no. 1 (2015): 1–22; Matthew Millkan, "Personality: The Science of Selfhood in Twentieth Century America" (PhD diss., University of Chicago, 2009).

18. *Jessie Taft: Therapist and Social Work Educator*, 69.

19. Margo Horn, *Before It's Too Late: The Child Guidance Movement in The United States, 1922–1945* (Philadelphia: Temple Press, 1989), 72–78.

20. Bulletin of the Alumni Association, Pennsylvania School of Social Work, May 1934; Jessie Taft, "The Significance of the Doctoral Program," in Alumni Association Bulletin, University of Pennsylvania School of Social Work, May 1952, box 3, Jessie Taft Papers, 1881–1961, Rare Book and Manuscript Library, Columbia University (hereafter JT Papers).

21. Jessie Taft, "What It Means to Be a Foster Parent," *Progressive Education*, 1926; "The Adopted Child," *Delineater*, 1933.

22. Robinson, "Influence of Otto Rank in Social Work," 88.

23. Virginia P. Robinson, *A Changing Psychology in Social Case Work* (Chapel Hill: University of North Carolina Press, 1930).

24. Jessie Taft, "Problems of Social Casework with Children," paper delivered at Mental Hygiene Section of the National Conference of Social Work, New Orleans, April 1920, reprinted in *Jessie Taft: Therapist and Social Work Educator*, 76–90, 77; Taft, "The Relation of Psychiatry to Social Work," *Jessie Taft: Therapist and Social Work Educator*, 56–63; John H. Ehrenreich, *The Altruistic Imagination: A History of Social Work and Social Policy in the United States* (Ithaca: Cornell University Press, 2014).

25. Taft, "Relation of Psychiatry to Social Work," 63.

26. Jessie Taft, "The Social Worker's Opportunity," Mental Hygiene Division of the National Conference of Social Work, Providence, June 1922, reprinted in *Jessie Taft: Therapist and Social Work Educator*, ed. Robinson, 90–98, 91.

27. Taft, "Problems of Social Casework with Children," 80.

28. "The Relation of the Child's Emotional Life to His Education," paper delivered at a meeting of Friends' Education Association, Coulter Friends School, Philadelphia, March 6, 1926, typescript, box 2, folder 1, JT Papers.

29. J. Taft, "Discussion of a Paper Delivered by Otto Rank," First International Congress for Mental Hygiene, 1930, reprinted in *Jessie Taft: Therapist and Social Work Educator*, 135–140.

30. Jessie Taft, "Living and Feeling," *Child Study*, January 1933, reprinted in *Jessie Taft: Therapist and Social Work Educator*, 140–153, 143.

31. Ibid., 152.

32. Ibid., 145.

33. Jessie Taft, "The Function of a Mental Hygienist in a Children's Agency," paper delivered at National Conference of Social Work, 1927, reprinted in *Jessie Taft: Therapist and Social Work Educator*, 108–118, 111.

34. Jessie Taft, *Otto Rank: A Biographical Study Based on Notebooks, Letters, Collected Writings, Therapeutic Achievements, and Personal Associations* (Oxford: Julian Press, 1958), 147–151.

35. Ibid., xv.

36. *The Letters of Sigmund Freud and Otto Rank: Inside Psychoanalysis*, ed. E. James

Lieberman, Robert Kramer, and Gregory C. Richter (Baltimore: Johns Hopkins University Press, 2012), 279; Taft, *Otto Rank*, 152. By 1945, Alexander saw Rank's approach in a more positive light as a way of strengthening the ego, in line with ego psychology.

37. *Letters of Sigmund Freud and Otto Rank*, 280.

38. Ibid., 282. Virginia Robinson formed the Otto Rank Association in 1965, and a symposium on the Rediscovery of Otto Rank was held in 1984 at the American Psychological Association.

39. Erich Fromm, "The Social Philosophy of 'Will Therapy,'" *Psychiatry* 2 no. 2 (1939): 229–237; E. James Lieberman, *Acts of Will: The Life and Work of Otto Rank* (New York: Simon and Schuster, 2010), 386–387, 400. Roazen argued that Rank has been woefully understudied, given his contributions on the rapport between patient and analyst and on the autonomy and creativity of the patient. Paul Roazen, "Otto Rank," *The Historiography of Psychoanalysis* (New Brunswick, N.J.: Transaction Publishers, 2001), 387–391.

40. Otto Rank to Freud, November 22, 1925, *The Letters of Sigmund Freud and Otto Rank*, 246–247; Theresa Aiello, "The Influence of the Psychoanalytic Community of Émigrés (1930–1950) on Clinical Social Work with Children," *Child and Adolescent Social Work Journal* 15, no. 2 (1998): 151–166; Nathan G. Hale, "From Berggasse XIX to Central Park West: The Americanization of Psychoanalysis, 1919–1940," *Journal of the History of the Behavioral Sciences* 14, no. 4 (1978): 299–315.

41. George Makari, *Revolution in Mind: The Creation of Psychoanalysis* (New York: HarperCollins, 2008), 164–166.

42. Otto Rank, *Der Künstler: Ansätze zu einer Sexual-Psychologie* (Vienna: Hugo Heller, 1907).

43. Lieberman, *Acts of Will*, 228.

44. *Letters of Sigmund Freud and Otto Rank*, August, 13, 1921, 111; Sigmund Freud, *Group Psychology* (New York: W. W. Norton, 1959), 50. The quote reads: " we are faced by the process which psychology calls 'empathy [Einfühlung]' and which plays the largest part in our understanding of what is inherently foreign to our ego in other people" and it is the "mechanism by means of which we are enabled to take up any attitude at all towards another mental life" (53). Lipps used the expression *fremden Ichen*, whereas Freud called it *Ichfremde*. Pigman supposes that Freud not only alluded to our knowledge of other selves, but also to what is alien to, or unknown to, the selves of others. Freud used "Einfühlung" twenty times in his oeuvre, although nine of these occurrences were translated in different ways by James Strachey in the Standard Edition of Freud's works. See G. W. Pigman, "Freud and the History of Empathy," *International Journal of Psycho-Analysis* 66 (1985): 237–54, 249. Lipps, "Das Wissen von fremden Ichen," *Psychologische Untersuchungen* 1, no. 4 (1907): 694–722.

45. Rank discussed the maternal libido in the Wednesday Society presentation of the "Rat-Man." Nunberg and Federn, eds., *Minutes of the Vienna Psychoanalytic Society*, vol. 1, 1906–1908 (New York: International Universities Press, 1962), 233, cited in Andre Haynal and E. Felzeder, "Empathy, Psychoanalytic Practice in the 1920s and Ferenczi's Clinical Diary," *Journal of the American Academy of Psychoanalysis* 21, no. 4 (1993): 605–621, 607.

46. Sandor Ferenczi and Otto Rank, *The Development of Psychoanalysis*, trans. Caroline Newton (New York: Nervous and Mental Disease Publishing, 1925).

47. Haynal and Felzeder, "Empathy, Psychoanalytic Practice in the 1920s," 613. For a description of Rank's and Ferenczi's active therapy, see Eli Zaretsky, *Secrets of the Soul: A Social and Cultural History of Psychoanalysis* (New York; Vintage 2004), 173–176.

48. Rank to Freud, August 6, 1924, *Letters of Sigmund Freud and Otto Rank*, 209.

49. Rank to Freud, November 22, 1925, *Letters of Sigmund Freud and Otto Rank*, 246–247.

50. Otto Rank, *Will Therapy*, authorized translation with preface and introduction by Jessie Taft (New York: W. W. Norton, 1978 [1936]). *Will Therapy* comprised volumes 2 and 3 of Rank's *Technique of Psychoanalysis*. Taft substituted the terms "therapy" and "therapeutic" for "analysis" and "analytic." Otto Rank, *Truth and Reality* (New York: W. W. Norton, 1978), 5. See preface.

51. Rank, *Truth and Reality*, 7–11.

52. Otto Rank, "Psychoanalysis as General Psychology," June 19, 1924, in Otto Rank, *A Psychology of Difference: The American Lectures*, ed. Robert Kramer (Princeton: Princeton University Press, 1996), 52–65.

53. Taft, *Otto Rank*, ix.

54. Ibid., xi.

55. Abram Kardiner, cited in *Letters of Sigmund Freud and Otto Rank*, 235.

56. *Letters of Sigmund Freud and Otto Rank*, 153 and 277. Karl Fallend, *Caroline Newton, Jessie Taft, Virginia Robinson: Spurensuche in der Geschichte der Psychoanalyse und Sozialarbeit* (Vienna: Erhard Löcker, 2012); Elizabeth Ann Danto, "A New Sort of 'Salvation Army': Historical Perspective on the Confluence of Psychoanalysis and Social Work," *Clinical Social Work Journal* 37 (2009): 67–76, 71. Ferenczi analyzed Clara Thompson and Harry Stack Sullivan. Lieberman, *Acts of Will*, 236–237.

57. Robinson, "Influence of Otto Rank in Social Work," 90.

58. Otto Rank, "Love, Guilt, and the Denial of Feelings" (1927), in *Psychology of Difference*, 153–165.

59. Taft, *Otto Rank*, 134.

60. Otto Rank, "Social Adaptation and Creativity" (1927), in *Psychology of Difference*, 189–200, 194.

61. Ibid., 194.

62. Otto Rank, "The Significance of the Love Life" (1927), in *Psychology of Difference*, 177.

63. Otto Rank, "The Prometheus Complex" (1927), in *Psychology of Difference*, 201–210, 209.

64. Kathleen Jones, "The Critique of Motherhood," in *Taming the Troublesome Child* (Cambridge: Harvard University Press, 1999), 174–204; Rank, *Psychology of Difference*, 11–12, 149–150.

65. Rank, "Prometheus Complex," 209. Italics in original.

66. Jessie Taft, "The 'Catch' in Praise," *Child Study*, February 1930, 6. Typescript, box 3, "Taft Papers 2," JT Papers.

67. Ibid.

68. Jessie Taft, "Loneliness," box 2, JT Papers.

69. Frederick Allen, "Evolution of Our Treatment Philosophy in Child Guidance," *Mental Hygiene* 14 (1930): 3–6; Frederick Allen, *Psychotherapy with Children* (New York: W. W. Norton, 1942).

70. Edward Strecker referred patients to Taft. *Jessie Taft: Therapist and Social Work Educator*, 130; Jessie Taft, "Case of Miss G, 1932," 35-page account, box 2, JT Papers.

71. Jessie Taft, "Experiment in a Therapeutically Limited Relationship with a Seven Year Old Girl," *Psychoanalytic Review*, 1931, reprinted in J. Taft, *The Dynamics of Therapy in a Controlled Relationship*, 29.

72. Taft, *Dynamics of Therapy*, 30.

73. Ibid., 121.

74. Ibid., 94.

75. Ibid., 106.

76. Ibid.

77. Robinson, *Changing Psychology in Social Case Work*, 114.

78. Taft, *Dynamics of Therapy*, 118.

79. Ibid., 108.

80. Ibid., 101.

81. William A. White to Jessie Taft, November 12, 1931; Taft to White, November 17, 1931, Correspondence, 1920–1943, box 1, folder 11, JT Papers. William A. White, *Mechanisms of Character Formation: An Introduction to Psychoanalysis* (New York: MacMillan, 1924 [1916]).

82. Virginia Robinson, *The Dynamics of Supervision under Functional Controls: A Professional Process in Social Casework* (Philadelphia: University of Pennsylvania Press, 1949).

83. Robinson, *Changing Psychology in Social Case Work*, 113; Taft, "The Relation of Function to Process in Social Case Work," in *Training for Skill in Social Case Work*, ed. Virginia Robinson (Philadelphia: University of Pennsylvania Press, 1942), 100–116, 101.

84. Jessie Taft, introduction to *A Functional Approach to Family Case Work*, ed. Jessie Taft (Philadelphia: University of Pennsylvania Press, 1944), 8.

85. John Ehrenreich, *The Altruistic Imagination*, 124–138. He credits Paul Federn, Melanie Klein, and Anna Freud with some of these trends.

86. Taft, *Dynamics of Therapy*, 290.

87. Jessie Taft, "Time as the Medium of the Helping Process," paper delivered to National Conference of Jewish Social Welfare, June 1949, reprinted in *Jessie Taft: Therapist and Social Work Educator*, 305–324, 309.

88. *Jessie Taft: Therapist and Social Work Educator*, 133.

89. "Courses in PA School of Social Work, 1918–1951," box 2, folder 6, JT Papers.

90. Jessie Taft to Ruth Benedict, October 29, 1935, box 1, JT Papers.

91. Robinson, *Changing Psychology in Social Case Work*, 175.

92. Ibid., 170; Robinson, *Dynamics of Supervision under Functional Controls*, 12.

93. Robinson, *Changing Psychology in Social Case Work*, 142.

94. Taft, "Function of the Personality Course in the Practice Unit," in *Training for Skill in Social Case Work*, ed. Virginia Robinson (Philadelphia: University of Pennsylvania Press), 55–74, 72.

95. Taft, "Function of the Personality Course in the Practice Unit," 69.

96. "First and Second Session of the Class in the Direct Treatment of Children, 1935–1936," 2, box 2, folder "Course Notes," JT Papers.

97. Letter from Taft to Mrs. Ethel Wannemacher, January 16, 1945, box 1, folder 7: Letters on Social Work Supervision, JT Papers.

98. Taft, "Function of the Personality Course in the Practice Unit," 74.

99. Ibid., 71.

100. Helen Padula to Jessie Taft, March 6, 1950, in box 1, folder 11, Correspondence 1948–1959, JT Papers.

101. Jessie Taft, "A Conception of the Growth Process Underlying Social Casework Practice," 1950, box 1, folder 7, 12, JT Papers.

102. Carl. R. Rogers, "Carl Rogers," *A History of Psychology in Autobiography*, vol. 5 (New York: Appleton-Century-Crofts, 1967), 343–384; Robert N. Sollod, "Carl Rogers and the Origins of Client-Centered Therapy," *Professional Psychology* 9, no. 1 (1978): 93–104.

103. Carl Rogers and Gerard Haigh, "I Walk Softly Through Life," *Voices: The Art and Science of Psychotherapy* 18 (1983): 6–14, 6. Counseling in a similar nondirective style was adopted in the Hawthorne studies at General Electric. See F. J. Roethlisberger and W. J. Dickson, *Management and the Worker* (Cambridge: Harvard University Press, 1939).

104. Excerpt of letter from Rank to Taft, June 10, 1936, in Jessie Taft, *Otto Rank*, 215. Robert Kramer, "The Birth of Client-Centered Therapy: Carl Rogers, Otto Rank and the Beyond," *Journal of Humanistic Psychology* 35, no. 4 (1995): 54–110; Roy J. deCarvalho. "Otto Rank, the Rankian Circle in Philadelphia, and the Origins of Carl Rogers' Person-Centered Psychotherapy," *History of Psychology* 2, no. 2 (1999): 132–148.

105. Carl Rogers, "A Theory of Therapy, Personality, and Interpersonal Rela-

tionships as Developed in the Client-Centered Framework," in *Psychology: A Study of a Science*, vol. 3, ed. Sigmund Koch (New York: McGraw-Hill, 1959), 184–256, 187; Rogers, "Carl Rogers," 360.

106. "D. E. Davis" is listed under the year 1938 in Taft's notes: "First MSW 1936" in Courses, box 2, folder 6, JT Papers. An Elizabeth Waples Davis was enrolled at the Pennsylvania School of Social Work in 1935, 1939, and 1940. She did not receive a master's degree. Information courtesy of Nancy R. Miller, Alumnae Records, University of Pennsylvania Archives, April 22, 2010. Rogers listed the staff member D. Elizabeth Davis in "The Services of the Rochester Guidance Center," nd, box 123, folder 10, Carl R. Rogers Papers, 1913–1989, MSS75853, Manuscript Division, Library of Congress, Washington D.C. (hereafter CR Papers).

107. Rogers, *Counseling and Psychotherapy*, 256; Rogers, *Clinical Treatment of the Problem Child* (Oxford: Houghton Mifflin, 1939), 284; Rogers, "Empathic," 1.

108. Rogers and Haigh, "I Walk Softly," 7.

109. Carl Rogers, *Counseling and Psychotherapy: Newer Concepts in Practice* (Oxford: Houghton Mifflin, 1942), preface, viii, 17, 28.

110. Rogers, "Carl Rogers," 343–384; Carl R. Rogers, "Therapy in Guidance Clinics," *Journal of Abnormal and Social Psychology* 38, no. 2 (1943): 284–289, 286.

111. Rogers, *Counseling and Psychotherapy*, 87.

112. Ibid., 255 (citation taken from Rogers, *Clinical Treatment of the Problem Child*, 281).

113. Rogers, *Counseling and Psychotherapy*, 86.

114. Ibid., 334.

115. Ibid., 18.

116. Ibid., 30.

117. Rogers, "Therapy in Guidance Clinics," 287–288.

118. The tradition of "verbatims" or writing out word-for-word exchanges was introduced in pastoral counseling. E. Brooks Holifield, *A History of Pastoral Care in America* (Eugene, Ore.: Wipf and Stock, 1983), 237; Rogers and Haigh, "I Walk Softly," 7.

119. Rogers, *Counseling and Psychotherapy*, 261–437.

120. William U. Snyder, "A Short-Term Nondirective Treatment of an Adult," *Journal of Abnormal and Social Psychology* 38, no. 2 (1943): 87–137, 90.

121. Ibid., 114.

122. Rogers, *Counseling and Psychotherapy*, 122, 246; Nathaniel Raskin, "The Development of Nondirective Therapy," *Journal of Consulting Psychology* 12, no. 2 (1948): 92–110.

123. Rogers, "Therapy in Guidance Clinics," 286.

124. Rogers, *Counseling and Psychotherapy*, 201.

125. Rogers, "Therapy in Guidance Clinics," 287.

126. Franz Alexander, "New Perspectives in Psychotherapy," *New Republic*,

January 8, 1945, 53–55. On the popularity of psychotherapy mid-century, see Jonathan Engel, *American Therapy: The Rise of Psychotherapy in the United States* (New York: Gotham Books, 2008).

127. Howard Kirschenbaum, *The Life and Work of Carl Rogers* (Alexandria, Va.: American Counseling Association, 2007), 147.

128. William Snyder, "The Present State of Psychotherapeutic Counseling," *Psychological Bulletin* 44, no. 4 (1947): 297–386, 300.

129. Carl Rogers, *Client-Centered Therapy: Its Current Practice, Implications and Theory* (Boston: Houghton Mifflin, 1951), 14.

130. Robert M. Yerkes, head of the Emergency Committee on Psychology, enlisted Carl Rogers to build bridges between the academic APA and the applied, clinical faction. http://www.apadivisions.org/division-19/about /history.aspx. Accessed January 11, 2016; Kirschenbaum, *Life and Work of Carl Rogers*, 252.

131. Kirschenbaum, *Life and Work of Carl Rogers*, 152–153.

132. Donald K. Routh, *Clinical Psychology since 1917* (Boston: Springer, 1994), 27–31.

133. Roderick D. Buchanan, "Legislative Warriors: American Psychiatrists, Psychologists, and Competing Claims over Psychotherapy in the 1950s," *Journal of the History of the Behavioral Sciences* 39, no. 3 (2003): 225–249, 236–241; Gerald N. Grob, *From Asylum to Community: Mental Health Policy in Modern America* (Princeton: Princeton University Press, 1991).

134. Letter from Carl Rogers to Dr. Forrest W. Kingsbury, Department of Psychology, University of Chicago, November 13, 1944, box 125, folder 1, CR Papers.

135. Frederick C. Thorne, "A Critique of Nondirective Methods of Psychotherapy," *Journal of Abnormal and Social Psychology* 39 (1944): 459–470.

136. William U. Snyder, "'Warmth' in Nondirective Counseling," *Journal of Abnormal and Social Psychology* 41, no. 4 (1946): 491–495, 491.

137. Note to Dr. Rogers, signed OHB, pp. 6–9, 2, box 80, folder 2, CR Papers. Bown later counseled Rogers during his psychological crisis. See Kirschenbaum, *Life and Work of Carl Rogers*, 185–186.

138. Carl Rogers, "Some Observations on the Organization of Personality," *American Psychologist* 2, no. 9 (1947): 358–368, 365. Rogers described the therapist a few years later as functioning as the "mirror-image of the self empathically perceiving the same situation in the same way but without the emotional involvement which the client himself feels." Rogers, "A Current Formulation of Client-Centered Therapy," *Social Service Review* 24, no. 4 (1950): 446.

139. Rogers, *Client-Centered Therapy*, 14.

140. Carl Rogers, "The Attitude and Orientation of the Counselor in Client-Centered Therapy," *Journal of Consulting Psychology* 13, no. 2 (1949): 82–94, 89.

141. Ibid., 87.

142. Kirschenbaum, *Life and Work of Carl Rogers,* 626, note 34. Howard Kirschenbaum, personal communication, April 17, 2012. See the concordance on Rogers's use of "empathy" and other terms by Juan M. Sánchez-Rivers Peiró, Carl R. Rogers Collection, 1902–1990, University of California, Santa Barbara.

143. Rollo May, *The Art of Counseling* (Nashville: Cokesbury Press, 1939); Robert P. Knight, "Psychotherapy with an Adolescent Catatonic Schizophrenia with Mutism: A Study in Empathy and Establishing Contact," *Psychiatry* 9 (1946): 323–339. Knight described literary empathy according to the early self-projection model: "I identify myself with the object mainly by projection of my own feelings onto him, so that I imagine him to be experiencing emotions that I am experiencing." Robert P. Knight, "Introjection, Projection and Identification," *Psychoanalytic Quarterly* 9 (1940): 334–341, 336.

144. In a list of references entitled "Read," Rogers included Angyal, Wolf, Chein, and others, as well as "Knight's paper" with a checkmark before it. Rogers, "Materials for September 1947 Speech," box 80, folder 2, CR Papers.

145. Rogers, "Some Observations on the Organization of Personality," 358. Harold G. Wolff, "Emotions and Gastric Function," *Science* 98, no. 2553 (1943): 481–484; Stewart G. Wolf and Harold G. Wolff, *Human Gastric Function: An Experimental Study of a Man and His Stomach* (London: Oxford University Press, 1943).

146. Anne Harrington, *The Cure Within: A History of Mind-Body Medicine* (New York: W. W. Norton, 2008), 177–178.

147. Rogers, "Outline," box 80, folder 2, CR Papers.

148. Rogers, "Some Observations on the Organization of Personality," 359.

149. Donald Syngg, "The Need for a Phenomenological System of Psychology," *Psychological Review* 48, no. 5 (1941): 404–424, 414. See Herbert Spiegelberg, *Phenomenology in Psychology and Psychiatry: An Historical Introduction* (Evanston: Northwestern University Press, 1972), 146–148.

150. Rogers, *Client-Centered Therapy,* 34; Rogers, "Some Clinical Observations," box 80, folder, 2, CR Papers.

151. Isidor Chein, "The Awareness of Self and the Structure of the Ego," *Psychological Review* 51, no. 5 (1944): 304–314, 307.

152. Rogers, *Client-Centered Therapy,* 33.

153. Ibid., 28, 34.

154. Rogers, "Theory of Therapy," 213.

155. Rogers, *Client-Centered Therapy,* x–xi.

156. Carl Rogers, "Attitude and Orientation of the Counselor," 86. He gave this exact definition in Rogers, *Client-Centered Therapy,* 29.

157. Rogers, "Theory of Therapy," 210.

158. Carl Rogers, "The Necessary and Sufficient Conditions of Therapeutic Personality Change," *Journal of Consulting Psychology* 21, no. 2 (1957): 95–103; Rogers, *Client-Centered Therapy,* 29.

159. Author interview with Rosalind Dymond Cartwright, October 1, 2009 (hereafter Interview, RDC).

160. C. Rogers, "Psychotherapy," in *Current Trends in Psychology*, ed. Wayne Dennis (Pittsburgh: University of Pittsburgh Press, 1947), 109–137, 111.

161. Rogers, *Client-Centered Therapy*, 13.

162. Interview, RDC.

163. Carl Rogers and Rosalind Dymond, eds., *Psychotherapy and Personality Change* (Chicago: University of Chicago Press, 1954); Kirschenbaum, *Life and Work of Carl Rogers*, 208–213.

164. Interview, RDC.

165. Carl Rogers, "Significant Aspects of Client-Centered Therapy," *American Psychologist* 1, no. 10 (1946): 415–422, 416.

166. Rogers, "Some Observations on the Organization of Personality," 358.

167. Rogers, *Client-Centered Therapy*, 40–41.

168. Ibid., 36.

169. Ibid., xi.

170. One historian writes that empathic immersion in psychotherapy bears a "striking similarity to what women have always done." Ilene J. Philipson, *On the Shoulders of Women: The Feminization of Psychotherapy* (New York: Guilford Press, 1993), 52.

171. Carl Rogers to Robert Yerkes, November 20, 1942, box 123, folder 8, CR Papers. The *Post* article was dated November 1, 1942.

172. George Adams to Talcott Parsons, October 14, 1947, box 1, folder 2: "Mental Health Conference, General and Miscellaneous," 1948 Mental Health, Summer School Conference Files UAV813.15, Harvard University Archive (hereafter HUA).

173. Press Release, "Excerpts of Remarks by Lawrence Kubie," 1–5; Harvard University News Office, in "Dissidents: Carl Rogers Correspondence," Unit ID 233376, Menninger Foundation Archives, Kansas State Historical Society, Topeka, Kansas (hereafter MFA).

174. "Transcript: Ways to Mental Health," 49, box 1, folder 4, 1948 Mental Health, Summer School Conference Files, HUA.

175. Ibid., 50.

176. Ibid., 54, 63.

177. George Adams to Karl Menninger, August 10, 1948, "Dissidents: Carl Rogers Correspondence," MFA.

178. Karl Menninger to Dean George Adams, August 2, 1948, "Dissidents: Carl Rogers Correspondence," MFA.

179. Lawrence Kubie to Richard Ludwig, August 18, 1948; see also Kubie to Dean George Adams, August 19, 1948, "Dissidents: Carl Rogers Correspondence," MFA.

180. Thomas Wilson (Harvard University Press) to George Adams, June 9, 1948; George Adams to Thomas Wilson, August 10, 1948, box 1, folder

3: "Mental Health Conference Speeches," 1948 Mental Health Conference, Summer School Conference Files, HUA.

181. Carl R. Rogers, "Divergent Trends in Methods of Improving Adjustment," *Harvard Educational Review* 19, no. 4 (Fall 1948): 209–219, reprint in "Dissidents: Carl Rogers Correspondence," MFA.

182. Nancy Tomes, "The Development of Clinical Psychology, Social Work, and Psychiatric Nursing, 1900–1980s," in *History of Psychiatry and Medical Psychology* (New York: Springer, 2008), 657–682, 671. See also John M. Reisman, *History of Clinical Psychology* (New York: Hemisphere Publishing, 1991).

183. "Transcript: Ways to Mental Health," 56, HUA.

184. Ibid., 58.

185. Taft, "A Philosophy of Helping in Social Work," 1947, *Jessie Taft: Therapist and Social Work Educator,* 273–290, 284.

186. Taft to Ethel Wannamacher, January 29, 1946, box 1, folder 7, JT Papers.

187. Taft to John M. Shlien, November 24, 1959, box 1, folder 7, JT Papers; Madge Lewis, C. Rogers, and John M. Shlien, "Time-Limited, Client-Centered Psychotherapy: Two Cases," in Arthur Burton, ed., *Case Studies in Counseling and Psychotherapy* (Oxford: Prentice-Hall, 1959), 309–352; J. M. Shlien, "A Client-Centered Approach to Schizophrenia: First Approximation," in *Psychotherapy of the Psychoses*, ed. A. Burton (New York: Basic Books, 1961), 285–317.

188. Taft to John M. Shlien, December 8, 1959, box 1, folder 7, JT Papers.

189. http://news.harvard.edu/gazette/2002/04.04/14-shlien.html. Accessed April 9, 2016.

190. Taft's book was reissued after her death by Dover Publications in 1962.

191. "Aims and Plans—CR 1947," letter to Dr. Ralph W. Tyler, Dean, Social Science Division, August 11, 1947, box 125, folder 1, CR papers.

192. "Psychology 450A Spring Quarter, 1952," box 127, CR Papers.

193. "Memo from Carl R. Rogers," May 26, 1954, box 128, folder 1, CR Papers.

194. C. Rogers and F. J. Roethlisburger, "Barriers and Gateways to Communication," *Harvard Business Review* 30, no. 4 (1952): 46–52, 50.

195. Ibid., 47.

196. Ibid.

197. Carl Rogers, "Divergent Trends in Methods of Improving Adjustment," *Harvard Educational Review* 18, no. 4 (1948): 209–19.

198. Rogers, "Psychotherapy," 117.

199. Eugene T. Gendlin, J. Beebe, J. Cassens, M. Klein, and M. Oberlander, "Focusing Ability in Psychotherapy, Personality and Creativity," in J. M. Shlien, ed., *Research in Psychotherapy*, vol. 3 (1968), 217–241; http://www.focusing.org/gendlin/docs/gol_2049.html. Marshall Rosenberg, *Nonviolent Communication: A Language of Life* (Del Mar, Calif.: Puddle-Dancer Press, 2003).

200. Fred E. Fiedler, "A Comparison of Therapeutic Relationships in Psychoanalytic, Nondirective and Adlerian Therapy," *Journal of Consulting and Clinical Psychology* 14, no. 6 (1940): 433–445, 443; Fred E. Fiedler, "The Concept of an Ideal Therapeutic Relationship," *Journal of Consulting Psychology* 14, no. 4 (1950): 239–245.

201. Stefano Bolognini, *Psychoanalytic Empathy* (London: Free Association Books, 1987), 41–53; Elizabeth Lunbeck, "Empathy as a Psychoanalytic Mode of Observation: Between Sentiment and Science," in *Histories of Scientific Observation*, ed. Lorraine Daston and E. Lunbeck (Chicago: University of Chicago Press, 2011), 255–276; E. Lunbeck, *The Americanization of Narcissism* (Cambridge: Harvard University Press, 2014); on psychoanalytic theorizing on the mother-child bond in the postwar period, see Marga Vicedo, *The Nature and Nurture of Love: From Imprinting to Attachment in Cold War America* (Chicago: Chicago University Press, 2013).

202. Roy Schafer, "Generative Empathy in the Treatment Situation," *Psychoanalytic Quarterly* 28 (1959): 342–373. For an examination of empathy between adults and children, see Austrian child analyst Christine Olden, "Notes on the Development of Empathy," *Psychoanalytic Study of the Child*, vol. 13 (New York: International Universities Press, 1958), 505–518, 514. See also Christine Olden, "On Adult Empathy with Children," *Psychoanalytic Study of the Child* 8 (1953): 111–126. David Stewart developed a group therapy method with alcoholics based on empathy, which he tried out at the Crichton Royal Mental Hospital in Scotland. "Empathy in the Group Therapy of Alcoholics," *Quarterly Journal of Studies on Alcohol* 15, 1 (1954): 74–110. Stewart drew on psychoanalytic and aesthetic concepts of empathy in his *Preface to Empathy* (New York: Philosophical Library, 1956).

203. Nathaniel J. Raskin, *Studies of Psychotherapeutic Orientation: Ideology and Practice*, No. 1. (Orlando, Fla: American Academy of Psychotherapists, 1974); *Empathy Reconsidered: New Directions in Psychotherapy*, ed. Arthur C. Bohard and Leslie S. Greenberg (Washington, D.C.: American Psychological Association, 1997); Ellen Singer More and Maureen Milligan, eds., *The Empathic Practitioner: Empathy, Gender and Medicine* (New Brunswick: Rutgers University Press, 1994).

204. Rogers, "Empathic: An Unappreciated Way," 5. Rogers sponsored the Association of Humanistic Psychology and the *Journal of Humanistic Psychology* in 1961. Kirschenbaum, *Life and Work of Carl Rogers*, 257.

205. Rogers, "Empathic: An Unappreciated Way," 4.

206. Ibid., 9.

Chapter 6. Measuring Empathy

1. In 1928, the George Washington University Social Intelligence Test was designed as a measure of "the ability to deal with people." Thelma Hunt,

"The Measurement of Social Intelligence," *Journal of Applied Psychology*, 12, no. 3 (1928): 317–334.

2. Rosalind Falk Dymond, "Empathic Ability: An Exploratory Study" (PhD diss., Cornell University, 1949), 83.

3. Fred Matthews, *Quest for an American Sociology: Robert E. Park and the Chicago School* (Montreal: McGill–Queen's University Press, 1977), 41–48. On the subjective meanings of social situations, see Edward Tiryakian, "Existential Phenomenology and the Sociological Tradition," *American Sociological Review* 30, no. 5 (1965): 674–688; Karen W. Tice, *Tales of Wayward Girls and Immoral Women: Case Records and the Professionalization of Social Work* (Urbana: University of Illinois Press, 1998), 66–69. See also Martin Bulmer, *The Chicago School of Sociology* (Chicago: University of Chicago Press, 1984), 6.

4. Richard Wright, introduction to St. Clair Drake and Horace R. Cayton, *Black Metropolis: A Study of Negro Life in a Northern City* (New York: Harper Torchbooks, 1962), xviii–xix.

5. William I. Thomas and Florian Znaniecki, *The Polish Peasant in Europe and America: Monograph of an Immigrant Group*, vol. 2 (Chicago: University of Chicago, 1918); Carla Cappetti, *Writing Chicago: Modernism, Ethnography and the Novel* (New York: Columbia University Press, 1993), 30–31.

6. Arnold M. Rose, "The Contributions of Ernest W. Burgess to Sociology," *Midwest Sociologist* 17, no. 1 (1955): 7–13; Ernest Burgess, American Sociology Association, http://www.asanet.org/about/presidents/Ernest_Burgess.cfm, accessed April 6, 2013; Matthews, *Quest for an American Sociology*, 105. Bulmer, *Chicago School of Sociology*, 94–95; see also Mark C. Smith, *Social Science in the Crucible: The American Debate over Objectivity and Purpose, 1918–1941* (Durham: Duke University Press, 1994).

7. Morris Janowitz, introduction to *Introduction to the Science of Sociology*, by Robert E. Park and Ernest W. Burgess, 3rd ed. rev. (Chicago: University of Chicago Press, 1969), vi. The excerpt from Yrjö Hirn, *The Origins of Art* (New York: Macmillan, 1900), 74–85, discussed inner imitation in the work of Vernon Lee, Anstruther-Thomson, Hogarth, and in the German tradition.

8. James Leiby, *A History of Social Welfare and Social Work* (New York: Columbia University Press, 1978), 122.

9. Mary Richmond, *Friendly Visiting among the Poor: A Handbook for Charity Workers* (New York: Macmillan, 1899), cited in Leslie Margolin, *Under the Cover of Kindness: The Invention of Social Work* (Charlottesville: University Press of Virginia, 1997), 23. Margolin offers a Foucauldian critique of sympathetic methods for gleaning social information. See also Mary Richmond, *Social Diagnosis* (New York: Russell Sage Foundation, 1917).

10. Tice, *Tales of Wayward Girls and Immoral Women*, 58.

11. M. J. Karpf, "The Relation between Sociology and Social Work," *Journal of Social Forces* 3, no. 3 (1925): 419–425, 420.

12. Ernest W. Burgess, "What Social Case Records Should Contain to Be
      Useful for Sociological Interpretation," *Social Forces* 6, no. 4 (1928): 524–
      532, 525; Ernest W. Burgess, "The Interdependence of Sociology and
      Social Work," *Journal of Social Forces* 1, no. 4 (1923): 366–370.

13. Ernest Burgess, "The Study of the Delinquent as a Person," *American
      Journal of Sociology* 28, no. 6 (1923): 657–680. On the use of social work
      records for the life history method in sociology, see Jennifer Platt, *A His-
      tory of Sociological Research Methods in America* (Cambridge: Cambridge
      University Press, 1996), 118–120.

14. Burgess, "What Social Case Records Should Contain," 526–527.

15. C. H. Cooley, "The Life-Study Method as Applied to Rural Social Re-
      search," *Sociological Study and Sociological Research* (New York: Henry
      Holt, 1930), 330–342, 334.

16. Gordon Hamilton, "Sharing Experience," *Survey Graphic* 59 (1927): 315.

17. Burgess, "What Social Case Records Should Contain," 527.

18. Clifford Shaw, *The Jack-Roller: A Delinquent Boy's Own Story* (Chicago:
      University of Chicago Press, 1930), 1.

19. Ibid., 21–23; Tice, *Tales of Wayward Girls and Immoral Women*, 70–71.

20. Shaw, *Jack-Roller*, 167.

21. Ibid., 187, 197.

22. Ernest Burgess, "Discussion," in *Jack-Roller*, 195.

23. Charles Ellwood, "Scientific Method in Sociology—Continued," *Social
      Forces* 11, no. 1 (1932): 44–50, 47.

24. Arnold M. Rose, "The Contributions of Ernest W. Burgess to Sociol-
      ogy," *Midwest Sociologist* 17, no. 1 (1955): 7–13, 9.

25. Ernest Burgess, "The Study of the Delinquent as a Person," 663; Shaw,
      Jack-Roller, 7.

26. Roger Salerno, *Sociology Noir: Studies at the University of Chicago in Loneli-
      ness, Marginality and Deviance, 1915–1935* (Jefferson, N.C.: McFarland,
      2007), 143–158.

27. Ernest Burgess, "Mental Health in Modern Society," lecture given at
      "Ways to Mental Health," July 22, 1948, p. 8, box 1, folder 3: "Mental
      Health Conference Speeches," 1948 Mental Health Conference, Sum-
      mer School Conference Files, Harvard Summer School, Harvard Uni-
      versity Archive.

28. Fern Lowry, "Current Concepts in Social Case-Work Practice," *Social
      Service Review* 12, no. 4 (1938): 571–597, 576.

29. Josephine Strode, *Social Skills in Case Work* (New York: Harper, 1942), 24.
      Strode defined empathy as a partial or full identification as well as the
      sharing of experience.

30. Herbert S. Langfeld, "The Ninth International Congress of Psychol-
      ogy," *Science*, n.s. 70, no. 1816 (1929): 364–368. John T. Metcalf, "Empa-
      thy and the Actor's Emotion" (presented at the congress), *Journal of Social
      Psychology* 2, no. 2 (1931): 235–238.

31. Josephine Strode, ed., *Social Insight through Short Stories: An Anthology* (New York: Harper and Brothers, 1946).

32. Ellwood, "Scientific Method in Sociology—Continued," 47.

33. Earle Edward Eubank, "The Vocabulary of Sociology," *Social Forces* 9, no. 3 (1931): 305–320, 306, 311; Eugenia Lea Remelin, "Students' Dissertations in Sociology," *American Journal of Sociology* 32, no. 6 (1927): 976; "Twenty-Sixth List of Doctoral Dissertations in Political Economy in Progress in American Universities and Colleges," *American Economic Review* 19, no. 3 (1929): 558.

34. Guide to the Cornell University Faculty Biographical Files, 1865–2004, Leonard Slater Cottrell, Jr., Division of Rare and Manuscript Collections, Cornell University Library. Cottrell's 1933 dissertation was titled "The Reliability and Validity of a Marriage Study Schedule."

35. Ernest W. Burgess and Leonard S. Cottrell, Jr., *Predicting Success and Failure in Marriage* (New York: Prentice-Hall, 1939).

36. Ibid., 341.

37. Ibid., 334.

38. Ibid., 335.

39. Ibid.

40. Ibid., 336, 337.

41. George Lundberg, review of *Predicting Success or Failure in Marriage*, *American Journal of Sociology* 45, no. 5 (1940): 805–807, 805.

42. Burgess and Cottrell, *Predicting Success and Failure in Marriage*, 338.

43. Milton Horowitz, "Review of Group Psychotherapy: A Symposium," *American Journal of Psychology* 60, no. 3 (1947): 465–470.

44. J. L. Moreno, *Who Shall Survive? A New Approach to Human Interrelations* (Washington, D.C.: Nervous and Mental Disease Publishing, 1934); George Lundberg, review of J. L. Moreno, *Who Shall Survive*, *American Sociological Review* 2, no. 4 (1937): 542–44.

45. Jonathan Moreno, *Impromptu Man: J. L. Moreno and the Origins of Psychodrama, Encounter Culture and the Social Network* (New York: Bellevue Literary Press, 2014), 118–133.

46. Gardner Murphy, "The Mind Is a Stage," *Forum and Century* 98 (1937): 277–280. René F. Marineau, *Jacob Levy Moreno, 1889–1974* (London: Tavistock, 1989), 98–99, 188.

47. J. L. Moreno, "Statistics of Social Configurations," *Sociometry* 1, no. 3/4 (1938): 342–374, 366; J. L. Moreno, "Inter-Personal Therapy and the Psychopathology of Inter-Personal Relations," *Sociometry* 1, no. 1/2 (1937): 9–76.

48. J. L. Moreno, "Contributions of Sociometry to Research Methodology in Sociology," *American Sociological Review* 12, no. 3 (1947): 287–292, 291; Moreno's biographer calls "tele" a kind of "mutual empathy"; see Moreno, *Impromptu Man*, 127.

49. Marineau, *Jacob Levy Moreno*, 143.

50. Francis Herriott and Margaret Hagan, "The Theatre for Psychodrama at St. Elizabeth's Hospital," *Sociometry* 4, no. 2 (1941): 168–176. Marineau, *Jacob Levy Moreno*, 137.

51. William S. White to Jessie Taft, January 5, 1936, box 1, folder 11, Jessie Taft Papers, 1881–1961, Rare Book and Manuscript Library, Columbia University (hereafter JT Papers).

52. J. L. Moreno and William S. Dunkin, "The Function of the Social Investigator in Experimental Psychodrama," *Sociometry* 4, no. 4 (1941): 392–417, 399. Moreno cited Theodore Lipps,"Das Wissen von Fremden Ichen," *Psychologische Untersuchungen* 1 (1907): 399.

53. Leonard Cottrell, Jr., "The Case-Study Method in Prediction," *Sociometry* 4, no. 4 (1941): 358–370, 367.

54. Ibid., 366; L. S. Cottrell, Jr., and Ruth Gallagher, *Developments in Social Psychology, 1930–1940* (New York: Beacon House, 1940).

55. Cottrell, "Case-Study Method," 368.

56. Ibid., 366.

57. Paul Wallin, "The Prediction of Individual Behavior from Case Studies," in Paul Horst, *The Prediction of Personal Adjustment* (New York: Social Science Research Council, 1941), 183–249, 224. See also J. G. Franz, "The Psychodrama and Interviewing," *American Sociological Review* 7, no. 1 (1942): 27–33.

58. Wallin, "Prediction of Individual Behavior from Case Studies," 201.

59. Cottrell, "Case-Study Method," 369–370.

60. Ernest R. Mowrer, "Recent Trends in Family Research," *American Sociological Review* 6, no. 4 (1941): 499–509.

61. Leonard Cottrell, Jr., "The Analysis of Situational Fields in Social Psychology," *American Sociological Review* 7 (1942): 370–382, 381.

62. Leonard Cottrell and Ruth Gallagher, "Important Developments in American Social Psychology during the Past Decade," *Sociometry* 4, no. 3, part 2 (1941): 302–324, 324; Gallagher's master's thesis was entitled "Technique of the Life History," listed in "Students' Dissertations in Sociology," *American Journal of Sociology* 46, no. 1 (1940): 58–74, 67.

63. Cottrell, "Analysis of Situational Fields," 370.

64. Ibid., 376.

65. Ibid., 382.

66. Ibid., 379. Kurt Lewin linked empathy to a "natural group unity," rather than to a formal organization. Kurt Lewin, "Field Theory and Experiment in Social Psychology: Concepts and Methods," *American Journal of Sociology* 44, no. 6 (1930): 868–896.

67. Cottrell, "Analysis of Situational Fields," 374.

68. Max Weber referred to *Einfühlung* (empathy) in different ways. He called it a means to access an actor's view through an emotional or artistic quality, and he usually connected it to *Evidenz* (verifiable certainty). See Richard Swedberg and Ola Agevall, *The Max Weber Dictionary: Key Words and*

Central Concepts (Stanford: Stanford University Press, 2005), 84–85. On Weber's concept of *Evidenz*, see Stephen Turner, "The Strength of Weak Empathy," *Science in Context* 25, no. 3 (2012): 383–399.

69. Carl Hempel, "The Function of General Laws in History," *Journal of Philosophy* 39, no. 2 (1942): 35–48. See also Carl G. Hempel and Paul Oppenheim, "Studies in the Logic of Explanation," *Philosophy of Science* 15, no. 2 (1948): 135–175, 146.

70. Hempel, "Function of General Laws in History," 45.

71. Edgar Zilsel, "Physics and the Problem of Historical-Sociological Laws," *Philosophy of Science* 8, no. 4 (1941): 567–579.

72. Ibid., 577.

73. E. Zilsel, "Problems of Empiricism," in *Foundations of the Unity of Science: International Encyclopedia of Unified Science*, 2 vols., ed. O. Neurath, R. Carnap, and C. Morris (Chicago: University of Chicago Press, 1941), vol. 2, 53–93.

74. George Lundberg, "Sociologists and the Peace," *American Sociological Review* 9, no. 1 (1944): 1–13, 9.

75. Ibid., 11.

76. Read Bain, "Comment," *American Sociological Review* 7 (1942): 383–387, 387.

77. Ibid.

78. Magda B. Arnold, *Emotion and Personality*, vol. 1, *Psychological Aspects* (New York: Columbia University Press, 1960). Arnold did not invoke "empathy" as a means for recognizing another's emotion but cited Max Scheler's theory of direct perception of another's emotion. See Arvid Kappas, "Appraisals are direct, immediate, intuitive, and unwitting . . . and some are reflective." *Cognition and Emotion* 20, no. 7 (2006): 952–975; Stephanie Shields, "Magda B. Arnold's Life and Work in Context," *Cognition and Emotion* 20, no. 7 (2006): 902–919, http://www.feministvoices .com/magda-arnold/. Accessed October 11, 2012.

79. Author interview with Rosalind Dymond Cartwright, October 1, 2009 (hereafter Interview, RDC).

80. Ibid.

81. Ibid.

82. Yuri Bronson-Brenner was on the committee, newly arrived from Michigan, Interview, RDC.

83. Ibid.

84. Ibid.

85. *Psychiatric Dictionary*, ed. Leland E. Hinsie and Jacob Shatzky (London: Oxford, 1940), 194. Freud's definition of empathy was cited here as an "intellectual understanding of what is inherently foreign to our own Ego in other people." Psychoanalyst Trigant Burrow called it an "organism's primary feeling motivation and response." In the *Dictionary of Psychology*, by Philip Lawrence Harriman (New York: Wisdom Library, 1947), 120,

empathy was defined as "a term used by Lipps (1903) to denote the act of projecting oneself into a work of art or a natural scene. . . . Psychoanalysts use the term to denote an objective, impersonal recognition of the significance of another person's behavior."

86. Dymond, "Empathic Ability," 28–31. She cites Roy Hoskins in chapter 4.

87. Ibid., 15.

88. Ibid., 14, 23–26; Lois Murphy found that sympathetic habits in schoolchildren depended on an individual's threshold for affection, ability to see similarities with others, and "empathic responsiveness." Lois Murphy, *Social Behavior and Child Personality: An Exploratory Study of Some Roots of Sympathy* (New York: Columbia University Press, 1937), 286.

89. Interview, RDC.

90. Ibid.

91. Rosalind F. Dymond, "A Preliminary Investigation of the Relation of Insight and Empathy," *Journal of Consulting Psychology* 2 (1948): 228–233.

92. Jason Miller, "Dredging and Projecting the Depths of Personality: The Thematic Apperception Test and the Narratives of the Unconscious," *Science in Context* 28 (2015): 9–30; Claire Douglas, *Translate This Darkness: The Life of Christiana Morgan* (New York: Simon and Schuster, 1993). Empathy was understood "as the amount of 'life' invested in the character by the subject." See Martin Mayman and Bernard Kutner, "Reliability in Analyzing Thematic Apperception Test Stories," *Journal of Abnormal and Social Psychology* 42, no. 3 (1947): 365–368.

93. Christiana D. Morgan and H. A. Murray, "Thematic Apperception Test," in Henry A. Murray, *Explorations in Personality* (New York: Oxford University Press, 2008 [1938]), 530–545, 531; Wesley Morgan, "Origin and History of the Thematic Apperception Test Images," *Journal of Personality Assessment* 65, no. 2 (1995): 237–254.

94. R. Wolf and H. A. Murray, "Judgments of Personality," in Henry A. Murray, *Explorations in Personality*, 243–281. They described "critical empathy" as a way to use objective facts to amend an initial "emotional hypothesis," 247.

95. Dymond, "Preliminary Investigation," 231.

96. Ibid., 232. A study of clinical psychologists in training supported Dymond: Ralph Norman, "The Inter-relationships among Acceptance-Rejection, Self-Other Identity, Insight into Self, and Realistic Perception of Others," *Journal of Social Psychology* 37 (1953): 205–235, 213.

97. Dymond, "Empathic Ability," 230.

98. Lawrence Frank, "Projective Methods for the Study of the Personality," *Journal of Psychology* 8 (1939): 389–413.

99. R. Dymond, "A Scale for the Measurement of Empathic Ability," *Journal of Consulting Psychology* 13, no. 2 (1949): 127–133.

100. Ibid., 128.

101. Ibid.

102. Ibid., 130.
103. Dymond, "Empathic Ability," 56. Italics my own.
104. R. Dymond, "Personality and Empathy," *Journal of Consulting Psychology* 14 (1950): 343–350, 344.
105. Ibid., 349.
106. Ibid., 344.
107. Dymond, "Empathic Ability," 135.
108. Leonard S. Cottrell and Rosalind F. Dymond, "The Empathic Responses: A Neglected Field of Research," *Psychiatry* 12, no. 4 (1949): 355–359.
109. Ibid., 355.
110. Leonard S. Cottrell, "Some Neglected Problems in Social Psychology," *American Sociological Review* 15, no. 6 (1950): 705–712. Cottrell argued that the topics of the self, situation, and motivation also deserved attention.
111. Ibid., 711.
112. Ibid., 708.
113. Leonard Slater Cottrell, Jr., Cornell University Faculty Biographical Files, Collection Number 47-10-3394, Division of Rare and Manuscript Collections, Cornell University Library.
114. John W. Riley, Jr., and Leonard S. Cottrell, Jr., "Research for Psychological Warfare," *Public Opinion Quarterly* 21, no. 1 (1957): 147–158, 148.
115. Cottrell's remarks were given in 1955. Leonard S. Cottrell, "Social Research and Psychological Warfare," *Sociometry* 23, no. 2 (1960): 103–119, 118.
116. R. Dymond, Anne Hughes, and Virginia Raabe, "Measurable Changes in Empathy with Age," *Journal of Consulting Psychology* 16 (1952): 202–206.
117. Ibid., 202. Italics my own.
118. Glenn Hawkes and Robert Egbert, "Personal Values and the Empathic Response: Their Inter-relationships," *Journal of Educational Psychology* 45, no. 8 (1954): 469–476.
119. Henry C. Lindgren and Jacqueline Robinson, "An Evaluation of Dymond's Test of Insight and Empathy," *Journal of Consulting Psychology* 17, no. 3 (1953): 172–176, 175.
120. N. L. Gage, "Explorations in the Understanding of Others," *Educational and Psychological Measurement* 13, no. 1 (1953): 14–26; Howard Halpern, "Empathy, Similarity and Self-Satisfaction," *Journal of Consulting Psychology* 19, no. 6 (1955): 449–452.
121. Rosalind Dymond, "Interpersonal Perception and Marital Happiness," *Canadian Journal of Psychology* 8, no. 3 (1954): 164–171.
122. Irving Bender, "Study in Integrations of Personalities by Prediction and Matching" (PhD diss., Syracuse University, 1935). Gordon Allport, *Personality: A Psychological Interpretation* (New York: Holt, 1937), 354–355.
123. Irving E. Bender and Chauncey Allen, "Psychology at Dartmouth, 1882–1962, a Brief History" (Hanover, N.H., May 18, 1962), 4, Dartmouth College Rauner Library Special Collections (hereafter DRL).

124. Irving Bender to Gordon Allport, July 14, 1943, HUG 4118.10, box 1, Miscellaneous Correspondence, 1930–1945, Bender File, Gordon Allport Papers, Harvard University Archive.

125. David Muhlinter, "Irving E. Bender: Psychology, 'Not Disjointed Stimuli,'" 1959, in Irving Edison Bender, Faculty Material, Dean of the Faculty Records, Dartmouth College (Collection #DA-165), box 10459, folder "Bender, Irving E. Psychology," DRL.

126. I. E. Bender and A. H. Hastorf, "The Perception of Persons: Forecasting Another Person's Responses on Three Personality Scales," *Journal of Abnormal and Social Psychology* 45, no. 3 (1950): 556–561.

127. Ibid., 557. The scales were the Minnesota Inventory, the Ascendance-Submission Scale, and the Study of Motives.

128. Ibid., 559.

129. A. H. Hastorf and I. E. Bender, "A Caution Respecting the Measurement of Empathic Ability," *Journal of Abnormal and Social Psychology* 47, no. 2S (1952): 574–576, 574.

130. Ibid., 574.

131. Ibid.

132. Ibid., 575.

133. Bender and Hastorf, "On Measuring Generalized Empathic Ability (Social Sensitivity)," *Journal of Abnormal and Social Psychology* 48, no. 4 (1953): 503–506. Of course, if the two subjects were actually similar, it was problematic to merely subtract out the projection score.

134. Bender and Hastorf, "On Measuring Generalized Empathic Ability," 505.

135. Erwin Singer at New York University delivered a paper on empathy in small groups, and N. L. Gage delivered a paper on forecasting strangers' interests, which depended on a "perseverative conventionality." Condensed Program of 59th Annual Meeting of the American Psychological Association, August 31–September 5, Chicago, Illinois, *American Psychologist* 6, no. 7 (1951): 225–407.

136. Ralph D. Norman and Patricia Ainsworth, "The Relationships among Projection, Empathy, Reality, and Adjustment, Operationally Defined," *Journal of Consulting Psychology* 18, no. 1 (1954): 53–58.

137. Albert H. Hastorf and Hadley Cantril, "They Saw a Game: A Case Study," *Journal of Abnormal and Social Psychology* 49, no. 1 (1954): 129–134. "Albert H. Hastorf, Stanford Historical Society Oral History Collections," a series of oral history interviews conducted by Susan Ward Schofield, Stanford University Archives, 27–28.

138. Hastorf and Cantril, "They Saw a Game," 132.

139. A recent evaluation of this study argued that viewers took a first-person point of view of their own team but a strongly negative third-person view of the other team, patterns found to parallel assessments of violence in other conflict situations. John Barresi, "Intentional Relations and Diver-

gent Perspectives in Social Understanding," in *Ipseity and Alterity: Interdisciplinary Approaches to Intersubjectivity*, ed. Shaun Gallagher, Stephen Watson, Phillipe Brun, and Philippe Romanski (Le Havre: Publication de l'Université Rouen, 2004), 89–111, 110.

140. The alumnus was lawyer Kenneth Montgomery. "Report of Special Committee on Instruction in Human Relations," by Irving E. Bender, Cecil A. Gibb, Francis W. Gramlich, six others, box 2, folder 62, Henry B. Williams Papers, DRL.

141. Stuart Chase, *Roads to Agreement: Successful Methods in the Science of Human Relations* (New York: Harper, 1951), http://harvardmagazine.com/2004 /09/stuart-chase-html. Accessed February 28, 2016.

142. Bender and Allen, "Psychology at Dartmouth, 1882–1962," May 18, 1962, 2, DRL.

143. George Theriault, "Instruction in Human Relations at Dartmouth, 1951–1976: A Retrospective Overview by One of Its Teachers," Dartmouth College, Associate Dean of Science records (Collection #CA-819), box 7620, DRL, http://libcat.dartmouth.edu/record=1517362.

144. George Theriault, "Appendix: Tentative Outline for Human Relations I and II," 6, in "Instruction in Human Relations at Dartmouth, 1951–1976," DRL.

145. Theriault, Appendix: "The Human Relations Course, an Introductory Statement by Professor Gibb," 1, in "Instruction in Human Relations at Dartmouth, 1951–1976," DRL.

146. Hugo Münsterberg, *Psychology and Industrial Efficiency* (Boston: Mifflin, 1913).

147. John Burnham, *Accident Prone: A History of Technology, Psychology, and Misfits of the Machine Age* (Chicago: University of Chicago Press, 2010), 150; F. J. Roethlisberger and William J. Dickson, *Management and the Worker: An Account of a Research Program Conducted by the Western Electric Company, Hawthorne Works*, Chicago (Cambridge: Harvard University Press, 1939).

148. H. H. Remmers, "A Quantitative Index of Social-Psychological Empathy," *American Journal of Orthopsychiatry* 20, no. 1 (1950): 161–65, 161.

149. Ibid., 164.

150. N. T. Smalzried and H. H. Remmers, "A Factor Analysis of the Purdue Rating Scale for Instructors," *Journal of Educational Psychology* 34, no. 6 (1943): 363–367, 366. The other main factor was professional maturity.

151. H. H. Remmers, A. Anikeeff, A. J. Drucker, and Ben Shimberg, "Understanding How Others Feel," Report No. 22—Supplement, *Purdue Opinion Poll for Young People* 8, no. 4 (1949), H. H. Remmers Papers, Archives and Special Collections, Purdue University Libraries.

152. Remmers, "A Quantitative Index," 162.

153. Lois June Remmers and H. H. Remmers, "Studies in Industrial Empathy, I," *Personnel Psychology* 2, no. 4 (1959): 427–436; Frank Miller and

H. Remmers, "Studies in Industrial Empathy II: Management's Attitudes toward Industrial Supervision and Their Estimates of Labor Attitudes," *Personnel Psychology* 3, no. 1 (1950): 33–40; Wendell M. Patton, Jr., "Studies in Industrial Empathy: III. A Study of Supervisory Empathy in the Textile Industry," *Journal of Applied Psychology* 38, no. 5 (1954): 285–288.

154. Willard A. Kerr and Boris J. Speroff, "Validation and Evaluation of the Empathy Test," *Journal of General Psychology* 50 (1954): 269–276, 269. Kerr and Speroff, "Manual of Instructions," *The Empathy Test* (Chicago: Psychometric Affiliates, 1955).

155. Kerr and Speroff, "Validation and Evaluation."

156. Willard A. Kerr and Boris J. Speroff, "Key 1962" (Chicago: Psychometric Affiliates, 1962).

157. Kerr and Speroff, "Validation and Evaluation," 271.

158. Ibid., 274.

159. Raymond H. Van Zelst, "Empathy Test Scores of Union Leaders," *Journal of Applied Psychology* 36, no. 5 (1952): 293–95.

160. Francis P. Tobolski and Willard A. Kerr, "Predictive Value of the Empathy Test in Automobile Salesmanship," *Journal of Applied Psychology* 36, no. 5 (1952): 310–311.

161. Boris J. Speroff and Willard A. Kerr, "Steel Mill 'Hot Strip' Accidents and Interpersonal Desirability Values," *Journal of Clinical Psychology* 8, no. 1 (1952): 89–91.

162. B. J. Speroff, "Empathic Ability and Accident Rate among Steel Workers," *Personnel Psychology* 6, no. 3 (1953): 297–300.

163. Other psychological factors were devotion to civil liberties and the tendency to participate. W. A. Kerr, "Untangling the Liberalism-Conservatism Continuum," *Journal of Social Psychology* 35 (1952): 111–125.

164. B. J. Speroff, "Empathy and Role-Reversal as Factors in Communication," *Journal of Social Psychology* 41–42 (1955): 163–165.

165. B. J. Speroff, "Group Psychotherapy in Labor Relations: A Case Study," *Personnel Journal* 39 (1960): 14–17.

166. R. L. Thorndike, "The Empathy Test," in *The Fifth Mental Measurements Yearbook*, ed. Oscar Krisen Buros (Highland Park, N.J.: Gryphon Press, 1959), 178.

167. Ibid.

168. Graham B. Bell and Harry E. Hall, "The Relationship between Leadership and Empathy," *Journal of Abnormal and Social Psychology* 49, no. 1 (1954): 156–157; C. F. Patterson, "A Note on the Construct Validity of the Concept of Empathy," *Personnel and Guidance Journal* 40, no. 9 (1962): 803–806.

169. Arthur Siegel, "An Experimental Evaluation of the Sensitivity of the Empathy Test," *Journal of Applied Psychology* 38, no. 4 (1954): 222–223.

170. Arthur H. Brayfield, comments in "Tests and Reviews: Diplomacy Test of Empathy," in *The Sixth Mental Measurements Yearbook*, ed. Oscar Krisen Buros (Highland Park, N.J.: Gryphon Press, 1965), 187.

171. Richard Hatch comments in "Tests and Reviews: Diplomacy Test of Empathy," in *The Sixth Mental Measurements Yearbook*, ed. Oscar Krisen Buros (Highland Park, N.J.: Gryphon Press, 1965), 188.

172. William Lesser, "The Relationship between Counseling Progress and Empathic Understanding" (PhD diss., Department of Psychology, Michigan State University, 1958).

173. Ronald Taft, "The Ability to Judge People," *Psychological Bulletin* 52, no. 1 (1955): 1–23, 12, 3. A test of "intuition" between European married couples in Durban, South Africa, found no differences between men and women on the tests. B. Notcutt and A. L. M. Silva, "Knowledge of Other People," *Journal of Abnormal and Social Psychology* 46 (1951): 30–37.

174. Harry S. Hall and Graham B. Bell, "The Relationship between Two Tests of Empathy: Dymond's and Kerr's," *American Psychologist* 8, no. 8 (1953): 361–362; Ralph D. Norman and Waldemar C. Leiding, "The Relationship between Measures of Individual and Mass Empathy," *Journal of Consulting Psychology* 20, no. 1 (1956): 79–82. Studies of empathy in leadership were not consistent. Bernard Bass, "The Leaderless Group Discussion," *Psychological Review* 51, no. 5 (1954): 465–492.

175. Taft, "Ability to Judge People," 3.

176. B. E. Chlopan, Marianne L. McCain, Joyce L. Carbonell, and Richard L. Hagen, "Empathy: Review of Available Measures," *Journal of Personality and Social Psychology* 48, no. 3 (1985): 635–653, 640.

177. R. Dymond Cartwright, "Comment on Walter M. Lifton, 'The Role of Empathy and Aesthetic Sensitivity in Counseling,'" *Journal of Counseling Psychology* 5, no. 4 (1958): 274–275.

178. Interview, RDC.

179. Dymond cited Bruno Klopfer, an interpreter of the Rorschach. Rosalind Dymond Cartwright, "Predicting Response to Client-Centered Therapy with the Rorschach PR Scale," *Journal of Counseling Psychology* 5, no. 1 (1958): 11–17, 14.

180. R. Dymond Cartwright and Barbara Lerner, "Empathy, Need to Change, and Improvement with Psychotherapy," *Journal of Consulting Psychology* 27, no. 2 (1963): 138–144.

181. Charles B. Truax, "A Scale for the Measurement of Accurate Empathy," *Psychiatric Institute Bulletin* 12 (1961), 1–21; Charles B. Truax, "Therapist Empathy, Genuineness, and Warmth and Patient Therapeutic Outcome," *Journal of Consulting Psychology* 30, no. 5 (1966): 395–401.

182. Truax, "Scale for the Measurement," 1.

183. Philip F. Caracena and James Vicory, "Correlates of Phenomenological and Judged Empathy," *Journal of Counseling Psychology* 16, no. 6 (1969):

510–515; Anne Wenegrat, "A Factor Analytic Study of the Truax Accurate Empathy Scale," *Psychotherapy: Theory, Research and Practice* 11, no. 1 (1974): 48–51; Julian Rappaport and Jack M. Chinsky, "Accurate Empathy: Confusion of a Construct," *Psychological Bulletin* 77, no. 6 (1972): 400–404.

184. G. T. Barrett-Lennard, "Dimensions of Therapist Response as Causal Factors in Therapeutic Change," *Psychological Monographs* 76, no. 43 (1962): 1–36, 34–35; G. T. Barrett-Lennard, "The Empathy Cycle: Refinement of a Nuclear Concept," *Journal of Counseling Psychology* 28, no. 2 (1981): 91–100.

185. James Chapman, "Development and Validation of a Scale to Measure Empathy," *Journal of Counseling Psychology* 18, no. 3 (1971): 281–282.

186. W. Robert Dixon and William C. Morse, "The Prediction of Teaching Performance: Empathic Potential," *Journal of Teacher Education* 12, no. 3 (1961): 322–329.

187. Robert Hogan, "Development of an Empathy Scale," *Journal of Consulting and Clinical Psychology* 33, no. 3 (1969): 307–316; Albert Mehrabian and Norman Epstein, "A Measure of Emotional Empathy," *Journal of Personality* 40, no. 4 (1972): 525–543; Chlopan et al., "Empathy: Review of Available Measures." Later studies saw it as a two-stage model: first one took the perspective of another, then responded with affect: J. Coke, C. Batson, and K. McDavis, "Empathic Mediation of Helping: A Two-Stage Model," *Journal of Personality and Social Psychology* 36 (1978): 752–766.

188. D. G. Cross and C. F. Sharpley, "Measurement of Empathy with the Hogan Empathy Scale," *Psychological Reports* 50, no. 1 (1982): 62; R. D. Froman and S. M. Peloquin, "Re-thinking the Use of the Hogan Empathy Scale: A Critical Psychometric Analysis," *American Journal of Occupational Therapy* 55, no. 5 (2001): 566–572.

189. Norma Feshbach and Seymour Feshbach, "The Relationship between Empathy and Aggression in Two Age Groups," *Developmental Psychology* 1, no. 2 (1969): 102–107; another study found that children experienced empathy as emotional imitation with those of the same gender. Norma Feshbach and Kiki Roe, "Empathy in Six- and Seven-Year-Olds," *Child Development* 39, no. 1 (1968): 133–145.

190. Clinicians listed elements of empathy as: minimal agreement, probing-reflection, repeating and understanding, unstructured invitation. The Interpersonal Reactivity Index has four subscales: perspective taking, fantasy, empathic concern, and personal distress. Chlopan, "Empathy: Review of Available Measures."

191. Orlo Strunk, Jr., "Empathy: A Review of Theory and Research," *Psychological Newsletter* (circulated at New York University), 1958, 47–57.

192. Ralph H. Turner, "Role-Taking, Role Standpoint, and Reference-Group Behavior," *American Journal of Sociology* 61, no. 4 (1956): 316–328.

193. Lee J. Cronbach, "Processes Affecting Scores on Understanding of Others and Assumed Similarity," *Psychological Bulletin* 52, no. 3 (1955): 177–193, 177. See also N. L. Gage, George Leavitt, and George Stone, "The Intermediary Key in the Analysis of Interpersonal Perception," *Psychological Bulletin* 53, no. 3 (1956): 258–266.

194. George Gunkle, "Empathy: Implications for Theatre Research," *Educational Theatre Journal* 15, no. 1 (1963): 15–23, 23.

Chapter 7. Popular Empathy

1. Edward Steichen, *The Family of Man* (New York: Simon and Schuster, 1955), 94–95.
2. Jacob Deshin, "Panoramic Show at the Museum of Modern Art" in Symposium: The Controversial Family of Man, in *Aperture* 3, no. 2 (1955): 8–9, 8.
3. Eric Sandeen, *Picturing an Exhibition: The Family of Man and 1950s America* (Albuquerque: University of New Mexico Press, 1995), 48.
4. Steichen, introduction to *Family of Man*, 4.
5. Roland Barthes, "The Great Family of Man," in *Mythologies* (New York: Hill and Wang, 2012 [1957]), 196–199.
6. Sandeen, *Picturing an Exhibition*, 10.
7. Fred Turner, "*The Family of Man* and the Politics of Attention in Cold War America," *Public Culture* 24, no. 1 (2012): 55–84, 56–57.
8. "Bibiliographical Addenda, The Controversial Family of Man," cited from *Modern Photography*, *Aperture* 3, no. 2 (1955): 18; Steichen, introduction, 4.
9. Barbara Morgan, "Theme Show: A Contemporary Exhibition Technique," *Aperture* 3, no. 2 (1955): 24–26, 26.
10. Erich Albrecht, "New German Words in Popular English Dictionaries," *German Quarterly* 22, no. 1 (1949): 10–16.
11. "Emphasis on 'Empathy': Mr. Lang Will Move an Audience Even If He Has to Make the Camera Weep," *New York Times*, January 24, 1937.
12. Empathy, seen as emotional hypnosis in some forms of new, expressionist dance, could have corrosive political consequences. "Physiological Aesthetics and Modernism Forum," Society for Literature, Science and the Arts, November 2016; Whitney Laemmeli, "The Choreography of Everyday Life: Rudolf Laban and the Making of Modern Movement" (Ph.D. diss., University of Pennsylvania, 2016); Susan Manning and Lucia Ruprecht, eds., *New German Dance Studies* (Urbana: University of Illinois Press, 2012).
13. Bertolt Brecht, "Indirect Impact of the Epic Theatre (extracts from the Notes to *Die Mutter*)," in *Brecht on Theatre: The Development of an Aesthetic*, ed. John Willet (New York: Hill and Wang, 1992 [1932]), 57–62; Magdalena Nowack, "The Complicated History of *Einfühlung*," *Argument* 1, no. 2 (2011): 301–326; Koss argues that Brecht saw the necessity

of both empathy and alienation. Juliet Koss, "On the Limits of Empathy," *Art Bulletin* 88, no. 1 (2006): 139–57, 152.

14. Herbert Blumer, *Movies and Conduct* (New York: MacMillan, 1933).
15. Ibid., 74.
16. Marc Connelly, "Fantasies and Their Audience," *New York Times*, September 19, 1948.
17. Rebecca Franklin, "Where Actors and Audience Meet: The Newest Theatre Is the Oldest," *New York Times*, June 11, 1950.
18. Milton Bracker, "New Showcase in the Village," *New York Times*, October 26, 1952.
19. Ellen Herman, *The Romance of American Psychology: Political Culture in the Age of Experts* (Berkeley: University of California Press, 1995). For a discussion of postwar interest in emotion, see Susan Lanzoni, reviews of Frank Biess and Daniel Gross, *Science and Emotions after 1945*, and David Cantor and Edmund Ramsden, *Stress, Shock and Adaptation in the Twentieth Century, Isis* 107, no. 1 (2016): 208–210.
20. Thomas Pyles, "Subliminal Words Are Never Finalized," *New York Times*, June 15, 1958.
21. "Veterinary Revolution," *Time* 71, no. 5 (February 3, 1958).
22. David Guy Powers, "The Secret of Personal Power: Sometimes Listening's Better than Talking," *Washington Post*, December 16, 1949.
23. "Goldwyn's New Ex-Model 'Find' Tosses $64 Word at Interviewer," *New York Times*, October 9, 1949.
24. "Why Do You Submit to These Indignities," *Washington Post*, August 8, 1950.
25. "After All, We Do Have the Time," *Los Angeles Times*, March 19, 1958.
26. On the uses of big data, including n-grams, see Michael Pettit, "Historical Time in the Age of Big Data: Cultural Psychology, Historical Change and the Good Books Ngram Viewer," *History of Psychology* 19, no. 2 (2016): 141–153.
27. Frank Colby, "Take My Word," *Los Angeles Times*, November 17, 1952.
28. "What's Your Question?" *Chicago Daily Tribune*, September 18, 1956.
29. John Crosby, "Mutants on TV: 'Tales of Tomorrow' Rouses No Empathy," *Washington Post*, May 2, 1952.
30. Roger Darling, "Scientists Study Why Fans Blow Their Tops at Favorite Sports Events," *Daily Boston Globe*, August 25, 1946.
31. Joan Culpepper, "She'll Love, Honor Mate but, She Won't Ski," *Washington Post*, February 22, 1948.
32. "Steeple," *Daily Boston Globe*, July 7, 1955.
33. Review of Overstreet's *The Mature Mind, New York Times*, August 10, 1949.
34. Harry A. Overstreet, *The Mature Mind* (New York: W. W. Norton, 1949), 14.

35. Ibid., 65.

36. Ibid.

37. Ibid., 286.

38. Ibid., 66.

39. Harry and Bonaro Overstreet, "Through Others' Eyes," *Washington Post*, September 30, 1956. They used the common misspelling "emphatic persons."

40. Wendell Wilkie, *One World* (New York: Simon and Schuster, 1943), 188.

41. Joseph Campbell, *The Hero with a Thousand Faces* (Novato: New World Library, 2008 [1949]), xiii. Hollinger describes an "extravagant universalism" to be common at this time. David Hollinger, *Postethnic America: Beyond Multiculturalism* (New York: Basic Books, 2006), 54. On the postwar universalizing discourse on "man" see also Mark Greif, *The Age of the Crisis of Man: Thought and Fiction in America, 1933–1973* (Princeton: Princeton University Press, 2015).

42. Dr. George W. Crane, "How to Cash in on Your Worries: Even One's Enemy Can Be Complimented," *Boston Globe*, July 11, 1956.

43. Uncle Dudley, "Now That You Have Graduated," *Daily Boston Globe*, June 8, 1956.

44. "The Ghouls," *Washington Post*, July 12, 1956.

45. "Running with the Pack," *Washington Post*, January 19, 1955; "The Young Primitives: An Editorial" *Washington Post*, August 11, 1957; "George Is 'Possibly' Mentally Ill—Doctor," *Afro-American*, March 22, 1958.

46. Ernest Burgess, "Our Dynamic Society and Sociological Research," *Midwest Sociologist* 17, no. 1 (1955): 3–6, 5.

47. Ernest Burgess, "The Family and Sociological Research," *Social Forces* 26, no. 1 (1947): 1–6.

48. Nelson N. Foote and Leonard S. Cottrell, Jr., *Identity and Interpersonal Competence: A New Direction in Family Research* (Chicago: University of Chicago Press, 1955).

49. Dorothy Barclay, "Six Essentials for Growing Up," *New York Times*, April, 22, 1956.

50. Helen Robinson "Educational News and Editorial Comment," *Elementary School Journal* 52, no. 8 (1952): 433–442.

51. Nelson Foote, "Research: A New Strength for Family Life," *Marriage and Family Living* 16, no. 1 (1954): 13–20, 17.

52. Ibid., 19.

53. Howard Stanton and Eugene Litwak, "Toward the Development of a Short Form Test of Interpersonal Competence," *American Sociological Review* 20, no. 6 (1955): 668–674, 672.

54. Marcia Winn, "Teach Child the Value of Honesty," *Chicago Daily Tribune*, March 6, 1952; "Topics," *New York Times*, August 3, 1958; "Former Teacher Writes What Pupils Taught Her," *Chicago Daily Tribune*, June 17, 1954.

55. Elizabeth Touchette, "Pack Empathy for Family Trip," *Washington Post*, June 23, 1968, F6.

56. Edith Weigle, "The Secret of Getting Along with People!" *Chicago Tribune*, February 26, 1956.

57. "Topic of the Times," *New York Times*, June 15, 1957; Edwin Diamond, "Empathy Is Key to Happy Marriage," *Washington Post*, December 11, 1956.

58. "Health for All: Love Need Fly out of the Window," *Philadelphia Tribune*, June 11, 1955.

59. Mary Haworth's Mail, *Washington Post*, February 12, 1950; she advised empathy, sympathy, and compassion: "Happiness in Married Life" *Washington Post*, February 2, 1955.

60. Haworth recommended the writings of analyst Margaret Ribble. On Ribble, see Marga Vicedo, *The Nature and Nurture of Love: From Imprinting to Attachment in Cold War America* (Chicago: Chicago University Press, 2013).

61. David Elkind, "'Good Me' or 'Bad Me': The Sullivan Approach to Personality," *New York Times*, September 24, 1972.

62. Gesell Institute, "Child Behavior: Teenage Love Is Stormy," *Washington Post*, June 8, 1959.

63. "Quotations," *New York Times*, December 15, 1968, E10.

64. "How's Your Empathy," *Reader's Digest* 66 (April 1955): 62–64.

65. John Kord Lagemann, "How's Your Empathy?" *Christian Century* 72, no. 1 (February 23, 1955).

66. "Eleanor," *Atlantic Daily World*, May 12, 1955; "How to get along with other people," advertisement, *Los Angeles Times*, March 24, 1955.

67. Lucy Freeman, "Good Psychiatrist Often an Ex-Rebel," *New York Times*, June 12, 1950.

68. Catherine Groves, "The Counseling Process," *Marriage and Family Living* 9, no. 3 (1947): 57–58.

69. Seward Hiltner, "Empathy in Counseling," *Pastoral Psychology* 1 (1950): 25–50.

70. University of Chicago Roundtable, "A New Approach to Solving Personal Problems," an NBC Radio Discussion by Seward Hiltner, James G. Miller, and Carl R. Rogers, pamphlet, August 12, 1951, Menninger Foundation Archives, Kansas State Historical Society, Topeka, Kansas.

71. E. Brooks Holifield, *A History of Pastoral Care in America* (Eugene, Ore.: Wipf and Stock, 1983), 227.

72. The translation of Buber's 1925 lecture, entitled "Education," appears in Martin Buber, *Between Man and Man* (New York: Collier Books, 1965), 83–103, 97.

73. Rollo May, *The Art of Counseling* (Nashville: Cokesbury Press, 1939); Holifield, *A History of Pastoral Care in America*, 250–251.

74. Buber, *Between Man and Man*, 96.

75. Carl Rogers, "Questions Not Used" and "Buber's Concept of Inclusion," April 18, 1957, box 80, folder 13; "Dialogue with Buber," box 80, folder 13, Carl Rogers Papers, Library of Congress.

76. "On Carl Rogers," *Time* 70, no. 1 (July 1, 1957): 36. Carlton Barrett, "What Does Family Life Ministry Do?" *New York Amsterdam News*, April 1, 1989.

77. Jean Murphy "Problems Aired by Hotline Workers," *Los Angeles Times*, May 28, 1971.

78. Daniel Goleman, "Carl R. Rogers, 85, Leader in Psychotherapy, Dies," *New York Times*, February 6, 1987.

79. Carolyn Coggins, "What Goes on Backstage at the Literary Pageant," *Atlanta Constitution*, August 19, 1945; Leonard Dubkin, "Savage Ritual Is Studied by Freud Pupil," *Chicago Daily Tribune*, November 24, 1946; Betsey Simon, "Why Women Don't Marry, Lack of Confidence Says One Expert," *Daily Boston Globe*, August 20, 1950; "Analyst," *New Yorker* 24 (July 17, 1948): 18–19; "Goethe and Dr. Reik," *The Nation* 69 (October 29, 1949): 424. For more on Reik, see Nathan G. Hale, Jr., *The Rise and Crisis of Psychoanalysis in the United States: Freud and the Americans, 1917–1985* (Oxford: Oxford University Press, 1995), 129–132.

80. Theodor Reik, *Surprise and the Psycho-Analyst: On the Conjecture and Comprehension of Unconscious Processes* (London: Kegan Paul, 1936), 193. Originally published as *Der überraschte Psychologe: Über erraten und verstehen unbewusster Vorgänge* (Leiden: A.W. Sijthoof, 1935).

81. Theodor Reik, *Listening with the Third Ear: The Inner Experience of a Psychoanalyst* (New York: Farrar, Straus, 1949 [1948]), 477.

82. Reik, *Surprise and the Psycho-Analyst*, 193.

83. Jule Eisenbud, "ABC's and X's of Psychiatry," *Saturday Review* 31, no. 40 (1948): 18–19.

84. Anthony Bower, "Friendly 'Third-Ear,'" *New York Times*, August 15, 1948.

85. Robert L. Katz, *Empathy: Its Nature and Uses* (New York: Free Press of Glencoe, 1963), 41; Robert L. Katz, "Aspects of Pastoral Psychology and the Rabbinate," *Pastoral Psychology* 5, no. 7 (1954): 35–42; Robert L. Katz, "Empathy in Modern Psychotherapy and in the Aggada," *Hebrew Union College Annual* 30 (1959): 191–215; Katz bemoaned the fact that his work on empathy was not picked up by analysts. Laura Sheinkopf Hoffman, "The Making of an American Rabbi: Examining the Life and Work of Robert Langdon Katz" (ordination thesis, Hebrew Union College–Jewish Institute of Religion, 2002), 72.

86. Katz, *Empathy: Its Nature and Uses*, 41.

87. Ibid., 44.

88. Pauline Lide, "An Experimental Study of Empathic Functioning," *Social Service Review* 41, no. 1 (1967): 23–30, 26.

89. Elizabeth Lunbeck, "Empathy as a Psychoanalytic Mode of Observation: Between Sentiment and Science," in *Histories of Scientific Observation*, ed.

Lorraine Daston and Elizabeth Lunbeck (Chicago: University of Chicago Press, 2011), 255–275; Geoffrey Cocks, *Treating Mind and Body: Essays in the History of Science, Profession, and Society under Extreme Conditions* (New Brunswick, N.J.: Transaction Publishers, 1998), 123–151.

90. Heinz Kohut, "Introspection, Empathy, and Psychoanalysis: An Examination of the Relationship between Mode of Observation and Theory," *Journal of the American Psychoanalytic Association* 7 (1959): 459–83.

91. Ibid., 464.

92. Heinz Kohut, "On Empathy," in *The Search for the Self: Selected Writings of Heinz Kohut, 1978–1981*, vol. 4, ed. Paul Ornstein (London: Karnac Books, 2011 [1981]), 525–535, 527.

93. Cover, *Time* 55, no. 9 (February 27 1950).

94. "Oceans of Empathy," *Time* 55, no. 9 (February 27, 1950).

95. Ibid.

96. Gilbert Millstein, "TV's Comics Went Thataway," *New York Times*, February 2, 1958.

97. Larry Wolters, "What Keeps Them Up?" *Chicago Daily Tribune*, September 29, 1957.

98. John Crosby, "Be Lovable, Says Lucy, and You've Got It Made," *Washington Post*, March 28, 1960.

99. Gilbert Millstein, "Its Creator Explains the $64,000 Appeal," *New York Times*, August 21, 1955.

100. William M. Blair, "Pit Farmer against City Slicker," *New York Times*, November 15, 1959.

101. Milton Bracker, "The Question about Quiz Shows," *New York Times*, December 1, 1957.

102. "Purchasing Power of Negroes Up," *Chicago Defender*, June 8, 1957; "Report Says Market Remains Untapped," *Atlanta Daily World*, May 31, 1957.

103. Carl Spielvogel, "Advertising: Empathy, One Man's Symbol," *New York Times*, June 30, 1957.

104. "How's Your Empathy?" *National Underwriter*, July 3, 1953, printed in *Journal of Applied Psychology* 37, no. 5 (1953): 431.

105. Gerald P. Hillman, "Question for Salesmen: How's Your Empathy and Ego?" *Boston Globe*, July 3, 1964; "Salesmen, How's Your Fund of Empathy and Ego Drive?" *Los Angeles Times*, February 23, 1965, B7; "Reading for Business," *Wall Street Journal*, December 11, 1957 (review of *Successful Selling Strategies* by Charles Lapp).

106. Classified Ad 3, *New York Times*, July 24, 1955, F12.

107. Edith Efron, "Psychotherapy for Executives," *New York Times*, April 28, 1957; "Bosses' English Not the Queen's," *New York Times*, June 5, 1960; "Reading for Business," *Wall Street Journal*, May 20, 1959.

108. "Novel Shows Author Must Travel Far," *Chicago Daily Tribune*, December 17, 1944.

109. Horace Reynolds, "A Man, a Mouse, a Wave," *New York Times,* July 16, 1950.

110. "The Chameleon Poet," *Time* 82, no. 17 (October 25, 1963).

111. Arthur Koestler, *Insight and Outlook: An Inquiry into the Common Foundations of Science, Art and Social Ethics* (New York: Macmillan, 1949); Arthur Koestler, "The Novelist Deals with Character," *Saturday Review of Literature,* January 1, 1949.

112. Koestler, "Novelist Deals with Character," 8.

113. Ibid., 30.

114. "Trapezoids and Empathy," *Time,* December 3, 1951. *Time* printed the same phrase in "Abstractions for Export," *Time,* February 11, 1952. For more on Hofmann, see Harold Rosenberg, "Hans Hofmann's 'Life' Class," *Portfolio and Art News Annual,* no. 6 (Autumn 1962): 17–31; 110–115; Clement Greenberg, *Hofmann* (Paris: Editions Georges Fall, 1961).

115. Hans Hofmann, *Search for the Real and Other Essays,* ed. Sarah T. Weeks and Bartlett H. Hayes (Andover Mass.: Addison Gallery of American Art, Phillips Academy, 1948), 68. Hans Hofmann, *Four Decades in Provincetown* (Provincetown, Mass.: Provincetown Art Association and Museum, 2000 [1958]).

116. Tina Dickey, *Color Creates Light: Studies with Hans Hofmann* (Canada: Trillistar Books, 2011), 127, 26.

117. Robert Ackart, "Readers Post Opinions," *New York Times,* June 19, 1960.

118. Richard L. Coe, "Olney Hangs Rich Mosaic," *Washington Post,* August 7, 1958.

119. "Drama Mailbag," *New York Times,* February 1, 1959.

120. Gilbert Millstein, "Actor Leads a Dog's Life," *New York Times,* January 30, 1955.

121. Richard L. Coe, "Big Crowd Thrills to Gielgud Artistry," *Washington Post,* December 21, 1958.

122. Jack Smith, "Of Smith and Men," *Los Angeles Times,* November 6, 1958.

123. Wilson McTeer, "Observational Definitions of Emotion," *Psychological Review* 60, no. 3 (1953): 172–180, 175.

124. Leon Howard, "The Tadpole Imprisoned in a Drop of Water," *Los Angeles Times,* January 21, 1954.

125. Robert Kirsch, "The Book Report," *Los Angeles Times,* July 16, 1958.

126. "A Star Is Born," *New York Times,* October 27, 1946.

127. Joyce Cary, "Speaking of Books," *New York Times,* June 26, 1955.

128. "Odd Work from Frank Norris," *Washington Post,* September 6, 1959.

129. W. H. Auden, "The Aliens (for William Gray)," in W. H. Auden, *Collected Poems,* ed. Edward Mendelson (New York: Modern Library, 1991) 849–851, 851.

130. Philip K. Scheuer, "Producer Analyzes Lost Film Market," *Los Angeles Times,* December 5, 1961, B11; "Wanted: Lay Missionaries," *Time,* Feb-

ruary 16, 1959; Harry Sylvester, "Working Blueprint for Friendship," *New York Times*, February 21, 1960.

131. Meryle Secrest, "A Head Start in Empathy," *Washington Post*, May 1, 1966, F17.

132. "South's Racial Powder Keg May Explode as JFK 'Cools Heels,'" *Philadelphia Tribune*, June 11, 1963, 6.

133. William A. Glenn, "Cousins in Korea," *Los Angeles Times*, November 24, 1953; Joseph Henry Jackson, "Bookman's Notebook," *Los Angeles Times*, December 18, 1953.

134. Toki Schalk Johnson, "Praise Theme of Aaronsburg Story as Inspiring Brotherhood of Man," *Pittsburgh Courier*, October 6, 1956.

135. "'Blacks Need Empathy,' African Grad Contends," *New Pittsburgh Courier*, November 14, 1970, 32.

136. "Black Priests Pushed," *Chicago Daily Defender*, April 4, 1970, 1.

137. Ursula Vils, "Black Psychologist Claims Empathy Edge in the Ghetto," *Los Angeles Times*, October 25, 1970, N4.

138. "Never Again Where He Was," *Time* 83, no. 1 (January 3, 1964).

139. Laurel Schackelford, "Liberian Model's Goal: To Black Out Prejudice with Education," *Washington Post*, September 2, 1968, C3. Another article described empathy as a "simpatico approach" and saw the press as using "empathy" for President Kennedy. "Press 'Empathy' for Kennedy Seen," *New York Times*, January 23, 1961. See also Milt Brouhard, "Truer Than Facts: Folklore Held Key to Ethnic Empathy," *Los Angeles Times*, February 16, 1969.

140. "Wanted: Lay Missionaries," *Time* 73, no. 7 (February 16, 1959).

141. Malvina Lindsay, "People-to-People South of the Border," *Washington Post*, February 23, 1959.

142. Chesly Manly, "Global Order Is School Aim, Council Told," *Chicago Tribune*, October 8, 1960.

143. Philip Scheuer, "Producer Analyzes Lost Film Market: Has Hollywood Lost Cultural Empathy? Foreman Says Yes," *Los Angeles Times*, December 5, 1961.

144. Robert Hogan, "Development of an Empathy Scale," *Journal of Consulting and Clinical Psychology* 33, no. 3 (1969): 307–316.

145. Ibid., 315.

Chapter 8. Empathy, Race, and Politics

1. Kenneth B. Clark, "Prologue," *Dark Ghetto: Dilemmas of Social Power* (Middletown, Conn.: Wesleyan University Press, 1989 [1965]).

2. Kenneth Clark, "Problems of Power and Social Change: Toward a Relevant Social Psychology," Kurt Lewin Memorial Award Address, *Journal of Social Issues* 21, no. 3 (1965): 1–20, 5.

3. John P. Jackson, "Creating a Consensus: Psychologists, the Supreme Court,

and School Desegregation, 1952–1955," Ian Nicholson, "'The Approved
Bureaucratic Torpor: Goodwin Watson, Critical Psychology, and the Dilemmas of Expertise, 1930–1945," and Ellen Herman, "Commentary,"
all in *Journal of Social Issues* 54, no. 1 (1998); David Krech and Dorin
Cartwright, "On SPSSI's First Twenty Years," *American Psychologist* 11,
no. 9 (1956): 470–473; Alexandra Rutherford, F. Cherry, and R. Unger,
eds., "75 Years of Social Science for Social Action: Historical and Contemporary Perspectives on SPSSI's Scholar-Activist Legacy," *Journal of
Social Issues* 67, no. 1 (2011): 1–202; Katherine Pandora, *Rebels within the
Ranks: Psychologists' Critique of Scientific Authority and Democratic Realities
in New Deal America* (Cambridge: Cambridge University Press, 1997);
Kurt Lewin, "Action Research and Minority Problems," in *Resolving Social Conflicts*, ed. G. W. Lewin (New York: Harper and Row, 1948), 201–
216.

4. Kenneth Clark, *Pathos of Power* (New York: Harper and Row, 1974): 19–
29, 22.

5. Gordon W. Allport, "The Study of the Undivided Personality," *Journal of
Abnormal and Social Psychology* 19, no. 2 (1924): 132–141.

6. Ian Nicholson, *Inventing Personality: Gordon Allport and the Science of Selfhood* (Washington, D.C.; American Psychological Association, 2003);
Nicole B. Barenbaum, "How Social Was Personality? The Allports'
'Connection of Social and Personality Psychology,'" *Journal of the History
of the Behavioral Sciences* 36, no. 4 (2000): 471–487.

7. Allport, "Study of the Undivided Personality," 140.

8. Ibid.

9. Gordon Allport, *Becoming: Basic Considerations for a Psychology of Personality* (New Haven: Yale University Press, 1955), 21.

10. G. W. Allport, "Conclusions," Social Relations 147, HUG 4118.29,
folder 26, Gordon Allport Papers, Harvard University Archive (hereafter
GWA Papers).

11. He continued: "We have no desire to fool ourselves: to be objective is our
high aim. Yet to understand why men act as they do, we have to understand their motives and how things appear to them. Can only do so by a
sympathetic act, projecting ourselves into their skins." "Conclusions,"
Social Relations 147, HUG 4118.29, folder 26, GWA Papers.

12. Gordon Allport, "Gordon Allport," *A History of Psychology in Autobiogra-
phy*, vol. 5 (New York: Appleton-Century-Crofts, 1967), 1–26, 7, 16, 19;
Frances Cherry, "The Nature of *The Nature of Prejudice*," *Journal of the
History of the Behavioral Sciences* 36, no. 4 (2000): 489–498, 490.

13. Allport, Sociology 32, Winter Term 1944–45, Seminar in Group Prejudice and Conflict, Course Materials, Syllabus, "My Personal Experience
with Racial, Religious, Class Attitudes (A Topical Life-History)," HUG
4118.20, folder 3, GWA Papers.

14. Allport, "Life Histories," Sociology 32, Winter Term 1944–45, Seminar

in Group Prejudice and Conflict, Course Materials, HUG 4118.20, folder 3, GWA Papers.

15. Gunnar Myrdal, *The American Dilemma: The Negro Problem and American Democracy*, 2 vols. (New York: Harper, 1944); Walter A. Jackson, *Gunnar Myrdal and America's Conscience: Social Engineering and Racial Liberalism* (Chapel Hill: University of North Carolina Press, 1990).

16. Allport to Fredrick W. Mansfield, chairman of the Governor's Committee to Recommend Fair Employment Practices Legislation, December 12, 1945, HUG 4118.10, box 1, folder 2, GWA Papers. Allport, "To Members of House Ways and Means Committee, June 15, 1945," HUG 4118.10, box 1, folder 2, GWA Papers.

17. Allport lectured to the American Association of Social Workers on January 13, 1944. Jane Abbot (director of social service) to Gordon Allport, January 29, 1944; Allport to Abbott, December 8, 1943, HUG 4118.10, box 1, folder 3, GWA Papers.

18. Allport to Harry Beaumont, University of Kentucky, September 28, 1938; Allport to Rudolf Arnheim, December 11, 1940, HUG 4118.10, box 1, folder 2, GWA Papers.

19. Allport, "History of Psychology in Autobiography," 17.

20. Gordon Allport, "Catharsis and the Reduction of Prejudice," *Journal of Social Issues* 1–2 (1945): 3–10.

21. Gordon Allport, *The Nature of Prejudice*, unabr. 25th anniversary ed. (Reading, Mass.: Addison-Wesley, 1979), 497.

22. Allport, *Nature of Prejudice*, 498.

23. Gordon Allport, "Psychology of Participation," *Psychological Review* 53, no. 3 (1945): 117–130, 130.

24. Ibid., 127.

25. Ibid., 129.

26. "Radcliffe Alumnae Behavioral Science, 1960—Development of Social Relations of Harvard," HUG 4119.50, box 3, folder 95, GWA Papers. The department admitted 40 graduate students, and by 1960 it had graduated 208 doctoral students.

27. Kenneth D. Benne, "History of the T Group in the Laboratory Setting," in *T-Group Theory and Laboratory Method; Innovations in Re-education*, ed. Leland Bradford, Jack Gibb, and Kenneth Benne (New York: John Wiley and Sons, 1964).

28. Gordon Allport, "The Historical Background of Modern Social Psychology," in *Handbook of Social Psychology: Theory and Method*, vol. 1, ed. Gardner Lindzey (Reading, Mass.: Addison-Wesley, 1954), 3–56, 3. On action research, group therapy, and empathy in postwar international relations, see Perrin Selcer, "The View from Everywhere: Disciplining Diversity in Post–World War II International Social Science," *Journal of the History of the Behavioral Sciences* 45, no. 4 (2009): 309–329.

29. Allport, "Historical Background of Modern Social Psychology," 4.

30. "Radcliffe Alumnae Behavioral Science, 1960—Development of Social Relations of Harvard," HUG 4119.50, box 3, folder 95, GWA Papers.

31. Allport, "Historical Background of Modern Social Psychology," 4, 3.

32. Nadine Weidman, "Popularizing the Ancestry of Man: Robert Ardrey and the Killer Instinct," *Isis* 102, no. 2 (2011): 269–299; Marga Vicedo, *The Nature and Nurture of Love: From Imprinting to Attachment in Cold War America* (Chicago: University of Chicago Press, 2013).

33. Allport, *Becoming*, 26.

34. See Ashley Montagu, *On Being Human* (New York: Hawthorn Books, 1966 [1950]), 121; Nadine Weidman, "An Anthropologist on TV: Ashley Montagu and the Biological Basis of Human Nature, 1945–1960," in *Cold War Social Science* (New York: Palgrave Macmillan, 2012), 215–232, 218–221.

35. Theodor Adorno, Else Frenkel-Brunswik, Daniel Levinson, and Nevitt Sanford, *The Authoritarian Personality* (New York: Harper, 1950).

36. Allport, *Nature of Prejudice*, 427.

37. Gordon Allport, "Prejudice in Modern Life," November 21, 1957, Series 25341, Open Reel Recordings, 1952–1967, box 1421, 1932–1957, folder 13. Guide to the Records of Dartmouth College, Public Affairs, Great Issues Course, 1946–1967 (Collection #DA-12), Rauner Special Collections, Dartmouth College.

38. Allport, *Nature of Prejudice*, 441.

39. Ibid., 437, 440.

40. Scheler's eight variations of sympathy and empathy were: *Miteinander-fühlung, Gefühlsansteckung, Einsfühlung, Nachfühlung, Mitgefühl, Menschenliebe,* and *Akosmistische Person- und Gottesliebe,* and *Einfühlung.* Max Scheler, *Wesen und Formen der Sympathie* (1923), trans. Max Scheler, *The Nature of Sympathy* (New Haven: Yale University Press, 1954).

41. Allport, "Historical Background of Modern Social Psychology," 20; Allport, *Nature of Prejudice*, 435.

42. Allport, "Historical Background of Modern Social Psychology," 21. He also used the term *Mitgefühl.*

43. Alvin Scodel and Paul Mussen, "Social Perceptions of Authoritarians and Nonauthoritarians," *Journal of Abnormal and Social Psychology* 48, no. 2 (1953): 181–184.

44. Gordon Allport, "Prejudice in Modern Life."

45. Theodore R. Sarbin, "Role Theory," in *Handbook of Social Psychology: Theory and Method*, vol. 1, ed. Gardner Lindzey (Reading Mass.: Addison-Wesley, 1954), 223–258, 247.

46. Allport, "Prejudice in Modern Life."

47. Gordon Allport, "Books: A Five-Volume Shelf about Sickness of Both Individuals and Society: Prejudice," *Scientific American* (1950): 56–58.

48. Allport, *Nature of Prejudice*, 262.

49. Ibid., 281.

50. Miles Hewstone and Rupert Brown, "Contact Is Not Enough: An Intergroup Perspective on the 'Contact Hypothesis,'" in *Contact and Conflict in Intergroup Encounters*, ed. Miles Hewstone and Rupert Brown (Oxford: Basil Blackwell, 1986), 1–44, 4.

51. Shafali Lal, "1930s Multiculturalism: Rachel Davis Dubois and the Bureau for Intercultural Education," *Radical Teacher* 69 (2004): 18–22.

52. Rachel Davis DuBois, "National Unity through Intercultural Education," Education and National Defense Series, Pamphlet no. 10, U.S. Office of Education (Washington, D.C.: U.S. Government Printing Office, 1942), 5.

53. Ibid., 24.

54. Ibid.

55. Ibid., 25.

56. Helen Trager and Marian Yarrow, *They Learn What They Live* (New York: Harper, 1952), 281.

57. Ibid., 277.

58. Allport, *Nature of Prejudice*, 491.

59. George and Fanny R. Shaftel, "Report on the Use of a 'Practice-Action Level' in the Stanford University Project for American Ideals," *Sociatry* 2, nos. 3–4 (1948): 243–253.

60. Gerhart Saenger, *The Social Psychology of Prejudice: Achieving Intercultural Understanding and Cooperation in a Democracy* (New York: Harpers and Brothers, 1953), 201; see Margaret M. Heaton, "Feelings Are Facts, National Conference of Christians and Jews: An Intergroup Education Pamphlet," 1954. Saenger headed a committee to analyze data on segregation and personality development and contributed to the initial drafting of the Social Science Report for the 1954 Supreme Court case.

61. Saenger, *Social Psychology of Prejudice*, 210.

62. Davis DuBois, "National Unity through Intercultural Education," 28.

63. Rachel Davis DuBois with Corann Okorodudu, *All This and Something More: Pioneering in Intercultural Education* (Bryn Mawr, Pa.: Dorrance, 1984), 121.

64. Allport, *Nature of Prejudice*, 489.

65. Allport to Rachel Davis DuBois, June 1, 1942, HUG 4118.10, Misc. Correspondence, 1930–1945, box 2, GWA Papers.

66. Rachel Davis DuBois and Mew-Soong Li, *Reducing Social and Conflict through the Group Conversation Method* (New York: Association Press, 1971), 48.

67. Carey McWilliams, *Brothers under the Skin* (Boston: Little, Brown, 1951), 17–22.

68. Allport to Stuart Cook, September 15, 1947. When Kurt Lewin, a mainstay of CCI, died suddenly in February 1947, the organization lost funding and had to reorganize. Cook to Allport, February 12, 1947; Cook to Allport, March 25, 1947; Allport, "Foreword," typescript, 3. Cook asked

Allport to represent the SPSSI in a press conference: Cook to Allport, April 27, 1949. See also Allport to Isidor Chein, June 5, 1951, all found in HUG 4118.10, box 24, folder Stuart Cook, GWA Papers.

69. Alfred J. Marrow, *Living without Hate: Scientific Approaches to Human Relations* (New York: Harper and Brothers, 1951), 205.

70. Saenger, *Social Psychology of Prejudice*, 204.

71. Abraham Citron, Isidor Chein, and John Harding, "Anti-Minority Remarks: A Problem for Action Research," *Journal of Abnormal and Social Psychology* 45, no. 1 (1950): 99–126.

72. Morrow, *Living without Hate*, 242–244.

73. Allport to Stuart Cook, September 23, 1949, HUG 4118.10, box 24, folder Stuart Cook, GWA Papers.

74. Morrow, *Living without Hate*, 253.

75. Allport, *Nature of Prejudice*, 491.

76. Ibid.

77. Virgina Axline, "Play Therapy and Race Conflict in Young Children," *Journal of Abnormal and Social Psychology* 43 (1948): 279–286. A political philosopher at Columbia University added poetry, discussion, and moral exhortation to drama as ways to thwart prejudice. See Robert MacIver, ed., *Unity and Difference in American Life: A Series of Addresses and Discussions* (New York: Harper and Brothers, 1947).

78. Lois Marin Hurwitz, "UCLA Offers Guides in Human Relations," *Los Angeles Times*, January 26, 1958.

79. Allport, *Nature of Prejudice*, 509.

80. "Equality of Religions," *Gleanings: Gathered at Bapu's Feet*, ed. Mira (Ahmedabad: Navajivan Publishing House, 1949), 3–5.

81. Gordon Allport, "Conquest of Bigotry," typescript for a 1956 lecture at the University of Chicago, 2, box 24, folder "University of Chicago, January 1956," HUG 4118.10, GWA Papers.

82. Allport, "Conquest of Bigotry," 33.

83. Allport, "Social Science and Human Values," Wellesley College address, May 17, 1955, HUG 4118.50, box 3, folder 79, GWA Papers.

84. Ibid.

85. Kenneth B. Clark to Gordon Allport, July 30, 1953, HUG 4118.10, box 23, folder Ca-Cn, 1951–1953, GWA Papers.

86. Kenneth B. Clark to Gordon Allport, September 26, 1944; Clark to Allport, October 4, 1944, "Procedure for a Social Psychological Study of Negro-White Conflicts," HUG 4118.10, Misc. Correpondence, 1930–1945, box 2, folder Ca-Cn, 1944, 1945, GWA Papers.

87. Gordon Allport to Kenneth B. Clark, August 4, 1953, HUG 4118.10, box 23, folder Ca-Cn, 1951–1953, GWA Papers.

88. Gordon Allport to Kenneth B. Clark, August 4, 1953, 2; Clark thanked Allport for this material on "contact." Kenneth B. Clark to Allport, August 10, 1953, HUG 4118.10, box 23, folder Ca-Cn, 1951–1953, GWA Papers.

89. Kenneth B. Clark, "The Civil Rights Act: 20th Anniversary," New York Society for Ethical Culture, November 17, 1984, 3, box 165, folder 7, Kenneth Bancroft Clark Papers, Manuscript Division Library of Congress, Washington, D.C. (hereafter KBC Papers).

90. James A. Bayton, "Francis Sumner, Max Meenes, and the Training of Black Psychologists," *American Psychologist* 30, no. 2 (1975): 185–186.

91. K. B. Clark, "Implications of Adlerian Theory for an Understanding of Civil Rights Problems and Action," *Journal of Individual Psychology* 23, no. 2 (1967): 181–190; Damon Freeman, "Reconsidering Kenneth B. Clark and the Idea of Black Psychological Damage," *Du Bois Review* 8, no. 1 (2011): 271–283.

92. Kenneth B. Clark, interview by Ed Edwin, February 23, 1976, in *The Reminiscences of Kenneth B. Clark* (Alexandria, Va.: Alexander Street Press, 2003), 74.

93. "K. B. Clark to Editors of *Time*," October 11, 1939, box 14, folder 1, KBC Papers.

94. Otto Klineberg, *Social Psychology* (New York: Henry Holt, 1940), 377. Edwin P. Hollander, "Otto Klineberg, 1899–1992," *American Psychologist* 48, no. 8 (1993): 909–910.

95. James M. Jones and Thomas F. Pettigrew, "Kenneth B. Clark, 1914–2005," *American Psychologist* 60, no. 6 (2005): 649–651; Richard Severo, "Kenneth Clark, Who Fought Segregation, Dies," *New York Times*, May 2, 2005.

96. For a history of the Northside Center, see Gerald Markowitz and David Rosner, *Children, Race and Power: Kenneth and Mamie's Clark's Northside Center* (Charlottesville: University of Virginia Press, 1996).

97. K. B. Clark and Mamie Clark, "The Development of Consciousness of Self and the Emergence of Racial Identification in Negro Preschool Children," *Journal of Social Psychology*, SPSSI Bulletin 10 (1939): 591–599; K. B. Clark and Mamie Clark, "Skin Color as a Factor in Racial Identification of Negro Preschool Children," *Journal of Social Psychology SPSSI Bulletin* 11 (1940): 159–169. The doll study was K. B. Clark and M. P. Clark, "Racial Identification and Preference in Negro Children," in *Readings in Social Psychology*, ed. T. M. Newcomb and E. L. Hartley (New York: Holt, 1947), 169–178.

98. K. B. Clark, *Prejudice and Your Child* (Middletown, Conn.: Wesleyan University Press, 1988 [1955]), 23; E. Franklin Frazier, *The Negro Family in the United States* (Chicago: University of Chicago Press, 1939); Kurt Lewin, "Self-Hatred among Jews," in *Resolving Social Conflicts*, ed. G. W. Lewin (New York: Harper and Row, 1948), 186–200.

99. K. B. Clark, Isidor Chein, and Stuart W. Cook, "The Effects of Segregation and the Consequences of Desegregation: A Social Science Statement," September 1952 in the *Brown v. Board of Education of Topeka* Supreme Court case, reprinted in *American Psychologist* 59, no. 6 (2004): 495–501.

100. Kenneth B. Clark to Gordon Allport, October 4, 1965, HUG 4118.10, box 41, folder Ca-Cn, GWA Papers.

101. Kenneth B. Clark, introduction to *The Nature of Prejudice*, by Gordon Allport, unabr. 25th anniversary ed. (Reading Mass.: Addison-Wesley, 1979), ix.

102. Clark, *Prejudice and Your Child*, 25.

103. Ibid., 81.

104. Ibid., 7.

105. Ibid., 73.

106. Ibid., 39–40. He cited Max Deutscher and Isidor Chein, and Natalie Sadigur, "The Psychological Effects of Enforced Segregation: A Survey of Social Science Opinion," *Journal of Psychology* 26, no. 2 (1948): 259–287.

107. Clark to Dr. Aaron Karush, September 20, 1948, box 14, folder 4, KBC Papers.

108. Clark to Louis Kronenberger, *PM*, May 15, 1946, box 14, folder 2, KBC Papers.

109. Letter in response to article "From Where I Stand," August 30 issue of the *Reporter*, September 7, 1949, box 14, folder 5, KBC Papers.

110. "Liberalism and the Negro: A Round-Table Discussion," with James Baldwin, Nathan Glazer, Sidney Hook, and Gunnar Myrdal, *Commentary* 37, no. 3 (1964): 38.

111. Ibid., 39.

112. Ibid., 39.

113. Ibid.

114. K. Clark, "Delusions of the White Liberal," *New York Times*, April 4, 1965, SM27. This article was drawn from Clark's book *Dark Ghetto: Dilemmas of Social Power*.

115. Martin Luther King, Jr., "Letter from a Birmingham Jail," April 16, 1963, http://www.africa.upenn.edu/Articles_Gen/Letter_Birmingham.html. Accessed April 15, 2013.

116. Daniel Patrick Moynihan to Clark, December 20, 1965, box 25, folder 7, KBC Papers. Clark was cited in Moynihan's defense in "The Negro Family: Visceral Reaction," *Newsweek*, December 6, 1965. See also Ben Keppel, *The Work of Democracy: Ralph Bunche, Kenneth B. Clark, Lorraine Hansberry, and the Cultural Politics of Race* (Cambridge: Harvard University Press, 1995), 166–169.

117. "Case of 'Benign Neglect,'" *Newsweek*, March 16, 1970, 25–28, 27.

118. Clark, *Dark Ghetto*, 224.

119. Clark, "Delusions of the White Liberal."

120. James Baldwin, "Everybody's Protest Novel," *Notes of a Native Son* (New York: Dial Press, 1955), 17.

121. Ibid., 15.

122. Scott argues that the conservative reaction to instituting social programs for the poor moved from pity to contempt by the 1970s. Darryl Michael

Scott, *Contempt and Pity: Social Policy and the Image of the Damaged Black Psyche, 1880–1996* (Chapel Hill: University of North Carolina Press, 1997).

123. Martin Luther King, Jr., *Where Do We Go from Here: Chaos or Community?* (Boston: Beacon Press, 2010 [1967]), 107.

124. James Baldwin, "Down at the Cross: Letter from a Region in My Mind," *The Fire Next Time* (New York: Vintage, 1993 [1962]), 93.

125. Clark to Joe King April 13, 1965, box 25, folder 4, KBC Papers.

126. Clark, *Dark Ghetto*, 20, 229.

127. Clark, "Delusions of the White Liberal."

128. Clark to Joe King, April 13, 1965, box 25, folder 4, KBC Papers.

129. Clark to Ross Thalheimer, May 26, 1964, box 24, folder 7, KBC Papers.

130. Clark, *Dark Ghetto*, 229.

131. Gunnar Myrdal, foreword to *Black Ghetto*, xxiv.

132. Keppel, *Work of Democracy*, 17, 279 note 29.

133. Clark, "Introduction to an Epilogue," *Dark Ghetto*, xxxiv.

134. Clark, *Dark Ghetto*, 87.

135. Ibid., 14–15.

136. Clark, "Observations on Little Rock," *New South*, June 1958, 8, cited in Keppel, *Work of Democracy*, 130.

137. K. Clark, "The Ghetto and Housing and *You*," speech at the symposium of the Committee on Civil Rights in Metropolitan New York, December 1, 1965, p. 2s, box 160, folder 1, KBC Papers.

138. Quoted by Myrdal in Clark, *Dark Ghetto*, xxiii.

139. Clark, *Dark Ghetto*, 222.

140. Ibid., 80.

141. Kenneth Clark, "Intelligence, the University and Society," *American Scholar* 36, no. 1 (1966–1967): 23–32, 28.

142. Clark, *Dark Ghetto*, 77.

143. K. Clark, "A Tribute to David Barry," 3–4, 1984, box 165, folder 7, KBC Papers; Kenneth Clark and Jeannette Hopkins, *A Relevant War against Poverty: A Study of Community Action Programs and Observable Social Change* (New York: Harper and Row, 1969), 128–129.

144. The Harlem novelist Albert Murray argued Clark had left out these aspects of ghetto life. See Mitchell Duneier, *Ghetto: The Invention of a Place, the History of an Idea* (New York: Farrar, Straus and Giroux, 2016), 121.

145. Methodological flaws in these studies included not controlling for order effects in asking subjects their preference for dolls, and in asking subjects which dolls looked more like them. Subjects also had no opportunity to express a relatively well-adjusted self-concept but could only indicate that their racial group held an inferior role in American society. See William E. Cross, Jr., *Shades of Black: Diversity in African-American Identity* (Philadelphia: Temple University Press, 1991), 3–73.

146. Ibid., 27–29.

147. Freeman, "Reconsidering Kenneth B. Clark," 280; Linwood J. Lewis, "Creating an Identity: An Analysis of Kenneth B. Clark's Influence on the Psychology of Identity," 54; and Frances Cherry, "Kenneth B. Clark and Social Psychology's Other History," in *Racial Identity in Context: The Legacy of Kenneth B. Clark*, ed. Gina Philogène (Washington, D.C.: American Psychological Association, 2004). For an understanding of Clark in an Afrocentric perspective, see Layli Phillips, "Recontextualizing Kenneth B. Clark: An Afrocentric Perspective on the Paradoxical Legacy of a Model Psychologist-Activist," *History of Psychology* 3, no. 2 (2000): 142–167, 145.

148. Keppel, *Work of Democracy*, 169.

149. Kenneth Clark, "The American White: A Social Science View," paper prepared for Symposium on Ethnic Minorities around the World, American Association for the Advancement of Science, Section on Anthropology, December 27, 1962, box 159, folder 1, p. 2, KBC Papers.

150. From K. B. Clark's unpublished 1979 notes "Beyond the Ghetto," cited in Mitchell Duneier, *Ghetto: The Invention of a Place, the History of an Idea*, 136.

151. K. Clark, "What Motivates American Whites," *Ebony* 20, no. 10 (August 1965): 69–74, 73; this material was also presented in Clark, "American White," 7. See also Baldwin, *Fire Next Time*, 102.

152. K. Clark, "Social Power and Social Change in Contemporary America," address to the Foreign Affairs Scholars Program, July 18, 1966 (Washington, D.C.: Government Printing Office, 1966), 1–20, 16, KBC Papers.

153. Clark, "Social Power and Social Change," 17–18.

154. K. Clark, "The Civil Rights Act," 10, KBC Papers.

155. Walter Goodman, "Kenneth Clark's Revolutionary Slogan: Just Teach Them to Read," *New York Times Magazine*, March 28, 1973.

156. K. B. Clark, "The Role of Social Scientists Twenty-Five Years after Brown," *Personality and Social Psychology Bulletin* 5, no. 4 (1979): 477–481, 481.

157. John P. Jackson, Jr., "The Triumph of the Segregationists? A Historiographical Inquiry into Psychology and the *Brown* Litigation," *History of Psychology* 3, no. 2 (2000): 239–261, 240.

158. Clark, "The Present Dilemma of the Negro," address to the Southern Regional Council, November 2, 1967, 14, typescript, HW BDZZ B, Widener Library, Harvard University. A version of this speech, given at the meeting of the Association of Negro Life and History in October 14, 1967, was published in *Journal of Negro History* 53, no. 1 (1968): 1–11.

159. Clark, "Social Power and Social Change," 7.

160. Clark, *Pathos of Power*, 92–119, 118.

161. Ibid., 118.

162. Clark, "Social Power and Social Change," 12.

163. Ibid., 16.

164. Damon W. Freeman, "Not So Simple Justice: Kenneth B. Clark, Civil

Rights, and the Dilemma of Power, 1940–1980" (PhD diss., Indiana University, 2004), 3.

165. Clark, "Present Dilemma of the Negro," 15.

166. Clark, "Ghetto and Housing and *You*," 9.

167. Ibid.

168. Clark, "Implications of Adlerian Theory." He cited Heinz and Rowena Ansbacher, eds., *The Individual Psychology of Alfred Adler: A Systematic Presentation in Selections from His Writings* (New York: Harper, [1956], 1964).

169. Alfred Adler, *The Problem Child* (New York: Capricorn Books, 1963), xii. This was a translation of Adler's 1930 book. Adler described Einfühlung in 1913 as an intuitive or artistic entry into the essential nature of the patient, revealing the often unconscious ways the analyst assumed likenesses or differences between himself and the patient. Alfred Adler, *Praxis und Theorie der Individual-Psychologie* (Munich: Verlag von J. F. Bergmann, 1920; reprint Ann Arbor: University of Michigan, 2012), 29. The English translation called it "artistic and intuitive self-identification with the patient's personality." Alfred Adler, *The Practice and Theory of Individual Psychology*, trans. P. Radin (New York: Harcourt, Brace, 1927), 42. Einfühlung was also translated in this volume as "absorption" and as "putting himself in the other person's place" (5, 25).

170. Clark, *Pathos of Power*, 33.

171. Ibid., 37; Kenneth Clark, "Some Problems in Human Intelligence," speech to Gamma Chapter of Phi Beta Kappa, November 9, 1964, New York, typescript, box 159, folder 4, 1–8, 8, KBC Papers.

172. Kenneth B. Clark, interview by Ed Edwin, September 9, 1976, in *The Reminiscences of Kenneth B. Clark* (Alexandria, Va.: Alexander Street Press, 2003), 379.

173. Clark, "Intelligence, the University and Society," 29–30.

174. Ibid., 27.

175. Clark, September 1976 interview by Ed Edwin, 368–369.

176. Kenneth Clark, "The Pathos of Power: A Psychological Perspective," *American Psychologist* 26, no. 12 (1971), 1047–1057, 1049–1050.

177. Clark, "Epilogue," *Pathos of Power*, 174.

178. Boyce Rensberger, "Kenneth Clark Asks New Drugs to Curb Hostility of Leaders," *New York Times*, September 5, 1971.

179. Howard M. Fish, "Gain the World," Letters to the Editor, New York Times, November 20, 1971.

180. Clark, September 1976 interview by Ed Edwin, 385.

181. Clark, foreword to *Pathos of Power*, xi.

182. Clark, "Prologue," *Pathos of Power*, 10.

183. Kenneth B. Clark, "Empathy, a Neglected Topic in Psychological Research," *American Psychologist* 35, no. 2 (February 1980): 187–190.

184. Kenneth B. Clark, "Rough Draft, August 31, 1979," box 165, folder 2, p. 3, KBC Papers.

185. Ibid.

186. Phyllis Newton Hallenbeck, "A Reply to Clark's 'Empathy,'" *American Psychologist* 36, no. 2 (1981): 225.

187. K. Clark, "Rough Draft, August 31, 1979," 5, KBC Papers.

188. Ibid., 7.

189. Clark, "Empathy, a Neglected Topic in Psychological Research," 189.

190. K. Clark, "Rough Draft 31 August, 1979," KBC Papers. Clark amended this statement in his published version, to read as follows: "The survival of the human species now appears to depend upon a universal increase in functional empathy." Clark, "Empathy, a Neglected Topic in Psychological Research," 190.

191. Highlights, Second Annual Dinner, Joint Center for Political Studies, March 1979, box 165, folder 2, KBC Papers. Clark helped create this organization in 1970 to provide support for elected black officials.

192. Clark, foreword to *Pathos of Power*, xiv.

193. K. Clark, "No Peace without Justice," Mercy College, the Dean's Lecture Series, March 9, 1983, p. 3, box 165, folder 6, KBC Papers.

194. Lynn Avery Hunt, *Inventing Human Rights: A History* (New York: W. W. Norton, 2007); *The Politics of Empathy*, ed. Barbara Weber, Eva Marsal, and Takara Dobashi (Berlin: LITverlag, 2011).

195. Michael Morrell, *Empathy and Democracy: Feeling, Thinking and Deliberation* (University Park: Penn State University Press, 2010), 2.

196. Carolyn Pedwell, *Affective Relations: The Transnational Politics of Empathy* (Houndsmill: Palgrave Macmillan, 2014), 46–47.

197. Claudia Rankine, "The Condition of Black Life Is One of Mourning," *New York Times Magazine*, June 22, 2015.

198. See "Epilogue" in Samuel Moyn, *Human Rights and the Uses of History* (London: Verso, 2014), 135–147; Samuel Moyn, *The Last Utopia: Human Rights in History* (Cambridge: Harvard University Press, 2010), 80–81.

Chapter 9. Empathic Brains

1. Marco Iacoboni and Mirella Dapretto. "The Mirror Neuron System and the Consequences of Its Dysfunction," *Nature Reviews Neuroscience* 7, no. 12 (2006): 942–951. The first study to publish these findings was G. di Pellegrino, L. Fadiga, L. Fogassi, V. Gallese, and G. Rizzolatti, "Understanding Motor Events: A Neurophysiological Study," *Experimental Brain Research* 91, no. 1 (1992): 176–80.

2. Amy Coplan, "Will the Real Empathy Please Stand Up? A Case for a Narrow Conceptualization," *Southern Journal of Philosophy* 49, Spindel Supplement (2011): 40–63.

3. Kenneth B. Clark, "Empathy, a Neglected Topic in Psychological Research," *American Psychologist* 35, no. 2 (1980): 187–190, 187.

4. Gerald A. Gladstein, "The Historical Roots of Contemporary Empathy

Research," *Journal of the History of the Behavioral Sciences* 20, no. 1 (1984): 38–59.

5. Clark, "Empathy, a Neglected Topic," 226.

6. Martin Hoffman, "Empathy: Its Development and Prosocial Implications," *Nebraska Symposium on Motivation* 25, ed. H. Howe and C. Keasy (Lincoln: University of Nebraska Press, 1977), 169–217.

7. Arnold P. Goldstein and Gerald Y. Michaels, *Empathy: Development, Training and Consequences* (Hillsdale, N.J.: Lawrence Erlbaum, 1985).

8. Mark H. Davis, "Measuring Individual Differences in Empathy," *Journal of Personality and Social Psychology* 44, no. 1 (1983): 113–126.

9. R. S. Lazarus, J. C. Speisman, A. M. Mordkoof, and L. A. Davison, "A Laboratory Study of Psychological Stress Produced by a Motion Picture Film," *Psychological Monographs* 76, no. 34 (1962): 1–35; S. M. Berger, "Conditioning through Vicarious Instigation," *Psychological Review* 69, no. 5 (1962): 450–466.

10. Ezra Stotland, "Exploratory Studies of Empathy," in *Advances in Experimental Social Psychology*, vol. 4, ed. L. Berkowitz (New York: Academic Press, 1969).

11. Ezra Stotland, Kenneth E. Mathews, Jr., Stanley E. Sherman, Robert O. Hansson, and Barbara Z. Richardson, *Empathy, Fantasy and Helping*, Sage Library of Social Research, vol. 65 (Beverly Hills: Sage Publications, 1978), 36. This volume includes research on birth order effects in empathy and emotional overarousal in nurses.

12. Dennis Krebs, "Empathy and Altruism," *Journal of Personality and Social Psychology* 32, no. 6 (1975): 1134–1148. The statistical significance was slight, but the author pointed out that all measures pointed in the same direction.

13. Robert W. Levenson and Anna M. Ruef, "Empathy: A Physiological Substrate," *Journal of Personality and Social Psychology* 63, no. 2 (1992): 234–246.

14. Paul D. MacLean, "The Brain in Relation to Empathy and Medical Education," *Journal of Nervous and Mental Disease* 144, no. 5 (1967): 374–382.

15. Ibid., 374.

16. For an excellent history of social neuroscience, see Nikolas Rose and Joelle M. Abi-Rached, *Neuro: The New Brain Sciences and the Management of the Mind* (Princeton: Princeton University Press, 2013), 143–148; Michael Gazzinga, *The Social Brain: Discovering Networks of the Mind* (New York: Basic Books, 1985).

17. Leslie Brothers, "A Biological Perspective on Empathy," *American Journal of Psychiatry* 146, no. 1 (1989): 10–19, 17.

18. Jean Decety and Julian Paul Keenan, "Social Neuroscience: A New Journal," *Social Neuroscience* 1, no. 1 (2006): 1–4, 4.

19. Sandra Blakeslee, "Cells That Read Minds," *New York Times*, January 10, 2006.

20. Ibid.

21. Giacomo Rizzolatti and Corrado Sinigaglia, *Mirrors in the Brain: How Our Minds Share Actions and Emotions*, trans. Frances Anderson (Oxford: Oxford University Press, 2008), 79.

22. Other studies found auditory mirror neurons in pianists: M. Bangert et al., "Shared Networks for Auditory and Motor Processing in Professional Pianists: Evidence from fMRI Conjunction," *NeuroImage* 30, no. 3 (2006): 917–926.

23. "Mirror neuron" was first used in V. Gallese, L. Fadiga, L. Fogassi, and G. Rizzolatti, "Action Recognition in the Premotor Cortex," *Brain* 119, no. 2 (1996): 593–609. See also G. Rizzolatti, G. Fadiga, V. Gallese, and L. Fogassi, "Premotor Cortex and the Recognition of Motor Actions," *Cognitive Brain Research* 3, no. 2 (1996): 131–141. For a history of the Parma laboratory and mirror neuron research, see Katja Guenther, "Imperfect Reflections: Norms, Pathology, and Difference in Mirror Neuron Research," in *Plasticity and Pathology: On the Formation of the Neural Subject*, ed. David Bates and Nima Bassiri (New York: Fordham University, 2016), 268–308.

24. M. A. Umiltà, E. Kohler, V. Gallese, L. Fogassi, L. Fadiga, C. Keysers, and G. Rizzolatti, "I Know What You Are Doing: A Neurophysiological Study," *Neuron* 31, no. 1 (July 19, 2001): 155–165.

25. G. Rizzolatti, L. Fogassi, and V. Gallese, "Neurophysiological Mechanisms Underlying the Understanding and Imitation of Action," *Nature Reviews/Neuroscience* 2 (September 2001): 661–670, 661.

26. Luciano Fadiga, Leonardo Fogassi, Giovanni Pavesi, and Giacomo Rizzolatti, "Motor Facilitation during Action Observation: A Magnetic Stimulation Study," *Journal of Neurophysiology* 73, no. 6 (1995): 2608–2611; Rizzolatti, Fogassi, and Gallese, "Neurophysiological Mechanisms Underlying the Understanding and Imitation of Action."

27. Marco Iacoboni, "Imitation, Empathy, and Mirror Neurons," *Annual Review of Psychology* 60 (2009): 653–670; L. Carr, M. Iacoboni, M. C. Dubeau, J. C. Mazziotta, and G. L. Lenzi, "Neural Mechanisms of Empathy in Humans: A Relay from Neural Systems for Imitation to Limbic Areas," *Proceedings of the National Academy of Sciences* 100, no. 9 (2003): 5497–5502.

28. R. Mukamel, A. D. Ekstrom, J. Kaplan, M. Iacoboni, and I. Fried, "Single-Neuron Responses in Humans during Execution and Observation of Actions," *Current Biology* 20, no. 8 (2010): 750–756.

29. Miralla Dapretto, Mari S. Davies, Jennifer H. Pfeifer, Ashley A. Scott, Marian Sigman, Susan Bookheimer, and Marco Iacoboni, "Understanding Emotions in Others: Mirror Neuron Dysfunction in Children with Autism Spectrum Disorders," *Nature Neuroscience* 9, no. 1 (January 2006): 28–30; Nouchine Hadjikhani, Robert M. Joseph, Josh Snyder, and Helen Tager-Flusberg, "Anatomical Differences in the Mirror Neuron System

and Social Cognition Network in Autism," *Cerebral Cortex* 16 (2006): 1276–1282.

30. B. Bower, "Goal-Oriented Brain Cells," *Science News* 167, no. 18 (April 30, 2005): 278; Leonardo Fogassi, P. F. Ferrari, B. Gesierich, S. Rozzi, F. Chersi, and G. Rizzolatti, "Parietal Lobe: From Action Understanding to Intention Understanding," *Science* 308, no. 5722 (April 29, 2005): 662–675.

31. Greg Miller, "Reflecting on Another's Mind," *Science* 308, no. 5724 (May 12, 2005): 945–947. Keysers reprised this talk seven years later in Dublin. See Dick Ahlstrom, "So, Why Does James Bond Make Our Skin Crawl?" *Irish Times*, July 16, 2012.

32. John Tierney, "Using MRIs to See Politics on the Brain," *New York Times*, April 20, 2004.

33. Marco Iacoboni, *Mirroring People: The Science of Empathy and How We Connect with Others* (New York: Picador, 2009), 210–211.

34. Ibid., 242.

35. "Politics on the Brain," *Toronto Star*, October 23, 2004.

36. Marco Iacoboni, Joshua Freedman, and Jonas Kaplan, "This Is Your Brain on Politics," *New York Times*, November 11, 2007.

37. "George Lakoff: Obama in a Bind," 90.9 WBUR, Open Source Radio, http://radioopensource.org/george-lakoff-obama-in-a-bind/. Accessed February 3, 2017.

38. Daniel Goleman, "Friends for Life: An Emerging Biology of Emotional Healing," *New York Times*, October 10, 2006.

39. Daniel Goleman, *Social Intelligence: The New Science of Human Relationships* (New York: Bantam Books, 2006), 43.

40. Daniel Goleman, "Flame First, Think Later: New Clues to E-Mail Misbehavior," *New York Times*, February 20, 2007.

41. Vilayanur S. Ramachandran and Lindsay M. Oberman, "Broken Mirrors: A Theory of Autism," *Scientific American* (November 2006): 63–69. See also Lindsay M. Oberman and V. S. Ramachandran, "The Simulating Social Mind: The Role of the Mirror Neuron System and Simulation in the Social and Communicative Deficits of Autism Spectrum Disorders," *Psychological Bulletin* 133, no. 2 (2007): 310–327.

42. Sharon Begley, "How Mirror Neurons Help Us to Empathize, Really Feel Others' Pain," *Wall Street Journal*, March 4, 2005.

43. Giacomo Rizzolatti, Leonardo Fogassi, and Vittorio Gallese, "Mirrors in the Mind," *Scientific American* (November 2006): 54–61, 59.

44. Sarah Kershaw, "Consumed with Guilt: Will Shopping Ever Feel Good Again?" *New York Times*, August 16, 2009.

45. Robert Lee Hotz, "How Your Brain Allows You to Walk in Another's Shoes," *Wall Street Journal*, August 17, 2007.

46. Alex Hutchinson, "Go Neurons Go!" *Globe and Mail*, November 2, 2013.

47. Iacoboni, *Mirroring People*; Christian Keysers, *The Empathic Brain* (Social

Brain Press, 2011); Rizzolatti and Sinigaglia, *Mirrors in the Brain;* V. S. Ramachandran, *The Tell-Tale Brain* (New York: W. W. Norton, 2011); see also Matthew D. Lieberman, *Social: Why Our Brains Are Wired to Connect* (New York: Crown, 2013).

48. For a selection of the large literature on motor resonance simulation, also called mindreading, see Alvin Goldman, *Simulating Minds: The Philosophy, Psychology and Neuroscience of Mindreading* (Oxford: Oxford University Press, 2006); Karsten Stueber, *Rediscovering Empathy: Agency, Folk-Psychology and the Human Sciences* (Cambridge: MIT Press, 2006); Vittorio Gallese and Alvin Goldman, "Mirror Neurons and the Simulation Theory of Mind-Reading," *Trends in Cognitive Science* 2, no. 12 (1998): 493–501; Shaun Nichols and Stephen P. Stich, *Mindreading: An Integrated Account of Pretence, Self-Awareness, and Understanding Other Minds* (Oxford: Oxford University Press, 2003); Alvin Goldman, "Empathy, Mind and Morals" *Proceedings and Addresses of the American Philosophical Association* 66, no. 3 (1992): 17–41; Nancy Eisenberg and R. Fabes, "Empathy: Conceptualization, Measurement, and Relation to Prosocial Behavior," *Motivation and Emotion* 14 (1990): 131–149; Simon Baron-Cohen, *Mindblindness* (Cambridge: MIT Press, 1995); C. D. Batson, *The Altruism Question* (Hillsdale N.J.: LEA, 1991).

49. See Stephen P. Turner, "Mirror Neurons and Practices: A Response to Lizardo," *Journal for the Theory of Social Behavior* 37, no. 3 (2007): 351–371.

50. Iacoboni, *Mirroring People*, 7. Italics in original. The original study is Marco Iacoboni, I. Molnar-Szakacs, V. Gallese, G. Buccino, J. C. Mazziotta, and G. Rizzolatti, "Grasping the Intentions of Others with One's Own Mirror Neuron System," *PLoS Biology* 3, no. 3 (March 2005): 529–535.

51. George Herbert Mead cited in Rizzolatti and Sinigaglia, *Mirrors in the Brain*, 50, 150.

52. Rizzolatti and Sinigaglia, *Mirrors in the Brain*, 125. See also Koen Nelissen, G. Luppino, W. Vanduffel, G. Rizzolatti, and G. A. Orban, "Observing Others: Multiple Action Representation in the Frontal Lobe," *Science* 310, no. 332 (2005): 332–336.

53. James J. Gibson, *The Ecological Approach to Visual Perception* (Boston: Houghton Mifflin, 1979).

54. Rizzolatti and Sinigaglia, *Mirrors in the Brain*, 51.

55. Vittorio Gallese, "The 'Shared Manifold' Hypothesis: From Mirror Neurons to Empathy," *Journal of Consciousness Studies* 8, no. 5–6 (2001): 33–50; Vittorio Gallese, "The Roots of Empathy: The Shared Manifold Hypothesis and the Neural Basis of Intersubjectivity," *Psychopathology* 36, no. 4 (2003): 171–180.

56. Maurice Merleau-Ponty, *Phenomenology of Perception*, cited in Vittorio Gallese, "'Shared Manifold' Hypothesis," 44.

57. Gallese, "'Shared Manifold' Hypothesis," 45. Gallese argues that the conceptual knowledge of action based in the mirror neuron system by-

passes the linguistic system and is thus also attributable to nonhuman primates: Vittorio Gallese, "A Neuroscientific Grasp of Concepts: From Control to Representation," *Philosophical Transactions of the Royal Society B: Biological Sciences* 358, no. 1435 (2003): 1231–1240.

58. Andrew J. Calder et al., "Impaired Recognition and Experience of Disgust Following Brain Injury," *Nature Neuroscience* 3, no. 11 (2000): 1077–1078.

59. A. Bechara, H. Damasio, and A. Damasio, "Emotion, Decision-Making, and the Orbitofrontal Cortex," *Cerebral Cortex* 10, no. 3 (2000): 295–307; Hannah Damasio, "Impaired of Interpersonal Social Behavior Caused by Acquired Brain Damage," in *Altruism and Altruistic Love: Science, Philosophy and Religion in Dialogue*, ed. Stephen G. Post, Lynn G. Underwood, Jeffrey Schloss, and William B. Hurlbut (Oxford: Oxford University Press, 2002), 272–283.

60. Stephanie D. Preston and Frans de Waal, "Empathy: Its Ultimate and Proximate Bases," *Behavioral and Brain Sciences* 25, no. 1 (2002): 1–75.

61. Ibid., 17.

62. Rick Grush, "The Emulation Theory of Representation: Motor Control, Imagery and Perception," *Behavioral and Brain Sciences* 27, no. 3 (2004): 377–442; W. Richter, R. Somorjai, R. Summers, M. Jarmasz, R. S. Menon, J. S. Gati, A. P. Georgopoulos, K. Tegeler, K. Ugurbil, and S. G. Kim, "Motor Area Activity during Mental Rotation Studied by Time-Resolved Single-Trial fMRI," *Journal of Cognitive Neuroscience* 12, no. 2 (2000): 310–320; Claus Lamm, C. Windischberger, U. Leodolter, E. Moser, and H. Bauer, "Evidence for Premotor Cortex Activity during Dynamic Visuospatial Imagery from Single-Trial Functional Magnetic Resonance Imaging and Event-Related Slow Cortical Potentials," *Neuroimage* 14, no. 2 (2001): 268–283.

63. Schwartz calls it "amodel spatial imagery": Daniel Schwartz, "Physical Imagery: Kinematic vs. Dynamic Models," *Cognitive Psychology* 38, no. 3 (1999): 433–464, cited in Grush, "Emulation Theory of Representation," 393.

64. David Freedberg and Vittorio Gallese, "Motion, Emotion and Empathy in Esthetic Experience," *Trends in Cognitive Sciences* 11, no. 5 (2007): 197–203.

65. G. Gabrielle Starr, *Feeling Beauty: The Neuroscience of Aesthetic Experience* (Cambridge: MIT Press, 2013).

66. Eric Kandel, "What the Brain Can Tell Us about Art," *New York Times*, April 4, 2013. See also Eric Kandel, *The Age of Insight: The Quest to Understand the Unconscious in Art: Mind, and Brain, from Vienna 1900 to the Present* (New York: Random House, 2012), chap. 11.

67. Some arguments for empathy as a higher-level processing include Frederique De Vignemont and Tania Singer, "The Empathic Brain: How, When and Why?" *Trends in Cognitive Sciences* 10, no. 10 (2006):

435–441; Pierre Jacob, "The Direct Perception Model of Empathy: A Critique," *Review of Philosophy and Psychology* 2, no. 3 (2011): 519–540; Shaun Gallagher, "Empathy, Simulation and Narrative," in "Varieties of Empathy in Science, Art and History," ed. Susan Lanzoni, Robert Brain, and Alan Young, special issue of *Science in Context* 25, no. 3 (2012): 355–381.

68. Pierre Jacob and Marc Jeannerod, "The Motor Theory of Social Cognition: A Critique," *Trends in Cognitive Sciences* 9, no. 1 (2005): 21–25.

69. Pierre Jacob, "What Do Mirror Neurons Contribute to Human Social Cognition?" *Mind and Language* 23, no. 2 (2008): 190–223, 211.

70. Fritz Heider and Marianne Simmel, "An Experimental Study of Apparent Behavior," *American Journal of Psychology* 57, no. 2 (1944): 243–259.

71. Giacomo Rizzolatti and Corrado Sinigaglia, "The Functional Role of the Parieto-Frontal Mirror Circuit: Interpretations and Misinterpretations," *Nature Reviews Neuroscience* 11, no. 4 (2010): 264–274.

72. Alison Gopnik, "Cells That Read Minds? What the Myth of Mirror Neurons Gets Wrong about the Human Brain," *Slate*, April 26, 2007, http://www.slate.com/id/2165123/.

73. Greg Hickok, *The Myth of Mirror Neurons: The Real Neuroscience of Communication and Cognition* (New York: W. W. Norton, 2014), 197–199.

74. Ibid., 178.

75. Ibid., 228.

76. Ibid., 142, 129–145. Hickok defines embodied cognitive models as interweaving higher-level cognition with affect and action in the sensorimotor system. He finds a parallel between mirror neuron theories of language and Alvin Liberman's 1950s motor theory of speech perception, which Hickok claims is now discredited. Liberman's model purported that a listener understood the speech of another by mimicking the motor gestures of speaking, 13–14.

77. Peggy Mason, "Empathy Is a Pain so Why Bother?" and Frans de Waal, "Do Animals Feel Empathy," *Scientific American* 24 (2015): 90–99.

78. Elisabeth Rosenthal, "When Bad People Are Punished, Men Smile (but Women Don't)," *New York Times*, January 19, 2006; Bjorn Carey, "Men Enjoy Physical Revenge, Brain Study Suggests," *LiveScience*, January 18, 2006. The medical anthropologist Allan Young calls the ability to imagine and take pleasure in another's punishment, empathic cruelty, which has not received much attention. Allan Young, "The Social Brain and the Myth of Empathy," *Science in Context* 25, no. 3 (2012): 401–424.

79. Tania Singer, Ben Weymour, John P. O'Doherty, Klass E. Stephan, Raymond J. Jolan, and Chris D. Frith, "Empathic Neural Responses Are Modulated by the Perceived Fairness of Others," *Nature* 439, no. 7075 (January 26, 2006): 466–469.

80. Cordelia Fine, *Delusions of Gender: How Our Minds, Society and Neurosexism Create Difference* (New York: W. W. Norton, 2010); Katherine Bou-

ton, "Peeling Away Theories on Gender and the Brain," *New York Times*, August 24, 2010.

81. Simon Baron-Cohen and Sally Wheelwright, "The Empathy Quotient: An Investigation of Adults with Asperger Syndrome or High Functioning Autism, and Normal Sex Differences," *Journal of Autism and Developmental Disorders* 34, no. 2 (2004): 163–175.

82. Ibid., 172–73.

83. Ibid., 170.

84. R. J. R. Blair, "Fine Cuts of Empathy and the Amygdala: Dissociable Deficits in Psychopathy and Autism," *Quarterly Journal of Experimental Psychology* 61, no. 1 (2008): 157–170. On autism and theory of mind, see Uta Frith and Christopher D. Frith, "Development and Neurophysiology of Mentalizing," *Philosophical Transactions of the Royal Society B: Biological Sciences* 358, no. 1431 (2003): 459–473; U. Frith and F. Happé, "Autism: Beyond 'Theory of Mind,'" *Cognition* 50, no. 1 (1994): 115–132.

85. Kimberley Rogers, I. Dziobek, Jason Hassenstab, Oliver T. Work, and Antonio Convit, "Who Cares? Revisiting Empathy in Asperger Syndrome," *Journal of Autism and Developmental Disorders* 37, no. 4 (2007): 709–715.

86. Simone G. Shamay-Tsoory, Syvan Shur, Hagai Harari, and Hechiel Levokovitz, "Neurocognitive Basis of Impaired Empathy in Schizophrenia," *Neuropsychology* 21, no. 4 (2007): 431–438.

87. C. Daniel Batson, Shannon Early, and Giovanni Salvarani, "Perspective Taking: Imagining How Another Feels versus Imagining How You Would Feel," *Personality and Social Psychology Bulletin* 23, no. 7 (1997): 751–758.

88. Claus Lamm, C. Daniel Batson, and Jean Decety, "The Neural Substrate of Human Empathy: Effects of Perspective-Taking and Cognitive Appraisal," *Journal of Cognitive Neuroscience* 19, no. 1 (2007): 42–58.

89. Jean Decety and Claus Lamm, "Human Empathy through the Lens of Social Neuroscience," *Scientific World Journal* 6 (2006): 1146–1163, 1157; Jean Decety and Claus Lamm, "Empathy versus Personal Distress: Recent Evidence from Social Neuroscience," in *The Social Neuroscience of Empathy*, ed. Jean Decety and William Ickes (Cambridge: MIT Press, 2009), 199–214.

90. Claus Lamm, Howard C. Nusbaum, Andrew N. Meltzoff, and Jean Decety, "What Are You Feeling? Using Functional Magnetic Resonance Imaging to Assess the Modulation of Sensory and Affective Responses during Empathy for Pain," *PLoS one* 2, no. 12 (2007): 1–15.

91. "Children Are Naturally Prone to Be Empathic and Moral, University of Chicago Study Shows," *ScienceDaily*, July 11, 2008, https://www.sciencedaily.com/releases/2008/07/080711080957.htm. Accessed January 20, 2017. Activation for seeing pain was localized to the insula, somatosensory cortex, anterior midcingulate cortex, periaqueductal gray and sup-

plementary motor area. When watching someone intentionally hurt another, the temporo-parietal junction, the paracingulate, orbital medial frontal cortices, and amygdala were also activated.

92. Jean Decety and Philip L. Jackson, "The Functional Architecture of Human Empathy," *Behavioral and Cognitive Neuroscience Reviews* 3, no. 2 (2004): 71–100.

93. Ibid., 93.

94. Decety and Lamm, "Human Empathy through the Lens of Social Neuroscience," 1147.

95. Ibid., 1153–1155; see also Rebecca Saxe and N. Kanwisher, "People Thinking about Thinking People: The Role of the Temporo-Parietal Junction in 'Theory of Mind,'" *NeuroImage* 19 (2003): 1835–1842.

96. Decety and Jackson, "Functional Architecture of Human Empathy," 71.

97. Ibid., 93.

98. Decety and Ickes, eds., *Social Neuroscience of Empathy* (Cambridge: MIT Press, 2009); Amy Coplan and Peter Goldie, eds., *Empathy: Philosophical and Psychological Perspectives* (Oxford: Oxford University Press, 2011); Jean Decety, ed., *Empathy: From Bench to Bedside* (Cambridge: MIT Press, 2011).

99. Stephanie Preston, Antoine Bechara, Hanna Damasio, Thomas Grabowski, R. Brent Stansfield, Sonya Mehta, and Antonia Damasio, "The Neural Substrates of Cognitive Empathy," *Social Neuroscience* 2, nos. 3–4 (2007): 254–275.

100. Ibid., 268.

101. Jamil Zaki and Daniel Ochsner, "The Neuroscience of Empathy: Progress, Pitfalls, and Promise," *Nature Neuroscience* 15, no. 5 (2012): 675–679.

102. Ruth Leys, "'Both of Us Disgusted in My Insula': Mirror-Neuron Theory and Emotional Empathy," in *Science and Emotions after 1945*, ed. Frank Biess and Daniel M. Gross (Chicago: University of Chicago Press, 2014), 67–95.

103. Tania Singer and Ernst Fehr, "The Neuroeconomics of Mind Reading and Empathy," *American Economic Review* 95, no. 2 (2005): 340–345.

104. Simone G. Shamay-Tsoory, "Empathic Processing: Its Cognitive and Affective Dimensions and Neuroanatomical Basis," in *Social Neuroscience of Empathy*, ed. Decety and Ickes, 215–232, 227.

105. Paul Bloom, *Against Empathy: The Case for Rational Compassion* (New York: HarperCollins, 2016).

106. Philip David Zelazo and William A Cunningham, "Executive Function: Mechanisms Underlying Emotion Regulation," in *Handbook of Emotion Regulation*, ed. James J. Gross (New York: Guildford Press, 2007), cited by William M. Reddy, "Neuroscience and the Fallacies of Functionalism," *History and Theory* 49, no. 3 (2010): 412–425.

107. Madga Arnold, *Emotion and Personality* (New York: Columbia University

Press, 1960); Martha Nussbaum, *Upheavals of Thought: The Intelligence of Emotions* (Cambridge: Cambridge University Press, 2003).

108. Daniel M. Gross and Stephanie D. Preston, "Emotion Science and the Heart of a Two-Cultures Problem," in *Science and Emotions after 1945*, 96–117; Lisa Feldman Barrett, *How Emotions Are Made: The Secret Life of the Brain* (Boston: Houghton Mifflin, 2017); Ruth Leys, *The Ascent of Affect* (Chicago: University of Chicago Press, 2017).

109. Zaki and Ochsner, "Neuroscience of Empathy," 678; a very recent review of the neuroscience of empathy calls empathy "a collection of dissociable processes." Abigail A. Marsh, "The Neuroscience of Empathy," *Current Opinion in Behavioral Sciences* 19 (2018): 110–115, 111.

110. Andrew Ferguson, "The End of Neurononsense," *Weekly Standard*, October 20, 2014.

111. David Brooks, "Beyond the Brain," *New York Times*, June 18, 2013. He cites Sally Satel and Scott Lilienfield, *Brainwashed: The Seductive Appeal of Mindless Neuroscience* (New York: Basic Books, 2013), and Robert Shulman, *Brain Imaging: What It Can (and Cannot) Tell Us about Consciousness* (Oxford: Oxford University Press, 2013).

112. Raymond Tallis, *Aping Mankind: Neuromania, Darwinitis and the Misrepresentation of Humanity* (Durham, Eng.: Acumen, 2011); Gary Marcus, "Neuroscience Fiction," *New Yorker*, December 2, 2012. See the blogs *Neuroskeptic* and *Neurocritic*.

113. http://deevybee.blogspot.co.uk/2011/06/brain-scans-show-that.html. Accessed January 3, 2017.

114. Charles Siebert, "What Does a Parrot Know about PTSD?" *New York Times Magazine*, January 28, 2016.

115. Jeneen Interlandi, "The Brain's Empathy Gap," *New York Times Magazine*, March 19, 2015.

116. http://www.slate.com/articles/health_and_science/science/2013/06/racial_empathy_gap_people_don_t_perceive_pain_in_other_races.html.

117. Matteo Forgiarini, Marcello Gallucci, and Angelo Maravita, "Racism and the Empathy for Pain on Our Skin," *Frontiers in Psychology* 2 (2011), published online May 23, 2011, doi:10.3389/fpsyg.2011.00108.

118. Sophie Trawalter, Kelly M. Hoffman, and Adam Waytz, "Racial Bias in Perceptions of Others' Pain," *PLoS one* 7, no. 11 (2012): e48546.

119. Jennifer H. Gutsell and Michael Inzlicht, "Empathy Constrained: Prejudice Predicts Reduced Mental Simulation of Actions during Observation of Outgroups," *Journal of Experimental Social Psychology* 46, no. 5 (2010): 841–845.

120. Michael Inzlicht, Jennifer N. Gutsell, and Lisa Legault, "Mimicry Reduces Racial Prejudice," *Journal of Experimental Social Psychology* 48, no. 1 (2012): 361–365.

121. Interlandi, "Brain's Empathy Gap."

122. Ibid.

123. Matthieu Ricard, *Altruism* (New York: Little, Brown, 2013), 56–61.

124. Ibid., 26. Italics in original.

125. Ibid., 11.

126. Ibid., 532–551.

Conclusion

Epigraph: Gordon Allport, *Personality: A Psychological Interpretation* (New York: Holt, 1937), 547.

1. Julien A. Deonna, "The Structure of Empathy," *Journal of Moral Philosophy* 4, no. 1 (2007): 99–116, 100; Susan Verducci, "Moral Empathy: The Necessity of Intersubjectivity and Dialogic Confirmation," *Philosophy of Education* (1998): 335–342. Accurate empathy has been studied for many years by psychologist William Ickes, who sees it as a performance variable—what one does in dialogue. William Ickes, "Empathic Accuracy: Its Links to Clinical, Cognitive, Developmental, Social and Physiological Psychology," in *The Social Neuroscience of Empathy*, ed. Jean Decety and William Ickes (Cambridge: MIT Press, 2009), 57–70.

2. Thomas Nagel, "What Is It Like to Be a Bat?" *Philosophical Review* 83, no. 4 (1974): 435–450.

3. Laurel Braitman, *Animal Madness* (New York: Simon and Schuster, 2014).

4. Stephanie D. Preston and Frans de Waal, "Empathy: Its Ultimate and Proximate Bases," *Behavioral and Brain Sciences* 25 (2002): 1–75, 19. De Waal has collected over two thousand anecdotal accounts of nonhuman primate empathy that include cognitive elements and helping behavior.

5. Jane Bennett, *Vibrant Matter: A Political Ecology of Things* (Durham: Duke University Press, 2009); Karen Barad, *Meeting the Universe Halfway: Quantum Physics and the Entanglement of Matter and Meaning* (Durham: Duke University Press, 2007).

6. Steven Shaviro, "Consequences of Panpsychism," in *The Nonhuman Turn*, ed. Richard Grusin (Minneapolis: University of Minnesota Press, 2015), 19–45, 20.

7. Jim Holt, "Mind of a Rock," *New York Times*, November 18, 2007; Peter Wohlleben, *The Hidden Life of Trees* (Vancouver: Graystone Books, 2016).

8. Dominick LaCapra, *Writing History, Writing Trauma* (Baltimore: Johns Hopkins University Press, 2001); Jill Bennett, *Empathic Vision: Affect, Trauma, and Contemporary Art* (Stanford: Stanford University Press, 2005), 10.

9. Edith Stein, *On the Problem of Empathy* (The Hague: Mijhoff, 1964). See also Welsh theologian Rowan Williams on Stein: "I Have No Idea How You Feel," *Harvard Magazine*, April 4, 2015; http://harvardmagazine.com/2014/04/paradoxes-of-empathy. Accessed January 6, 2017.

10. Edward B. Titchener, *A Beginner's Psychology* (New York: Macmillan, 1915), 198.

11. Anthony M. Clohesy, *Politics of Empathy: Ethics, Solidarity, Recognition* (London: Routledge, 2013), 36.

12. Colum McCann, *Letters to a Young Writer* (New York: Random House, 2017), 12.

13. Arthur Koestler, "The Nightmare That Is the Reality," *New York Times*, January 9, 1944, SM5.

14. Emile G. Bruneau, Mina Cikara, and Rebecca Saxe, "Minding the Gap: Narrative Descriptions about Mental States Attenuate Parochial Empathy," *PloS one* 10, no. 10 (2015): e0140838.

Index

abstract formalism, 93
Adler, Alfred, 232, 246, 367n169;
 Adlerian theory, 235, 243
aesthetic perception: bodily effects of,
 21–23, 26–30, 32–34; and empathy,
 9–10, 18, 44–45, 51, 57, 67–81, 86,
 93–97; and imitation, 34–35, 39. *See
 also* art; Einfühlung; modern dance;
 poetry
affect theory, 286n57
age suits, 4
Alexander, Franz, 132
Allen, Frederick, 129, 135
Allport, Floyd, 312n111
Allport, Gordon, 13, 119, 172, 177, 277,
 279; as advisor to Kenneth Clark,
 231, 234; as advocate for community
 activism, 220–221; background of,
 217–218; on child-rearing, 222–223;
 and experiments on empathy and
 personality type, 90–93, 218–219;
 The Nature of Prejudice, 217, 222,
 230; and photographic images
 evoking empathy, 78–79; on racial
 prejudice, 224–231
altruism, 6, 105, 269, 276
American Psychological Association
 (APA), 76, 120, 146–148, 151, 179,
 244, 246

Americans All, Immigrants All, 225,
 226
Angyal, Andras, 122
animals: empathy with, 6, 278
Anstruther-Thomson, Clementina
 (Kit), 21–22, 26, 35, 290n33;
 aesthetic experiments conducted by,
 23, 27–30, 32–34, 40, 43; concerns
 about experiments by, 33–34
anthropocentrism, 278
architecture: as experienced, 30;
 Gothic, 88
Aristotle, 55
Armitage, David, 16, 286n62
Arnheim, Rudolf, 94, 96, 220
Arnold, Magda B., 342n78
art: abstract versus representational,
 88–89; aesthetic response to lines
 in, 84–87, 211; by people with
 mental illness, 114–115; psychological and physiological responses to,
 22–23, 25–30, 69, 84–87; and
 semblance, 49–50. *See also* aesthetic
 perception; color; poetry
Art Brut movement, 114
Asperger's syndrome, 269
association of ideas, 25, 35, 52, 86
Auden, W. H., 213
autism, 115–116, 269

Bain, Alexander, 25, 26

Baldwin, James, 236, 237, 239

Baldwin, James Mark: on Einfühlung and semblance, 48, 49–51, 56, 57, 277; and psychological nomenclature, 47–49

Baldwin effect, 48

Ball, Lucille, 208

Baron-Cohen, Simon, 268

Barrows, B. E., 85–86

Bartlett, Frederic, 53

Bastian, H. Charlton, 26

Batson, C. Daniel, 7–8, 269, 270

Bavelas, Alex, 180

Bazzi, Giovanni Antonio (Il Sodoma), 35–36

beauty: physiological responses to, 23, 25–30

Bell, Charles, 26

Bellah, Robert N., 285n53

Bender, Irving, 177–180

Benedict, Ruth, 141, 232

Bennett, Jill, 278

Benny, Jack, 208

Berenson, Bernard, 27, 290n33

Binet-Simon intelligence test, 70, 104, 111

Binswanger, Ludwig, 113

Bishop, Dorothy, 274

Blackman, Nathan, 124

black nationalism, 245

Blake, William, 71

Bleuler, Eugen, 110, 115–116

Bloom, Paul, 7

Blumer, Herbert, 196

Boas, Franz, 232

Boisen, Anton, 120

Boston Psychopathic Hospital, 109–112, 119–120

Botticelli, Sandro, 36

Bown, Oliver, 147

brain. *See* mirror neurons; neuroscience

Brecht, Bertolt, 15, 195–196

Brill, Abraham A., 108–109, 132

Brooks, David, 274

Brothers, Leslie, 255

Brown v. Board of Education, 231, 234

Bruneau, Emile, 5, 274, 275

Bruno, Giuliana, 295n102

Buber, Martin, 37, 205

Bullough, Edward, 52, 74–75, 87

Bunche, Ralph, 232

Burgess, Ernest, 11, 152, 153, 158, 201, 262; and sociological case studies, 159–163, 164–165

Burke, Edmund, 5

Burns, Robert, 101–102, 181, 315n3

Burrow, Trigant, 342n85

Cabot, Richard C., 103, 120

Cacioppo, John, 255

Calkins, Mary Whiton, 33

Campbell, Joseph, 200

Canavan, Myrtelle, 316n11

Cannon, Walter, 116, 121, 123

Cantril, Hadley, 179, 180

Cartwright, Desmond, 186

Cartwright, Rosalind Dymond. *See* Dymond, Rosalind

Cary, Joyce, 213

case studies: psychological, 92, 219, 230, 313n123, 341n62; sociological, 158, 159–165

Cason, Hulsey, 184

Cattell, James McKeen, 47

Chalmers, David, 1

Charon, Rita, 6, 283n28

Chase, Stuart, 180

Chein, Isidor, 149, 234

Chicago Area Project, 163

child psychology: Taft as trailblazer in, 129, 131, 138–139

civil rights: and empathic reason, 216, 244–250; struggle for, 215, 216, 230. *See also* civil rights movement

Civil Rights Act (1964), 244

civil rights movement: backlash
   against, 244; and the black power
   movement, 245; and Kenneth
   Clark, 236–244; liberals' ambivalence toward, 236–241, 244–245
Clark, Andy, 1
Clark, Kenneth B., 13, 255; as advocate
   for racial equality, 217–218,
   238–244; background of, 232–233;
   Dark Ghetto, 216, 240, 241; on
   empathic reason, 246; empathy as
   advocated by, 238–239, 241,
   247–250, 252–253, 279, 368n190;
   Prejudice and Your Child, 234–235;
   research on racial discrimination,
   231–238, 240–244; on white
   liberalism, 236–238
Clark, Mamie, 216, 233
Clarke, Helen, 64
Cohen, Ted, 18
color: empathic responses to, 74–75
Colvin, Stephen, 60
Commission on Community Interrelations (CCI), 228–229
consciousness: elements of, 62;
   psychology of, 53
controlled identification, 127, 136,
   144
Cook, Stuart, 234
Cooley, Charles, 161, 162
Cottrell, Leonard, 11, 158, 164, 165,
   166, 170–171, 201; as advocate for
   empathy as societal benefit,
   167–169, 175, 176, 248
Council for the Clinical Training of
   Theological Students, 120
curved lines: and Einfühlung, 39–42
Cushing, Harvey, 103

Dallenbach, Karl, 60–61
Damasio, Antonio and Hannah, 263
Davis, D. Elizabeth, 144
Davis, Mark, 253
Davis DuBois, Rachel, 224–228

Decety, Jean, 255–256; empathy
   research by, 269–271
dementia praecox. *See* schizophrenia
De Vries, Alma, 63
de Waal, Frans, 6, 263–264, 267, 278,
   378n4
Dewey, John, 75, 95, 143
Dick, Philip K., 213
Downey, June, 10, 61, 68; and psychological tests relating to empathy,
   69–75, 91–92, 94
drama theory: and empathy, 15–16.
   See also role-playing
Du Bois, W. E. B., 242
Duchamp, Marcel, 103
Duncan, Isadora, 81
Dymond, Rosalind, 11, 150–151, 248;
   background of, 170; critics of,
   176–177; empathy as defined by,
   171–172; empathy tests developed
   by, 158–159, 171–175, 176–178,
   186–187, 188, 189

Early, Shannon, 269
Einfühlung, 2, 133, 286n61; and
   aesthetic response, 23, 37–45,
   303n80; as "aesthetic sympathy,"
   48, 49–50; "empathy" as English
   translation for, 47, 50–53, 54, 60,
   277; experiments relating to, 38–39;
   as fusion of self and object, 32–33;
   Vernon Lee's research on, 37–38;
   Lipps's theory of, 30–33, 37–39, 42,
   48, 58, 90, 93, 133, 171, 205,
   291n52; and motor response, 41,
   44–45; origins of the concept of,
   32–33; scope and meanings of, 37,
   48–49, 318n48; as semblance,
   49–51, 277; translations of, 9,
   47–53, 54, 60, 298n20; types of,
   42–43. *See also* empathy
emotion: in advertising, 209; as applied
   in social work, 128–129, 131–132,
   139, 159; bracketing of, 202–204;

emotion (*continued*)
    debates on, 14–15, 17; and empathy,
    14–15, 109, 195–196; William
    James's theory of, 25, 26; versus
    judgment, 5, 12; as a physiological
    concept, 25–26; in politics, 245,
    350n12; in psychoanalysis, 11,
    132–137; in racial and intercultural
    understanding, 225, 227, 234
emotional contagion, 196, 252,
    259–260
emotional intelligence, 3
empathic distress, 253
empathic dynamism, 83
empathic index: for diagnosing
    schizophrenia, 109–112, 115; as
    psychiatric concept, 10–11,
    101–102, 104–109
empathic projection. *See* projection
empathic psychotherapy: Rogers as
    advocate for, 11, 126, 144, 147–151,
    152, 154–157
empathy: and abstract art, 88–89;
    accurate, 176–181, 187, 378n1; in
    advertising, 209–210; as aesthetic
    response, 9–10, 18, 42, 44–45, 51,
    57, 67–75, 86, 93–97, 195, 210–211,
    278; aesthetic roots of, 166;
    Allport's research relating to, 90–93,
    218–219, 223–224; and anthropo-
    morphic projection, 55–56, 96, 207;
    as aspirational value, 12–13,
    155–157, 194–195, 213–215; as
    bridge between racial and cultural
    divides, 213–215; chauvinistic,
    249, 279; and the clinician, 112,
    113–114, 115; complexity of, 6, 15,
    273–274, 277–280; controversy over
    use of, 67; and creativity, 69–71;
    cultural, 194–195; and cultural
    norms, 176–177; definitions of, 3,
    9–10, 12, 21, 122, 124–125, 163,
    164, 171–172, 176, 178, 182, 248,
    276, 306n131, 342–343n85; and

design practice, 4; as distinguished
    from sympathy, 5–6, 66; and drama
    theory, 15–16; elements of,
    349n190; and emotions, 14–15, 109,
    195–196; experimental studies of,
    11–12, 27–30, 32–34, 40, 43, 52–53;
    and the family, 201–203; and
    feminine instincts, 203; history of,
    2, 8–14, 15–18; and the imagina-
    tion, 57, 65–66, 201; in industrial
    contexts, 181–185; and intelligence,
    246; and kinesthetic imagery, 9–10,
    46–47, 58–67, 198–199, 264–265;
    lack of, in schizophrenic patients,
    112, 115–116, 121–124; Langfeld's
    theories of, 10, 75–77, 84–85,
    96–98; and leadership, 3, 184, 214;
    in literature, 4, 210–211, 213;
    measurement of, 158–159, 165,
    169–170, 171–175, 176–180,
    187–189; and mental imagery, 46,
    56, 71; and mirror neurons, 7, 13,
    252, 256–265; as motor response,
    76–81, 315n154, 325n156; multiple
    meanings of, 8–14, 47, 197–198,
    279–280, 297n3, 341n68; as mythic
    impulse, 47; neuroscientific studies
    of, 7, 13, 18, 251–252, 255–256,
    268–276; as outmoded aesthetic,
    93–97; paradox inherent in, 17–18;
    parochial, 279; and personality type,
    69, 87–93; as personification, 55–56;
    and physicians, 6–7; physiological
    indicators for, 253–255; political
    implications of, 215, 231–250,
    350n12; popular awareness of,
    12–13, 189, 194–195, 198–199,
    201–203; projection as opposed to,
    176–181; in psychiatry, 105–107; as
    psychological concept, 11–12,
    52–53, 68–69, 105–109, 122–125,
    196–201, 203, 328n44; in psycho-
    therapy, 11, 126–127, 134–137,
    148–151, 154–157, 187–189,

203–207, 337n202; questions about validity of empathy tests, 185–186; and racial prejudice, 217, 223–224, 230, 238–239, 241, 247–250, 274–275; and relationships, 200–201; and role–playing, 165–168, 202; and self–object fusion, 73–74, 75, 90; as simulation, 261–265; and social inequality, 5, 14, 217; as social value, 3–4, 122–125; in social work, 136–137, 163–164, 207; and sociological case studies, 160–165; and sympathy, 54–55; on television, 208–209; in theater, 196, 212; as translation for Einfühlung, 47, 50–53, 54, 60; types of, 42–43. *See also* Einfühlung; empathic index; kinesthetic empathy; relationship therapy

empathy gap, 4–5; and brain studies, 274

Empathy Quotient Scale (EQ), 268–269

empathy scales, 13, 157; developed by Dymond, 158–159, 170, 171–175, 176–178, 182, 186–187, 188; developed by Hogan, 188; developed by Kerr and Speroff, 182–186; developed by Mehrabian and Epstein, 188; developed by Truax, 187; emotional, 188; for rating therapists and clients, 187–189

Endell, August, 42, 43

Epstein, Norman: empathy scale developed by, 188

equimindedness, 230–231

evolutionary continuity, 52, 53

extroversion: Allport's research on, 90–93; in Jung's typology, 69, 87, 89–90

Family of Man, The, 193; critics' response to, 194

Fechner, Gustav, 22–23

Ferenczi, Sandor, 11, 134, 135

Feshbach, Seymour and Norma, 188

Fine, Cordelia, 268

Fogassi, Leonardo, 260

Foote, Nelson, 170, 201–202

form: perception of, 94. *See also* Gestalt psychology

Foster, Michael, 52

Foucault, Michel, 16–17, 317n38

Fouillée, Alfred, 26

Frazer, James, 54–55, 56

Frazier, E. Franklin, 234

Freedberg, David, 264–265

Freeman, Damon, 243

Freeman, Frank, 171

Freud, Anna, 139

Freud, Sigmund, 32, 67, 132, 206, 232, 291–292n54; on empathy/Einfühlung, 328n44, 342n85; *Totem and Taboo*, 113

Fromm, Erich, 133

Gage, N. L., 345n135

Gallese, Vittorio, 260, 263, 264–265

Galton, Francis, 25

Gandhi, Mahatma, 230

Gardner, Isabella Stewart, 27

Geiger, Moritz, 37

Gendlin, Eugene, 156

Gestalt psychology, 75, 94–96, 141, 218, 220, 221

Gibson, J. J., 262–263

Gielgud, Sir John, 212

Giuliani, Rudy, 259

Gladstein, Gerald, 253

Glazer, Nathan, 236

Goddard, Henry H., 70

Godfrey, Arthur, 208

Goldberg, Clara, 101

golden section, 22–23

Goleman, Daniel, 3, 259–260

Gopnik, Alison, 266–267

Gordon, Kate: and empathic projection, 77–78, 81, 171

Gothic architecture, 88
Graham, Martha, 81–82, 83, 309n61
graphology. *See* handwriting analysis
Greenberg, Clement, 93, 313n130
Groos, Karl, 42, 43, 48, 49, 82; on
    inner imitation, 34–35, 36, 39
Gross, Daniel, 273

Hacking, Ian, 16
Halpern, Jodi, 6–7, 8
handwriting analysis: and personality
    type, 70–71, 91–92
Harlem Youth Opportunities Unlim-
    ited (HARYOU), 233
Hastorf, Alfred, 177–180
Hatch, Orrin, 5
Haworth, Mary, 202–203
Hays Code (film rating system), 196
Helmholtz, Hermann, 25
Hempel, Carl, 169
Herder, Johann, 32, 286n61
Hickok, Gregory, 267, 374n76
Hildebrand, Adolph von, 26–27
Hiltner, Seward, 204
Hoch, August, 117
Hoffman, Martin, 253
Hofmann, Hans, 42, 211, 313n130
Hogan, Robert: empathy scale
    developed by, 188, 215
Hook, Sidney, 236, 237
Horney, Karen, 141
Hoskins, Roy, 171, 175, 325n161; as
    schizophrenia researcher, 11, 102,
    116–119, 121–124
Hume, David, 5, 299n24
Humphrey, Doris, 82
Husserl, Edmund, 37, 263, 294n84
hypnotism, 25
hysteria, 87

Iacoboni, Marco, 258–259, 261–262
Ickes, William, 378n1
images: and abstract thought, 57–59,
    61. *See also* kinesthetic imagery

imagination: and empathy, 49, 57,
    65–66, 201; and memory, 63;
    psychology of, 57
Imagist poets, 70
imitation, 13, 48, 90; and aesthetic
    enjoyment, 3–36, 39; bodily, 9–10,
    30; inner, 39, 49, 84, 160
intercultural understanding, 224–230
Interpersonal Reactivity Index, 253,
    269, 349n190
intersubjectivity, 263
introversion: Allport's research on,
    90–93; in Jung's typology, 69, 87,
    89–90, 102, 114; and schizophrenia,
    87, 89, 102, 114

Jackson, Henry, 55
Jackson, Philip, 271
Jacob, Pierre, 266
James, Henry, 24
James, William, 24–26, 48, 53, 103,
    107
Jarrett, Mary, 106, 131
Jarzombek, Mark, 94, 314n133
Jaspers, Karl, 113
Jeannerod, Marc, 266
Jelliffe, Smith Ely, 117
Jolson, Al, 212–213
Jones, Caroline, 313n130
Jung, Carl: personality types as
    described by, 69, 87, 89–90, 102,
    114, 172, 311n91

Kandel, Eric, 265
Kandinsky, Wassily, 42, 296n117,
    313n130
Karush, Aaron, 235
Katz, Robert Langdon, 206–207,
    354n85
Keats, John, 71, 210; aesthetic
    responses to poetry of, 72, 94
Kelley, David and Tom, 4
Kempf, Edward, 117
Kennedy, John F., 214

Kenworthy, Marion, 135
Kerr, Willard: empathy test developed by, 182–186, 188
Keysers, Christian, 258
kinesthetic empathy, 305n119; and modern dance, 69, 81–84
kinesthetic imagery: and empathy, 9–10, 46–47, 61–67, 264–265, 302n65; Southard's theories regarding, 104–105; Titchener's concept of, 9–10, 58–67, 71, 303n74
kinesthetic sense, 58; and aesthetic perception, 26–27; and meaning, 304n108
King, Martin Luther, Jr., 214, 237, 239
Kirsch, Robert, 212
Klee, Paul, 114
Klein, Melanie, 139
Klineberg, Otto, 232
Knight, Robert P., 148, 334n143
Koestler, Arthur, 210–211, 279
Koffka, Kurt, 94, 141
Köhler, Wolfgang, 95–96
Kohut, Heinz, 156, 207
Kraepelin, Emil, 110, 113, 117
Kristof, Nicholas, 3–4
Kubie, Lawrence, 152–153
Külpe, Oswald, 38–39, 42, 43, 57

Lakoff, George, 259
Lamm, Claus, 270
Lang, Fritz, 195
Langfeld, Herbert: and aesthetic empathy, 10, 75–77, 84–85, 96–97, 164, 171, 218
Lazarsfeld, Paul, 166
leadership: and empathy, 3, 184, 214
Lee, Vernon (Violet Paget), 9, 21–22, 68, 82, 104, 290n33; aesthetic experiments conducted by, 27–30, 32–37, 40, 43, 95; background of, 23–24; The Beautiful, 44, 67; Beauty and Ugliness, 42; "Gallery Diaries" of, 35–36; and kinesthetic imagery,

67, 265; and the psychology of the beautiful, 25–30; research and writing on Einfühlung, 37–38, 42, 43–45
Leibniz, Gottfried Wilhelm, 54, 105
Levy, David, 137
Lewin, Kurt, 180, 221, 234, 341n66
Lewis, Clarence I., 107
Lide, Pauline, 207
lines (in art): aesthetic response to, 84–87
Lipps, Theodor, 82, 104; The Aesthetics of Space, 37; Einfühlung as defined by, 9, 21; empathic aesthetics of, 74, 86; on optical illusions, 30–31, 104; theory of Einfühlung as developed by, 30–33, 37–39, 42, 48, 58, 90, 93, 171, 205, 291n52, 294n84
Listowel, Earl of, 42
literature: and empathy, 4, 210–211, 213, 334n143
Livingston, James, 326n10
Lowry, Fern, 163
Lundberg, George, 169–170
Lundholm, Helge, 85–86, 310n81

MacGregor, Geddes, 96–97
MacLean, Paul, 254–255
MacLeish, Archibald, 212
manic depression: as distinguished from schizophrenia, 109, 110, 111
married couples: case studies of, 164–165; empathy as measured in, 177
Martin, John: on empathy as response to modern dance, 81–84
Masefield, John, 193
May, Rollo, 148, 205
McCain, John, 259
McCann, Colum, 278
McCormick, Katherine Dexter, 116–118, 124
McCormick, Stanley, 124; diagnosed with schizophrenia, 116–117

Mead, George Herbert, 11, 127, 159, 168, 262; as Burgess's mentor, 159; as Taft's mentor, 127–128

Mead, Margaret, 166, 228

Mehrabian, Albert: empathy scale developed by, 188

memory: Bartlett's theory of, 53; and imagination, 63

Menninger, Karl, 152, 153–154

Menninger Clinic, 148

mental hygiene, 102, 130–131. *See also* psychiatry; psychology

mental illness: challenges of diagnosing and classifying, 110–112

mental imagery: and aesthetic response, 69–75. *See also* images; kinesthetic imagery

Merleau-Ponty, Maurice, 263

Metropolitan Applied Research Center, 233

Meyer, Adolf, 102, 117, 119, 166

mind: as extended, 1–2

mirror neurons: critique of theories based on, 266–267; and empathy, 7, 13, 252, 256–261; in humans, 257–265

Miterleben, 34

modern dance: and kinesthetic empathy, 69, 81–84

Molière, 45

Montagu, Ashley, 222

Moreno, Jacob, 165–167

Morgan, Barbara, 194

Morgan, Christiana, 172

mother, the, 14, 203; and empathic contagion to infant, 109, 203; as model of therapist, 127, 136–137, 141; Rank's theories of, 133–134, 136–137

motor response: empathic, 41, 44–45, 76–81, 82–84, 315n154

movies: impact of, on children, 196

Moyn, Samuel, 250

Moynihan, Daniel Patrick, 237–238

Mukamel, Roy, 257–258

Müller-Lyer illusion, 30–31

Mundt, Ernest, 67, 93

Münsterberg, Hugo, 26, 41, 181, 218, 295n102

Murphy, Gardner, 166, 315n154

Murphy, Lois, 343n88

Murray, Henry, 172

muscle sense. *See* kinesthetic sense

music: and empathy, 184, 186, 302n69; movement as perceived in, 95; physiological responses to, 28, 325n156

Myers, Charles S., 52–53

Myrdal, Gunnar: *The American Dilemma*, 219–220, 231, 235, 236, 241

Nagel, Thomas, 277

National Institute of Mental Health (NIMH), 147

neuroscience: empathy as researched in, 7, 13, 18, 251–252, 255–256, 268–276. *See also* mirror neurons

neurosyphilis, 111

Newton, Caroline, 135

nonviolent communication, 156

Nussbaum, Martha, 14, 273

Obama, Barack, 5, 259

Oberman, Lindsay M., 260

Ochsner, Daniel, 272–273

optical illusions, 291n50; and Einfühlung/empathy, 30–31, 104

outsider art, 114

Overstreet, Harry and Bonaro, 199–200

Paget, Violet. *See* Lee, Vernon

panpsychism, 9, 53–54, 56

Park, Robert E., 159, 160

Parks, Larry, 213

Parsons, Talcott, 152

Pasternak, Boris, 212
pathetic fallacy, 107
Peirce, Charles Sanders, 48, 53–54
Pennsylvania School of Social Work, 127, 129, 135; casework as practiced at, 140; curriculum at, 141
Perky, Cheves, 63
personality types: empathy as related to, 69, 91, 92–93. See also extroversion; introversion
personification: and empathy, 55–56
Perugino, Pietro, 77, 78
Piaget, Jean, 50, 299n22
Picabia, Francis, 103
pity, 5, 217, 238–239, 364–365n122
Podhoretz, Norman, 236
Poe, Edgar Allan, 72; aesthetic responses to poetry of, 72–73
poetry: empathic engagement with, 69–73
Poffenberger, A. T., 85–86
prejudice: Allport's studies relating to, 13, 93, 219–220, 224–231. See also Clark, Kenneth B.; racial prejudice
Preston, Stephanie, 263–264, 271–272, 273
Prinzhorn, Hans, 321n91; Artistry of the Mentally Ill, 114–115
projected kinesthesis, 65–66
projection: and abstraction, 88; anthropomorphic, 55–56, 96, 207; and art objects, 195, 197; as childlike, 86–87; as complement to empathy, 172–173, 176; as opposed to empathy, 11–12, 14, 124–125, 127, 159, 176–186, 272; Rosalind Dymond on, 171, 173, 176; and Einfühlung, 23, 33, 37, 41, 57; empathic, 67, 77–78, 94, 96, 106–107, 114, 122, 124–125, 166; into form, 77–81; and Gestalt psychology, 94; Theodor Lipps on, 9, 23, 32, 33, 37, 264, 291n52, 294n84; and literature, 210–211; in

psychotherapy, 105–107, 124, 139, 166; Otto Rank on, 133, 135–136; Jessie Taft on, 137, 139; and transference, 32; as unconscious, 16, 17, 23, 90, 172, 173, 211
psychiatry: early research relating to, 103–104; empathy as diagnostic tool in, 101–102, 104–109; at odds with psychology, 152–154; social dimensions of, 104, 105, 317n38; and social work, 130–131. See also empathic index; schizophrenia
psychodrama, 165–167
psychology: of the beautiful, 25–30; clinical, 146, 155, 197, 221; empathy as aspect of, 11–12, 52–53, 68–69, 105–109, 122–125; growing influence of, 196–201; of the imagination, 57; in industrial contexts, 159, 181–185; laboratory protocols for, 57; standardized terminology for, 47–49
psychopathy: later use of term, 249, 269; original definition of, 102, 111
psychotherapy: for children, 141, 144; client–centered, 147–151, 152, 154–155, 163, 180; empathy as aspect of, 11, 126–127, 134–137, 148–151, 152, 154–157, 187–189; role-playing in, 165–168. See also relationship therapy
Puffer, Ethel, 41–42, 43–44, 265

racial prejudice: Kenneth Clark's research relating to, 231, 232–238; empathy as antidote to, 217, 223–224, 230, 238–239, 241, 247–250; and empathy gap, 274–275; as inherent in American life, 235–236; interventions to alleviate, 224–231; sentimentality as factor in, 238–239; social forces contributing to, 224
Ramachandran, Vilayanur S., 260

Rank, Otto: as advocate for emotional connection in psychoanalysis, 11, 127, 132–133, 141, 328n39; controversy surrounding, 132–133; and Freud, 133–134; on identification and projection, 135–137; and Carl Rogers, 143–144
Rankine, Claudia, 250
Raphael, 77, 79
Read, Herbert, 90
Reik, Theodor, 8, 206–207
relationships: empathy as important to, 200–201
relationship therapy, 11, 138–143, 154. *See also* psychotherapy
Remmers, Hermann H., 181–182
Reynolds, Dee, 313n130
Ricard, Mathieu, 276
Richmond, Mary, 160
Riegl, Alois, 88
Rifkin, Jeremy, 3, 281n4
Rizzolatti, Giacomo, 7, 260, 262, 263, 266
Robinson, Virginia, 128, 135, 141–142; as Taft's partner, 127, 129–130, 140
Rogers, Anna Sophie, 64
Rogers, Carl: as advocate for empathic psychotherapy, 11, 126, 144, 147–151, 152, 154–157, 171, 180, 187, 204–205, 207, 325n1, 333n138; as APA president, 147; growing prominence of, 146–147; nondirective methods advocated by, 143, 144–146, 153, 220; and Otto Rank, 143–144; and training for USO workers, 146
role-playing: and empathy, 180, 200, 202; in industrial settings, 185, 210; and intercultural understanding, 225–227, 230; in psychotherapy, 165–168
Rorschach, Hermann, 64
Rorschach inkblot test, 64, 187, 304n109

Rosenberg, Marshall, 156
Rotman, Brian, 281n1
Rouse, W. H. D., 55
Rowe, Allan, 117, 118
Royce, Josiah, 53, 54, 103
Ruskin, John, 107
Russell, Bertrand, 245

Saenger, Gerhart, 227
Safire, William, 5
Salvarini, Giovanni, 269
Sargent, John Singer, 24
Saxe, Rebecca, 274
Schafer, Roy, 157, 283n28
Scheler, Max, 37, 223, 294n84, 360n40
Scherner, Karl, 32
Schiller, Friedrich, 34, 71
schizophrenia (dementia praecox), 10–11, 269, 319n62; and animistic thinking, 113, 114; art by people with, 114–115, 321n91; causes of, 118; feelings of isolation associated with, 120, 121; and hormone therapy, 117–118; and introversion, 87, 89, 102, 114; neuropathological studies of, 110; research at Boston Psychopathic Hospital on, 109–112, 119–120; research at Worcester State Hospital on, 102, 115–125; symptoms of, 117–118; use of empathic index for diagnosis of, 109–112, 115
Schopenhauer, Arthur, 32
Schroeder, Theodore, 318n48
Scott, Darryl Michael, 239
Sebastian, Saint, 35–36
selfhood: and empathy, 13–14; expanded sense of, 1–2; and relationship therapy, 139
selfishness, 6
Selye, Hans, 121
semblance: as translation for Ein-fühlung, 47, 49–51

sentimentalism/sentimentality, 129, 137, 250; in contrast to empathy, 108, 124, 144, 194, 207, 217, 238–239

Sergi, Giuseppe, 25

serial contextualism, 16

Shakow, David, 119–120, 323n128

Shaw, Clifford, 161–163

Shelley, Norm, 212

Shelley, Percy: aesthetic responses to poetry of, 73, 94

Shlein, John, 154–155

simulation theory, 261–265; flaws in, 265–267

Singer, Tania, 268, 272, 276

Smith, Adam, 5

Smith, Robertson, 55

Snyder, William, 145

Snygg, Donald, 149

social emotions, 255

social inequality: empathy as response to, 14; and failure of empathy, 5. See also intercultural understanding

social neuroscience, 7, 255

social psychology, 104, 127, 221–222, 223, 255, 274

social science: emotion as aspect of, 128–129, 131–132, 138

social work: and case records, 160–161; empathy as important in, 136–137, 163–164, 207; functional school of, 140; psychoanalysis as aspect of, 130–131. See also Taft, Jessie

Society for the Psychological Study of Social Issues (SPSSI), 217

sociology, 104, 122, 153–165

sociometry, 165–166

Sodoma, Il (Giovanni Antonio Bazzi), 35–36

Solomon, Harry, 152

Sorokin, Pitirim, 222

Sotomayor, Sonia, 5

Southard, Elmer Ernest, 131, 181, 316n11; empathic index developed by, 10–11, 101–102, 104–109, 115, 119; philosophical and psychological training of, 103–104; as schizophrenia researcher, 110–112, 121

Speroff, Boris: empathy test developed by, 182–185

Stanislavsky, Konstantin, 81

Steichen, Edward, 193

Stein, Edith, 37, 263, 278, 294n84

Stewart, David, 337n202

Stonequist, Everett, 160

Stotland, Ezra, 253–254

Strachey, Alix and James, 67, 328n44

Stratton, George, 40–41

Strecker, Edward, 135

Strode, Josephine, 163–164

structural similarity (isomorphism), 94–95

Stumpf, Carl, 75

Sullivan, Alice, 65–66

Sullivan, Harry Stack, 109, 132, 175, 203

Sullivan, Helen, 46

Sully, James, 25

Sumner, Francis Cecil, 232

Swinburne, Algernon Charles, 71

sympathy: aesthetic, 49; as distinguished from empathy, 5–6, 66, 96, 105, 108, 124, 161–164, 168, 172, 197, 199, 203, 253

synesthesia, 70

systematic introspection, 10, 23, 35, 46–47; and kinesthetic images, 58, 62–63

Taft, Jessie, 11, 126–127, 133, 159, 161, 166, 262, 279, 326n3, 326n10; as advocate for emotion in social science, 128–129, 131–132, 139, 159; on error of projection, 137; and Otto Rank, 135–136; on relationship therapy, 11, 138–143, 151, 154–155; as Robinson's partner, 127, 129–130, 140; on the therapist as assistant ego, 148; on women's role in society, 127, 128

Tamiris, Helen, 82

Thematic Apperception Test (TAT): as a measure of empathy, 172–174

Thomas, Dylan, 212

Thompson, Fred, 259

Thorndike, Robert, 185–186

Titchener, Edward B., 35, 42, 48, 104, 170, 302n69, 303n80; and empathy as translation for Einfühlung, 9–10, 47, 50–51, 57–58, 278; and kinesthetic images, 10, 46–47, 58–67, 71, 171, 264, 303n74; and systematic introspection, 46–47, 56–57

Tomkins, Silvan, 286n57

Trilling, Lionel, 133

Trout, J. D., 4, 282n14

Truax, Charles, 187

Tufts, James, 127

Turner, Ralph, 189

Tylor, Edward B., 55

unconscious, the: and empathy, 206; Freud's conception of, 32

Urban, Wilbur M., 48, 50, 298n20

Valentine, Charles, 39–40, 53

Van Doren, Charles, 209

Vernon, Philip, 91–92

Vischer, Friedrich Theodor, 32

Vischer, Robert, 32

Voting Rights Act (1965), 244

Vygotsky, Lev, 50

Ward, James: and "empathy" as translation for Einfühlung, 9, 47, 50–53; and James Frazer, 54–55; and panpsychism, 53–56

Washington, Booker T., 159

Watson, John B., 58, 137

Weber, Max, 341n68

Weidman, Charles, 82

Weizenbaum, Joseph, 147

Wells, Frederic, 120

West, Rebecca, 68, 212

Wheelwright, Sally, 268

White, William A., 107–108, 113–114, 117, 135, 140, 166

white liberalism: James Baldwin on, 236–237; Kenneth Clark on, 237–238, 239–240

Wilkie, Wendell, 200

Willis, Irene Cooper, 36

Wirth, Louis, 160

Wispé, Lauren, 6, 16

Worcester State Hospital: schizophrenia research at, 102, 115–125

Worringer, Wilhelm, 42; and *Abstraction and Empathy* 87–89

Wright, Richard, 160

Wundt, Wilhelm, 26, 47, 56, 57, 291n50, 301–302n62

Yerkes, Robert, 104, 152

Young, Allan, 374n78

Zaki, Jamil, 272, 273

Zilsel, Edgar, 169